*S*panish in
the *A*mericas

GEORGETOWN UNIVERSITY PRESS
Romance Languages and Linguistics Series

See p. 379 for additional titles of interest.

Spanish in the Americas

Eleanor Greet Cotton

John M. Sharp

Georgetown University Press, Washington, D.C.

Library of Congress Cataloging in Publication Data

Cotton, Eleanor C.
  Spanish in the Americas.

  1. Spanish language—Dialects—Latin America.
I. Sharp, John M.   II. Title.
PC4821.C68   1988   467'.98   87-12005
ISBN 0-87840-094-X

Dedication

To those who inspired this work and prepared the authors to write it: Amado Alonso, who awakened the interest of one of the authors in Hispanic dialectology and provided basic orientation in this field; Juan M. Lope Blanch, who familiarized the authors with the present status of this discipline and made available to them much of the material used in this study; Ray Past, who, in founding the Department of Linguistics at The University of Texas at El Paso, brought the authors together and encouraged them; Leland Sonnichsen and Marie Mason Hughes for sharing their dedication to learning.

Contents

Part Three: Contemporary Spanish dialects in the Americas

Tables

Figures

Maps

Tapes

Acknowledgements

This guide to Latin American dialectology is not simply the product of its two authors but of hundreds of scholars who have done research and formed theories on this complex and multifaceted subject. The authors, in fact, are comparable to the compilers of an encyclopedia or anthology in their structuring of this mass of information. A glance at the bibliography will give the reader an idea of the very numerous sources of the material to be presented.

We are particularly grateful to the following authors and publishers for their permission to reprint selections illustrative of many variants of Spanish and other languages which have influenced it: Alurista for his poem "We've Played Cowboys"; D.C. Health for samples from Henry Hare Carter's *Contos e anedotas brasileiros*; Ediciones Ibéricas for José Mercado's "La lengua castellana"; Editorial Cultural for René Marqués' *La carreta*; Espasa-Calpe for parts of Benavente's *Doña Ama*; E. R. Goilo for a passage from *Papiamentu Textbook*; and the Instituto Caro y Cuervo for their model of a dialect map.

The value and the interest of a work such as this is enhanced by the contributions of speakers of the varieties of the language that are being dealt with. Some of these who have given of their valuable time to make recordings for us are Fermín Rodríguez, Alberto Bagby, Lino Landy, Félix Bultrón, Domingo Ricart, Víctor Sánchez, Pilar Monte, Miren Marcaida, Carlos Vizcarra, Virgilio Veletti, Alexander Santiago, and Carmen Acosta.

Others whose research into dialects has proven beneficial to us are Jon Amastae, María Rayen Catrileo, Lurline Coltharp, Adela Berry Dávila, Timothy Lawrence, Gertrude Muro, Deborah Nathan, and Marcia Lagos-Sandoval.

We have also benefited from the wise guidance of our colleagues Edward Blansitt, Chester Christian, Ray Past, and Richard Teschner, as well as Professor Thomas Walsh and others on the staff of Georgetown University Press. We are grateful to President Diana Natalicio for the institutional support she provided for the typing of the manuscript and to Flo Dick for her meticulous work as the word-processor.

Finally, for their patience and moral support we thank our families, Gladys Sharp, Cabell Cotton Capshaw, Stephanie, Brooke, and Donald Reed.

E. G. C.

El Paso   J. M. S.

June, 1987

Part One: Hispanic dialects

Chapter 1
What is a dialect?

If you were to remark to someone newly met that he spoke a dialect, he might well be embarrassed or offended. Yet your observation would inevitably be true. Anyone who speaks, speaks a dialect. Because of this, it is extremely difficult to give a definition of dialect that is not also a definition of language. However, in a treatment of dialectology, a definition of 'dialect' is indispensable. Let us then attempt to modify the generally accepted definition of language so that it will apply specifically to the special variety of language called a 'dialect'.

For a linguist, language is 'an arbitrary system of arbitrary vocal symbols used by a human society in carrying on its affairs' (Past 1970:3). That language is arbitrary is easily seen in that different languages employ different sounds, different words, and different grammatical structures to convey the same meanings. For example, when the men of Ephraim were defeated by those of Gilead, we are told:

5 . . . and it was so, that when those Ephraimites which were escaped said, Let me go over; that the men of Gilead said to him, Art thou an Ephraimite? If he said, Nay;
6 Then said they unto him, Say now Shibboleth: and he said Sibboleth: for he could not frame to pronounce it right. Then they took him, and slew him (Judg. 12:5-6).

The presence or absence of *sh*, in this case, was a matter of life or death. Further, the component parts of a language are systematically arranged, that is, bound by rules. English may use *-ng* only at the end of a syllable, whereas Japanese may use it syllable-initial or medial but not final. If a Texas rooster is carried to Ciudad Juárez, his native *Cock-a-doodle-do* will be heard by Mexicans as *Ki-*

1

kiri-kí, and if by some chance he is shipped to Colombia, he will cry *Ko-koro-kó*. So we see that even symbols which are supposedly onomatopoeic are arbitrary too.

The general system of a language consists of four subsystems, just like the general vital system of the body with its several subsystems (e.g., circulatory, respiratory, digestive) which work in close coordination with each other. In language, these subsystems are (1) phonology: sounds which are important in that they distinguish between one word and another; (2) morphology: forms of words and significant parts of words; (3) syntax: grammatical constructions; (4) lexicon: vocabulary items and their meanings.

How then can 'dialect' be distinguished from 'language'? If, within the general system of a language, one (or more) of these subsystems differs consistently in some way, these differences constitute a dialect. Even in languages used by a relatively small number of speakers, such as Tarahumara with 50,000, dialectal differences are the norm rather than the exception. In the United States, phonological differences are seen in the Midwesterner's *thirty-third* which corresponds to the Georgian's *thutty-thud* and the Brooklynite's *toity-toid*. A morphological difference is *et* for the past tense of *eat*, viewed as substandard by some but socially acceptable among cultured persons of the older generation in Virginia. In syntax, children in Minneapolis will ask *Can I go with?* or *Can I spend?*, while speakers of all ages in some areas of Pennsylvania say *The sugar is all* if the sugar is all gone. Extremely common is lexical variation: one man's *skillet* is another man's *spider*, and *Hang ten* communicates in California but not elsewhere. A *godfather* to a pious Catholic is different from a *godfather* to a mafioso.

When one mentions 'dialect', probably the first thing most people think of is regional speech, and indeed that is one of the principal types of language variation. In many areas, it is possible for even the most linguistically naive listener to guess the origin of a speaker after he has uttered but a few words. In some countries, such as Italy and Switzerland, geographical dialects may prove a real barrier to communication; in others, such as Mexico and the United States, they may simply provide local color. Some dialects are found to be charming or amusing and are affected by entertainers for their cultural value—for example, the country western accent of a popular singer who has never left New York City. And a parent north of the Mason-Dixon line will call out to his child *Albert* with falling pitch while a southern parent will shout *Albert* on the upswing.

People's speech also varies according to their socioeconomic status, often a function of education, life style, and peer group. Professor Higgins of *Pygmalion* and *My Fair Lady* is able to identify not only the geographical but also the social source of his informants on hearing them speak. It may be assumed that within each regional variant there exist a number of social dialects.

Also to be considered are subdialects. Prominent among these are jargons, ways-of-speaking characteristic of groups closely united by professions or avocations. God help the outsider at a doctor's cocktail party, who will be unlikely to understand anything but his host's welcome and farewell. Equally murky to the nonaficionado are sports headlines, such as *AMERICAN LEAGUE KICKS OUT STREAK*, with the subheading *Lynn's grand slam ignites 13-3 rout* (*The El Paso Times*, 7 July 1983). *Kicking, slamming,* and *igniting,* only metaphoric here, are suggestive of underworld mayhem, which has itself given rise to numerous jargons, most recently one for users of narcotics. Criminal cant, designed for private use by an in-group, is often colorful enough to make its way into general speech, especially when it is adopted by authors such as Dickens or Cervantes.

Moreover, one generation does not speak in exactly the same way as either its forebears or its descendants. Research in generational differences in both Temuco, Chile, and Juárez, Mexico reveals that slang usage varies distinctly among four age groups: teenagers, young adults, the middle-aged, and the elderly. Slang flourishes among teenagers and may not even be understood by older people, who use little of it, having discarded their own for fear of ridicule (Lagos-Sandoval 1980; Dávila 1975).

Not only age but also sex is important in determining usage. In many languages, there are some words that are preferred by one sex and zealously avoided by the other. *What a darling little purse!* would be unlikely, man-to-man. In some cultures, profanity and obscenity are accepted among men, if not necessarily expected of them, but proscribed for women in the presence of men. In Mexico, the United States, and especially in Japan, men and women also differ in their intonation patterns (stress, pitch, and juncture): women have higher highs and lower lows, a range which would be considered effeminate of men. To a nonnative speaker in Japan, women seem to warble and men to growl.

There are also variations in 'register', the style of speech appropriate to a given social situation. A college professor addressing a formal lecture to his students does not employ the same locutions that he uses when bulling with his buddies in the bar or chatting with his wife and children at home. Playwrights have long used inappropriate registers to achieve comic effects. Cantinflas, as Romeo in *Romeo y Julieta*, does this when he greets her sedate and noble father with ¡*Quiúbole, joven!* 'Hiya, guy!'. Further, the casual register, in families, underlies the creation of a special vocabulary, a kind of verbal shorthand understood only by kin and intimate friends.

Some people have so distinctive a way of speaking that they can be recognized by the differences in their 'idiolects'. *Cantinfladas* are well known throughout the Hispanic world and are characterized by rapid-fire delivery, exaggerated intonation, scrambled syntax, and meaningless words created at the moment in order to camouflage the fact that one is making no sense. Idiolects, however, need not be so extreme, for, after all, no two people speak in an identical way, and it may be said, therefore, that each of us has his own idiolect. This is one reason why it is so difficult to design a computer which will respond to voice commands.

While each of us in every act of speaking is influenced by regional, social, and situational factors, we all like to feel that we can express ourselves in what is called the 'standard' dialect. Though this is a fictional construct, it nevertheless serves as an ideal form to which we aspire and which binds us together in a speech community. It is the kind of language which is the aim of the Voice of America in its international broadcasts, to express our best possible image, and, insofar as possible, is devoid of individual or group coloration. It is, in short, public language, and, in it, the laws of the land are written, scientific articles are published, and public education is conducted. Training in this dialect begins early. Who of us has not been admonished, like Johnny in the following dialogue:

Johnny: I ain't got no crayons!
Teacher: Johnny, you should say 'I don't have any crayons'. Nice people don't say 'ain't got no'.
Johnny: Why, teacher?
Teacher: Because 'ain't got no' is incorrect English.

Why is it 'incorrect English'? Because it is not the way we think that the people we most admire would speak (the prestige dialect). These may be people who have achieved success in a given society. In the West, the hallmarks of success are wealth and educational level, especially that which leads to a professional degree in medicine, law, or research science. How can one ascertain the careers that provide prestige? Ask a mother, 'What would you like your little boy to be when he grows up?' She probably would not answer 'a sharecropper', 'panhandler', or 'a burglar'! We may also admire the speech of people who live in a certain area, perhaps the center of political power, such as Paris, Tokyo, or Moscow, or a place historically renowned for its cultural achievements, such as Florence. Finally, there are some countries in which regional considerations have little or no bearing on determining the 'standard' dialect (the United States and Mexico). While few linguists would ever say that any dialect which meets the needs of its speakers is inferior, few would oppose the use of the standard dialect in schools, believing sincerely that it will open doors which might otherwise be closed.

Why do dialects evolve? Why is Latin no longer spoken in Spain nor Anglo-Saxon in England? Generally, in language evolution, two kinds of factors are involved: internal, that is, changes caused by the very nature of language itself, and external, changes due to sociological phenomena affecting speakers of the language. Of the two, the more generally predominant is internal change. For example, a linguistic system may be altered enough by generational differences eventually to produce a dialect. Also, analogy may cause irregular forms such as *dove* (past tense of *dive*) in English and *satisfizo* in Spanish to become regularized as *dived* and *satisfació*.

Moreover, language must be transmitted at a speed sufficient for practical communication but not so great as to lose comprehensibility. Rapidity in articulation tends to modify speech sounds through 'assimilation', that is, making one sound more similar to those which are adjacent. For instance, in some dialects of Spanish, before a voiced consonant any other consonant becomes voiced. Therefore, in the Spanish of Mexico and Castile, [s] in *desde* and *mismo* is pronounced [z]. In Mexico, the second [ð] in *desde* may disappear in the speaker's output but the listener will supply it mentally because of the linguistic context, as in *Estuve allí desde las ocho hasta las nueve* 'I was there from eight until nine'. Also, as a result of the speed of articulation, part of a message may be lost in transmission. Contributing factors may be a noisy environment or an inattentive listener. To overcome such obstacles, all languages use a variety of means to be 'redundant', that is, to provide the same information in several ways. In most Western European languages, a noun modified by a numeral (*three men*, *tres hombres*, *drei Männer*) is also plural in its morphology, much to the surprise of Orientals, for whom the numeral seems enough.

Another internally caused alteration is compensatory change. Since the four subsystems of language are closely interrelated, a change in one tends to produce a change in one or more of the others in order to maintain comprehensibility. For example, in some dialects of Spanish, an [s] before another consonant or a pause may vanish: in these dialects, in order to distinguish the plural of a noun from its singular, speakers modify the nature of the vowel preceding the inflection. Thus, [líβros] becomes [líβrɔ].

Similar is the internal accommodation which will differentiate among a group of sounds that are so much alike that they might easily be confused with one another. Here there are two possible solutions—either to abandon some of these sounds or make them more distinct.

Different languages and different dialects assimilate differently, use different means of providing redundancy, and have different devices for compensation and accommodation. Extralinguistic, social, and environmental factors often explain why the various dialects of a language do not solve their problems in the same way.

Prominent among these factors is separation within a formerly united people. This may be actual physical separation by geographical barriers such as mountains, rivers, or deserts within the same country or due to emigration of a group from its homeland to a distant locale. Or the separation may be social within the same community. Where there exists a sharp division among social classes, each may develop its own dialect owing to lack of association and/or pride of identity. In highly stratified Britain, domestics do not mix socially with their employers, and the dialect of neither one influences the other. Furthermore, there is occasionally a strong sense of class identification which is manifested in deliberate dialect maintenance. Cockney girls, for example, accept training in 'standard English' to better themselves economically, but steadfastly speak in their mother dialect off the job! Both the Texas cowboy and the Argentine gaucho would refuse to imitate the highfalutin' speech of the city slicker or *currito*, unless in mockery.

Language adapts rapidly to cultural change, the only constant, according to Xeno, and with the incorporation of new elements in a given culture, there arises a need for new names. If the innovations develop within the culture itself, they may be named in one of three ways. One is to attribute a new meaning to a word already current in the lexicon. *Coach*, for example, which once meant a four-wheeled horse-drawn vehicle, now may refer to a section of a 747! Or, drawing on native stock, the language may create a compound such as *tocadiscos* 'record player' or *matasanos* 'physician' (literally, 'killer of healthy people'). A third way is to borrow from foreign languages, either entire words or morphemes, as in *automobile* or *television*, where the first half is Greek and the second Latin.

Another kind of cultural and corresponding linguistic change occurs when speakers of a language take up residence in another country. Here, as above, a new element may be named with an existing word or, as more frequently happens, both the element and its native signifier will be adopted simultaneously, as in English *raccoon* and *wigwam* from Algonkin, or Spanish *chocolate* and *tequila* from Nahuatl.

Linguistic borrowing tends to be a two-way street. Spanish affected the indigenous languages of the New World tremendously. Those it did not obliterate were changed in all four subsystems. For example, the Aztecs, upon borrowing the Spanish *jarro* 'pot', were faced not only with a lexical problem but also a phonological one, since it could only be produced as [ʃálo]. As they became bilingual they added /r/ and other sounds to their phonemic stock. Although to a lesser extent, Spanish was also affected by languages with which it came into contact. Most of the Amerindians who learned Spanish in the sixteenth century were adults, and, as any foreign language teacher knows, few adults can master the phonology of a second language. One may safely assume that their Spanish was accented in accordance with the phonological pattern of their first language. It has been estimated that in the Mexico of 1600 there were but 50,000 Peninsular Spaniards as compared to several million Indians and mestizos who spoke Spanish with Amerindian intonation and taught it to their children. Linguists describe this sort of phenomenon as a dominant language both affecting and being affected by one or more substratum languages. Another example closer to home can be seen in the English spoken by monolingual Mexican Americans in Los Angeles, whose pronunciation is clearly different from that of Anglo Americans.

Social upheavals and cataclysms (such as the fall of the Roman Empire or the Moorish invasion of Spain) can cause important changes in languages. In most societies, the speech of the dominant group, the aristocracy, is different from that of the masses, and with the onset of drastic restructuring of a civilization, the prestige dialect may be superseded by that of the new upper class. Or it may be artificially preserved as the language of scholarship or ritual, like Latin in the Middle Ages and Pueblo Indian languages in New Mexico at the present time.

How are dialects studied? They have elicited comments, often charged with emotion, since the dawn of written literature and probably even earlier. One of the first writers on dialects was Aristotle, who was chiefly concerned with the appropriateness of different varieties of Greek for different applications. He held that the Spartan dialect was the most suitable for lyric poetry and the Attic for politics. Equally subjective in attitudes toward dialects were educated urban Romans, who felt that there were two ways of speaking, their way and 'the rustic and boorish kind of speech' of the less fortunate. Cicero compared the 'sweetness of utterance' characteristic of the city (Rome) with the 'harshness' of the language of provincials (Ramage 1973:68-69). Dante, a Florentine, lashed out at all Romans, whose 'vulgar tongue . . ., or rather, hideous jargon, is the ugliest of all the Italian dialects' (1940:36). Other dialects fared no better. Some, he says, lead to confusion as to the sex of the speaker:

> One of these, on account of the softness of its words and pronunciation, seems so feminine that it causes a man, even when speaking like a man, to be believed to be a woman. . . . There is also. . .another type of dialect, so bristling and shaggy in its words and accents that, owing to its rough harshness, it not only distorts a woman's speech, but makes one doubt whether she is not a man (1940:46-47).

But despite his subjectivity, Dante was perhaps the first serious dialectologist in Europe in that he was systematic in attempting to enumerate the variations in Italian, exemplify them, and explain their origin. He found fourteen major dialects with subdialects exceeding 1,000! The cause, he felt, was geographic, the mountain ranges which divide Italy into numerous linguistic compartments (1940:31-33). Dante recognized that all of these variants had one system at their base and proposed that it become the prestige dialect:

> . . .we declare the illustrious, cardinal, and curial vernacular language in Italy to be that which belongs to all the towns in Italy but does not appear to belong to any one of them (1940:55-56).

Further, Dante codified this curial dialect, based upon Florentine (his own native speech), which has since become the standard for all of Italy.

Only recently has dialect study attempted to free itself from intuitive influences. It was not until the late nineteenth century, with the birth of linguistics, that more systematic and scientific efforts to study dialects objectively were made. Georg Wenker published the first fascicle of his *Linguistic Atlas of Germany* in 1881, followed by Jules Gilliéron's *Atlas linguistique de la France* between 1902 and 1908 (Montes Giraldo 1970:70). Wenker's monumental work was never published in full because of the expense that would have been entailed in reproducing his colored overlays. The more cost-conscious Gilliéron profited by his rival's ambitious but impractical plans and chose a more modest format, employing symbols as a kind of shorthand.

Since then, most of the major countries of the world have followed suit. In Europe, linguistic atlases have been completed for Italy, France, Switzerland, England, and parts of Spain, among others, and, in the Western Hemisphere, work is finished in some areas such as Mexico and Puerto Rico and is in progress in the United States and Colombia.

An objective survey of a dialect, whether of its phonology, morphology, syntax, lexicon, or all four of these, begins with a research design for gathering data. These data, of course, will be synchronic, i.e., characteristic of the dialect at one point in time, in this case the present. The investigation may continue to be synchronic. It may focus on theoretical issues such as the expression of linguistic universals or significant contrasts within the dialect. It may focus on a comparison of one dialect with others, including the 'standard' or different regional or social variants. A second step to be taken is to record data on a map. Deviations 'involving groups of different features' then allow us to draw 'isoglosses', like isobars on a weather map, to show their distribution and boundaries. Since dialect boundaries are often not clearcut, an alternate method to indicate speech variations on a map is to use symbols indicating the areas in which neighboring dialects are mingled (Reed 1977:6) (see Figure 1 of the United States and Colombia).

Once the present nature of a linguistic variety has been determined, then the investigation may become diachronic, that is, the study of the dialect as it evolved over time. This may shed light on dialect formation in general, on the historical development of the parent language, on temporal relationships among sister dialects, or on the growth of this dialect alone. For instance, *The Linguistic Atlas of New England* carefully records speech from both quite young and very old informants, commenting on differences where they occur. Yiddish can be seen to have arisen out of a Low German variety which was influenced for centuries by Slavic elements after the Jews' flight from Germany to Western Russia. Social influences can be seen in Chicano Spanish with its sixteenth-century rogue terms borrowed from the lexicon of Mexican outlaws forced into military service in northern Mexico, now the southwestern United States.

Knowledge about a contemporary language variety is elicited from informants who are representative of the whole body of its users. It is important, therefore, to select as informants people whose speech has been influenced as little as possible by other dialects. The investigator prefers a speaker who was born in

Figure 1 Two types of dialect maps.

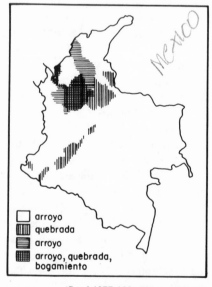

(Reed 1977:108; Flórez 1963:88)

the area. For one who is researching a nonurban dialect, the ideal informant is one who lives in the country and has had little contact with city folk. He has not traveled much nor been subject to much prescriptive training in school. A high school graduate is better than someone who has attended college, and one who has gone only to grade school is better yet. An older informant is more apt to be sought after than a younger one, because his language is less likely to be innovative. To the contrary, it may be archaic. Moreover, investigators are cautioned to beware of elderly speakers who have lost their teeth or wear ill-fitting dentures. Otherwise, their data might be of more interest to a dentist than to a linguist. Experienced field-workers in dialectology generally feel that the female is more conservative than the male in her manner of speaking since she is, in many cultures, less likely to mix with people outside her domestic sphere. Usually the first teacher of language to her progeny, she is concerned that their speech seem 'normal', so she will avoid neologisms and slang.

Criteria for selecting informants, of course, vary according to the goals of the investigation. Nonurban and urban inquiries would be directed to entirely different populations. In general, information is sought regarding not only the birthplace of the informant but also that of his parents, the informant's ethnicity, sex, age, educational level, occupation, socioeconomic status, and area of residence (Reed 1977; Shuy, Wolfram, and Riley 1968; Buesa Oliver and Flórez 1954).

Not just anyone can be a successful investigator. One must be well prepared in linguistics or willing to be trained. He must also possess certain personality traits. He must have a *don de gentes* 'a gift for working with people'. Since human beings are unpredictable, he must be resourceful, especially in a culture which may be alien to him, so that if his best laid plans go awry he can replace them with others as needed. Further, he must be guileful without seeming so. If he betrays to his informants what language behavior he is looking for, they will attempt to oblige him by providing it, whether it is natural or not. Some informants are made nervous by tape recorders or note-taking, so he must have a retentive memory. He must also be able to 'rough it', since he may well visit primitive areas where the niceties of sanitation and hygiene are as yet unknown. In some cultures, the sex of the field-worker may be of critical importance. To some groups, women are not acceptable investigators as they are expected to attend to matters domestic, not linguistic.

By way of preparation, investigators will probably conduct an inquiry into what is already known about the dialect they have chosen to work with. They will then define their goals and may even conduct a pilot study. After forming hypotheses, they will determine the best methods and equipment for testing them. These may vary widely. If they are studying a phonological problem and are allowed to use a recorder, they will probably make many hours of tapes for later transcription and analysis. Or, if a field worker is in the Philippines, where some informants believe that the machine will steal their voices, he may have to conceal his recorder or resort to abbreviated symbols or phonetic or phonemic shorthand. If the focus is lexical, the equipment can be much simpler. Based upon what he knows, the researcher can devise a questionnaire containing alternate forms that need only a quick check mark to record the answer. (See Appendix 1 for sample questionnaires.) Or the informant may be shown line drawings (as people in some remote areas cannot interpret photographic images).

Perhaps most difficult is the study of syntax because extensive texts are required to discover what structures are used and how frequently. Lengthy samples of popular speech in Mexico have recently been collected by the Centro de Lingüística Hispánica, directed by Juan Lope Blanch, at the Universidad Nacional Autónoma de México. This corpus consists of three kinds of dialogues: (1) between informant and investigator, (2) between two informants, and (3) 'secret recordings' of type (1) or type (2) (Lope Blanch 1976:5). Subjects were both men and women of high and low socioeconomic status from three generations, speaking informally on topics of interest to them, such as their work, their children, and their amusements, to an investigator who was at all times interested and sympathetic. The data were transcribed by the investigator who had conducted the interview and edited by several other readers. The results were then published for use by future dialectologists.

Gaining the confidence of the people being interviewed is of primary importance. Another successful venture was that carried out by a professor at the University of Texas at Austin. His modus operandi was to disguise himself as a ranch hand, go to a saloon in a country town, order a beer, and swap yarns with the cowboys. He had no tape recorder, no notebook, but an excellent memory, and after a few beers he would retire to his motel and type up his findings.

Country people in Latin America are often distrustful of city dwellers who, they think, propose to exploit them. Luis Flórez, director of the linguistic atlas of Colombia, overcame this problem by arranging for investigators to be introduced to the village by the resident priest, who explained that they were not evil *fiscales* 'tax collectors' but simple schoolteachers and harmless drudges, just curious about the way people talk.

If you have a lively curiosity about language, and are warm and friendly, and have a taste for adventure, you might find field work in dialectology a rewarding profession or avocation!

References

Buesa Oliver, Tomás, and Luis Flórez. 1954. El atlas lingüístico-etnográfico de Colombia. Bogotá: Caro y Cuervo.

Dante Alighieri. 1940. The 'De Vulgari Eloquentia'. In: A translation of the Latin works of Dante Alighieri. Trans. A.G.F.H. London: J.M. Dent and Sons, Ltd. 3-115.

Dávila, Adela B. 1975. El habla popular de Ciudad Juárez. M.A. thesis, The University of Texas at El Paso.

Flórez, Luis. 1963. El español hablado en Colombia y su atlas lingüístico. Bogotá: Caro y Cuervo.

Lagos-Sandoval, Marcia. 1980. Non-standard lexical usage in the Spanish of Temuco, Chile: A case study. M.A. thesis, The University of Texas at El Paso.

Lope Blanch, Juan M. 1976. El habla popular de la Ciudad de México. México: Universidad Autónoma de México.

Montes Giraldo, José Joaquín. 1970. Dialectología y geografía lingüística. Bogotá: Caro y Cuervo.

Past, Ray. 1970. Language as a lively art. Dubuque, Iowa: Brown.

Ramage, Edwin S. 1973. Urbanitas: Ancient sophistication and refinement. Norman: University of Oklahoma Press.

Reed, Carroll E. 1977. Dialects of American English. Amherst: University of Massachusetts Press.

Shuy, Roger, Walter A. Wolfram, and William K. Riley. 1968. Field techniques in an urban language study. Washington, D.C.: Center for Applied Linguistics.

Chapter 2
A brief description
of the Spanish language

2.1 The sounds of Spanish. Before examining the specific varieties of a language, one must first be familiar with its general characteristics, its system of sounds, forms, grammatical structures, and vocabulary. Each of the sections in this chapter treats one of those aspects of the Spanish language, while also introducing the student to standard linguistic terminology.

The sounds of a language may be described in two ways: how they are produced and how they are used. They are produced by organs which human beings share with other higher mammals. What enables man to use these organs for speech is his brain. Is the brain preprogrammed for language at birth? Some linguists think so, likening the mind of a newborn child to a computer which will process certain kinds of information while rejecting others. Or is the brain so constructed that it has a general propensity if not a driving need to learn, a process which, based at the outset exclusively on reflexes, comes to use the environment to construct its mental schemata? Although the answers to these questions are slowly emerging through neurolinguistic research, the functioning of the mind is largely hidden from human view. Much more accessible is knowledge of the other organs involved in speech production. These may be divided into three groups, (1) those located in the thoracic cavity, (2) the laryngeal group, and (3) those situated in the upper respiratory tract.

The thoracic cavity contains the rib cage, the lungs, and the diaphragm. When the rib cage and diaphragm contract, a column of air is expelled from the lungs through the trachea to the buccal and nasal cavities, suffering certain modifications as it proceeds, the ultimate result being the sounds we recognize as speech. It is believed that the vigor and number of pulsations of the column of air differ for different languages. It is certain that the modifications do. The first modification occurs in the tracheal area when the flow of air reaches the larynx. In simple terms, the larynx may be described as a barrel-shaped tube of cartilage housing two shelves of flexible muscle. These shelves are thick at the point where they are attached to the wall of the barrel but taper as they extend toward its center and toward each other (see Figure 2).

During respiration, these shelves (the vocal cords) are retracted to form an opening (the glottis) through which air freely passes. In the production of many speech sounds, such as [t], [s], and [tʃ], the glottis remains open and the vocal cords play no part in their articulation. These sounds are 'voiceless'. However, in the pronunciation of sounds such as [d], [z], and [ĵ], the thin edges of the vocal cords are brought together and made to flutter or vibrate by the passage of the airstream, producing sounds which are 'voiced'. Observe this phenomenon for yourself. Place your fingertips—lightly—on your Adam's apple (the barrel).

Figure 2 A schematic view of the vocal cords.

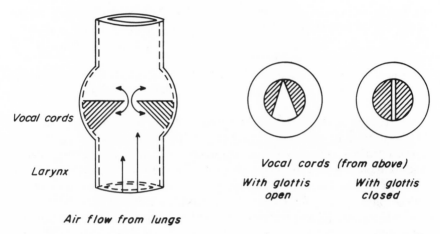

Vocal cords

Larynx

Air flow from lungs

Vocal cords (from above)

With glottis
open

With glottis
closed

Then say rapidly, in sequence, the sounds *ssss* like a snake and *zzzz* like a buzzer. If your equipment is standard, you should feel the vibration of [z] and the lack of it in [s]. Or the shelves may be clapped together to create a closure, either brief or of some duration. If the closure is momentary, it may produce an audible click or it may simply be used to separate *three* from *eagles* in *three eagles*, *night-rate* from *nitrate*, or be characteristic of words like *kitten* and *bottle* in the English of Brooklyn or some parts of Scotland. Though rare in Spanish, that sound does occur in at least one dialect. (For phonetic symbols, see Appendix 3.)

The column of air, with or without accompanying vibration, approaches the buccal (oral) and nasal cavities, where it is further modified to produce consonants and vowels. Consonants are generally associated with more turbulence and vowels with less. In the articulation of consonants, the air may be stopped, constricted, or both of these in succession. We call these 'manners' of articulation. When the stream of air is completely interrupted, the noise produced is called a 'stop' or 'occlusive'. Which stop occurs depends upon where the air is interrrupted, the 'point of articulation', usually an immovable part of the mouth. It also depends on the 'articulator', generally a movable organ, often the tongue. (For the sounds of Spanish, listen to Tape 1, selection a, the text of which is in Appendix 4.)

There are three pairs of stops in Spanish: /p/b/, /t/d/, and /k/g/. The first member of each of these pairs is voiceless and the second voiced. There are both differences and similarities between the Spanish stops and their English counterparts. No Spanish stop is aspirated, while an English voiceless stop is aspirated if it occurs at the beginning of a word. To put it in another way, in Spanish the vocal cords begin to vibrate at the moment of release of the stop, or even before, while in English release of the stop is followed by a brief instant before the vibration begins, during which time a puff of air escapes. Spanish /p/ and /b/ are like their English counterparts in both point of articulation and articulator, the two lips, but Spanish /t/ and /d/ are dental while the English pair are alveolar in point of articulation. Both pairs have the same articulator, the tip or apex of the tongue. Very similar for the two languages are /k/ and /g/, stops produced by the juxtaposition of the back of the tongue, the 'dorsum', and the soft palate or 'velum' (see Figure 3).

Spanish is characterized by a relatively high number of fricatives, sounds in whose production air is not stopped but forced under pressure through a small opening between the articulator and the point of articulation, with audible friction. In general, the muscular tension involved is less in Spanish than in English. Similar in point of articulation to the stop /p/ is the voiceless bilabial fricative [ɸ], condemned by prescriptive speech teachers but frequent in actual usage in place of more standard [f], a labiodental. For example, *fuera, fuego,* and *fogón* are often produced as [ɸwéra], [ɸwéɣo], and [ɸoɣón]. Represented in regular orthography by *f*, it is often spelled by dramatists and semiliterates with *j*, because it sounds less like [f] and more like [h]. (Some linguists speculate that [ɸ] may have been implanted in Spain by Roman legionnaires who were speakers of Oscan, since [ɸ] is thought to have been a significant sound in that ancient language spoken in Southern Italy.)

Since the stops and fricatives of Spanish occur in voiceless/voiced pairs, [ɸ] predictably has a voiced counterpart [β]. This is standard and occurs in all dialects. Tradition has dictated, since the Renaissance, whether this sound is to be written with a *b* or a *v*. In addition to the pair [β/ɸ], some speakers use the labiodental

Figure 3 The upper areas of the vocal tract.

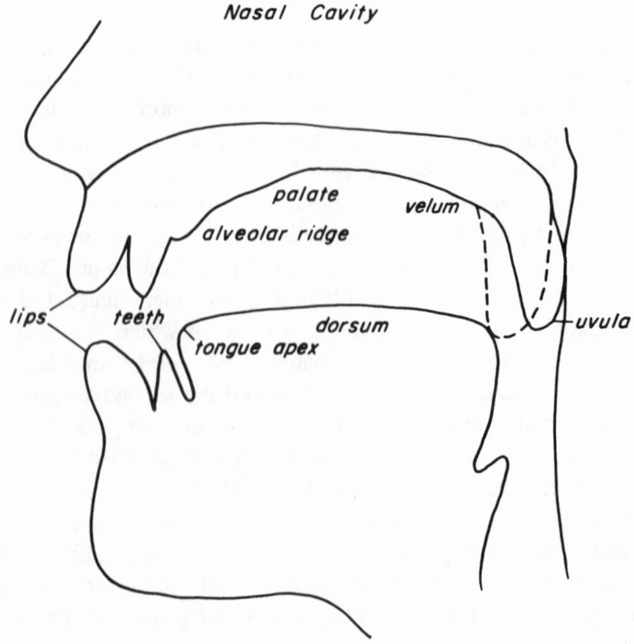

[f] and, less frequently, [v]. There is considerable variation on this point from dialect to dialect.

Another pair of fricatives, voiceless and voiced, consists of the interdentals /θ/ and [ð], as in English *ether* and *either* or *thigh* and *thy*. (Here the articulator is not named, on the assumption that the only vocal organ that one can safely and consistently put between the teeth is the tongue!)

As to sibilants, written *s* can be pronounced in three ways, depending upon dialect. One of these is laminoalveolar [s], similar to that of English, produced with the blade (i.e., front) of the tongue near the alveolar ridge. Another, [ş], is produced when the apex (i.e., tip) of the tongue approaches a point farther back on the alveolar ridge, and the dorsum of the tongue is concave, like a spoon. A third is [ş], with the apex right at the gumline and the dorsum of the tongue convex. Inexperienced listeners may easily mistake this *s* for [θ], a lisp. When *s* is voiced, its point of articulation is the same as that of its voiceless counterpart, alveolar, postalveolar, or dental.

Another sibilant in some dialects is voiceless [ʃ], where the front of the tongue nears the front of the palate, as in English *sheep*. This sibilant tends in Spanish to be mutually exclusive with [č]; that is, dialects may have one or the other but not both. The voiced counterpart of [ʃ] is [ʒ], common pronunciation of *y* in the River Plate area, as in English *azure* and *treasure*. Even farther forward, about halfway between [s] and [ʃ] is voiceless [ç], similar to standard German *ich*. This sound has no voiced counterpart.

A final voiceless/voiced pair of fricatives is that articulated when the dorsum of the tongue is raised toward the velum, represented by the symbols /x/ and [γ]. These have no equivalents in modern American English, although /x/ appears in Scots *loch*, and [γ] was a part of the sound system in Old English, word-final in *through* and *though*. The sound /x/ is represented orthographically in Spanish by *j* or *g* before *e* and *i*, while [γ] is written as *g* before all other than *e* and *i*.

Spanish is very short on affricates. An affricate may be defined phonetically as stop plus fricative. English has the voiceless affricate /tʃ/ (as in *church*), which is a combination of the alveolar [t] and the palatal [ʃ]. In the Spanish affricate /č/, however, there is no alveolar element, and the air is both stopped and released with friction at the same point, the palate, with a few dialectal exceptions. The voiced equivalent of English [tʃ] is /dʒ/ (as in *judge*), a combination of [d] and [ʒ]. The voiced Spanish [ǰ], however, has no alveolar element; again, the air is stopped and then given friction at the palate. In short, the only difference between /č/ and [ǰ] is the matter of voice. Spanish [ǰ] occurs most frequently after *n* and in vigorous, emphatic speech for *y*. For example, as a retort to *¿Quién hizo esto?* a speaker might reply *¡Yo!* ([ǰo]).

All of the preceding consonants are obstruents, that is, sounds produced by obstructing to a considerable extent the flow of air. The remaining consonants are nonobstruents. All are continuants (the air is not obstructed), and all are voiced. First are the liquids, /l/, /λ/, /r/, and /r̄/. The subclass of laterals, /l/ and /λ/, are so called because the air flows at the sides of the mouth, between the edges of the tongue and the lower molars. The articulator of /l/ is the apex, and its point of articulation is the alveolum (as for English /d/ or /t/). The articulator for [λ], however, is the body of the tongue, which rises to the anterior part of the palate. These are usually represented by written *l* and *ll*. Spanish /l/ is 'light' [l] as in the English word *light*; Spanish lacks 'dark' [ł] as in English *vulgar* or *full*. The vibrants /r/ and /r̄/ are both apicoalveolar, spelled *r* and *rr*. The single flap /r/ never occurs word-initially in any dialect. It has been likened to the 'double d' in American English *ladder*. The /r̄/ occurs word-initially (even when spelled *r*) and word-medially, but not word-finally. It may be thought of as several flap [r]s pronounced in rapid succession.

Second among the nonobstruent groups are the nasals. In all nonnasal sounds, the velum is raised so that the stream of air is kept from the nasal cavity and issues from the mouth. (Some people, however, have velums which are 'lazy', and some of the air does indeed enter the nasal cavity. You have doubtless heard this in what is popularly referred to as a 'nasal twang'.) When the velum is lowered deliberately, all of the air is directed into the nasal cavity, where it creates a resonance which enables a listener to identify a consonant as a nasal (see Figure 3). Which nasal one hears depends upon the articulator and the point of articulation in the mouth. In English, the three nasals /m/, /n/, and /ŋ/ (as in *sing* versus *sin*) are articulated at the same point as the stops /p/b/, /t/d/, /k/g/, but this is not altogether true of Spanish. The Spanish /m/, a bilabial, does correspond to /p/b/, and [ŋ], dorsovelar, to /k/g/. But two other nasals are mavericks. Spanish /n/ is apicoalveolar, like English /n/, and therefore does not correspond to Spanish /t/d/, which are apicodental. And Spanish [ɲ] corresponds to the affricates /č/ and [ǰ]. Originally an /n/ in Latin, in words such as *signo* and *senior*, the nasal [ŋ] assimilated to the preceding sound in the first case and the following sound in the second, thereby becoming the palatal nasal [ɲ]. Originally alveolar, it has lost this feature entirely. It is not like English *canyon*, although some books claim it is; not [n] plus [j], but purely the unitary palatal nasal [ɲ].

In contrast to the articulation of the consonants, the production of the vowels may be likened to the formation of notes by a musical instrument. Why is this true? In an old-fashioned pipe organ, the low notes are sounded by the long thick pipes, the high notes by the short thin ones. A brass player extends the slide of his trombone to play a low note and retracts it for one which is higher. In both cases, this is because a low note resonates best (is louder and heard better) in a large cavity and a high one in a small cavity. For any vowel, two cavities are created by the different positions of the tongue (see Figure 4). Vowels, therefore, consist of two simultaneous tones, the base tones formed by the vocal cords and the modifications (i.e., overtones) formed in the cavities. In order to pronounce /i/, the speaker raises the tongue front toward the front of the palate, creating a small cavity in the front of the mouth near the open lips where its high tone will be emitted. The large cavity in the back of the mouth is less influential—its low tone is less audible, less accessible to the hearer because it is partially blocked by the tongue. These two tones, or 'formants', constitute what the hearer perceives as /i/. To pronounce /a/, the speaker lowers his tongue

Figure 4 Tongue positions for Spanish vowels.

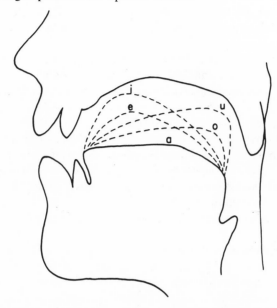

to a central position, creating two cavities of approximately the same size and shape. The two ensuing tones are very close in pitch, and the hearer perceives them as /a/. For /u/, the speaker raises the dorsum of the tongue toward the velum, creating in this instance a large cavity in the front of the mouth and a small one in the back. If one plots the closest points of approach of the tongue to the roof of the mouth for /i/, /a/, and /u/ and connects these points, a triangle results. On this triangle, /e/ is about halfway between /i/ and /a/, and /o/ about midway between /a/ and /u/ (see Figure 4).

The position of the tongue is not the only factor that determines the quality of a vowel. Whether or not the lips are rounded also contributes, as they modify the stream of sound in much the same way as does the mute or derby hat of a jazz musician like Louie Armstrong. In Spanish, as in English, all front vowels are unrounded, while all back vowels are rounded, even more rounded than in English.

In Spanish, as in other languages, there are also sounds that cannot be classified as purely consonantal or vocalic since they share some qualities of both. These are called semivowels. If a speaker tenses his tongue and raises it to a position above that for the pronunciation of /i/, the stream of air is forced through an even narrower opening with audible friction and is heard as a *y*. This sound, represented phonetically by [j], does not occur in English and is heard by English speakers sometimes as *y* and sometimes as *j*. It is neither, but it has some features of both (Bowen and Stockwell 1960:81).

For [w], exactly the same process occurs, but the highest part of the tongue is in the back of the mouth, above /u/. If the speaker raises his tongue so high that it touches the velum, he may introduce a fricative [ɣ], and [wéso] will become [ɣwéso]. Since [ɣ] is acoustically similar to [β], it often replaces it in popular speech, so that one hears [estáɣwéno], considered substandard, but nonetheless widespread.

When [j] and [w] occur in front of a vowel, they seem to be consonants, as in *hielo* and *huevo*, *vaya* and *agua*, and words in which they appear often have consonantal symbols accompanying or representing them. Their sound, however, is nevertheless vocalic. This can easily be demonstrated by taping a word such as *yo* or *ya* and running the tape backwards to produce [oj] and [aj]! That is to say that a semivowel, when it occurs after a vowel, seems to the hearer to be a vowel and to produce a diphthong, but the converse is not true. We even define a diphthong as one vowel plus another, a glide wherein the highest part of the tongue moves rapidly from one position on the vowel triangle foward and up to [j] or backward and up to [w].

Spanish is thought to have either five or eight diphthongs:

Figure 5 Diphthongs of Spanish.

	Vj	Vw
i	—	(iw)
e	ej	ew
a	aj	aw
o	oj	(ow)
u	uj	—

(Bowen and Stockwell 1960:38)

The commonest of these are [ej], [aj], [oj], and [aw]. The diphthong [uj] may also be pronounced [wi], and [iw] may become [ju], according to individual preference. Navarro Tomás says that the preposing of the semivowel is more characteristic of popular usage and that the preposed vowel is more typical of 'careful and select pronunciation' (Navarro Tomás 1932:166). The diphthong [ow] usually occurs over a word boundary as in *lo usual* [lowswál], or *lo unido* [lowníðo]. The only diphthong that poses a problem for native speakers is [ew], which maintains its identity when word-medial as in *deuda* [déwða], but frequently is reduced to [u] if word initial as in *Euphemia* [ufémja]. Compared to diphthongs in English, Spanish diphthongs rise farther and are produced with greater speed and more muscular tension.

Phones, the sounds of a language, are of interest in communication only insofar as they are of significance or are variations that are considered significant. For example, in Spanish the difference between [d] as a stop and [ð] as a fricative is never meaningful. In English, however, it is. Contrast [dej], *day* and [ðej] *they*. Each language, almost as if by agreement, selects a stock of phones, usually

30 to 60, which are thought to be sufficiently different from one another to distinguish otherwise identical words. In Spanish, *mar* and *mal* have distinct referents; therefore, we say that /r/ and /l/ are in contrast, i.e., are separate phonemes. Though Japanese possesses both of these phones, they do not contrast: [radio] and [ladio] not only mean the same thing, but sound the same, to a native speaker. In English, /s/ and /z/ are separate phonemes, as can be seen in the minimal pair /sip/ and /zip/, but in Spanish they are simply allophones. One can say [mísmo] or [mízmo] because these allophones are in free variation before a voiced consonant. The speaker is free to choose either one or indeed may vary his pronunciation at will.

The allophones of a phoneme may relate to each other in such a way that one always prefers the position word-initial, while another may occur only word-medially, or word-finally. We call this relationship 'complementary distribution'. Two allophones of the English phoneme /p/ are aspirated [p'], used at the beginning of a word, and unaspirated [p], which occurs in the middle. Compare your pronunciation of /p/ in *pin* and *spin*. In Spanish, allophones of the phoneme /d/ are also in complementary distribution. When /d/ is initial after a pause, or when it follows /l/ or /n/, it is realized as stop [d], as in [dónde está], [fálda], [andándo]. In all other environments, /d/ is realized as [ð], as in [berðáð].

In certain environments, the contrasts between separate phonemes are generally neutralized, although neither speaker nor listener is consciously aware of this. For example, /m/ and /n/ are separate phonemes, but before a bilabial /p/ or /b/, the contrast disappears: /n/ becomes [m] through assimilation, as in [umpéso] *un peso*. It will become [ŋ] in [uŋgáto]. All Spanish nasals assume the point of articulation of a following consonant.

Every language has considerably more phones than it has phonemes, but since only the phoneme determines meaning, it is the key element in understanding and making ourselves understood.

Spanish may be said to have nineteen consonantal phonemes and five simple vowels. Its eight diphthongs, if counted as phonemic, would bring the total number of syllabic nuclei to thirteen and the subtotal of phonemes to thirty-two. (These figures, of course, vary somewhat from one dialect to another.) Phonemes are often called 'segmental' since as parts they combine to make up the stream of speech. Also phonemic, however, is another group, the so-called 'supraseg-mentals', 'suprasegs' for short. The melody, which seems to be a secondary overlay on the segmentals, actually occurs simultaneously and contributes equally to meaning, often indicating part of speech, inflection, grammatical structure, or the attitude of the speaker. Suprasegmentals include stress, pitch, and juncture. Stress is of primary importance in Spanish. An example of this, often used by teachers, is the triplet *término*, *termino*, and *terminó*—the first, 'end', a noun, the second, 'I finish', a verb in the first person singular, present tense, and the last a verb in the third person singular of the preterite. Spanish has two degrees of stress, as opposed to the four degrees in certain analyses of English. Stressed syllables are longer than unstressed, so Spanish will have several short syllables in sequence, as opposed to English, which rarely has more than two. Moreover, the English long syllable is longer and the short syllable shorter, in comparison with Spanish (Bull 1965:78-79). For that reason, Spanish seems to native English speakers to have a staccato delivery. Stress is relatively uniform over different dialects of Spanish, but there do exist variations.

Similar to degrees of stress are levels of pitch, and the two interact in that greater stress usually is accompanied by higher pitch. Pitch plays a very important role: where stress differentiates in morphology or syntax, pitch and length serve to make a syllable prominent. In general, Spanish has three levels of pitch in contrast to English four. The Spanish third level, high pitch, is usually reserved for emphasis, as is English pitch four, and in both languages, high pitch appears relatively infrequently, but it is phonemic. Compare [2]*Hijo*[1] for a man calling his son and [3]*Hijo*[1], the oath, for a man expressing delight, surprise, disgust, or anger. Because of the enormous differences in the intonation patterns in an intercontinental language such as Spanish, it is risky at best to generalize about them. Nevertheless, cultured speakers tend to exhibit similar if not identical patterns. In a normal sentence with several breath groups, intermediate groups tend to resemble one another, while the initial and the final groups are different. The initial group begins at a low tone, rises to a level, and ends on a slightly higher tone. An intermediate group begins low, but not as low as the first group, and ends on a rising tone unless it is parenthetical. The last group is like the intermediate except that it falls to the same low as group one, unless it terminates a Yes-No question (Brun 1966:63). There are, of course, as many variations of this pattern as there are sentences with different grammatical structures and speakers with different intentions.

The 'uncolored statement' contour, according to Bull, is $1-2-1-1 \downarrow$, that is, low, rising, low, falling, as in *Hacemos mucho*. An emphatic statement raises the pitch to the highest level on the last stressed syllable to produce the contour $1-2-3-1 \downarrow$ as in ¡*Hacemos mucho*! Information questions—those beginning with *cuándo, de dónde, cómo,* etc.—have the same contour as statements. If emphatic, they have the same contour as emphatic statements. For Yes-No questions, there are two possibilities. If one expects an affirmative answer, the contour is $1-2-3-1$ ending on a level tone. If one is not sure of the answer, the contour is $1-2-2-2 \uparrow$ ending on a rising tone (Bull 1965:87).

The last component of intonation, juncture, is very different in Spanish and English. In Spanish, there is less tendency to mark word boundaries than in English. The boundary which is more likely in Spanish is that which marks a breath group or a phrase. If a learner of a second language fails to acquire its intonational characteristics, he may ask a question without receiving a reply, or offend his hearer by seeming derisive or indifferent. On the other hand, if he knows intonation, according to an old story, he can become a success at a party in Mexico City with only one sentence, *No me diga*, with varying contours and the right look on his face!

2.2 The forms of Spanish. While phonemes may determine meaning, they have no meaning in themselves. The smallest meaningful unit of a language is called a 'morpheme'. A morpheme may be a complete word such as Eng. *dog* or Sp. *papel*, or a part of a word such as the *-s* in *dogs* and the *-es* in *papeles*, both of which add to the base the meaning of plural. Some morphemes may appear to be meaningless but nonetheless serve to distinguish the meaning of one word from another, such as *cran-* in *cranberry*. Other morphemes have syntactic if not lexical significance—for example, the *-a-* in *tomamos*, which classifies this verb as belonging to the first conjugation. *Dog*, *papel*, and *berry* can occur by themselves and are thus considered 'free', while *-s*, *-es*, *cran-*, and *-a-* cannot and are thus 'bound'. Generally in English and Spanish, most free morphemes are bases while bound morphemes are affixes. In the same way that phonemes have as constituent members their allophones, so do morphemes have allomorphs. The English noun plural morpheme may be realized as /s/ in *pits*, /z/ in *pins*, and /ɨz/ in *peaches*. The Spanish morpheme signifying third person singular in the preterite of the verb has as its allomorph *-ó* or *-ió* as in *tomó* and *comió*.

As to the morphological structure of Spanish, it is considerably more complex than that of English since a great many more bound morphemes may be added to a base. Spanish is perhaps intermediate between the highly inflected or synthetic languages such as Latin, Classical Greek, and Russian, and the more analytical languages such as English and Chinese.

Affixation in Spanish, as in English, may be inflectional or derivational. Spanish inflectional affixes enter into the composition of verbs, nouns, adjectives, adverbs, noun determiners, and pronouns.

The Spanish verb is like its Latin forebear in that it has numerous inflectional affixes which mark person, number, tense, aspect, mood, and, if one includes verb phrases, voice (active or passive). The synthetic forms of any one verb total 51 (see Table 1).

If one includes verb phrases used to express the perfect, progressive, and passive systems, the total is increased to 437 (see Table 2).

The progressive system in the active voice, exclusive of the perfect, consists of the auxiliary *estar* plus the present participle as in *están hablando* 'they are talking'. Its 50 forms correspond to those of the synthetic verb in Table 1, with the exception of the past participle. Only the auxiliary is inflected.

The perfect progressive system, active, is made up of the auxiliary *haber* plus *estado* plus the present participle, as in *han estado hablando* 'they have been talking'. Again, only the auxiliary is inflected. There are 50 forms in this system which match those of the perfect tense active on a one-to-one basis.

Unlike Latin, Spanish has no synthetic passives but a rather complex set of verb phrases. For nonperfect tenses, the constituents are a form of *ser* or *estar* followed by a past participle which agrees with the subject in number and gender, as in *son/están escritos* 'they are written' (see Table 3).

The passive system perfect forms, like the nonperfects, total 100 and consist of *haber* plus *sido* or *estado* plus a past participle agreeing with the subject in number and gender, as in *han sido/estado escritos* 'they have been written'.

The elements of a synthetic form may be as many as four, in the order (1)

Table 1 The 51 Spanish synthetic verb forms.

	Finite (51)			
Indicative		**Subjunctive**		
Present	6	Present		6
Imperfect	6	Imperfect -*ra*		6
		-*se*		6
Preterite	6			
Future	6			
Conditional	6			
Total	30		Total	18
Infinitive	1			
Present Participle	1			
Past Participle	1			
Total	3			

Table 2 Analytical verb phrases.

	Perfect System (*haber* + Past Part.) (50)			
	Active			
Indicative	Finite (48)	**Subjunctive**		
Present	6	Present		6
Pluperfect *había*	6	Pluperfect -*ra*		6
hube	6	-*se*		6
Future Perfect	6			
Conditional Perfect	6			
Total	30		Total	18
	Nonfinite (2)			
Present Perfect Infinitive	1			
Present Perfect Participle	1			

base, which carries the meaning of the action or state; (2) thematic vowel (if present), which signifies the conjugational type; (3) the marker which shows tense and/or mood; and (4) personal suffixes. For example, the form *gritábamos* 'we were shouting' is made up of the following morphemes:

(1) *grit-*: base ('shout')

(2) -*a-*: thematic vowel (first conjugation)

Table 3 The passive system, nonperfect forms (100).

Finite (96)					
Indicative			Subjunctive		
Present	12		Present		12
Imperfect	12		Imperfect *-ra*		12
			-se		12
Preterite	12				
Future	12				
Conditional	12				
Total	60			Total	36

Nonfinite (4)			
Present Infinitive	*ser*		1
	estar	+ past participle	1
Present Participle	*siendo*		1
	estando	+ past participle	1

(3) *-ba-*: tense marker (imperfect indicative)

(4) *-mos*: personal suffix ('we', first person plural)

The base morpheme of a regular Spanish verb is invariable in form. Many 'irregular' verbs, however, mark some tenses by a change in the base, analogous to *run*, *ran* in English. For example, with *tener*, the basic stem is *ten-* but the preterite stem is *tuv-*. The most highly irregular verbs have suppletive bases (cf. *go*, *went* in English), such as *ir* with *v-* in the present and *fu-* in the preterite. Prefixed or not, the base always precedes its inflections. Its thematic vowel is *a*, *e*, or *i*, determining which inflections will occur (see Table 4).

Theme vowel *a* has been maintained in 30 of the 33 synthetic forms (91%); *i* in 29 (88%); *e* in only 19 forms (57.6%). Historically, *e* has not been preserved in the imperfect and preterite indicative because at an early stage in the development of Spanish these forms coalesced with those of *i* theme verbs.

Maintenance of all three theme vowels is strongest in the present indicative. In the case of *-ir* verbs, *e* takes the place of *i* in the second singular and the third singular and plural as in *vivir* 'live', *vives* 'you live'. Maintenance is weakest in the preterite indicative. Future and conditional, now synthetic, are derived from verb phrases beginning with an infinitive which almost invariably retains its thematic vowel as in *comer* 'eat', *comerá* 'he will eat', and *comería* 'he would eat'. Because of their history, these are not really comparable to the other synthetic forms.

The thematic vowel in subjunctive verbs has been less preserved than in the indicative. Present tense subjunctive forms are marked by *-e-* for *-a-* theme verbs and by *-a-* for *-e-* or *-i-* theme verbs. Only *-a-* has been retained in the remaining tenses of the subjunctive of *-a-* theme verbs; *-e-* and *-i-* have either been replaced

Table 4 Synthetic indicatives preserving thematic vowels.

	-a-		*-e-*		*-i-*	
			Finite			
	Sg.	Plur.	Sg.	Plur.	Sg.	Plur.
Pres.	2	3	2	3	0	2
Imp.	3	3	0	0	3	3
Pret.	1	3	0	0	3	3
Fut.	3	3	3	3	3	3
Cond.	3	3	3	3	3	3
			Nonfinite			
Infinitive		1		1		1
Pres. Part.		1		1		1
Past Part.		1		0		1
Totals		30		19		29
Percentage of 33 Possible Forms		91%		57.6%		88%

by *-ie-*, or the *-i-* in forms such as *luciera* may be assumed to be the theme vowel and the *-e-* to descend from Latin *-era-*. The latter of these two possibilities is the more likely but is unprovable.

The morphemes which serve to mark tense are both segmental and suprasegmental. In the indicatives, present is signalled by the lack of a tense morpheme: base + theme vowel + personal suffix as in *compran* 'they buy'. Imperfect is marked by *-ba-* for *-a-* theme verbs and *-ía-* for *-e-* and *-i-* as in *compraban* 'they were buying' and *vendían* 'they were selling'. Preterite has affixes which are unique (except for *-mos*, first plural), designating both tense and person as in *compraron* 'they bought' and *vendieron* 'they sold'. The synthetic future is triply marked: to the base are added the infinitive ending, the present tense of the irregular *haber* in the requisite person and number, and primary stress on the final syllable for all persons except first plural *(h)emos*, as in *comprará* 'he will buy' or 'he is probably buying' and *venderá* 'he will sell' or 'he is probably selling'. The conditional affixes are apocopated forms of the imperfect of *haber*, *(h)ía*. Since these are identical to the imperfect suffixes of *-er* and *-ir* verbs, they are probably responsible for the frequent confusion between these two tenses and the use of the imperfect for the conditional, such as *comía* for *comería*, which has come to be acceptable in colloquial speech.

In the subjunctives, present is again signalled by the lack of a tense morpheme: base + substitute vowel + 0 + personal suffix as in *trabaje* and *coma*. One imperfect affix is *-ra-*, quite productive, and the other is *-se-*, relegated to literary usage in some dialects, and both occur following base + theme vowel or *-ie-* (for *-er* and *-ir* verbs) as in *trabajara* and *comiera*, *trabajase* and *comiese*. The future subjunctive, signalled by *-re-*, *trabajare*, *comiere*, is obsolete, occurring only in poetry, legal language, and folk archaisms.

The final suffixal morphemes of the verb are the person and number markers, as seen in Table 5.

Table 5 Personal suffixes.

Tense (except Pret)	First Person Sg.	Pl.	Second Person Sg.	Pl.	Third Person Sg.	Pl.
Pres. Ind.	*-o*	*-mos*	*-s*	*-ís*		*-n*
Imp. Ind.		*-mos*	*-s*	*-ís*		*-n*
Fut. Ind.	*-é*	*-mos*	*-s*	*-ís*	*-á*	*-n*
Cond. Ind.		*-mos*	*-s*	*-ís*	*-ía*	*-n*
Pres. Subj.		*-mos*	-s	*-ís*		*-n*
Imp. Subj.		*-mos*	-s	*-ís*		*-n*

Where the personal suffix is 0, the preceding morpheme (the theme vowel or *-e-* for *-ir* verbs) is word final.

The preterite personal suffixes in Spanish, as in Latin, also serve as tense markers. In the first singular there is always an accented vowel, *-é* for *-ar* verbs and *-í* for *-er* and *-ir* verbs. The second singular suffix is *-ste* for all three classes. The third singular is *-ó* for *-ar* verbs and *-ió* for *-er* and *-ir* verbs. First person plural is suffixed by *-mos*, second plural by *-steis*, and third, for *-ar* verbs, by *-a-* + *-ron* and, for *-er* and *-ir* verbs, by *-ie-* + *-ron*. A fairly numerous group of irregular verbs share a set of personal endings in the preterite which differ from those of regular verbs of any conjugation.

As has been seen, the analytic forms are composed of far more numerous elements than the synthetics and they also outnumber the synthetics by about eight to one. Among the most frequent substitutions for a synthetic are the several verb phrases used to express future tense, one of which is similar to English and two of which are quite different. Like the English construction is *ir a* + infinitive 'to be going to':

John is going to kiss Mary.
Juan va a besar a María.

This analytical phrase is in competition with the supposedly synthetic inflected future:

Juan besará a María.

Here *besará* is *besar* + *ha* as it was written in medieval Spanish, cf. Latin *basiare habet*. A more definite future is formed by *haber de* + infinitive:

John is to kiss Mary.
Juan ha de besar a María.

Also with a future sense are some verb phrases containing modals such as *deber* (*de*) 'must' or in some tenses 'should', *hay que* 'must' or 'should', and *tener que* 'have to'. In all of these, as in the perfect tense system, the modal is inflected and the accompanying form is nonfinite.

This complexity of the Spanish verb is observed in all dialects, even by illiterates, although there are some 'literary' forms that are reserved for the written language and are seldom heard in colloquial speech—for example, in most of Latin America the *-se* imperfect subjunctive, the future subjunctive, and the pluperfect formed with the preterite of *haber*.

In contrast to the morphemic structure of the verb, that of the other parts of speech seems relatively simple. The noun has only two basic forms, singular and plural. English distinguishes between 'count' nouns, which can be pluralized and cooccur with only certain quantifiers, and 'mass' nouns which do not pluralize and occur with other quantifiers. In Spanish, however, most mass nouns may be pluralized, thereby becoming counts. The Spanish noun does not inflect for possessive as does English with -'*s*. Another difference between English and Spanish nouns lies in gender. English has 'natural' gender as does Spanish in the case of nouns referring to people or the higher animals such as *perro* and *perra*. However, Spanish also has 'grammatical' gender. That *una mesa* is feminine is meaningless and merely demonstrates that its Latin etymon was feminine.

Occasionally, gender is used in Spanish to distinguish between two applications of the same word as in *la policía* 'the police force' and *el policía* 'the policeman', where the collective noun is feminine. Perhaps two-thirds of all Spanish nouns are marked for gender by their endings. However, in the case of nouns designating people, natural gender takes precedence over the marker. For example, *el comunista* would be applied to Fidel Castro while *la comunista* would designate Madame Mao Zedong. Modern Spanish, like English, is replete with loanwords from Greek, French, English, and other sources, and unschooled speakers frequently are deceived by the endings of such nouns into attributing gender wrongly. For example, *sistema*, from Greek, is masculine but frequently occurs with a feminine article. There also exist words whose gender is uncertain, even to members of the Royal Spanish Academy, such as *sartén* 'frying pan' and *orden* 'order'.

The Spanish adjective, unlike its English counterpart, agrees with the noun it modifies and thus is always inflected for number and frequently for gender as well if its morphology permits. The general rule is that adjectives which end in *-o* in the masculine singular have four forms and those ending in any other phoneme have only two, singular and plural. *Azul/azules* is normally a two-form adjective while *blanco/-a/-os/-as* is four-form. A very small group of adjectives of high frequency have five forms, where the fifth is due to apocope, such as *buen/-o/-a/-os/-as* or *mal/-o/-a/-os/-as*. Other exceptions to the general rule include adjectives of nationality and those with terminal *-dor*, or the augmentatives *-ote*, or *-ón* and others, which have four forms. *Gran/grande/grandes* with three forms is a special case.

Some of the most common adjectives in Spanish use suppletive forms for their comparative and superlative degrees, for example, *buen(-o)*, *mal(-o)*, respectively, *mejor* and *peor*. Comparison is not a matter of *more* versus *most*, as in English, since *más*, which precedes the adjective, means both 'more' and 'most'. Compare dialogue 1 and dialogue 2:

Carlos: ¿Por qué ya no sales con Eufemia?
Roberto: Busco una muchacha más inteligente.

Carlos: Why don't you go out with Eufemia anymore?
Roberto: I'm looking for a more intelligent girl.

Carlos: ¿Por qué prefieres a Rafaela?
Roberto: Porque es la muchacha más inteligente de nuestra clase.

Carlos: Why do you prefer Rafaela?
Roberto: Because she is the most intelligent girl in our class.

Más occurs in both dialogues, but in the first the lack of the definite article *la* signals the comparative while its presence in the second dialogue indicates the superlative. While the comparative must follow the noun it modifies, the superlative may precede, as can be seen in Góngora's '*La más bella niña / de nuestro lugar* . . .' The preposing of the superlative here shows that the poet thinks all the girls in his town are beautiful, but the one to whom he is referring is the loveliest.

Adjectives that are regularly compared have a second, 'absolute' superlative, the very productive *-ísimo/-a/-os/-as* as in *bellísimo* 'extremely pretty' and *feísimo* 'terribly ugly'. Some comparative forms are used only in particular contexts: *máximo* 'highest' or 'most supreme' in politics, as in *el Máximo Jefe* (Castro). *Facílimo* 'easiest' and *libérrimo* 'most free' occur only in formal oratory or in poetry. Comparison of adverbs is similar, but the comparative and superlative are identical in form (*más despacio* 'more/most slowly'), with no definite article preceding. Only context disambiguates.

Noun determiners, which as their name implies, signal a nominal, are also generally subject to inflection. Unlike descriptive adjectives, they precede their noun, if one is present. They fall into discrete classes such as articles, deictics (demonstratives), numerals, quantifiers, and possessives. The indefinite articles include *un/-o/-a/-os/-as* and *algún/-o/-a/-os/-as*. The definite article has four forms plus the neuter *lo* which occurs before an adjective and nominalizes it, as in *lo importante*, *lo cierto*, *lo malo*, 'the important thing', 'the truth of the matter', 'the bad part'. The deictics, like the definite article, have five forms apiece:

este/esta/estos/estas + the neuter *esto*
ese/esa/esos/esas/ + the neuter *eso*
aquel/aquella/aquellos/aquellas + the neuter *aquello*

With the meanings of 'this', 'that', and 'that over there', they are roughly comparable to the three persons of the verb. The neuters only rarely precede adjectives and serve as nominals in their own right.

Spanish possesses both cardinal and ordinal numbers, some of one morpheme and some of many, some inflected and some not. The forms *un/-o/-a* serve a double function, acting not only as indefinite articles but also as cardinals. The same is not true of their plurals *unos/unas*, which serve as indefinites only. Cardinals from two to 199 are invariant except for compounds containing *un(-o)/un(-a)* as in *cien muchachos, ciento un muchachos, ciento una muchachas*. In cardinals from 200 to 999, the hundreds agree in number and gender as well (*doscientos setenta y tres hombres* '273 men' and *setecientas ochenta y ocho mujeres* '788 women'). Spanish has a full set of ordinal numbers, presumably up to infinity, but even the well-educated speaker in ordinary conversation will ignore them beyond *décimo* 'tenth'. Higher ordinals are *cultismos* 'learned words' borrowed from Latin, most of which never became established either in continental or in Latin American speech. In their place in Mexico are substituted shortened forms with *-avo* (*el veintavo hombre* 'the twentieth man', *la veintava mujer* 'the twentieth woman'), perhaps by analogy with *ochavo* 'eighth' and *centavo* 'hundredth'. In academic Spanish, *-avo* is used to form the denominator of a fraction.

Quantifiers also precede nouns and agree with them in number and gender (*pocos cigarros y muchas cervezas* 'few cigarettes and many beers') and often occur following an article or deictic and preceding a nominal (*las muchas ciudades mexicanas* 'the many Mexican cities').

Similar to adjective inflection is that for possessive pronouns. If they end in *-o* they have four forms showing number and gender, and if they end in any other phoneme they have only two, singular and plural (*nuestro/-a/-os/-as* and *mi/-s*). The possessives fall into two groups: possessive determiners which are unstressed and precede their noun and possessive pronouns which are stressed and never precede their noun. Possessive pronouns are usually preceded immediately by the definite article except when they follow their noun or the verb *ser*:

La mía está en casa.	'Mine is at home.'
¡Hijo mío, ven acá!	'My son, come here!'
Este libro es mío.	'This book is mine.'

Even if the possessive pronoun follows the verb *ser*, the article may occur to add emphasis, as in *Este libro es el mío* 'This book is *mine*', if ownership of the book is in dispute, for example.

Like the possessive pronoun is the personal pronoun, which also has two sets: unstressed and stressed. The unstressed consist of three sets, direct, indirect, and the reflexive objects (see Table 6).

Only the direct object pronouns, third person, are inflected for gender, and these forms do double duty for second person when the addressee merits the formality of *Ud.* or *Uds.* It has been said that the entire Hispanic world is divided into *loístas* and *leístas*, that is, those who say *lo* (historically correct) or *le* for the masculine direct object. There is no inflection for gender among the indirect forms and none for number in the third person of the reflexives, necessitating an additional phrase, *a él, a ellas*, for clarification of meaning. Unstressed pronouns invariably accompany a verb, preposed if the verb form or the first element in the verb phrase is finite, as in *Lo hago* 'I do it'/'I am doing it' and

Table 6 Unstressed object pronouns.

Person	Direct		Indirect		Reflexive	
	Sg.	Pl.	Sg.	Pl.	Sg.	Pl.
First	me	nos	me	nos	me	nos
Second	te	os	te	os	te	os
Third	lo/le (masc.)		le	les	se	se
	los/les (masc.)					
	la (fem.)					
	las (fem.)					

Lo estoy haciendo 'I am doing it'. With a nonfinite verb form, these pronouns must be suffixed as in *Haciéndolo bien se acaba más pronto* 'By doing it well, one finishes sooner'. In the case of verb phrases consisting of a finite form followed by an infinitive or present participle, unstressed pronouns may either precede or follow the entire phrase, as in *Lo tengo que hacer* or *Tengo que hacerlo* 'I have to do it' and *Lo estoy haciendo* or *Estoy haciéndolo* 'I am doing it'. In a sentence containing both a direct and an indirect object pronoun, the indirect always precedes the direct, as in *Me lo dió* 'He/she gave it to me'. If the two pronouns begin with *l-*, the first becomes *se*, as in *Se lo dió a María* 'He gave it to Mary'.

The stressed personal pronouns serve as subjects and as the objects of prepositions. All are inflected for both number and gender except for the first and second singular, in which one form is used to express the subject of the verb and another the object of a preposition, as in *Yo voy/A mí me gusta* 'I go/I like it' and *Tú vas/A ti te gusta* 'You go/You like it'. A stressed form cannot be used as a direct or indirect object without a corresponding unstressed pronoun (*A él lo admira toda la ciudad* 'The entire city admires him'). The stressed reflexive in the third person is *sí*: (*Se*) *lo compró para sí* 'He bought it for himself'. The indefinite pronoun *alguien* and the negatives *nadie* and *nada* are uninflected.

Most European tongues, including all Romance languages, distinguish between formal and informal speech in the second person singular and plural of the pronoun and corresponding verbal suffix. In Spain, in general, the formal *usted* is used in speaking with a person addressed by a title, such as *señor*, *señora*, *general*, or *profesor*, in contrast to the informal *tú*, reserved for a person one knows well enough to call by his first name. Traditionally, one addresses the father as *usted* and mother, sisters, and brothers as *tú*. All children are addressed as *tú*, as are people occupying menial positions. University professors speak to students as *tú* and classes as *vosotros*. If one should be angry enough to swear at a person who has perhaps run into his car, *tú*, naturally, is the form of address used and an expletive is preceded by *so*, a very special pronoun used only in this kind of situation: ¡*Tú no sabes manejar, so imbécil!* 'You don't know how to drive, you imbecile!'

In Latin America, the same general pattern is followed, but with some variations. There, the plural of *tú* is *ustedes*, not *vosotros*, which has been completely lost. In Mexico, the father may be addressed as *usted* or as *tú* with the appropriate verb form, depending upon family tradition. A menial in Mexico, however, is not invariably *tú*. A waiter is entitled to formal address. A professor in Mexico speaks to a student as *usted*, while a student calls another student *tú*. A wife refers to her husband as *tú* unless she is angry, when he becomes *usted*. A teenager and his date call each other *tú*, but if they become engaged they symbolize their new formal relationship with *usted*. In some Latin American countries (e.g., Argentina, Costa Rica), the familiar subject pronoun is not *tú* but *vos*, and the verb form used with it varies from dialect to dialect. The object and possessive forms, however, are *te*, *tu*, and *tuyo*, in all of Latin America.

The relative pronouns in Spanish are *que*, *quien/-es* and the four-form *el/la cual*, *los/las cuales*. The first, *que*, is uninflected and can refer to both animates and inanimates. The second, *quien/-es*, inflects for plural and refers only to humans. The last group, inflected for number and gender as well, refers to both animates and inanimates. Where there are two possible referents of different number and/or gender, *el/la/los/las* identifies the referent as such: *Las maestras y los alumnos, las cuales trabajan en esta escuela, están en sus clases a las ocho* 'The teachers and the students who (teachers) work in this school are in their classes at eight'. Where two antecedents have the same number and gender, the first will be assumed to be the referent: e.g., in *Los vaqueros y los patrones, los cuales trabajan todos los días con el ganado* 'The cowboys and their bosses, who work with the herd everyday', . . . *los cuales* refers to *los vaqueros*. *Cuyo*, with four forms, is the possessive relative 'whose'.

Interrogative pronouns are essentially the same in form as the relatives except that *cuál* is not preceded by an article and *cúyo* is considered substandard. *Qué* as an interrogative can only be used with inanimates: *¿Qué es ese hombre?* 'What is that man?' does not ask for the identity of the man but for his civil or his economic status, his profession or his nationality, for example. (A question of human identity demands *quién*.) *Qué* asks for a definition (*¿Qué es la lingüística?*) while *cuál* asks that a choice be made. *¿Cuál es su apellido?* asks 'What is your surname?' among all surnames that are possible.

Inflection in English is limited to members of the form classes noun, verb, adjective, and adverb while function group members have only one form (noun determiners, numerals, et al.). In Spanish, however, inflection is not confined to the form classes, and in a given Spanish utterance, most of the lexical bases are accompanied by inflectional morphemes. The two languages are similar, however, in that all inflectional morphemes are suffixes.

There are other affixes which differ from inflectional morphemes in several ways. Inflections may be affixed to all members of an appropriate form class while derivational suffixes have limited privileges of occurrence and hence much narrower distribution. If a member of this second group cooccurs with an inflectional affix, the inflectional affix must be final. Derivational suffixes often serve to convert one part of speech to another. This process has been especially productive in Spanish morphology. A verb can be created from a noun or adjective by the addition of *-ar*, *-ear*, or *-izar* to the nominal or adjectival base, as in *camino* > *caminar*, *golpe* > *golpear*, and *autor* > *autorizar*. No longer productive is the verbal suffix *-ecer* as in *flor* > *florecer* and *oscuro* > *oscurecer*. Most popular at the present time is *-ar*.

Nouns are often derived with the suffixes *-mento/-miento* and *-ción* added to the base of a verb as in *nacimiento* and *asociación*. Other suffixes that derive nouns from verbs are *-ada/-ida*, *-ador/-edor/-idor*, *-anza*, *-dura*, *-eo*, *-ón*, and *-zón* (Ramsey and Spaulding 1960:638-654). Among other morphemes marking nouns are *-dad*, *-eza*, *-ura*, *-ía*, and *-ismo*, usually affixed to adjective bases as in *bondad*, *limpieza*, *hermosura*, *cortesía*, and *machismo* ('goodness', 'cleanliness', 'beauty', 'courtesy'), but not always, as can be seen in *pintura*, *costura*, *lectura* ('painting', 'sewing', 'reading'), verb-based, and *criminalidad*, *penitenciaría*, noun-based ('criminality', 'penitentiary').

Adjectives may be formed by several morphemes such as *-ado*, *-al*, *-oso*, *-ico*, *-able/-ible*, and *-eño* suffixed to a noun stem as in *naranjado*, *monumental*, *chistoso*, *asmático*, *respetable*, *terrible*, and *risueño* ('orange', 'monumental', 'funny', 'asthmatic', 'respectable', 'terrible', and 'smiling'), or they may derive by the suffixation of *-ivo* or the like to verbal bases as in *combativo*, *bebedizo*, and *hablador* ('combative', 'alcoholic', and 'talkative'). Adverbs are frequently coined by the addition of *-mente* to the feminine singular of an adjective: *rápidamente*, *lentamente* ('rapidly', 'slowly'). Many of these forms are ancient, having been copied from Latin or formed in primitive Romance. For instance, a Spanish adverb ending in *-mente* descends from a Latin noun phrase consisting of an adjective followed by the free morpheme *mente*, meaning 'of a mind' or 'in a mood', e.g., *ciertamente* (Patterson and Urrutibéheity 1975:19).

Other derivational suffixes do not change a part of speech classification but do change the meaning, and this process is especially common among nouns:

cuchara 'spoon' *cucharada* 'spoonful'
conde 'count' *condado* 'county'
lengua 'language' *lenguaje* 'manner of speaking, etc'.
mezquite 'mesquite bush' *mezquital* 'mesquite forest'
olivo 'olive tree' *olivar* 'olive orchard'
dicción 'diction' *diccionario* 'dictionary'
político 'politician' *politicastro* 'crooked politician'
mayor 'elder' *mayorazgo* 'primogeniture'
bala 'bullet' *balazo* 'shot wound'
álamo 'cottonwood' *alameda* 'grove' or 'park'
tabaco 'tobacco' *tabaquera* 'tobacco pouch'
filosofía 'philosophy' *filósofo* 'philosopher'
mecánica 'mechanics' *mecánico* 'mechanic'
manzano 'apple tree' *manzana* 'apple' (Ramsey and Spaulding 1960:638-654)

Derivatives may serve as bases for further derivatives as in *libro* 'book', *librero* 'bookseller', and *librería* 'bookstore'.

There is an especially interesting group, augmentative and diminutive affixes, which add overtones of meaning in expressing the speaker's attitude. For example, among verbs one may choose a base, add an augment, followed by frequentative *-e-* and the appropriate inflectional *-ar* ending, as in *mirojear* 'ogle' from *mirar* 'look at' with the augment *-oj-*. Other augments that can be used in this position include *-ac-*, *-et-*, *-iq-*, *-isq-*, *-ol-*, *-on-*, *-or-*, *-ot-*, *-uel*, *-uch-*, *-uq-*, and *-usq-*. Verbs formed with these augments as a rule criticize behavior and are derisive in tone. Those with front vowels mid to high suggest smallness, triviality, or contemptibility while those with the low or back vowels *o* or *u* usually denote large size, dullness, absurdity, or repulsiveness (Cotton and Sharp 1980a:229-246). Noun and adjective augments are similar:

-ón	*-acho*
-azo	*-ucho*
-ote	*-ujo*
-ajo	*-uco* (Ramsey and Spaulding 1960:630-633)

These inflect for gender and number. Diminutive affixes also capitalize on the potential of front vowels and at times express the notions of smallness, endearment, pity, or ridicule. Again, these derivatives may be cumulative:

-ete	*-cete*	*-ecete*	
-ito	*-cito*	*-ecito*	*-ececito*
-ico	*-cico*	*-ecico*	*-ececico*
-illo	*-cillo*	*-ecillo*	*-ececillo*

And *-ito* may recur for intensification and become *-itito* or *-ititito* like its opposite *-ote/-otote/*and *-ototote*. Intensification is also achieved by combining both augments and diminutives, the ordering of which provides subtle differences of meaning. For example, *picarillón* is applied to a 'large man who is somewhat of a rascal' and *picaroncillo* to a 'small person who is a great rascal' (Ramsey and Spaulding 1960:634). All of these affixes can be appended to nouns or adjectives, and all are inflected for gender and number. Which augment or diminutive may be used is subject to phonological restrictions (Ramsey and Spaulding 1960:623-637).

The prefixes in Spanish morphology are of Latin origin and retain their original meaning. Five of the most common prefixes are *a-*, *en-/em-*, *in-/im-/ir-*, *des-*, and *re-*. The first of these frequently occurs in verbs derived from nouns involving the use of an implement or the idea of temporary attachment as in *abozalar* 'to muzzle' and *apuntalar* 'to prop up'. Verbs with this prefix are often spontaneously coined in rustic speech. The second prefix, *en-*, also appears with verbs based on nouns. These often refer to more permanent attachment as in *encespedar* 'to sod' or to insertion within a container as in *embotellar* 'to bottle'. The negativizers *in-/im-/ir-* can be prefixed to a few nouns and many adjectives such as *impaciencia* and *incapaz* ('impatience' and 'incapable'). Similarly, *des-*, prefixed mainly to verbs, negates the meaning of the base as in *descansar* and *desocupar* ('rest' and 'leave vacant'). *Re-* as a verbal prefix indicates that the action or state expressed by the verb is repeated or revived as in *rearmar* 'rearm' and *reanimar* 'revive'. Prefixed to adjectives, *re-* is an intensifier: *rebonita* is 'very pretty'. For even more intensity, *re-* may be followed by *-te-* and, for the superlative degree, by *-que-* as in *retebonita* and *retequebonita*. There are many other prefixes such as *con-*, *entre-*, and *sub-*, each with its own addition of meaning.

All of these prefixes are very productive and are used by every level of society in the spontaneous creation of neologisms, in contrast to their appearance in many words of Latin descent so ancient that the original meanings of the prefixes have disappeared, as in:

apuntar 'jot down'	*resultar* 'result'
enojarse 'become angry'	*contentarse* 'become happy'
invitar 'invite'	*entretener* 'entertain'
despertar 'awake'	*subir* 'go up'

In Spanish as in English, suffixes and prefixes often cooccur. Perhaps the ultimate example of this process is the term *desanalfabetizacionismo* 'the policy of reducing illiteracy', coined by an editor of the Mexico City daily *El Universal* in 1937. Less sensational are words such as *reproducción*, *infumable* (said of terrible tobacco), and *descamisados* 'shirtless ones', made famous by Perón.

Two other productive morphological processes in Spanish are compounding and agglutination. In both of these, two or more elements are fused into a single lexical item which functions syntactically as a unit and, if affixed, is affixed as a unit. Many parts of speech may appear, usually in their normal syntactic order. For example, if the elements of a compound are a verb and a noun in the relationship of verb and object, the verb always precedes the noun and creates a new noun. Compositions of this type are among the most common. Quite literal are some referring to household equipment:

abrelatas 'can opener'	*sacacorchos* 'cork screw'
lavaplatos 'dish washer'	*tocadiscos* 'record player'

Others refer to people and express varying degrees of irony:

espantapájaros 'scarecrow'	*matasiete* 'bully'
picapleitos 'shyster lawyer'	*salvavidas* 'brawler'

If the constituent parts of a compound are a preposition and a noun, they occur in this order and also create a new noun. Very productive is *para* as in:

parabrisas 'windshield'	*paraguas* 'umbrella'
parachoques 'bumper'	*parasol* 'parasol'

Also productive are *contra*, *entre*, and *por* as in:

contraseña 'countersign' *entrevista* 'interview'
contrasentido 'contradiction' *pormenor* 'detail'
entremés 'intermission' *pordiosar* 'beg from door to door'

If an adjective cooccurs, it too is in its customary position as in *enhorabuena* 'congratulations'. The preposition may also be followed by an adverb as in *pafuereño*, a derisive epithet for 'an outsider', or by a verb form as in *paracaidista* 'parachutist' (or in Mexico, 'squatter').

Infrequently, the fusion consists of a noun plus an adjective. If a new adjective is formed which denotes a physical attribute, the usual noun + adjective order is maintained but the final vowel of the noun becomes *-i-*:

boquiabierto 'openmouthed'
carilargo 'long faced'
patizambo 'bowlegged'

The adjectives coined in this way are usually derisive but not always, as can be seen in *ojinegro* 'black-eyed' and *puntiagudo* 'sharp-pointed'. Other noun-adjective compounds derive new nouns. The components of some are in the usual syntactic order as in *aguardiente* 'brandy', while in others the order is reversed as in *altavoz* 'loudspeaker'. Compounds of noun + noun are not quite so rare and often are composed of a more general noun followed by a more limiting one:

aguamiel 'juice of the maguey' *madreselva* 'honeysuckle' (from 'forest-
bocacalle 'street intersection' mother')
  plumafuente 'fountain pen'

Modified compounds or blends are often composed of two verbs, the first of which is phonologically altered as in *jirimiquear* 'whimper' from *gemir* plus *lloriquear* and *muraguear* from *morir* plus *haga* 'murder'.

Sometimes an entire clause may be agglutinated into a single word which functions as a noun:

correveidile 'busybody'
hazmerreír 'laughingstock'
sábelotodo 'know-it-all'

Another derivational process is abbreviation in which a compound loses its final segment/s:

automóvil > *auto*
cinematografía > *cinema* > *cine*
(*la*) *radiodifusión* > (*la*) *radio*
(*el*) *radiorreceptor* > (*el*) *radio*

(The last two of these are a source of confusion to many speakers who are not sure of the difference in meaning between these two apocopated forms.) Or the compound may be abbreviated by dropping its first component: *autobús*/*ómnibus*

> *bus* (Colombia). An extreme kind of abbreviation is the acronym, deliberately manufactured by advertisers, journalists, and politicians as in:

ProNaF 'Programa Nacional Fronterizo'
ETA 'Basque terrorist organization'
ETArrista 'member of *ETA* '
PAN 'Programa Acción Nacional'
PRI 'Partido Revolucionario Institucional'

As can be seen, the Hispanic system of derivation is highly complex. Nonetheless, it is quite lively and popular, not only with the cognoscenti but also with those less fortunate.

2.3 The structure of Spanish. Syntax may be viewed as the combination of morphemes (words and significant particles) into meaningful utterances. To communicate in a language, it is not sufficient simply to know what things are called; one must also know how to put things together. For example, a tourist in Mexico, after finishing dinner in a restaurant, decided to practice his Spanish by asking the waiter how much his meal had cost. His pocket dictionary told him that 'how' was *cómo* and 'much' was *mucho*, so he inquired *¿Cómo mucho?* The waiter nodded gravely and replied, *Sí, señor*. This time-honored anecdote illustrates the fact that knowledge of vocabulary is not enough to make oneself understood.

Different languages use a variety of devices to structure clauses and phrases. Among these are four major syntactic means: (1) strict word order, in which the position of a word indicates its grammatical function, (2) separate grammatical function markers, (3) inflections, and (4) agglutination, where words, markers, and inflections are often fused into 'word-phrases' or 'word-sentences'. Perhaps the simplest of these means is word order. Many languages put the grammatical subject first, followed by the verb, and then the object (SVO). Others, like the Semitic tongues, put the verb first, followed by subject and object (VSO). Yet others, like Latin and Japanese, put the verb in final position (SOV). The subject almost always precedes the object, wherever the verb may be; languages which reverse these two elements are so extremely rare as to be considered oddities.

In languages using the second device, i.e., separate markers, each major element of the clause is accompanied by a particle which specifies it as the subject of the clause or the object. For example, 'I buy tobacco' in Japanese is:

Watashi	*wa*	*tabako*	*o*	*kaimasu*
1st per. sg. pro.	subj.-marker	'tobacco'	DO marker	'buy'
				+ present
				+ polite

The third device, inflecting, works just as the separate markers do, but inflections are bound morphemes, inseparable from the words to which they are attached. 'Mark loves Mary' in Latin is:

Marcus	*Mariam*	*amat*
'Mark' + subj.-marker	'Mary' + obj.-marker	'love' + 3rd-per. sg.
		[+ present]

Languages that base their syntax on word-sentences produce utterances in which the component units are not independent words but ordered series of bases and affixes, most of which are bound. Paul Garvin, investigating the Kootenai language, in Victoria, Canada, found no word for 'wife'. He was told that /kapaʓke/ means 'my wife', and his informant explained to him that a speaker cannot talk about a wife without specifying whose wife she is. 'My' is /ka/, and /paʓke/ refers to 'wife' but these never appear as independent forms.

In the past, linguists attempted to classify languages on the basis of which syntactic device they employed, but it eventually became apparent that no language depends exclusively on any one device. English, which has been described as a word order language, nevertheless still inflects nouns for plural and possessive, verbs for person and tense, one-syllable adjectives and adverbs for comparative and superlative, and pronouns for person, number, and case. Japanese, which uses independent markers to indicate grammatical function, also has fairly rigid word order. Classical Latin and Greek, with bound markers, also depend upon word order at the phrase level: in Greek, *pros ten polin* is 'to the city' while **polin ten pros* would not have been understood except by a most sympathetic listener. In Nahuatl, we see the extensive use of agglutination in formations such as *ika.wka.tahto.htinemi* 'talk forcefully while walking' (Bolinger 1975:28), but word order is important as well.

Like many other languages, Spanish does not restrict itself to one syntactic device, but indeed may be said to use all four of those mentioned. As to (1) word order, Spanish has been called an SVO language, but in actual fact it often exhibits VSO order, not only in literary language, but in ordinary everyday usage as well. Word position is grammatically functional, but to a lesser extent than in English, and many nuances of meaning accompany positional change. In English,

John kisses Mary

but in Spanish,

Juan (la) besa a María
Besa Juan a María
A María la besa Juan
Juan a María la besa
A María Juan la besa

In literary language,

La besa a María Juan

is also conceivable. Displacement from regular SVO order, usually through fronting of an element, often serves for emphasis.

Another similar variation in word order can be seen in nouns modified by descriptive adjectives. The customary dictum that such adjectives follow nouns is true much of the time, but they may occur before nouns occasionally to emphasize a quality or characteristic implicit in the noun, but to which the speaker nonetheless desires to draw attention. In *la blanca nieve* 'the white snow', for example, whiteness is intensified. *El gigante pequeño* 'the little giant' distinguishes this *gigante* from the ordinary species of giant—he is a giant, but small. *El pequeño gigante* might be used in a fairy tale in which it had already been established that the story was about a dwarf giant, i.e., his smallness is not new information.

The subtle implications of word order in Spanish may set a trap for the unwary foreigner. To ask an acquaintance *¿Cómo está su hermana hermosa?* may be offensive since the listener may think it is being implied that one of his sisters is pretty and the others unattractive. *¿Cómo está su hermosa hermana?* will keep the speaker safe.

In Spanish as in English, when descriptive adjectives cooccur, they must be ordered. The first to follow the noun delimits the general category and defines a subcategory. The second distinguishes within the subcategory. *El toro bravo español* contains the subcategory of bulls bred for the ring and within this subcategory the bull is distinguished as Spanish rather than Mexican, while *el toro español bravo* implies that within the category of Spanish bulls the particular one referred to is fierce. If the speaker wishes to avoid this subcategorization, he may insert between the adjectives a conjunction, usually *y*, as in *un libro interesante y nuevo* or *un libro nuevo e interesante*, 'a book which is equally new and interesting'.

Past participles which modify nouns are also ordered. If they follow the noun, they differentiate it in a factual way, while if they precede it, they typify or express a value judgment. *Una criada cansada* is 'a tired maid', but *una cansada junta* is 'a boring meeting'. Two past participles both following the noun are either (1) linked by a conjunction or (2) separated by a comma and followed by a clause or phrase, as in *un hombre abandonado y olvidado* 'a man abandoned and forgotten' or *un hombre abandonado, olvidado de todos* 'a man abandoned, forgotten by all'. Alternatively, one past participle may precede the noun and the other follow it, as in *una cansada junta alargadísima* where, in the speaker's judgment, meetings are usually boring but this one was also very prolonged.

As to present participles, Spanish has two, each with its own uses. The *-nte* form, often literary, is basically adjectival, as in *recurrente* 'recurring', *abusante* 'abusive'. The *-ndo* form (called *gerundio* in Spanish), primarily adverbial, describes the circumstances accompanying the action of the main verb, as in

El perro salió aullando
'The dog ran away howling'

These constructions, along with their restrictions and attendant implications, are common to all Spanish dialects, regional and social.

In regard to use of separate grammatical function markers to structure phrases and clauses, Spanish is, on the whole, quite parallel to English, with a few minor exceptions:

Elías le dio una caja de dulces a Nena
'Eliot gave a box of candy to Nena'

Here, Spanish *a*, like English *to*, marks the indirect object, while *le* does so redundantly.

A Nena le dio Elías una caja de dulces
'Eliot gave a box of candy to Nena'

This Spanish structure is not analogous to the English structure:

'Eliot gave Nena a box of candy'

where word order alone signifies indirect object. Another difference between Spanish and English in the use of particles is in the marking of possessives. Spanish has no option but to use *de* with personal possessors, whereas English has both singular and plural bound markers. A third difference lies in the infinitive phrase, which in English is introduced with *to*, while the Spanish infinitive may be preceded by one of a variety of particles, such as *a*, *de*, *que*, or others.

Spanish, unlike English, has retained to a considerable extent its ancestral heritage of inflections (device (3)). In every sentence these serve to establish agreement, a basic characteristic of the language. In a typical noun phrase, all noun modifiers agree with the head noun in number and, if possible, in gender. The verb phrase must reflect the number of the noun phrase, and, if passive, will reflect its gender as well:

Las tazas están rotas
'The cups are broken'

If a noun phrase is replaced by any kind of pronoun, the replacer is inflected for the person, number, and gender of the noun replaced as well as for grammatical case:

Los González les dieron su casa vieja a sus hijas
'The Gonzalezes gave their old house to their daughters'
Ellos les dieron la suya a ellas
'They gave theirs to them'

Agglutinative processes (device (4)), though more easily observable at the word level, function syntactically as well, albeit to a lesser extent. *La/lo* as object markers occur free and bound, a distinction which may be merely orthographic.

Voy a comprarla
'I'm going to buy it'
Se lo voy a dar
'I'm going to give it to him'

Voy a dárselo
'I'm going to give it to him/her'
Se la compró por veinte pesos
'He/she bought it for/from him/her/them for twenty pesos'
Comprósela por veinte pesos (Literary usage)
'He/she bought it for/from him/her/them for twenty pesos'

Se as a replacement for *le* or *les* is not to be confused with the reflexive *se*:

Se la compró en la tienda
'He/she bought it for himself/herself in the store'
Comprósela en la tienda
'He/she bought it for himself/herself in the store'

Other particles or inflections, once free, have since lost their separate identity and now always occur bound. *Siéntense*, in which *se* is bound, in the popular speech of a semiliterate may become *siéntesen*, where *se* has become an infix, perhaps unbeknownst to the speaker!

Basic clause patterns in Spanish closely parallel those in English, predictably enough, since both languages are fairly closely related members of the Indo-European family. The frequency of occurrence of these patterns, however, differs, especially with reference to subordination and coordination. Some languages, like Classical Latin, tend to subordinate while others, like modern American English, more often coordinate. Spanish stands in between these two extremes, subordinating less than Latin and coordinating less than English. The tendency to subordinate can be seen in this example of upper class colloquial usage from *Lo cursi*, a twentieth-century comedy by Jacinto Benavente, in which Valentina explains why they have not put a little coat on their dog:

como veníamos a pie y la gente baja, hija, está cada día más insolente, dicen unas cosas cuando ven a los perros con manta (Benavente 1942:91).

'since we were coming on foot and (since) the lower classes, dear, are becoming more insolent everyday, they say some (shocking) things when they see dogs in a blanket'

There are two subordinate clauses, one main clause, followed by another which is subordinate. In an English conversation among intimates, the structure would most probably be more like:

'We were walking, and the lower classes are becoming more insolent everyday, and they say shocking things when they see dogs with a blanket on'

In Spanish, subordination is prominent even in the speech of the semiliterate, as in *La carreta*, a recent play by the Puerto Rican dramatist René Marqués, where Doña Isa says:

Donde las que no pueden mantener un hijo tienen seis, yo, que podría mantener seis, no puedo tener ninguno (1963:95).

'Where those who cannot support one son have six, I, who could support six, cannot have any'

For a functional illiterate, this is a rather complicated sentence! In English, she would more likely say

'Some women have six children and they can't support one, but I could support six, and I can't have any'

One may suspect that the frequent use of subordination in Spanish is inherited directly from Latin.

Ruth Brend's tagmemic analysis classifies Spanish clauses as primary, secondary, and tertiary, all but one of which may occur as independent or dependent. The three primary types are transitive, intransitive, and equative:

Independent transitive: El público aplaudió al actor
       'The public applauded the actor'
Dependent transitive: . . . después de que el público aplaudió al actor
       '. . . after the public applauded the actor'
Independent intransitive: Federico fuma demasiado
       'Federico smokes too much'
Dependent intransitive: . . . cuando Federico fuma demasiado
       '. . . when Federico smokes too much'
Independent equative: Toledo era la capital
       'Toledo was the capital'
Dependent equative: . . . que Toledo era la capital
       '. . . that Toledo was the capital'

The secondary types, which derive from the primary, are passive, impersonal, and descriptive:

Independent passive: El actor fue aplaudido por el público
       'The actor was applauded by the public'
Dependent passive: . . . después de que el actor fue aplaudido por el público
       '. . . after the actor was applauded by the public'
Independent impersonal: No se fuma en esta sección del avión
       'There is no smoking in this section of the airplane'
Dependent impersonal: . . . porque no se fuma en esta sección del avión
       '. . . because there is no smoking in this section of
       the airplane'
Independent descriptive: Toledo es muy antigua
       'Toledo is very old'
Dependent descriptive: . . . que Toledo es muy antigua (Brend 1968:16-17)
       '. . . that Toledo is very old'

The tertiary types, which derive from the primary and/or secondary, are the interrogative and the imperative:

Independent transitive interrogative: ¿Aplaudió el público al actor?
'Did the public applaud the actor?'
Dependent impersonal interrogative: . . . que no se fuma aquí?
'. . . that there is no smoking here'
Independent intransitive imperative: No fume tanto (Brend 1968:29)
'Don't smoke so much'

It is difficult to exemplify an imperative which is dependent, unless with a subjunctive form in a jussive construction such as *Que vengan a vernos* 'Have them come see us', where the addressee is instructed to give the command to someone else—and, even here, there might be some discussion as to whether *que vengan* is independent or dependent.

Gili Gaya's clause categories are somewhat different but no less valid and perhaps more inclusive. Clauses, analyzed as to the speaker's attitude, may be

exclamativas
de posibilidad
dubitativas
interrogativas
afirmativas
negativas
optativas
exhortativas (Gili Gaya 1961:40)

He adds that these descriptors apply equally to both independent and dependent clauses, but that the structures of the two may differ. His second categorization, less psychological, depends upon the nature of the predicate:

	intransitivas
	transitivas
atributivas o cualitativas	*pasivas*
predicativas	*reflexivas*
	recíprocas
	impersonales (1961:40)

The attributive predicate classifies the subject and is thus 'nominal' in force, consisting of a copula plus an adjective, substantive, adverb, pronoun, or a descriptive phrase (Gili Gaya 1961:57). Most frequently, the copulas are *ser* and *estar*—*ser* for qualities considered permanent and *estar* for those which are transitory or accidental, according to most grammar books. Gili Gaya, however, finds this description incomplete. *Ser* deals with qualities from an imperfective point of view in which the duration of time involved is of no importance, as in *Este jarro es blanco* 'This jug is white'. *Estar*, on the other hand, is perfective in that it portrays a quality as the result of a change which has been completed in the past, as in *Este jarro está roto* 'This jug is broken' (Gili Gaya 1961:62). The fact that the attributive adjective *muerto* is ordinarily used with the copula *estar* bears out his contention. While death may be accidental, it is anything but transitory (Gili Gaya 1961:60)! Other verbs often used as copulas are *parecer*, *venir*, *ser llamado*, *ser tenido por*, and intransitive statives such as *quedar*, *vivir*, and *dormir*. All of these, including *ser* and *estar*, also occur in other kinds of constructions. For example, *ser* occurs with attributes that are substantives, pronouns, determiners, and infinitives, while *estar* is used to indicate location (Gili Gaya 1961:64).

A predicate which does not describe the quality of the subject but expresses an event or change in which the subject participates is called 'predicative'. In this type of clause, verbs, the essential words, may or may not be accompanied by complements. If a verb has no complements, Gili Gaya says that it alone serves as a complete predication. If it has complements, they may be direct, indirect, and circumstantial. The last of these categories expresses notions of place, manner, time, means, cause, or instrument of the verbal action. Only a very few verbs are intransitive by nature: *quedar* and usually *morir*, *vivir*, and *dormir*. There are also a few verbs which are transitive by nature: e.g., *dar*, *dejar*, *entregar*, *abandonar*, and *mostrar* (Gili Gaya 1961:67).

A subgroup of intransitive verbs is made up of statives. These designate facts and express a fixed situation with regard to the subject:

Mi tío vive en El Paso
'My uncle lives in El Paso'
Quedaron muy contentos
'[as a result] they were very happy'
Llegué cansada
'I arrived tired'

Here the subject does not produce the action; rather the action or state is produced in the subject. These clauses are intermediate between active voice, with subject as agent, and passive voice, with subject as patient. Gili Gaya adds that they also stand on the dividing line between attributive clauses expressing a quality of the subject and predicative clauses referring to an event (1961:72).

Passive voice, infrequent in Spanish, is used when the main interest of the speaker is in the recipient of the action, as in *Granada fue reconquistada por los cristianos en 1492*. Agent may be expressed, as in the foregoing example, or it may be omitted, as is also the case with reflexive passives such as *Se expulsaron los judíos de España por decreto de los Reyes Católicos* or *Se expulsaron los judíos*. This construction can be used only with third person singular or plural, and if the agent is not expressed, it is on the borderline between passive and impersonal. A true reflexive is used when the action of the subject falls upon or is reflected in the subject; this is to say that the referent of the subject and the complement are the same. These structures may express physical actions or psychological states:

Me bañé anoche
'I took a bath last night'
Nos asustamos del fantasma

'We were frightened by the ghost'
Me arrepiento de haber pecado
'I am sorry to have sinned'

Verbs of eating and drinking are often reflexive when both the subject and the direct object are definite and specific, in contrast to nonreflexive forms for general statements: *Alfredo se tomó una Coca-Cola*, but, on an advertising sign, *Tome Coca Cola*. Another use of the reflexive can be seen in constructions where the subject of the clause is not a true agent, but merely influences or intervenes in an action which benefits him, but is performed by another, as in *Me construí una casa* 'I had a house built for me' (Gili Gaya 1961:74).

Certain verbs which are normally nonreflexive can be made reflexive if the speaker wishes to convey heightened emotion. One might read this headline in Madrid or Buenos Aires: CIEN CHINOS MURIERON EN EL ACCIDENTE. But a speaker might say ¡Se murió mi canario! or ¡Se me murió el canario! The difference lies in the fact that the newspaper reader, unacquainted with the victims of the accident, is not moved by their fate, while, as a canary owner, he is emotionally involved and is either distressed or (in the *se-me* construction) feels resentful at the selfish bird for leaving him!

A reciprocal clause in English and Spanish is one in which two or more subjects are both agents of the action and recipients of it. However, the syntax of such statements in the two languages is different. In English, one might say *The children are hitting each other*! In Spanish reciprocals, on the other hand, the verb is made reflexive in form but not in sense. *Los niños se están golpeando* would not be understood as 'The children are hitting themselves', but hitting each other. The clues here are provided by the context. Where they are lacking or ambiguous, an explanatory phrase must be appended. In *Los bandidos se mataron*, one would have to add the phrase *el uno al otro*, if these criminals killed each other, or *a sí mismos* if they jointly committed suicide.

Meteorological clauses in Spanish, as in English, are impersonal, probably because of the impossibility of assigning a subject-agent in phenomena such as rain, snow, hail, and the like. As in other Indo-European languages, such constructions are invariably in third person singular and are felt to contain a subject internally: *Está lloviendo*. If a separate subject-agent is provided, the result is usually figurative: *El general tronó de rabia* 'The general thundered with rage'.

There are two other types of impersonal clauses in Spanish, one similar to English and the other quite different. In the first, *They want you in the office* is analogous to *Quieren que pase Ud. a la oficina*—the identity of the subject is either unimportant or unknown. In the second type, the verb is in the third singular and is accompanied by *se*: *Se vende muchas curiosidades a los turistas en México* 'People sell many curios to tourists in Mexico'. This impersonal construction differs from the *se* passive (1) in the lack of subject-verb agreement, which shows that *curiosidades* is the object, not the subject, and (2) in the absence of a specified agent.

Gili Gaya summarizes his analysis of Spanish clauses with the following figure, commenting on its validity not only for main clauses but for subordinate clauses as well.

General diagram of possible clauses in Spanish

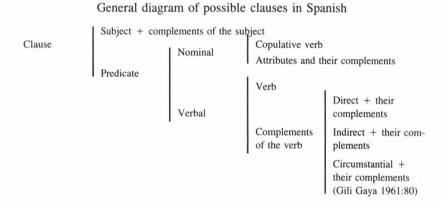

Subordinate clauses in Spanish are often in the subjunctive mood, which contrasts with the indicative in many Indo-European languages. In general, the indicative is used for events which the speaker views as factual or within his control, while the subjunctive is used for events about which the speaker is uncertain because he sees them as hypothetical and not wholly subject to his will. For example, consider a verb of volition with a noun clause as its object:

Quiero que Juan venga a mi fiesta
'I want John to come to my party'

I want is factual, but there is no certainty that John will come nor that he will come because of the speaker's desire that he do so. In contrast, consider

'I want to go to John's party'
Yo quiero ir a la fiesta de Juan

I want here is again factual, and the speaker's attendance at the party is presumably within the domain of his will.

The subjunctive is also used in a noun clause which is the object of a verb expressing emotion:

Me alegro de que Juan haya venido
'I'm glad John came'

Here, that the speaker is glad and that John came are both factual propositions, but again, John's having come is the result of a choice made by him and not by the speaker. Compare

Me alegro de haber ido
Me alegro de que haya ido

Both of these mean

'I am glad that I went'

The first, in the indicative, presents an emotion and a fact that was the result of the speaker's choice. The second, however, is subjunctive because the speaker feels that he might not have made this decision. In short, the hypothetical nature of the event is the focus here, even if the event has already taken place—because it might not have! Many languages have lost the subtleties which the subjunctive can express or have developed certain verb phrases as substitutes. In English, the subjunctive has been fossilized and occurs only in contrary to fact conditions and in certain verb phrases, while many of its previous functions have been assumed by the modals: *if I were you, I insist that he go, be it ever so humble.* French has kept its subjunctive intact, but as in English, it is used automatically in certain fixed constructions and is not a matter of the speaker's choice, not dependent upon his feelings.

In Spanish, the greater the probability of an event, the more likely it is to be expressed by the indicative. Conversely, the less strong the probability, the more likely it is that the subjunctive will be used. This is especially well illustrated by conditional sentences such as

Si llueve mañana, no iremos
'If it rains tomorrow, we won't go'
Si lloviera mañana, no iríamos
'If it should rain tomorrow, we wouldn't go'

In the first set of sentences, the speaker feels that the probability of going is rather strong, but in the second set, he is more pessimistic.

The same conditions apply to adjective clauses. Consider, if the speaker is in the southwestern part of the United States,

Busco a una mujer que habla español
'I'm looking for a woman who speaks Spanish'
Busco una mujer que hable chino
'I'm looking for a woman who speaks Chinese'

In the first Spanish sentence, the speaker has a specific woman in mind, whether he knows her name or not. In the second, the existence of such a woman is hypothetical from the speaker's point of view, so the definitizer *a* does not appear and the subjunctive is used in the verb. Where the speaker feels sure of the existence of the referent but is uncertain as to her identity, he might say

Busco a una persona que me traduzca esta carta
'I'm looking for someone to translate this letter for me'

Perhaps the speaker is in the modern language office of a western university, where he is a complete stranger. He knows that there must be a specific person who can translate Spanish, hence the definitizer *a*, but he has no idea who, hence the subjunctive.

Volition of the speaker and probability of the event no doubt also explain why the subjunctive is used in formal commands: the compliance of the listener is hypothetical, as anyone knows who has called the plumber and asked him politely to come. In contrast, the informal imperative is not a subjunctive, because presumably the speaker is in a position to impose his will.

Spanish syntax, thus, is highly complex. No matter how a speaker structures his phrases and clauses, he is bound by strict rules of agreement that are often semantically empty. On the other hand, the wealth of inflection and the supple word order of Spanish place at his command an instrument through which to impart fine nuances of meaning. The conscious use of these devices by great Hispanic authors has been responsible for the peculiar texture of Spanish literature, in which many major works are all but untranslatable. But the manipulation of these linguistic resources is not limited to literature: even the illiterate make telling use of them, particularly to lend subtle attitudinal overtones to their expression.

2.4 The lexicon of Spanish. In morphology, one analyzes the constituent parts of words. In lexicon, by contrast, one deals with the end result of morphological processes, the word stock of a given language. Yet vocabulary, which appears to be the simplest and most tangible component of speech, is in reality the least understood. It is becoming evident that lexical structure is no less systematic than other components of language, and much research is currently under way to determine its features—but the results are not yet conclusive.

Obviously, the lexicons of members of a family of languages can be expected to resemble one another, and that of Spanish, a Romance language, is similar in many ways to those of French and Italian. The processes of phonological evolution for all three are more or less analogous in the case of words directly inherited from Vulgar Latin. For example, VL *bŏna* became Sp. *buena*, It. *buona*, and Fr. *bonne* by regular rules. Another even greater similarity is the propensity in all three, once formed, to create new words through combining inherited bases and affixes. A third likeness is their tendency to borrow directly from Latin, from each other, or from other linguistic sources. Celtic, for example, contributed words in two historical periods, the earlier beginning in 600 B.C. at the time of massive migrations from Gaul, and the later in 200 B.C. with the Roman legionnaires who spoke a Latin which had already borrowed from Celtic stock. Some of these lexical items are *carro* 'cart', *camino* 'road', *cambiar* 'change', and *camisa* 'shirt' (Patterson and Urrutibéheity 1975:12). The Romans also borrowed over 300 Germanic words such as *blanco* 'white', *banco* 'bench', *guardar* 'guard', and *guerra* 'war'. Beginning in A.D. 411, the invading Visigoths introduced about a hundred more in active use today, such as *fresco* 'fresh', *ganar* 'win', *rico* 'rich', and *sacar* 'take out'. Also Visigothic are many common given names such as *Alfonso, Elvira, Fernando,* and *Ricardo,* and surnames such as *Álvarez, Gómez, González,* and *Rodríguez.*

However, the lexicon of Spanish (as well as that of Portuguese) has one major characteristic which it does not share with its sister languages. In Peninsular

Spanish there are lexical items, small in number but great in frequency, of non-Indo-European origin. Some of these are attributed to pre-Roman Iberian, such as *cama* 'bed', *arroyo* 'ravine', *gordo* 'fat', and possibly *perro* 'dog' from onomatopoeic *prrr* or *brrr*, imitative of a growl (Corominas 1961:449). From Basque came *izquierdo* 'left', *pestaña* 'eyelash', and *vega* 'river bank'. Arabic contributed more than 4,000 terms, some of which are extremely common in Spanish:

aceite 'oil'	*asesino* 'murderer'
alcalde 'mayor'	*azúcar* 'sugar'
alcoba 'bedroom'	*barrio* 'neighborhood'/'ward'
alcohol 'alcohol'	*rincón* 'corner'
almacén 'warehouse'	*ronda* 'police patrol'/'serenader'
(now 'department store')	*taza* 'cup'
arroz 'rice'	

Also from Arabic are *limón, naranja, toronja, algodón*, and *hasta*, the only function word in Spanish of non-Latin origin.

The hospitality to foreign loan words has continued in the Spanish of the New World, which has accepted an enormous number from African languages in the Caribbean, Amerindian languages throughout, and, in the Southwestern United States and Puerto Rico, from English.

The lexical analysis of any language can be approached in two ways, according to Patterson and Urrutibéheity. Using both ways, these authors based their study on a compilation of the 5000 words of highest frequency in contemporary Spanish, the frequency dictionary of Juilland and Chang-Rodriguez, 1964. Patterson and Urrutibéheity found that words inherited from Vulgar Latin, both popular and semilearned, account for about 24% of the total. Words created in Spanish by different kinds of affixation, compounding, and agglutination make up 35%. But borrowings comprise the largest group, 41%, and these have the following origins: Classical Latin 81%, other Romance languages 11%, Greek 5%, and Arabic and others about 2% each (Patterson and Urrutibéheity 1975:21).

The second way to analyze a lexicon is to include data concerning frequency of use, and their figures yielded by this method are in sharp contrast to the first set:

Table 7 The lexical composition of modern Spanish.

	Percentage share of total membership	Percentage share according to frequency
Inherited	24	81
Created	35	8
Borrowed	41	11

(Patterson and Urrutibéheity 1975:21)

Table 7 shows that the smallest group, words inherited from Vulgar Latin, has by far the greatest frequency of occurrence. The largest group, borrowings, is used much less often. The second largest group, created words, has the smallest frequency of all.

The historical periods that saw the most rapid growth in the Spanish lexicon correspond to times in which Spain was experiencing important cultural development. According to Patterson and Urrutibéheity, borrowings were especially numerous in the fifteenth century and amount to 35% of the loanwords in their sample; in the thirteenth century, 21% of the total were borrowed; in the sixteenth, 12%; and in the seventeenth, 11%. Thus, the fifteenth, sixteenth, and seventeenth centuries, which correspond to the Renaissance and the transitional period immediately preceding it, contributed 58% of the loan words in their sample. A smaller percentage, 21%, were borrowed in the thirteenth century (Patterson and Urrutibéheity 1975:32-34)—the time of Alfonso el Sabio, a period of intense literary and intellectual activity.

It was also during these same eras that the Spanish lexicon was increased by the largest numbers of created words: in the fifteenth through the seventeenth centuries, 48%, and in the thirteenth century, 20%. The remarkable similarity of the figures for both borrowing and creating is an example of cultural expansion resulting in lexical growth.

Patterson and Urrutibéheity state that number of items and frequency of use are also helpful in analyzing lexicon according to parts of speech (see Table 8).

As can be seen, form class or lexical words comprise 98% of the total of the Patterson and Urrutibéheity sample but occur only 47% of the time, while the function group members consist of less than 3% of the total but occur 53% of the time. Nouns are more than twice as numerous as verbs, but the two classes occur with almost the same frequency. Adjectives are more numerous than verbs in the sample but their usage is one-third less. Among the function words, prepositions and articles are the most often used, 19% and 16%, while pronouns and conjunctions appear with almost equal frequency. These figures obviously would vary from region to region in the Hispanic world, but those for the high-frequency words are presumably relatively constant.

Quite common in Spanish is functional shift, the creation of a new part of speech by altering the syntactic function of an old one. For example, new nouns have arisen from adjectives (*obrero* 'workman', *desierto* 'desert'), from infinitives (*placer* 'pleasure', *saber* 'knowledge'), from past participles (*soldado* 'soldier', *sorpresa* 'surprise'), and from present participles (*habitante* 'inhabitant', *continente* 'continent'). New adjectives have been formed from past participles (*casado* 'married', *satisfecho* 'satisfied' (Patterson and Urrutibéheity 1975:20).

The average length of a Spanish word in the Patterson and Urrutibéheity corpus is about three syllables (see Table 9). High frequency items are likely to be function words, short, and old, a part of the vocabulary inherited from Vulgar Latin. Long items are apt to be lexical words, new, and either borrowed or created (Patterson and Urrutibéheity 1975:160).

Table 8 Parts of speech: Membership and frequency.

Part of speech	Percentage share of total membership	Percentage share according to frequency
Form class or lexical words:		
Noun	51	15
Verb	19	16
Adjective	24	10
Adverb	4	6
Total percentages	98	47
Function words:		
Pronoun	1	9
Preposition	.3	19
Article	.1	16
Conjunction	.4	8
Interjection	.2	.2
Number	.7	1
Total percentages	2.7	53.2

(Patterson and Urrutibéheity 1975:72)

A special group within the Spanish lexicon consists of numerous idioms, clauses or phrases whose meanings are not the sum of their component parts. The constituent which is most likely to lose its normal semantic value is the verb around which the idiom is constructed, such as *dar*, usually 'give', in *La ventana da a la calle* 'The window faces the street'. Another 'emptied' verb is *echar*, usually 'throw', in *Te echo de menos* 'I miss you'. A third is *poner*, usually 'put'/'place', in *Se pone triste* 'He becomes sad'.

Like lexicons in all languages, the vocabulary of Spanish has its weak and its strong areas as a vehicle for communication. One of the weaknesses is the attribution of masculine and feminine gender to inanimates. That a cup (*taza*) is feminine and a saucer (*platillo*) masculine and that their modifiers must agree in gender can be viewed as a complication that does not contribute to meaning and is, in effect, 'excess baggage'. Moreover, Spanish has no neuter nouns, and their absence causes problems in reference. Consider:

Juan está en la cocina con su esposa. Ella está en malas condiciones.

Which is in need of attention, the wife or the kitchen? In this respect, Spanish, as well as its sister languages, lost a useful part of its heritage when the Latin neuter case endings coalesced with those of the masculine before the birth of Romance.

Table 9 Word length according to origin.

	Number of members	Frequency (%)
Inherited:		
One syllable	88	68
Two syllables	731	28
Three syllables	313	3
Average		2.27 syllables
(The longest are four syllables and are of low frequency)		
Borrowed:		
One syllable	12	.4
Two syllables	432	27
Three syllables	1037	52
Average		3.1 syllables
(The longest are six syllables and are of low frequency)		
Created:		
One syllable	12	.6
Two syllables	228	32
Three syllables	683	38
Average		3.5 syllables
(The longest are eight syllables and are of extremely low frequency)		

(Patterson and Urrutibéheity 1975:26-28)

Culturally, Spain and Latin America lagged behind the rest of Western Europe and the United States in technological development. Consequently, most technical terminology has been acquired through borrowing or the creation of calques from other languages. As a result, there is little homogeneity in many scientific and technical areas. For instance, the Carter Carburetor Company has had to publish five different service manuals in Spanish for five different dialect regions.

A minor weakness lies in the lack of specificity in Spanish verbs of motion. *Andar*, for example, may mean either 'walk' or 'ride' and if a distinction must be made, it necessitates the addition of a phrase such as *a pie* 'on foot', *a caballo* 'horseback' or *en coche* 'by car'.

Also weak is the range of color terms. Spanish, like its ancestor, lacks a generic adjective for 'brown', and therefore has had to compensate for this deficiency either by borrowing (*marrón* in Argentina and Uruguay from Italian *marrone*) or by comparing (*color café* and *chocolate*, in general use). The nuances of English *purple, violet, lavender*, and *mauve* are not easily expressed in Spanish, where *morado* covers the entire range. Modern English is replete with color terms coined by dress designers and manufacturers of automobiles, such as cinnamon, rust, aquamarine, baby blue, teal, wine, maroon, hot pink, and charcoal, which have no Spanish counterparts.

Spanish, further, is burdened by many phonological/orthographic problems. In most dialects, [b] and [v] sound identical, creating confusion in that two words, once separate, become homonyms:

barón 'baron'	*varón* 'male'
basto 'coarse'	*vasto* 'vast'
botar 'pick out'	*votar* 'vote for'
sabia 'wise woman'	*savia* 'sap of tree' (Mosterín 1981:121)

A child learning to write is faced with memorizing one spelling for each meaning with no phonological cue. Similar is the lack of differentiation for many speakers between *ll* and *y*:

valla 'fence'/'wall'	*vaya* 'go'
calló 'was silent'	*cayó* 'fell'
pollo 'chicken'	*poyo* 'bench'
arrollo 'I roll up'	*arroyo* 'ravine'

There is no problem in Castile in contrasting *s* with *z* or *c* before *i/e*, where the first is pronounced [s] and the last [θ]. In Andalusia and Latin America, however, the phonemes coalesced into one, [s], again creating homonymns and orthographic difficulties:

beso 'kiss'	*bezo* 'snout'
casar 'marry'	*cazar* 'hunt'
coser 'sew'	*cocer* 'cook'
serrar 'saw'	*cerrar* 'close'

Another spelling problem is caused by *h* when it is not silent, as in *holgorio* and *halar*, which has led people in some countries to write these words with *j*. Rustic speakers throughout the Hispanic world tend to pronounce initial *h* in several words that began with *f* in Latin such as *harto* [hárto] 'fed up with,' *hierro* [hjɛřo] 'iron,' *hervir* [hɛrβír] 'boil', and *hijo* [hího] 'son' in certain contexts. In general, however, *h* in Spanish orthography is a fossil, retained out of respect for tradition, analogous to *h* in English *honor* and *honest*. In neither language is it likely to disappear.

Efforts to reform Spanish spelling began with Gonzalo Korreas' little known *Ortografía kastellana nueva i perfeta* in 1630. They were renewed, nearly successfully, by Andrés Bello in Chile, whose innovative spellings endured there from 1844 to 1927. The most recent attempt is under way at the present time, in the work of the Spaniard Jesús Mosterín (1981:121). It is unlikely that his efforts will meet with more success than those of his predecessors in the face of Hispanic conservatism.

The strengths of the Spanish lexicon lie in its expressive power, richness of color, and ease of understanding. Like English and unlike French, Spanish possesses a great wealth of synonyms which provide means for subtlety and variety in expression. Often there coexist in a speaker's vocabulary two terms with the same referent, one inherited from Vulgar Latin and another, a *cultismo* borrowed from Classical Latin at a later time, offering different shades of meaning and greater and lesser degrees of formality in one's choice of register. Other nuances are derived from the flexibility in altering Spanish words through affix-ation, functional shift, and compounding, processes which often serve to express attitudinal factors. Further meaning potential comes from the traditional hospi-tality of Spanish toward loanwords. Such borrowings from Amerindian languages have additionally provided local color without interfering seriously with com-munication.

In Spanish, as in German, words formed by composition are usually transparent in their meaning since the semantic values of their constituent parts are well known, thus facilitating the understanding of complex neologisms. English, in contrast, is more opaque in its non-Germanic words because they have been borrowed as wholes and the meanings of their components have become obscure. As a result of composition and inflection, Spanish words tend to be longer than their English equivalents and thus, as any translator knows, a page in English is likely to be four-fifths of a page in its Spanish version.

These then are the phonological, morphological, syntactic, and lexical systems upon which all varieties of Spanish are ultimately based, and from which all depart to a greater or lesser extent. Let us now examine the historic and cultural causes that are responsible for the ways in which Hispanic dialects differ from one another and, specifically, what these differences consist of.

References

Benavente, Jacinto. 1942. La fuerza bruta y lo cursi. Buenos Aires: Espasa-Calpe Argentina.

Bolinger, Dwight. 1975. Aspects of language. 2nd ed. New York: Harcourt, Brace, and Jovanovich.

Bowen, J. Donald, and Robert P. Stockwell. 1960. Patterns of Spanish pro-nunciation. Chicago: University of Chicago Press.

Brend, Ruth. 1968. A tagmemic analysis of Mexican Spanish clauses. The Hague: Mouton.

Brun, Gerard. 1966. La lingüística aplicada a la enseñanza del español como lengua extranjera. Madrid: Instituto de Cultura Hispánica.

Bull, William E. 1965. Spanish for teachers: Applied linguistics. New York: Ronald Press.

Corominas, Joan. 1961. Breve diccionario etimológico de la lengua castellana. Madrid: Gredos.

Cotton, Eleanor Greet, and John M. Sharp. 1980a. Hypersemanticization in neologistic Mexican Spanish verbs. Papers in Romance 2.4.229-246.

Gili Gaya, Samuel. 1961. Curso superior de sintaxis española. 13th ed. Barcelona: Biblograf.

Juilland, Alfonse, and E. Chang-Rodríguez. 1964. Frequency dictionary of Spanish words. The Hague: Mouton.

Marqués, René. 1971. La carreta. 8th ed. Río Piedras, Puerto Rico: Editorial Cultural.

Mosterín, Jesús. 1981. La ortografía fonémica del español. Madrid: Alianza.

Navarro Tomás, Tomás. 1932. Manual de pronunciación española. 4th ed. Madrid: Centro de Estudios Históricos.

Patterson, William, and Hector Urrutibéheity. 1975. The lexical structure of Spanish. The Hague: Mouton.

Ramsey, Marathon Montrose, and Robert K. Spaulding. 1960. A textbook of modern Spanish. New York: Holt.

Chapter 3
The contemporary languages of Spain

3.1 Castilian. Miguel de Unamuno has compared the geography of Spain to the architecture of a castle: a high structure surrounded by battlements constituted by chains of mountains running parallel to the coastline. There is a relatively narrow strip of land between the mountains and the sea. Going inland from the coast and crossing the mountains, one finds an immense tableland that continues to the mountains on the other side of the country (like the *altiplano* of Mexico, curiously enough; see Map 1).

The dialect spoken on the northern three quarters of the plateau is the 'official dialect' of Spain, that used in the public school system, telecommunications, radio and TV, laws, public signs, and so on. It is popularly known as Castilian. Actually, it has no special name, as the words Castilian and Spanish are synonymous in both Spain and in the New World, since no one recognizes it as a dialect! It is, of course, as much a dialect as is any other variety of Spanish.

That dialect shows a number of distinctly regional traits. Its pronunciation is characterized by widespread velarization, a throatiness which has, at least to Navarro Tomás, 'a lordly and aristocratic effect' (1968:32), intensified by the

Map 1 The regions of Spain.

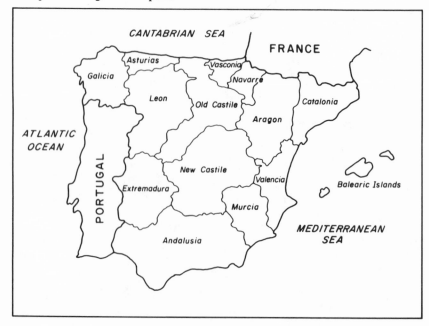

'calm and measured tone' supposedly used by Ferdinand the Catholic and speakers in Spain today (1968:104-105). Within Castile, speakers of subdialects differ enough in their intonation so that a fellow Spaniard can tell whether they come from the areas of Madrid, Toledo, Segovia, or elsewhere. As to segmental phonemes, /p/, /t/, and /k/ are pronounced uniformly in the Hispanic world. In contrast, however, Castilian fricatives display several characteristics unique to this variety. Especially prominent is /θ/ for z and for c before i and e, a pronunciation which proclaims the speaker a *castellano* to the rest of the Spanish-speaking world. Equally distinct is /s/, which, though a retroflex apicoalveolar, has an acoustic effect similar to that of palatal /ʃ/. There is also a voiceless velar fricative /x/ corresponding to j or g before i and e which has been described as 'scrapy', almost like German velar *ch*. Only in the Castilian dialect is this phoneme pronounced with such vigor and muscular tension. A third fricative is the interdental voiced phoneme written d, which in Castile is normally very weak in intervocalic position, much more so than in, say, Mexico. At the ends of words it is often left unpronounced, even by cultured speakers, except in formal situations. When it is pronounced, it is frequently devoiced and becomes /θ/.

The phonemes /j/ and /ll/ are regularly distinguished on most of the plateau (e.g., *cayó* vs. *calló*) but there are islands of *yeísmo* where both are pronounced /j/. Among these are the cities of Santander, Toledo, and Valladolid, and the working-class sections of Madrid. Some linguists believe that *yeísmo*, typical of the south, is gaining ground in northern Spain at the present time. The other consonants and the five vowels are essentially the same as those described in the previous chapter.

The following texts illustrate the wide variance between urban and rural usage. The first is a selection from an informal address 'Cómo hacerse actor' by the well-known writer Lino Landy, who was born in Toledo and lived for many years in Madrid.

Los griegos—que en paz descansen—llamaron "hipócritas" a los actores, o sea, "hipócrita" tenía esa acepción. Hoy día, tiene una acepción un poco más amplia. ¿Por qué?—pues porque el hipócrita, el actor, finge ser otro individuo, otra persona, otro carácter. Ahora la pregunta es, ¿cuál es el carácter verdadero del "hipócrita", del actor? ¿El que vive, o mejor dicho, el que siente y sufre en la vida real, la llamada "real", o el que vive y goza en la escena? El escenario es seguramente el único lugar donde *se vive*. Fuera del escenario no se vive, no se goza la vida: la vida se siente, y se siente a través del sufrimiento, porque lo único positivo es el dolor. El "hipócrita" del actor no vive esa vida, y si la vive, la sufre, la siente. Pero en el escenario el actor sí vive, sí goza la vida, y ésa es su vida verdadera, y antes y después que se alza el telón vuelve a su casa y se encuentra con su esposa, seguramente una señora gorda, con tres o cuatro niños, o cinco, o seis, quizás. Bien. Esa no es la vida del actor: ese es el entreacto de su vida. Díganme si no, ¿dónde puede Don Juan gozar de sus hazañas mejor que en el escenario? En el escenario Don Juan goza, vive sus hazañas. En el escenario goza su vida no solamente

Don Juan, también Quasimodo. Y goza su vida Barba Azul, y goza cuando diga frente al cadalso y cae en la guillotina, "¡Gozo!" ¿Gozó Barba Azul y vivió Barba Azul con esa intensidad cuando llegó al cadalso? ¡No! ¿Sintieron Romeo y Julieta el amor tan intensamente como los sienten los actores que los encarnan en el escenario? ¡No! ¿Qué muchacha puede gozar, puede vivir el amor, poseyendo y cantando, como Mimí, —por muy tuberculosa que se crea—, en la vida real, más banal que real, una muchacha no con la vida y el amor como Mimí, cantando, viviendo? O sea, aquí la vida del escenario es la vida del papel, es la única que se vive. Y, por lo tanto, los actores son los únicos seres vivientes en este mundo. (Tape 1, selection b, records this address.)

The second text, a scene from Jacinto Benavente's drama *Señora Ama*, contains a conversation between two peasant women, Pola and Gumersinda. Pola's daughter has found herself in a delicate condition as a result of the sexual advances of the *patrón* of the *hacienda*, Don Feliciano. The conversation turns from Pola's daughter to Feliciano's wife Dominica, who accepts his philandering with resignation. While Benavente's representation of rustic Castilian may be somewhat stereotyped, Spanish critics agree that the country dialect in this play is accurately portrayed. Note the frequent omission of intervocalic and final [ð] (*toos, verdá*) and in some cases [ð] initial (*ecirle 'decirle'*). Another omission is intervocalic [r] in the imperfect subjunctive (*fuéamos 'fueramos'* and *tuvián 'tuvieran'*, where there is a stress shift as well). There are at least three apocopes of common verbs (*tie 'tiene'*, *quies 'quieres'*, and *puen 'pueden'*). The archaic quality of rural Hispanic speech is obvious in *haiga 'haya'*, *naide 'nadie'*, *pa 'para'*, and *ande 'donde'*, as it is in the proverb '*Siempre perdices, cansan*'. These special traits are immediately evident when the rural text on the left is compared to the urban Castilian version on the right.

Pola. ¿Y qué puen decir en el pueblo? Que mi chica y ha tenío una desgracia. . . No ha sío la primera ni será la última, y si se casa, naide tie que decir na. . . Después de too, como muchas y de más alto que ella; y si fuéamos a ver, las que más hablan.

Pola. ¿Y qué pueden decir en el pueblo? Que mi chica también ha tenido una desgracia. No ha sido la primera ni será la última, y si se casa, nadie tiene que decir nada. . . Después de todo, como muchas y de más alto que ella; y si fuéramos a ver, las que más hablan.

Gubesinda. ¡Y si las que más tenéis hablao de toas en vuestra vida habéis sido vosotras! Pa al fin y a la postre venir a caer en lo mismo, que no hay como hablar pa que too caiga encima . . . ¿Qué no tendréis hablao de la Jorja y de la Engracia y de la Cisela y de toas? . . .

Gumersinda. ¡Y si las que más habéis hablado de todas en vuestra vida habéis sido vosotras! Para al fin y al cabo venir a caer en lo mismo, que no hay como hablar para que todo caiga encima. . . ¿Qué no habréis hablado de Jorga y de Engracia y de Cisela y de todas? . . .

Pola. ¡En el nombre del Padre! . . . ¡Bendito y alabao! Pero ¿es que de mi hija y hay quien puea decir otro tanto? Es que tú también has ido a creerte de más de cuatro, que bien las conozco, y serán las que habrán ido a ecirle al ama lo que haigan querío. . . Que a eso vengo, a hablarle y también, y que sepa de mi boca la verdá de too.

Gubesinda. ¡Mejor te hubieas estao en tu casa! Lo que el ama quie es no verte ni oírte, a ti ni a ninguna. . .! ¡Sinvergonzonas! ¡Desastrás! Que no sé cómo tenéis cara pa presentaros ande ella pisa. . . ¡Ah, si no fuea una santa, que de puro santa, paece boba, como le digo yo y le yo y le decimos todos!. . . ¡Ay, si vosotros tuviáis vergüenza!¡Y si tuvián vergüenza vuestros maridos, que con eso bastaba, aunque no la tuvieais vosotras!

Pola. ¡Mira, Gubesinda, que si no mirase y que eres tú la que me lo dices! . . .

Gubesinda. ¡Y tanto como has de mirarte! Y si quies hacerte caso de mí, vuélvete a la Umbría y no te pongas delante del ama, y tu chica menos.

Pola. ¡Eso es! Pa consentir y que la Jorja, que está más cerca del ama, le haga ver lo que no ha sío, y el ama se crea de ella más que de nosotras, que ésa tie mucha miel y trae engañá a mucha gente.

Gubesinda. Descuida que ni al ama ni a mí, ni la Jorja ni tú ni ninguna nos traéis engañás, que toas sois lo mismo. . . . ¿Conque dices y que tu hija se casa? Con Francisco, ¿verdá? ¡Si mientras haiga hombres pa too, tan ricamente! ¿Y el amo el padrino. . . , con su buen regalo?

Pola. ¡En el nombre del Padre! . . . ¡Bendito y alabado! Pero ¿es que de mi hija también hay quien pueda decir otro tanto? Es que tú también has ido a creerte de más de cuatro, que bien las conozco, y serán las que habrán ido a decirle al ama lo que hayan querido. . . Que a eso vengo, a hablarle yo también, y que sepa de mi boca la verdad de todo.

Gumersinda. ¡Mejor te hubieras estado en tu casa! Lo que el ama quiere es no verte ni oírte, a ti ni a ninguna. . .! ¡Sinvergonzonas! ¡Desastradas! Que no sé cómo tenéis cara para presentaros donde ella pisa. . . ¡Ah, si no fuera una santa, que de puro santa, parece boba, como le digo yo y le decimos todos!. . . ¡Ay, si vosotros tuvierais vergüenza ! ¡Y si tuvieran vergüenza vuestros maridos, que con eso bastaría, aunque no la tuvierais vosotras!

Pola. ¡Mira, Gumersinda, que si no mirase también que eres tú la que me lo dices!. . .

Gumersinda. ¡Y tanto como has de mirarte! Y si quieres hacerte caso de mí, vuélvete a la Umbría y no te pongas delante del ama, y tu chica menos.

Pola. ¡Eso es! Para consentir también que Jorga, que está más cerca del ama, le haga ver lo que no ha sido, y el ama se crea de ella más que de nosotras, que ésa tiene mucha miel y trae engañada a mucha gente.

Gumersinda. Descuida que ni al ama ni a mí, ni Jorja ni ninguna nos traéis engañadas, que todas sois lo mismo. . . ¿Conque dices también que tu hija se casa? Con Francisco, ¿verdad? ¡Si mientras haya hombres para todo, tan ricamente! ¿Y el amo el padrino. . . , con su buen regalo?

Pola. No hará más que por otros. . .

Gubesinda. ¡Y que la Dominica lo consienta y no coja y se vaya a casa de su padre a estar como una reina, como estaba de moza, con too el regalo del mundo!

Pola. ¿Regalo? Yo no sé qué le falte; que si ella vino de buena casa, el amo no vino desnudo ni descalzo. . . Y bien enamoradicá d'él andaba, que su padre de ella no quería casarla . . . Y sus padres d'él querían casarle con la Dacia. Y bien supo ella plantarse con toos, y buen mozo se llevó, y bien orgullosa está ella de habérselo quitao a muchas más principales que andaban desatinás por él.

Gubesinda. ¡Así es, desatinás! Que la mujer que no mira más que la presencia del hombre, too le está muy merecío. . . Y así ha sío con la Dominica. ¿Pa qué le ha servío el buen mozo? Pa las demás.

Pola. ¿Dejará ella de ser su mujer y el ama de su casa?

Gubesinda. ¡Buen consuelo! Pa verse siempre rebajá. . . ¿Y por quién? Por quien no le llega a la suela del zapato, por cualquier lao que se mire.

Pola. ¿Qué hemos de hacerle? Siempre perdices, cansan. ¡El mundo es así y así son los hombres!

Gubesinda. Si yo de los hombres no digo naa. . . , que ellos naa tienen que perder por naa. . . Pero las mujeres son las que no tenían que ser como son.

Pola. No hará más que por otros. . .

Gumersinda. ¡Y que Dominica lo consienta y no coja y se vaya a casa de su padre a estar como una reina, como estaba de moza, con todo el regalo del mundo!

Pola ¿Regalo? Yo no sé qué le falte; que si ella vino de buena casa, el amo no vino desnudo ni descalzo. . . Y bien enamoradita de él andaba, que su padre de ella no quería casarla. . . Y sus padres de él querían casarle con Dacia. Y bien supo ella plantarse con todos, y buen mozo se llevó, y bien orgullosa está ella de habérselo quitado a muchas más principales que andaban desatinadas por él.

Gumersinda. ¡Así es, desatinadas! Que la mujer que no mira más que la presencia del hombre, todo le está muy merecido. . . Y así ha sido con Dominica. ¿Para qué le ha servido el buen mozo? Para las demás.

Pola. ¿Dejará ella de ser su mujer y el ama de su casa?

Gumersinda. ¡Buen consuelo! Para verse siempre rebajada. . . ¿Y por quién? Por quien no le llega a la suela del zapato, por cualquier lado que se mire.

Pola. ¿Qué hemos de hacerle? Siempre perdices, cansan. ¡El mundo es así y así son los hombres!

Gumersinda. Si yo de los hombres no digo nada. . . que ellos nada tienen que perder por nada. . . Pero las mujeres son las que no tenían que ser como son (Benavente 1947:80–81).

(This part of *Señora Ama* is recorded on Tape 1, selection c.)

3.2 Andalusian. The southern quarter of the Iberian peninsula speaks Andaluz, the second most widely spoken Spanish dialect in Spain (see Map 1). In its homeland it enjoys great prestige. An aristocratic Andalusian is no more likely to switch to Castilian than a cultured Virginian to Midwestern. Andalusians in general consider their speech amusing and witty, often poetic, and this view is shared by many Spaniards in other areas. As a result, comedians and popular singers often adopt an Andalusian accent as their stage dialect. Whereas Castilian is spoken gravely and deliberately, Andalusian has a more rapid delivery and the range of pitch is wider with higher highs and lower lows.

Phonemically, the stops are the same as in Castilian, voiced or voiceless. The fricatives differ, however, in being pronounced less vigorously, with less muscular tension. Intervocalic [β] is not only more relaxed but also tends to drop out, as in [akáa] for *acaba* 'he finishes'. The *f* tends to be a voiceless bilabial fricative rather than a labiodental, a pronunciation also found in other parts of Spain. Most importantly, the phonemic distinction between [s] and [θ] is not observed in most of Andalusia, where both are pronounced [s]. Further, the typical Andalusian [ş] is dental as opposed to the apicoalveolar [ş] of Castile. If the /θ/ most immediately identifies Castilian, its absence identifies Andalusian, except for southernmost regions, where there is no [s] at all and *s* is pronounced [θ] as in [θómoh] for *somos* 'we are'. Where [ş] occurs before another consonant or a pause, it is reduced to an aspiration or disappears entirely, as in [εhtámɔh] and [εtámɔ] for *estamos* 'we are', and a preceding /e/, /a/, or /o/ becomes more open. Most of Andalusia is *yeísta* in that *ll* is pronounced [j]. The voiceless velar fricative /x/ is different from that of Castile. In the production of Castilian /x/ the postdorsum of the tongue is raised into actual contact with the velum, while in Andalusia it is raised close to the velum but does not quite touch it, so the resulting sound is not as 'scrapy' as in Castile, but sounds more like an *h*.

Among the nasals, *n* before another consonant or a pause, especially the latter, often becomes velar [ŋ].

In the case of the vibrants, /r/, if word-final before a pause, tends to disappear. Similarly, the lateral /l/ is dropped if word-final before a pause, and /r/ and /l/ are frequently interchanged in certain regions. Multiple vibrant /r̄/ is often pronounced as a postalveolar voiced fricative rather than as a vibrant.

In Andalusia, some speakers use [ʃ] for the spelling *ch*, as in other regions of the Hispanic world. There is also a strong tendency to shorten many high-frequency words: *tiene* to *tie*, *puede* to *pue*, and *quiere* to *quie*. While this is common in rustic Castilian, it is typical of urban speech as well in Andalusia.

As to lexicon, Andalusian has numerous borrowings from Arabic and from gypsy *caló*, such as *pistear* 'drink', *jamar* 'eat', *sardo* 'soldier', *camellar* 'to desire ardently', and two that mean 'money', *jando* and *parné*. Many of these were exported to the Americas.

Despite these regional differences, Castilian and Andalusian are very similar. In oral communication they are mutually intelligible and, if written by the educated, identical.

The following dialogue, from *El peregrino*, a farce by the brothers Álvarez

Quintero, illustrates some of the traits of Andalusian pronunciation in the lines spoken by Antoñuelo. Note his *seseo* in *ofisio* ('*oficio*') and *relasiones* ('*relaciones*'), the omitted [ð] in *quemao* ('*quemado*') and *tos* ('*todos*'). Further, the use of [r] for [l] can be seen in *er* ('*el*') and *ocurtis* ('*ocultis*'). Word-final [r] and [l] are often lost, as in *humó* ('*humor*') and *cabá* ('*cabal*'). Antoñuelo consistently pronounces *ll* as [y] and *pues* as [pos]. His *pa* is typical of substandard Spanish universally. *Pue* is an apocopated form in his speech, as in Pola's.

buena pieza	ANTOÑUELO. ¡Sopla! . . . Y dime, *güena piesa,*
chiquillos	¿tienes muchos *chiquiyos* ya?
	SOTILLO. No; hasta ahora no tengo más que ocho. Menedemo, que es el primero de la dinastía; Eutiquiano, Amandino, Filadelfo, Nemorato. Vitálico y Magnisio, que son gemelos, y Onesífero, que es el chiquitín. . .
camarada	ANTOÑUELO. (¡*Camará*, qué nombres! ¿En dónde
bautizado, todos	le habrán *bautisao* los niños a éste?) Y ¿son *tos* varones?
	SOTILLO. Todos. Niña sólo tuve una: Tirifila.
	ANTOÑUELO. Tiri. . . ¿qué?
	SOTILLO. Tirifila. Se murió a poco de bautizado.
	ANTOÑUELO. (¡No podía menos!)
	SOTILLO. Pero es particular que siendo todos varones salgan más bien a su madre que a mí. El corte de cara, la subida de ojos, el modo de rascarse. . . Todo, todo es de ella. Mío tienen muy poco.
el	ANTOÑUELO. ¡Mira que *er* modo de rascarse!. . .
oficio, variado	Veo que *er* cambio de *ofisio* no te ha *variao* el *humó.*
humor	No hay quien te dé una pena.
	SOTILLO. Ni falta, querido Antoñuelo. Y a ti ¿quién te la da, con el cañuto de licenciado en el bolsillo y camino ya de tu tierra?
pues, quemado	ANTOÑUELO. *Pos*, sin embargo, estoy más *quemao* que las ánimas.
	SOTILLO. Tú dirás por qué.
	ANTOÑUELO. Y de este pueblo no me voy como
-ado	no me vaya bien acompaña*ao.*
	SOTILLO. ¡Hola, hola!
aquella	ANTOÑUELO. ¿Te acuerdas de *aqueya* Maruja, más
onza	bonita que una *onsa* de oro, con quien en Saragosa entré
relaciones	en *relasiones*?
	SOTILLO. Sí; que por cierto tenía un tío muy bruto. . . criado de un marqués o de un duque. . .
cabal	ANTOÑUELO. *Cabá.* Ese duque o ese marqués le
plaza	dió a ese tio la *plasa* de jardinero y guarda de aqueya
allí	finca que ves *ayí*. . .SEÑALANDO HACIA LA DE-
allí, hace	RECHA. Y *ayí* vive con mi morena desde *hase* dos meses.

	SOTILLO. Allí está. . . Dadme el laúd. . . en trova
	triste y llorosa, en endecha lastimosa. . .
para	ANTOÑUELO. Si, ¿eh? *Pa* versitos está este cura.
el, empeñado	¿Tú no sabes que *er* viejo se ha *empeñao* en casarla con
	un hijo suyo que vive ahora en América, y que a
puede ver, pintado	mí *pué vé* ni *pintao*?
	SOTILLO. No, no sabía nada.
Pues	ANTOÑUELO. *Pos* ya lo sabes. Y aquí me tienes
para hablar	que no sé cómo componérmelas *pa hablá* de *ocurtis* con
ocultis, aquello	la muchacha y cantarle *aqueyo* de:
chocita	"Vente conmigo y haremos una *chosita* en er campo y
ella	en *eya* nos meteremos" (Álvarez Quintero and Álvarez
	Quintero 1923:142-143). (This part of *El peregrino* is
	recorded on Tape 1, selection d.)

3.3 Leonese. Farther removed from Castilian are two dialects found in northwest and northeast Spain. In the northwest, the dialect of Leon (paradoxically no longer spoken in the city of Leon) extends from the northern fringe of the historical kingdom of Leon through Asturias to the Cantabrian coast (see Map 1) and coexists with Castilian in that it is used by rural speakers and lower class urban dwellers, while Castilian is the dialect of the urban upper class. Unlike Andalusian, Leonese and Castilian are not mutually intelligible in many cases in both spoken and written forms. Leonese resembles Galician, the northernmost dialect of Portuguese, its neighbor to the west. This resemblance is referred to in the popular saying *Gallegos y Asturianos, primos hermanos* 'Galicians and Asturians, first cousins'. For example, word-final [o] becomes [u] and [e] becomes [i]; initial [l] is often palatalized (e.g., *lluna* 'moon'), while postconsonantal [l] may become [r] as in *praza* and *cravo*, as in Portuguese. Verb inflection in the perfect tenses is somewhat like Portuguese in that the pluperfect is synthetic: *Preguntóme lo que me dixeran* as compared to Portuguese *Perguntou-me o que me dixeram* and Castilian *Me preguntó lo que me habían dicho* 'He asked me what they had told me'. As can be seen, object pronouns follow an initial verb. An oddity in Leonese equational sentences is the lack of agreement between an adjective and the substantive it modifies, as in *La tsitsi ta cuayao* (= Sp. 'La leche está cuajada') 'The milk is curdled' (Alvar 1960:1:23).

Leonese is not uniform but varies greatly from one area to another. A well-known Asturian variety is *bable*, restricted to rustic usage or jokes deriding country people. Samples of *bable* are provided in the two following texts. Note that, in contrast with the Andalusian selection, this dialect differs from Castilian not only in its phonology, but in morphology and lexicon as well. Compare, for example, *faime* with Castilian *me hace*, *biei* with *velada*. The syntax, however, is not significantly different from Castilian: *Yo nun pedí un hermanín* corresponds word for word to *Yo no pedí un hermanito*, despite the lexical and phonological differences. And some clauses are exactly the same, *Yo quiero una bicicleta* and *Pido un patín*. The first text comes from a Christmas card:

Reyes Magos, Palestina:
Por el furacu la puerta
déxovos ista cartina,
un cachín arrugadina
y la lletra un pocu tuerta.

Reyes Magos, yo soy Pin.
De los catorce hermaninos
yo soy el más piquiñín.
Nací 'n Tudela Veguín
y ya tengo siete añinos.

Pe la mañana tempranu,
con la barriga toa inchá,
foi mió madre 'ncamillá,
pa traeme utru hermanu
que nun lu quiero pa na.

Illa dizme que los Reyes
tan muy probinos isti añu,
que la biei faime dañu
y si nun pe les oreyes,
de cabeza voy p'al bañu.

Y metiosei entre 'l ceñu,
de traeme un rapacín,
com' un xatu de gordín,
pa que xugara col neñu
en Tudela de Veguín.

La mió má ta maxareta
y mió pá ta del coquín.
Yo nun pedí un hermanín.
Yo quiero una bicicleta
y si non. . . Pido un patín!
(Tape 1, selection e.)

Reyes Magos, Palestina:
Por la puerta abierta
os dejo esta cartita,
un poquito arrugadita
y la letra un poco tuerta.

Reyes Magos, yo soy Pin.
De los catorce hermanitos
yo soy el más pequeñito.
Nací en Tudela Veguín
y ya tengo siete añitos.

Por la mañana temprano,
con la barriga toda hinchada
fue mi madre encamada,
para traerme otro hermano
que no lo quiero para nada.

Ella me dice que los Reyes
están muy pobrecitos este año,
que la velada me hace daño
y si no por las orejas,
de cabeza voy para el baño.

Y se le metió entre ceja y ceja,
de traerme un rapazuelo,
como un piojo de gordito,
pera que jugara con el niño
en Tudela de Veguín.

Mi mamá está encantada
y mi papá está como un gallo.
Yo no pedí un hermanito.
Yo quiero una bicicleta
y si no. . . Pido un patín!

The second text comes from the Maragatería region south of Oviedo in northwest Spain.

Cantar de pastores
San Juanico, San Juanico,
¡cuándo acabas de veniri!
Soy pastor y guardu ugüeyas;
tiengu ganas de saliri.
Adiós, ugüeyas del alma,
curdeiros del alma miya;

Cantar de pastores
San Juanico, San Juanico,
¡cuándo acabas de venir!
Soy pastor y guardo ovejas;
tengo ganas de salir.
Adiós, ovejas del alma,
corderos del alma mía;

Dios vus traya outru pastor	Dios os traiga otro pastor
que vus dé mejor guarida,	que os dé mejor amparo,
que vus llieve monte abajo,	que os lleve monte abajo,
que vus traya monte arriba,	que os traiga monte arriba,
ea ruyier de la carqueixa	y a roer la carqueja
ya beber del agua fria,	y a beber del agua fría,
a ruyier la urz albar	a roer el brezo blanco
que vus lliene la barriga.	que os llene la barriga
	(Alvar 1960:1:227).

3.4 Aragonese. Aragonese, now spoken only in the northernmost reaches of Aragon (see Map 1) is the counterpart of Leonese in many respects. Like Leonese, it coexists with Castilian (and, in some border areas, also with Catalan). It is likewise spoken primarily by rural people and by the laboring classes in the cities of the region. Just as Leonese shares a number of the important characteristics of nearby Galician, so Aragonese has many traits in common with its larger neighbor, Catalan. Phonologically, both retain initial Latin *cl-*, *fl-*, and *pl-* without the palatalization often observable in Spanish (though in some subdialects of Aragonese an [l] following an initial stop may become [λ]; thus, forms such as *cllau 'clavo'*, *fllama 'llama'*, and *pllat 'plato'* are found). Initial [f], frequently lost in Castilian, is maintained: *forno 'horno'*. Initial *j* changes to [č]: *choven 'joven'*, while word-medially it becomes [ʒ]: *festejar*. Also similar to Catalan is the preservation of final consonant clusters once separated by a vowel (*calders* 'calderos' and *fuanz* 'fuentes') with the loss of *o* and *e* in final position (Alvar 1960:1:300).

Aragonese differs from both Castilian and Catalan in some aspects of verb morphology. In the present tense, the inflection for first person plural *-mos* often becomes *-nos* in popular speech. The imperfect of *-er* and *-ir* verbs has kept the Latin marker *b* lost in Castilian (*bebeba 'bebía'* and *moriba 'moría'* (Zamora Vicente 1979:266). This loss may be an archaism or may result from analogy with the imperfect of the first conjugation. The preterite seems capricious in several ways: some verbs are analogic in that the same vowel precedes the personal suffixes in all preterite forms:

cantó	cantomos
cantos	cantoz
cantó	cantoron (Zamora Vicente 1979:269)

Also, some verbs which are irregular in Castilian have been regularized through analogy in Aragonese, where the stems for the present and the preterite are again identical: *estaron 'estuvieron'*, *sabió 'supo'*, and *tenión 'tuvieron'* (Zamora Vicente 1979:275).

The morphology of other parts of speech reveals further traits peculiar to Aragonese. For all nouns, even those ending in a consonant, the plural inflection is [s], as in *arbols*, *calcetins*, and *señals*. Many two-form adjectives in Castilian have four forms in Aragonese, with feminine singular and plural forms such as *granda/grandas* 'big', *proba/probas* 'poor', and *verda/verdas* 'green'. These feminine forms by false analogy have led to masculines such as *grando* and *tristo*. The masculine singular definite article is *o*, *lo*, or *ro*, while the feminine is *a* or *ra* and the plural forms are *os*, *los*, *ros*, or *es*, and *as* or *ras* (Zamora Vicente 1979:251, 256-257). The personal pronouns closely resemble those of Castilian except for *mos* 'nos', and *le lo* instead of *se lo*. The possessive pronoun for third person plural is *lur*, avoiding the ambiguity of *su* in Castilian. The archaic relative *qui* is used in place of Castilian *quien*, and *cual* has a masculine *cualo* and a feminine *cuala*. The indefinite pronoun is *otri* instead of *se* or *uno* (Zamora Vicente 1979:254-256).

The pronouns of Aragonese also differ syntactically. *Yo* and *tú* are used as the objects of prepositions as in Catalan: *con yo* and *para tú*. If an inanimate direct object pronoun cooccurs with an animate indirect, the inanimate precedes as in

Lo te diré	*'Te lo diré'*
Bébelate	*'Bébetela'* (Zamora Vicente 1979:253)

In the lexicon of some subdialects, *haber* is still used to express possession, and *ser* and *estar* are often interchangeable. In the Pyrenees, many pre-Roman words survive, and loanwords from Gascon, spoken in southwestern France, are abundant. Ever since the Middle Ages, Aragonese has borrowed extensively from Catalan: *clau* 'clavo', *festejar* 'festejar', and *seo* 'sebo' ('tallow') (Alvar 1960:1:302).

As the *Romance de Marichuana* shows, Aragonese differs from Castilian to about the same extent as Leonese, but in different ways:

De los altos Pirineos
m'en baché ta tierra plana,
pa ver un amor que tiengo,
que se llama Marichuana.

Ye una moza muy rolliza,
güellos negros, nariz chata;
tiene más juerza que un güey
y más ancas que una vaca.

En a pocha d'o gamboy
t'he bachato unas manzanas,
pa que tú veigas l'amor
que te tengo, Marichuana.

Juntaremos o bodoño
y toda la parentalla,
y as alhajas que yo tiengo
te las diré en dos palabras.

De los altos Pirineos
he bajado hasta la tierra llana,
para ver un amor que tengo
que se llama Marijuana.

Es una moza muy rolliza,
ojos negros, nariz chata;
tiene más fuerza que un buey
y más ancas que una vaca.

En el bolsillo de la chaqueta
te he bajado unas manzanas,
para que tú veas el amor
que te tengo, Marijuana.

Juntaremos el regalo de bodas
y toda la parentela,
y las alhajas que yo tengo
te las diré en dos palabras.

Tengo una sartén sin coda,
y una olla desansata,
y os espedos para asar
yo me los faré de bucho,
os tenedós y as cucharas,
y a rueca con o fuso
pa filar en as bilatas.

Ya nos claman ta la ilesia;
nos dijon cuatro palabras;
me preguntó iñó retor
si quereba a Marichuana.

Le dije: siñor retor,
a pregunta ya escusata:
¿No sabe que yo la sigo
como lo buco a la crapa?

Tengo una sartén sin mango,
y una olla sin asas,
y los espetos para asar
yo me los haré de boj,
los tenedores y las cucharas,
y la rueca y el huso
para hilar en las veladas.

Ya nos llaman a la iglesia;
nos dijeron cuatro palabras;
me preguntó el señor rector
si quería a Marijuana.

Le dije: Señor rector,
la pregunta está excusada:
¿No sabe que yo la sigo
como el macho cabrío a la cabra?
(Alvar 1960:1:457)

3.5 Portuguese and Galician. Spanish in its several dialects shares the fringes of the Iberian Peninsula with three other languages. That spoken by the largest number is Portuguese, between Spain and the Atlantic Ocean to the west. Are Portuguese and Castilian two variants of the same language or not?

In the court of Alfonso X el Sabio in Toledo, a poet was free to use either tongue, depending on his theme—Portuguese for love lyrics and more martial Castilian for heroic ballads. But the early independence of Portugal (in the time of the Cid) and subsequent invasions by the Spanish crown created enmity which has continued unabated to the present day. Hence the dictum that 'Espanhol è português mal falado' and the corresponding retort 'El portugués es español mal hablado'. These sayings reveal a popular awareness of the similarities between the two. Their lexicons coincide to a great extent, as does their morphosyntax. Phonologically, however, they are very different. For example, Portuguese, unlike Spanish, has 12 vowel phonemes, five of them nasal, and [s] before another consonant or pause becomes palatal [ʃ] or [ʒ] in many dialects. Another difference is that in Portugal unaccented e and o word-final become [ə] and [u], respectively (in Brazil, [i] and [u]), and there are many other dissimilarities. In fact, Castilian phonology bears considerably less resemblance to Portuguese than to standard Italian, and as a result any educated Spaniard is able to read Portuguese easily but cannot understand it when spoken.

The resemblance between Portuguese and Castilian is obvious in the following Brazilian anecdotes. The marginal glosses should enable you to read these texts without difficulty. Bear in mind that similarities between these languages are sometimes disguised by their different orthographic conventions. (Tape 1, selection f, recorded by Dr. Alberto Bagby, from Porto Alegre.)

Sorpresa	*Espanto*
son las, de los niños	Interessantes *são as* impressões *das crian-ças.* . .
padre	Comentava um *pai:*
Yendo	*Indo* a Santos esperar uma família amiga, que
llegaba, lleve, los dos	*chegava* da Europa, *levei* a mulher e *osdois* pe-quenos, vestidos à marinheira.
Llegamos al muelle, allá	*Chegámos ao cais. Lá* estava un navio de gue-rra.
de los, viendo	Um *dos* pequenos, *vendo* desembarcar os ma-
reéndose	rinheiros, gritou *a rir:*
Mira allá, Hombres tan	—*Oi lá,* papai! *Tamanhos homens* vestidos de
grandes	criança!

O presente

En la Nochebuena, van	*Na noite de Natal vão acordar* O Pedrinho,
a despertar,	*no seu leito.*
en su lecho,	—Pedrinho! Pedrinho! *acorda!* O *Pai Noel*
despiértate, el Padre	*trouxe-te um irmãozinho agora de noite.*
Navidad, te trajo, un	—*É* de açúcar?—pergunta Pedrinho, *acor-*
hermanito, esta noche	*dando.*
Es	—Não.
despertándose	—É de carne?
	—É.
acostándose	E Pedrinho, *deitando* outra vez:
Entonces, échalo fuera	—*Então* . . . *bota fora!*

Caso estranho

Se hablaba en una	*Falava-se numa* reunião familiar sôbre os lu-
personas	gares de onde eram as diversas *pessôas.*
	Luizinho começou a mostrar-se intrigado e
	perguntou ao pai.
dónde es que, usted	—Papai, *onde é que o senhor* nasceu?
	—Em Campinas.
	—E mamãe?
En el	—*No* Rio de Janeiro.
Y yo	—*E eu?*
Usted nació	—*Você nasceu* aquí em São Paulo.
extraña	—Que coisa *esquisita!* Como é que conse-guimos nos reunir aquí os três?

Justo motivo

enojada, llama	A mamãe, *zangada, chama* o Olavo.
hace un poco, duraznos	—Olavo! Agora *há pouco* estavam dois *pêssegos* alí em cima do aparador: como é que agora
sólo hay uno	*só há um*?
yo no vi	—É porque *eu não vi* o outro, mamãe (Carter 1942:6-7).

The use of Portuguese extends beyond its political borders, continuing all the way up the western coast and crossing the Spanish border. The Portuguese dialect spoken in northwestern Spain is Galician (Gallego), which has over the centuries been massively invaded by Castilian. For example, upper class speakers have adopted the [θ] for *z* or for *c* before *i* or *e*. The [s] does not always palatalize to [ʃ] or [ʒ], but can be apicoalveolar like that of Castile. And like Castilian, Galician lacks the nasal vowel phonemes of Portuguese. Further, the lexicon, though generally archaic, exhibits many loanwords from Castilian. Also, Galician makes use of the Castilian orthographic system, albeit inappropriately at times. In spite of these borrowings, Galicians, like Asturians, are felt to be inferior, stereotyped as rustics, and made the butt of Castilian jokes.

Galician, however, has a literary tradition at least as old as that of Castilian and even older than that of Portuguese. In the Middle Ages, it was the language preferred for lyric poetry in the court of Alfonso X el Sabio. The linguist Silveira Bueno believes that Galician would have become the prestige dialect of Portuguese, if Galicia had not, at an early date, been incorporated into Spain (Silveira Bueno 1967:295).

A court poet who wrote in Gallego in fifteenth-century Spain was Alfonso Álvarez de Villasandrino, whose poem 'Desexo' is cited below. One of the traits it exemplifies is the use of a stop plus [r] where Castilian has a stop plus [l] (e.g. *prazer* 'placer'). Also, it shows the retention of Latin /f/ word-initially (*facer* 'hacer'), regularly lost in Castilian. The fricative *x*, voiceless [ʃ], is the equivalent of Portuguese voiced *j* [ʒ], so *xa = já*. The analytical future, still recognized as such, as opposed to Spanish where it no longer exists, is seen in *desprezer ei* 'penaré' 'I will suffer'. The syntax of this text is closely parallel to that of Castilian, as is its orthography, which is quite different from the spelling conventions of Portuguese.

Desexoso con desexo	Deseoso con deseo
Desexoso con desexo,	Deseoso con deseo,
desexando todavía,	deseando todavía,
ando triste, pois non vexo	ando triste, pues no veo
a xentil señora mía,	la gentil señora mía,
a que amo sen falía	la que amo sin falta
desexando todavía.	deseando todavía.
De prazer xa non me praze	El placer ya no me place
desprezer ei noite e día,	penaré noche y día,

pois ventura así me faze	pues la ventura así me tiene
apartado todavía	apartado todavía
de aquesta señora mía,	de esta señora mía,
desexando todavía.	deseando todavía.
Pensar outro pensamento	Pensar otro pensamiento
penso que non ousaría,	pienso que no osaría,
meu ben e consolamento	mi bien y consuelo
é loar sa louzanía	es loar su lozanía,
desta linda en cortesía,	de esta linda en cortesía,
desexando todavía.	deseando todavía.
Cuido con gran cuidado	Me inquieto con gran inquietud
cuidando sen alegría,	inquietándome sin alegría,
onde pois vivo apartado	ya que vivo apartado
de quem me fazer soía	de quien solía hacerme
moito ben sen vilanía,	mucho bien sin escatimármelo,
desexando todavía.	deseando todavía (Álvarez de Vi-llasandrino 1967:296).

3.6 Catalan, Valencian, and Majorcan. Within the political boundaries of Spain, the most important minority tongue is Catalan, with nine to ten million speakers. It is one of a series of closely related Romance languages spread in a crescent shape along the Mediterranean coast, from northern Italy through southern France to the east coast of Spain. Scholars disagree as to whether Catalan should be classed as Ibero- or Gallo-Romance, and as to whether it is a dialect or a separate language in its own right, though current scholarly opinion leans strongly toward the latter position (Entwistle 1951:82). Regardless of origin, in the Middle Ages Catalan and Provençal shared a common literary language, called Lemosín, which was not viewed as foreign by either. As a result of political and geographic separation, the two drifted apart, Provençal under the influence of northern French and Catalan under that of Castilian in Spain.

Despite their minority status, the Catalans play a leading role in Spanish industry and finance and consider themselves superior to Castilians in all respects. A Catalan has compared Spain to a freight train: 'Catalonia is the locomotive—pulling a string of empty cars!' And for their part, Castilians have repeatedly tried to stamp out the Catalan language. Its use was forbidden in schools, radio, television, and the public press during Franco's dictatorship. Consequently, several generations of Catalans have grown up with no formal education in their mother tongue.

Notwithstanding this mutual animosity, the language systems of Catalan and Castilian have interacted, principally in the area of lexicon. One of the features that sharply differentiates Catalan from Provençal is its great number of Castilian borrowings, while there are also numerous common words in Castilian that go unrecognized as Catalanisms, such as *bosque*, *palenque*, *patio*, and *salvaje*.

Catalan has served as a conduit for transmitting into Castilian many words from Italian, German, and French (*balance* and *artisano*; *esquife* 'skiff'; *entremés* 'intermission' and *linaje* 'lineage') (Consejo Superior de Investigaciones Científicas 1967:2:227-234).

In its phonology, Catalan is like Castilian in some respects and unlike it in others. Its stops and their fricative allophones are similar to those of Castilian. In its fricatives, there is a phonemic distinction in some dialects between /β/ and /v/, and /f/ is labiodental rather than bilabial. Some sibilants which may occur as allophones in Castilian are phonemic in Catalan, such as /s/, /z/, /ʃ/, and /ʒ/. There are two allophones of /l/, a light [l] and a dark [ł] which occurs before a pause or another consonant as in English. Also like English are two affricates /č/ and /ĵ/. The nasals, however, are like Castilian in that they assimilate to the point of articulation of a following consonant. As to vowels, there are seven phonemes: /i/, /e/, /ɛ/, /a/, /ɔ/, /o/, and /u/. Both /a/ and /e/ if unstressed become [ə]. These phonemes have privileges of occurrence inadmissible in Castilian: *tots els cors* 'todos los corazones', *menys* [méɲs] 'menos', *aquells* [akɛʎs] 'aquellos'. On seeing these consonant clusters, especially word-finally, a tourist in Barcelona may well think he is looking at some sort of Hispanized French.

Catalan morphology is so different from that of Castilian as to defy comparison. Consider, for example, the present tense forms of the verb *poder* 'to be able':

puc	*podem*
pots	*podeu*
pot	*poden*

The past participle is *pogut* (Gili 1967:76). While Catalan, like other Romance languages, has a synthetic preterite, it also has an analytic one made up of *anar* 'ir' plus infinitive, as in *vaig fer*, with forms equivalent to *voy a hacer* but with the meaning of 'hice'. Despite these morphological contrasts, Catalan syntax closely parallels Castilian, as can be seen in the following text and literal translation of a chapter of a short story by Víctor Catalá in *Contrallums*:

COMENÇA EL TRAMAT

COMIENZA LA TRAMA

A X regnava una calma relativa. Conseqüència de les veus que corrien i de les primeres espurnes de que ès tenia més o menys contradictòries referències, ja el dia avans habien deixat d'acudir la majoria de les externes i aquell matí no n'havia comparegut ni una, però encara seguia donant-se qualque classe per a fer passar l'estona a les pensionistes—poquíssimes—que restavan i que, al mateix que les mestres, estaven distretes, sense poder fixar

A X reinaba una calma relativa. Consecuencia de las voces que corrían y de las primeras chispas de que se tenía más o menos contradictorias referencias, ya el día antes habían dejado de acudir la mayoría de las externas y aquella mañana no había comparecido ni una de ellas, pero todavía seguía dándose alguna clase para hacer pasar el rato a las pensionistas — poquísimas — que quedaban y que, lo mismo que las maestras, estaban distraídas, sin pol'atenció, bo i cap temença particular les hi anunciés la proximitat del perill.

De sobte, a cosa de les onze, la recadera féu irrupció, sense ni demanar vènia, a la cella de la Mare Superiora i confegí amb un tartamudeig:

—*Madre, Madre*! Hi ha el senyor Doctor, que diu que ha de parlarli de seguida!

La Superiora quedà parada, car no hi havia cap malalta a la casa i el Doctor no venia més que quan era cridat. I com que la inquietud jeia, aquells dies, condormida o desperta, al fons de tots els cors, fins dels que es creien menys amenaçats, la Reverenda Mare ordenà que el Doctor passès a la saleta de visites, i ella, acte seguit, espolsant-se els plecs de les faldilles i estenent-se correctament el vel desarreglat, hi acudí, no sense un leu baticor.

El Doctor estava en peus, amb el barret a la mà, al centre de la habitació.

—Bon dia, Doctor!. . . Prengui seient i digui'm què el porta per aquesta santa casa—feu ella amb amable cordialitat.

—Perdoni, *Madre*; no és hora de seure—declarà el metge amb greu resolució.

—Ai, Verge puríssima! Què hi ha?

—Després en parlarem del què hi ha. Però ara, digui'm: tenen encara nenes aquí?

—Alguna pensionista. . .

—Doncs, de seguida, abans de què sigui tard, les enviï a casa seva. . .

La Superiora restà esglaiada.

—Impossible, Doctor! Una és

der fijar la atención, aunque ningún temor les hubiese anunciado la proximidad del peligro.

De súbito, a cosa de las once, la recadera hizo irrupción, sin ni siquiera pedir permiso, a la celda de la Madre Superiora y declaró con un tartamudeo:

—¡Madre, Madre! ¡Allí está el señor Doctor, que dijo que tiene que hablarle en seguida!

La Superiora quedó parada, porque no había ningún enfermo en la casa y el Doctor no venía más que cuando era llamado. Y como la inquietud yacía, aquellos días, dormida o despierta, al fondo de todos los corazones, hasta de los que se creían menos amenazados, la Reverenda Madre ordenó que el Doctor pasase a la salita de visitas, y ella, acto seguido, sacudiendo les pliegues de las faldillas y exteniéndose correctamente el velo desarreglado, acudió allí, no sin un leve sobresalto.

El Doctor estaba de pie, con la boina en la mano, en el centro de la habitació.

—¡Buenos días, Doctor!. . . Tome asiento y dígame qué le trae por esta santa casa—dijo ella con amable cordialidad.

—Perdone usted, Madre, no es hora de sentarse—declaró el médico con gran resolución.

—¡Ay, Virgen Purísima! ¿Qué hay?

—Después hablaremos de lo que hay. Pero ahora, dígame: ¿tienen todavía niñas aquí?

—Alguna pensionista. . .

—Entonces, en seguida, antes de que sea tarde, envíelas a su casa. . .

La Superiora quedó espantada.

d'Amèrica, altres, orfes, amb els tutors lluny, altres. . .

(Listen to Tape 1, selection g.)

—¡Imposible, Doctor! Una es de América, otras, huérfanas, con los tutores lejos, otras. . . (Catalá 1930:28).

The dialect of Catalan spoken south of the Ebro River, Valencian, is orthographically similar to Catalan but phonologically so like Castilian that the two are to some extent mutually intelligible. Valencia was occupied by the Moors for several centuries and has many Arabic importations that Catalan lacks. Also, it was reconquered by Castilians, invaded again by the Almoravids and again liberated by Castilians, whose influence in the region has been constant and pervasive, as can be seen in the following selection from a short story *Una vida romántica* by Visént Mallent:

UNA VIDA ROMANTICA

Dedicat a ma mare, a eixa mare que tant vullc. . .

    Qui era Malva

Amadeo Malva había naixcut en lo carrer del Portalet.

Son pare, mestre d'escola, ya había fet els cuaranta cuant Amadeo vingué al mon.

Desde chicotet, el carácter de Amadeo responía cumplidament al seu apellido: era una verdadera malva.

Els autors dels seus díes ho eren, naturalment, també dels de la seua chermana Amparito, que tenía dos añs més qu'ell.

La póbra chica era llecheta. La Naturaleza, tan pródiga en Amadeo, s'había portat carroña en Amparito. Al mascle el feu molt guapo, a la femella molt llecha.

Amadeo se criaba delicat com una chiqueta masa mimá. Pareixía una porselana, un anchelet dels que revolotechen per els cuadros de les vérches de Murillo.

Hasta que li posaron pantalóns tots el preníen per chiqueta.

Desde que pogué articular silábicament demostrá memória y condicións pera'l estudi, y segóns conten

UNA VIDA ROMANTICA

Dedicado a mi madre, a esa madre que tanto quiero. . .

    Quién era Malva

Amadeo Malva había nacido en la carrera del Portalet.

Su padre, maestro de escuela, ya había cumplido los cuarenta cuando Amadeo vino al mundo.

Desde chiquito, el carácter de Amadeo correspondía cumplidamente a su apellido: era una verdadera malva.

Los autores de sus días lo eran, naturalmente, también los de su hermana Amparito, que tenía dos años más que él.

La pobre chica era feúcha. La Naturaleza, tan pródiga en Amadeo, se había comportado tacaña con Amparito. Al varón le hizo muy guapo, a la hembra, muy fea.

Amadeo se criaba delicado como una chiquita mimada. Parecía una porcelana, un angelito de los que revolotean por los cuadros de los vergeles de Murillo.

Hasta que le pusieron pantalones todos lo tomaban por muchacha.

Desde que pudo articular silábicamente demostró memoria y condiciones para el estudio, y según

molts disipuls de son pare, als ca-
torse mesos ya día ben clar el a, e,
i, o, u.

cuentan muchos discípulos de su
padre, a los catorce meses ya decía
bien claro el a, e, i, o, u (Mallent
1914:1:283).

Mallorquín, the Catalan dialect spoken on the Balearic Islands, is extremely archaic because of its isolation. Mainland Catalonians visiting there experience difficulty in communicating in this older dialect of their language, a sample of which comes from a collection of Mallorcan folk tales by D'en Jordí des Recó:

UN FESTETJADOR

Això era una mare que tenia un fil, bajoca de tot, que havia nom Pere.

Ja havia doblegats es trenta, i no era estat capaç mai de escometre cap al•lota.

Sa mare li arribà a dir:

—¡Hauries de veure si vas a fes-tetjar qualque poc!

—¡Si jo no sé què tenc de dir!—va respondre ell.

—Mira,—digué sa mere d'es cap d'un parei de dies,—ses raons sien acabades; ¡a festetjar has d'anar, surta d'allà on surta!

—¿I a on voleu que vaja?—diu ell.

—Ves a Na Maria-Aina d'es fil.

Na Maria-Aina d'es fil era fia d'una que per temps era estada vei-nada seua.

—¿I què li he de dir?—demanà En Pere.

—¡Foi, què li has de dir!—diu sa mare. Tot-d'una convé que digues: ¿com va?

UN GALANTEADOR

Érase que era una madre que tenía un hijo, imbécil de todo, que se lla-maba Pedro.

Ya había cumplido más de treinta años, y no había estado nunca capaz de echar un piropo.

Su madre le llegó a decir:

—¡Habrías de ver si vas a ga-lantear un poco!

—Sí yo no sé qué tengo que decir!—respondió él.

—Mira,—dijo su madre al cabo de un par de días,—que se acaben las razones; ¡a galantear has de ir, salga de allá lo que salga!

—¿Y adónde quiere que vaya?—dijo él.

—Vayas a doña María-Aina (la) de los hilos.

Doña María-Aina (la) de los hilos era hija de una que un tiempo había sido vecina suya.

—¿Y qué le he de decir?—pre-guntó Pedro.

—¡Imbécil, qué le has de de-cir!—dijo su madre. De una vez conviene que digas: ¿Cómo va? (Recó 1953:22)

3.7 Basque. The most exotic language in Spain is Basque, *Euskara* to its speakers. The Basque country, Viscaya, extends from the eastern Cantabrian coast to the central Pyrenees, with an additional smaller area in southwestern France (see Map 2). Far from uniform, Basque has five major dialects, three in Spain and two in France, not all of which are mutually intelligible. A non-Indo-European tongue, Basque is thought by some linguists to be related to a family

Map 2 The languages and dialects of Spain.

of languages spoken in the Caucasus between the Black and Caspian Seas and to have been brought to Spain around 2000 B.C. In ancient times, its speakers were scattered throughout the peninsula, as is evidenced by the many Basque place names extending as far south as Andalusia (Consejo Superior 1960:1:96, 68).

According to anthropological research, the Basque people are racially distinct from the rest of the Spanish population in their blood type and cranial measurements (Consejo Superior 1960:1:69). Fiercely independent throughout history, they have maintained their culture and language in the face of dominant majorities. The Roman conquest of Spain, which began in the early second century B.C., succeeded in wiping out all of the indigenous languages there except for Basque. In the Middle Ages, it withstood the occupation of Spain by the Visigoths and Arabs. In recent times, like Catalan, it has been subject to persecution by the Spanish government, which forbade its use in education and public affairs. Since the fall of the Franco regime, however, there has been a resurgence of Basque, and it has been established juridically as one of the official languages of Spain, to be used in the Basque Parliament and in public schools. A Basque extremist party, the E.T.A., not appeased by these reforms, is vociferously demanding national independence for the Basque country and unification with the Basques in France.

Basque is spoken by perhaps 600,000 Spaniards and 100,000 Frenchmen (Consejo Superior 1960:1:68), who are reputedly proud of the difficulty outsiders experience in attempting to speak their tongue. According to a folk tale, the Devil came to Vizcaya to tempt the people to become his followers but departed crestfallen when he found himself unable to learn their language.

The phonology of Basque offers some interesting analogies with that of Castilian. The stops /p/, /t/, /k/, /b/, /d/, /g/ are the same. Both Basque and Castilian diachronically found a syllable-initial stop plus /l/ to be a problem, and their solutions to this problem were in some ways similar and in others different. Both chose the alternative of dropping the stop and keeping the liquid as in Latin *placet*, which became Basque *laket* 'agreeable', and Latin *glande*, which became Spanish *lande*. In Basque, /r/ presented a similar problem, which unlike Castilian, was solved by the insertion of a vowel. Thus Latin *libru* gave *liburu* 'book' (Consejo Superior 1960:1:72-73).

The Basque sibilants are similar to those posited for late medieval Castilian: alveolar *z* (like English /s/), postalveolar *s* (like Castilian /s/), and palatal *x* (like English *sh* as in *shop*). In both Basque and Spanish, *n*, *l*, *t*, and *d* can be palatalized, as *n* and *l* still are in Castilian. No word in Basque may begin with labiodental [f] or [v]. In Spain, Basque *j* is the [x] of Castile but in France it is [ʒ]. Basque has three affricates which correspond in position to the sibilants: alveolar *tz*, postalveolar *ts*, and palatal *tx* (Consejo Superior 1960:1:72).

The vowels of Basque are similar to those of Castilian although they occur in words etymologically and morphologically unrelated. A Basque who has learned Castilian 'accurately gives the pronunciation of the Spanish vowels the degree of openness, tension, and quality that corresponds to them' (Navarro Tomás 1968:72).

Words of all four form classes in Basque are highly inflected. The conjugation of the verb reflects 'two planes of thought: that of the real (present or future) and that of the non-real (eventual, optative, and past)'. The idea of reality thus supersedes that of time or aspect. Verbs are also marked for informal address in all persons. In the second person singular, an additional affix specifies the sex of the person spoken to. Other affixes denote subject, object, and indirect object, prefixal or suffixal depending on tense (Consejo Superior 1960:1:83, 81). For example:

I-aki-t 'I know it' (real)
it know I

n-aki-en 'I knew it' (nonreal)
I know past

d-u-t 'I have it'
it have I

d-u-k 'You have it'
it have 2nd person/singular/masculine/familiar

d-u-n 'You have it'
it have 2nd person/singular/feminine/familiar

Further, verbs are divided into two classes, stative and active, each of which demands different auxiliaries, and there are five verbal moods: indicative, imperative, subjunctive, potential-conditional, and suppositive (Consejo Superior 1960:1:90-91, 80-83).

While verb stems are both prefixed and suffixed, nouns are suffixed only, marked in 11 ways: subject stative, subject active, comitative, dative, animate and inanimate possessive, instrumental, locative, allative, ablative, and partitive. Nouns are not suffixed for gender. Definite nouns may be pluralized, but indefinites and proper names may not. Adjectives follow the nouns they modify, and there is a full set of pronouns (Consejo Superior 1960:1:76-78). More generally, Basque is SOV, but the word order may vary, and deviations predictably add emphasis. The subject of an intransitive verb and the object of a transitive verb are unmarked, whereas the subject of a transitive verb is marked, as in other ergative languages.

The basic lexicon of Basque shows many dialectal variations. It has a number of loan words from Germanic, Celtic, and especially Latin and the modern Romance languages with which it has been in contact: Spanish, French, and Provençal (Consejo Superior 1960:1:86). Borrowings are adapted to the native stock as in *errege* and *erregiñ* 'king' and 'queen' from Latin *rege* and *regina*. The agglutinative tendency of Basque allows the formation of other lexical items composed of base plus numerous bound morphemes:

dut 'lo tengo'
dugu 'lo tenemos'
dugun 'que tenemos'
duguna 'lo que tenemos'
dukegu 'podemos tenerlo'
dukegun 'que podemos tener'
dukeguna 'lo que podemos tener'
dukegunarentzat 'por lo que podemos tener' (Consejo Superior 1960:1:74)

An amusing Basque text is a song sung by children to taunt the town black sheep in Pío Baroja's novel *Zalacaín el aventurero*:

Tellagorri	Tellagorri,
Galchagorri	Red Trousers,
Ongui etorri	Be welcome
Onerá.	Here.
Ostutzale	Fond of stealing,
Erantzale	Fond of drinking,
Nescatzale	Fond of the girls
Zu cerá.	Are you (Baroja 1928: 25).
(Tape 1, selection h.)	

Almost all of these lexical items are compounds. *Gorri* 'red' combines with both *tella* 'tile' and *galcha* 'pants', in the miscreant's surname and in the sobriquet applied to him. Further, *Galchagorri* is homonymous with 'red Devil', where *galcha* is the 'evil doer'. *Ongui* is 'well' and *etorri* is 'come', a formation which is probably calqued from Spanish *bienvenido*. *Onerá* consists of *one* 'this' and the allative suffix *-ra* 'to'. *Zale 'aficionado'* or 'lover' combines with the verbs *ostu* and *eran* 'drink' and the noun, *nesca* 'girl'. *Zu* means '*usted*', as opposed to *hi 'tú'*, and *cerá* is second person singular, present tense of '*be*'.

Spain thus can be seen to have within its borders a rich variety of tongues which reflect the cultural diversity of their speakers. But a powerful unifying force exists in the fact that most Spaniards are either bidialectal or bilingual in Castilian and the regional speech of their own *patria chica*.

References

Álvar, Manuel. 1960. Textos hispánicos dialectales: antología histórica. Madrid: Revista de Filología Española, anejo LXXIII. 2 vols.

Álvares de Villasandrino, Alfonso. 1967. Desexoso con desexo. In: Francisco da Silveira Bueno, A formação histórica da língua portuguesa. São Paulo: Paraiva. 296.

Álvarez Quintero, Serafín y Joaquín. 1923. Teatro completo. vol. 1. Primeros ensayos. Madrid: Imprenta Clásica Española.

Baroja, Pío. 1928. Zalacaín el aventurero. Eds. S. L. Millard Rosenberg and Laurence D. Bailiff. New York: Knopf.

Benavente, Jacinto. 1947. Señora Ama. Buenos Aires: Espasa-Calpe Argentina.

Carter, Henry Hare. 1942. Contos e anedotas brasileiros. Boston: Heath.

Catalá, Víctor. 1930. Conversió. In: Contrallums. Barcelona: Gost. 9-68.

Consejo Superior de Investigaciones Científicas. 1960-1967. Enciclopedia lingüística hispánica (E.L.H). 2 vols. Madrid: Consejo Superior de Investigaciones Científicas.

Entwistle, William J. 1951. The Spanish language together with Portuguese, Catalan and Basque. London: Faber and Faber.

Gili, Joan. 1967. Catalan grammar. Oxford: Dolphin.

Mallent, Visént. 1914. Una vida romántica. In: El Cuento del Dumenche. 1.15.283-298.

Navarro Tomás, Tomás. 1968. Studies in Spanish phonology. Trans. Richard D. Abraham. Coral Gables, Florida: University of Miami Press.

Recó, D'en Jordí des. 1953. Aplec de rondaies mallorquines. Palma de Mallorca: Gráfiques Miramar.

Silveira Bueno, Francisco da. 1967. A formação histórica da língua portuguêsa. São Paulo: Paraiva.

Zamora Vicente, Alonso. 1979. Dialectología española. 2nd ed. Madrid: Gredos.

Part Two: The spread of Spanish

Chapter 4
The Spanish that
was brought to America

What kind of Spanish was spoken at the time of the discovery and colonization of many areas of the Western Hemisphere? The answer must include both the several varieties spoken over a span of at least 200 years in Spain and the dialects used in the different areas from which the Conquistadores and settlers had originated.

The central meseta, which had been occupied by the Moslems since A.D. 711, was largely reconquered by men from the Cantabrian coast, speakers of different varieties of Spanish Romance, some of which may not have been mutually intelligible. Under these circumstances, it is thought that a levelling process took place in which regional differences were abandoned, similarities were made more pronounced, and linguistic elements were fused into a new manner of speaking which could be understood by all. Thus was born the dialect since called Castilian.

As the Reconquest of the Central Plateau continued, speakers of this dialect who had fought valiantly were rewarded by their kings with land grants in the country or holdings in the newly won cities, with local autonomy granted in return for allegiance to the monarchic courts which at that time were being threatened by the growing power of the nobles. Once central Spain had been retaken (eleventh and twelfth centuries), political power moved south to Toledo, where the new dialect became the language of the court. When the *Reyes Católicos* Fernando and Isabel were married in 1474, Castile and Aragon were united to form the first nation-state in Europe, with Castilian as its national tongue.

And what was the language like? Fortunately, there are several sources of information which answer this question. As to phonology, there are two of these sources which confirm one another. One is the speech of the Sephardic Jews, expelled from Spain in 1492. They carried into exile with them the dialect of that time and place and, as a ritual language, it has been kept virtually unchanged for five centuries in their adoptive homes in Yugoslavia, Greece, Turkey, and, now, Israel. The following exemplifies Sephardic as it is spoken in Ankara:

NISSIM BUENO NOS ESKRIVE NOVEDADES DE TURKIA

En Istanbol se avṛio el kongreso general de los lavoradores del petrolyo. En este kongreso tomaron parte komo delegados ajenos el delegado de la Amerika, de la Israel y del Levanon. De una parte bolava la bandiera de Israel, de otra parte la bandyera del Levanon, i en medio entre las dos bandyeras bolava la bandyera Amerikana, komo ke se metyo entre las dos bandyeras.

Ansi los delegados estavan asentados ansi, de una parte el delegado de Israel, Sr. Yadlin de la Histadrut, de otra parte el delegado del Levanon, i en medio los dos el delegado Amerikano.

Denpues de la primera seduta del kongreso, fue dado ala notche un pranso muy riko onde fuimos envitados i los jurnalistos. En el pranso los delegados estavan asentados de la mesma manera, el amerikano entre el Israelyano i el Arabo.

Denpues del pranso una kantadera Libaneza enpeso a kantar en Turko, denpues kanto en Arabo, i los reprezentantes de la Turkia demandaron de la kantadera de kantar i alguna koza en honor del delegado de Israel, alora la kantadera Araba enpeso a kantar en Ivrit (Ava Nagila, Ava Nagila ve Nismeha, Ava Nagila i la Ava). Todos se levantaron a baylar la Horra Israelyana, solo el delegado Libanezo no se levanto a bayla este bayle Israelyano i prefero kedar asentado en la meza.

The first aspect of Sephardic in this text to strike the eye is its spelling—which is wholly phonetic—as in *ke*, *bolava*, and *metyo* as opposed to *que*, *volaba*, and *metió* of Standard Spanish today. This seemingly aberrant orthography has two causes. One is that prescriptive spelling had not yet developed in Spain, and the other is that the exiles wrote Spanish with Hebrew characters, as they had throughout the Middle Ages. They continued to do so until 1928, when the dictator Kemal Pasha decreed that all writing in Turkey must be in the Latin alphabet. In Greece, on the other hand, the use of Hebrew characters was maintained, so the informant who recorded this text, Itzaak Beracha, a native of Salonika, experienced some difficulty in reading the Latin alphabet, which was unfamiliar to him. (The text, with his hesitations in the third paragraph, can be heard on Tape 1, selection i.) Phonologically, [s] is distinguished from [z] and [b] from [v], phonemic contrasts which existed in Peninsular Spanish at that time. The morphosyntax does not differ significantly from that of modern colloquial Spanish. The lexical entries in this passage include several archaisms: *denpues 'después'*, *onde 'donde'*, and *mesmo 'mismo'*, widespread in rural usage today, and *i* as an adverbial particle with the meaning of *'también'*. There are also four Italian loanwords: *alora 'luego'*, *bandyera 'bandera'*, *pranso 'cena'*, and *seduta* 'sesión' as well as two analogical formations *arabo/-a* 'árabe' and *israelyano* 'israelí'.

Another valuable source of information lies in sixteenth-century textbooks published not only in Spain but also in Portugal, France, Italy, and England. These were designed for teaching Spanish as a second language to adults, due to the recognition of the vernacular as a respectable means of communication on serious subjects and the awareness that Spain was the most powerful country in Western Europe. The textbooks cast light on the pronunciation of Spanish at that time and also identify sounds that were in the process of change.

Before the sixteenth century, Latin had served as an international language for professional men and had been viewed as the sole legitimate vehicle for scholarly writing. Moreover, from Germany to the Mediterranean, Latin was used in all higher education. Indeed, university students were required to speak only Latin among themselves, even in taverns and boarding houses. This rule was strictly enforced by the university beadles and its violation was punishable by expulsion.

With the national unification movements in France and Spain, patriotism brought with it pride in all things viewed by citizens as characteristic of their respective cultures, not the least of these their language. The ancient prestige of Latin began to wane. In France, one of the foremost poets, Joachim du Bellay, published in 1549 *La Deffence et illustration de la langue Francoyse* [*sic*], in which he exhorted his countrymen to use French rather than Latin in composing works of lasting significance. French, he declared, is in no way inferior and may be likened to a fertile field which through cultivation can produce an abundance of rich fruit (Du Bellay 1966:24-25).

In Spain, 36 years later, Fray Luis de León, Rector of the University of Salamanca, published his theological treatise entitled *De los Nombres de Cristo*. The fact that it was written in Spanish scandalized many of his conservative colleagues, who threatened to bring him before the Inquisition for this 'blasphemy'. A peppery Andalusian, he answered his detractors in the Prologue to the second volume in the vein of du Bellay, that all languages can become equally expressive. He ridiculed the commonly held notion that the use of Latin added nobility to an idea. Do these people really believe that a Roman's request for a dozen turnips in the marketplace is more profound than a Spaniard's? he asked. He derided the thinking of those who claimed that their understanding would have been enhanced if he had written in a dead language rather than their mother tongue. Like Du Bellay, Fray Luis urged his compatriots to enrich their native language by employing it for noble purposes (León 1944:674).

This use of the vernacular, combined with the great prestige of Spanish and French culture, prompted a keen interest in learning languages and a consequent flurry in the production of manuals for their study, most of which followed a standard format. Typically, the first chapter presented a brief historical sketch of the language, and the second chapter the particular alphabet and its phonological values described in two different ways, either through comparing the sounds of the target language with those of a system already known or, where they were not comparable, indicating how they could be produced, in a crude but effective attempt at articulatory phonetics.

These descriptions show that the vowels and most of the consonants of Spanish in the sixteenth century were essentially as they are today. Only certain of the fricatives and affricates have undergone significant change. A phonemic contrast between /b/ and /v/ is attested, but the opposition between them seems to have been weakening. William Stepney in *The Spanish Schoolmaster* (1591) describes their status as separate phonemes:

> Of the letter *B*. This letter is all one with the Latin *b* which is called *literam labialem*, the labiall letter, and it is sounded in joyning both the lippes together.
> Of the letter *V*. This letter . . . must be pronounced as in English *vaunt*, *valiant*, *verie*: or as the Graecians do sound *vita*. Example, *vida*, life, *voto*, a vowe, &c (Alonso 1967a: 1:51).

Benito Ruiz, in *Declaración de bozes y pronunciaciones que aí en nuestra lengua castellana* (1587), says that /b/ is bilabial while /v/ is sometimes labiodental:

> La diferencia que aí de la pronunçiaçión de la *be* a la de la *eve* es que la *be* se pronunçia al nombrarla juntos los labios, i con más fuerça que la *eve*. I la *eve* se pronunçia con más blandura, tocando algunas vezes el labio de abaxo en los dientes de arriba. Son letras que muchas vezes se truecan ansí en la pronunçiaçión como en la escritura; i assí en muchas palabras, no es rregla çierta (Alonso 1967a: 1:51).

Yet Villalón, in *La viñaza* almost 30 years earlier, declares flatly that 'no real Castilian knows how to distinguish between *b* and *v*':

> La *B* se pronuncia al abrir de la boca teniéndola antes cerrada y llena de viento. Y la *V* se pronuncia teniendo la boca abierta, los labios redondos echando el ayre de la garganta afuera amorosamente y sin passión (Alonso 1967a: 1:46).

As for the affricates, texts of the late sixteenth century are in general agreement that *ç* represented the voiceless [ts] and *z* its voiced counterpart. According to John Minsheu, in his *Spanish Grammar* of 1591, *ç*

> going before *e* or *i* [is pronounced] almost as the Italian *z* as *Prudenza*, *Discalzo*, or their *t* before *ia* or *io*, as *Prudentia*, *Iustificatione* . . . (Alonso 1967a: 1:204).

His examples describe *ç* as [ts], and Francisco Brito seems to hold the same view, although his articulatory description suggests an evolution toward [θ] (Alonso 1967a: 1:130). Amado Alonso writes that in Mexico *ç* was commonly used to transcribe Nahuatl [ts], but he states that by 1580 in Castile [ts] coexisted with dental [ş] in free variation (Alonso 1967b: 100-102).

The voiced affricate [dz] has a similar history. Comparable to [ts] except for vibration, it may have tended toward the dental fricative [ẓ], 'the sound that a bumblebee or horsefly makes', according to Benito Ruiz (Alonso 1967a: 1:252). Closely akin is another phonemic pair of sibilants, the alveolar [s] and [z], written respectively *ss* and *s* word-medially as in *passar* and *casa* (Alonso 1967a: 2:7). The distinction between these two became blurred in Castilian by the end of the sixteenth century. Still another contrasting pair are /ʃ/, spelled *x*, and /ʒ/, spelled *j* or *g* before *e* and *i* (Lapesa 1968:146). These lost their status as separate phonemes, and both were pronounced [ʃ] in Castile by around 1600 (Lapesa 1968:245).

Many of these changes came about because Spanish by the sixteenth century had developed a phonemic inventory containing no fewer than six sibilants, too similar to each other for clear communication. Lapesa calls attention to the resultant confusion in forms such as *quijo* [kíʒo] for *quiso* [kízo] and *vigitar* [viʒitár] for *visitar* [vizitar] (Lapesa 1968:244). Alonso describes this situation as '*la crisis lingüística de las sibilantes*' (Alonso 1967b: 122). Speakers of Spanish were faced with two problems, first, whether to make these phonemes more distinct or to abandon their differences and, second, how to go about the alternative chosen. In any event, different choices were made by different speakers. The Castilians differentiated these sounds by moving the point of articulation of the dental sibilants forward to an interdental position and that of the palatals to velar, leaving the alveolars unchanged. Andalusians also moved the palatals to velar (later glottal) articulation but allowed the dentals and alveolars to coalesce, well before the discovery of America (Lope Blanch 1968:42). Whatever the point of articulation, for all speakers the feature of voicing was abandoned.

After this 'great phonetic revolution' between 1560 and 1630, the most important change, according to Alonso, was that of *ll* to *y* (*yeísmo*), which is older in Andalusian but occurred in some varieties of Castilian as well, probably some time in the eighteenth century; in the sixteenth century it had not yet developed in either dialect (Alonso 1967b: 162).

The important changes in Spanish phonology that occurred precisely at the time of the conquest and initial colonization of the Americas have been in large measure responsible for the celebrated 'Great Polemic' among Hispanic linguists as to the origin of Latin American Spanish: is it a Castilian or an Andalusian subdialect? The resolution of this question has been vastly complicated by the fact that either conclusion can be objectively supported by data available to modern linguists.

Scholars who believe that the Spanish of the New World has developed from Andalusian call attention to the phonological resemblance between many varieties of Latin American speech and that of Southern Spain. Among these are: (1) *seseo*; (2) the lack of [θ]; (3) the aspiration or loss of [s] before another consonant or a pause; (4) the free variation of [r] and [l] when syllable-final; and (5) the pronunciation of syllable-final /n/ as /ŋ/ before a pause and, occasionally, before nonvelars, i.e., 'entrar' [eŋtrar].

Historical evidence, too, is cited for supposing Latin American dialects to have descended from Andalusian. Among Spaniards emigrating to the Americas in the early sixteenth century, Andalusians accounted for at least 40% (Lope Blanch 1968:44), or, if those from Extremadura and Murcia (areas that speak subdialects that share many Andalusian traits) be included, about 49% (Lapesa

1968:350). During the early years of conquest and colonization, only Spanish males were permitted to sail to the mainlands of the New World; however, once Spanish women were admitted to Mexico and Peru, the great majority of them (perhaps 67%) (Lope Blanch 1968:45) were from Southern Spain. Furthermore, the motivation to seek a better future in the New World must have been higher among Andalusian than Castilian peasants, in view of the relatively more prosperous status of small farmers in Castile.

These convincing arguments are rebutted on equally good grounds by linguists who believe that Latin American varieties of Spanish are of multiple rather than singular origin. Amado Alonso, a prominent proponent of this view, noted that by the time of the conquest of Mexico and Peru, Castilian had become officially recognized as the prestige dialect of Spain. It is unlikely, he holds, that a form of speech viewed as regional rather than national would have become dominant in the Americas (Alonso 1967b: 44-46). If only 40% of the sixteenth-century conquerors were from Andalusia, then obviously the majority were from other parts of Spain—such as Castile, Cantabria, Vizcaya, and Galicia. Catalans were excluded from participation in New World affairs until 1778 (Peffer 1984:101).

While 'anti-Andalucistas' admit that many varieties of Latin American Spanish do indeed parallel Andalusian pronunciation, they are quick to point out that the phonology of the Mexican *altiplano* and of the Andean highlands shows great similarity to that of Castile. Specifically, (1) /s/ is not aspirated or lost as in Andalusian; (2) syllable-final /r/ and /l/ are not in free variation; (3) syllable-final /n/ is not velarized except before a velar consonant; and (4) if [θ] does not exist in any variety of Hispanic-American Spanish, this cannot be attributed to Andalusian influence, for this phoneme had not yet appeared in Castilian until many decades after the conquest of the Aztec and Inca empires.

Accordingly, linguists of Amado Alonso's persuasion posit two major categories of Latin American dialects: (1) those resembling Castilian, that is, the varieties spoken in 'highland' regions of Hispano-America, Mexico, Guatemala, and the Andes; (2) those more similar to Andalusian, specifically, dialects of 'lowland' areas, i.e., the Caribbean, much of Central America, South American coastal zones, and the *'Cono Sur'* (the River Plate countries and Chile).

This distribution of New World Spanish into 'highland' and 'lowland' varieties is attributed by these linguists to historical reasons. When the Spaniards first undertook the conquest of the mainland, they were attracted to lands such as Mexico and the Andes that had riches and civilized (hence exploitable) populations to offer. Whereas in Europe, as a result of Mediterranean trade, the great civilizations were coastal, on the American *tierra firme* the most advanced cultures had developed on the cool plateaus of the interior. Here it was that sixteenth-century Conquistadors (only a minority of whom were Andalusians, according to the 'anti-Andalucistas') established Spanish rule and, with it, their *'lengua nacional'*, Castilian. Castilian, as the official dialect of the government, was the language of the great centers of Hispanic power, Mexico and Peru.

Toward the end of the sixteenth century, this situation was to change as domination over the Indies began to pass into the hands of the Andalusians, when the Spanish crown granted to the Casa de Contratación in Seville the privilege of administering trade with the New World. This monopoly placed Andalusia in a position to dominate shipping between Spain and her colonies; to determine who might emigrate and who not; and to reap the wealth produced by the New World.

Under these circumstances, the Caribbean, daily visited by galleons from southern ports, soon became an Andalusian lake. South American coastal and lowland areas, hitherto neglected by explorers and colonists, underwent vigorous development by the Casa de Contratación throughout the seventeenth century. In these areas, economically and culturally dominated by Andalusians, the Andalusian dialect was implanted.

Both of these hypotheses as to the source of Latin American Spanish seem well supported by the objective data cited by their proponents. The difference in their conclusions is probably attributable to the ambiguous character of some of the available facts. For example, if 40% of the Spanish emigrants to the Indies in the 1500s were Andalusians, would this plurality have been large enough to impose its speech habits on the remaining 60%? How much influence would the southern women (undoubtedly a majority) have had on the language of their children? Why did Lima, seat of one of the two most potent viceroyalties, develop an Andalusian variety of Spanish, while the Andes, a few kilometers to the east, remained 'Castilian'? Why did supposedly 'Castilian' speakers in the New World simplify the profusion of sibilants in the same way as the Andalusians? These and a host of other questions remain unanswered and continue to offer interesting possibilities for research.

References

Alonso, Amado. 1967a. De la pronunciación medieval a la moderna en español. 2 vols. Madrid: Gredos.

Alonso, Amado. 1967b. Estudios lingüísticos: Temas hispanoamericanos. 3rd ed. Madrid: Gredos.

Du Bellay, Joachim. 1966. La deffence et illustration de la langue francoyse. Ed. Henri Chamard. Paris: Didier.

Lapesa, Rafael. 1968. Historia de la lengua española. 7th ed. Madrid: Escelicer.

León, Luis de. [1585] 1944. Los nombres de Cristo. In: Obras completas castellanas. Ed. Félix García, O.S.A. Madrid: Biblioteca de Autores Cristianos. 339-759.

Lope Blanch, Juan M. 1968. El español de América. Madrid: Ediciones Alcalá.

Peffer, Randall. 1984. Catalonia: Spain's country within a country. National Geographic. January. 95-127.

Chapter 5
Spanish as an exported language

Since the end of the fifteenth century, several European languages have been 'transplanted' to overseas colonies, where they have either supplanted the languages of the native populations or have continued to coexist with them until the present. English, for example, has been adopted as the dominant tongue of such far-flung areas as North America, Australia, and New Zealand, and serves as a lingua franca in many Third-World countries, such as India, Pakistan, and several African states. The linguistic 'empire' of France, comprising Québec and many of the Lesser Antilles, is hardly less extensive than that of Britain. As a second language, it is used for international communication throughout Western Europe; like English, it serves a number of African countries as a neutral language for intertribal affairs. In the Union of South Africa, Afrikaans, an archaic variety of Dutch, coexists with English as an official language, and Dutch continues to be spoken by many educated Asians in Indonesia. Portuguese, the national tongue of Brazil, most populous of the neo-Latin countries, is also used in such Asian areas as Goa in India, Macao, and two important former colonies of Portugal in Africa, Angola and Mozambique.

These transplanted languages share a number of traits which are also observable in Latin American Spanish. A mother country in all likelihood will have several dialects, but speakers of these dialects in the new country will erase differences which hinder easy understanding, in the process called levelling. The result is usually similar to the 'standard' dialect of the time in the homeland. Afrikaans, for example, is based on the prestige dialect of seventeenth-century Holland, not on the numerous other dialects coexistent with it; and Québec French, Jouval, stems from accepted usage in eighteenth-century France. There is no evidence that the English spoken in colonial North America differed significantly from that of London or Liverpool. Australia, however, is an exception to this general rule since the great majority of its settlers were a homogeneous group, speakers of a dialect viewed as substandard by native English speakers in Great Britain. From this dialect grew the new prestige dialect, the accepted norm for cultured speakers since that time. Spanish speakers of sixteenth-century Latin America were not a homogeneous group but represented many social classes and many geographical areas in a mixture similar to that of Spain. Thus the prestige dialect continued to exercise the same pressure abroad as at home, while differences due to influence of local dialects such as Leonese and Aragonese tended to be eliminated. In the seventeenth century, when the Andalusians became dominant in the New World, levelling continued, but on the basis of southern Spanish rather than Castilian, producing a second major manner of speaking.

Another trait shared by transplanted languages is their proclivity to retain traditional forms abandoned in their land of origin. In American English, for example, pronunciations such as *heist* 'hoist' and *pizen* 'poison', once acceptable in English, are widespread in rustic usage. Similar to these are *chaw* 'chew', *critter* 'creature', *hant* 'haunt', and *tetched* 'touched'. Morphological maintenance can be seen in *holp* 'helped', *et* 'ate', and *hit* 'it' (Reed 1977:14-15). In the English of Australia, there are also many British terms no longer common in England, such as *billy* 'rancher's teapot', *swag man* 'a tramp', and *tucker bag* 'big knapsack'. The phonology of eighteenth-century France has been preserved in the French-speaking provinces of Canada in the use of a front flap /r/ as opposed to the current continental velar /r/, and in the diphthongs of such words as *roi* 'king' and *loi* 'law', [rwé] and [lwé], in France now [rwá] and [lwá]. Afrikaans contains fossilized vocabulary, morphology, and syntax from Dutch translations of the Bible in the late seventeenth century (Breyne 1956:2). And the Portuguese of Brazil and the Azores preserves remnants of sixteenth-century continental phonology in its treatment of [d] and [g] as stops with no fricative allophones.

Like these languages, Latin American Spanish exhibits a number of archaic features. Phonologically, it has been seen to resemble sixteenth- and seventeenth-century usage more closely than it does that of present-day Spain. Morphologically, the single most important archaism is *vos*, the intermediate level of formality in the sixteenth century. Alongside *vos* are its accompanying verb forms such as *cantás*, *tenés*, *decís*, and *sos* (equivalent to *sois*), and the imperatives *andá*, *poné*, and *vení*. Throughout Latin America in popular speech an *-s* is added to the second person singular of the preterite (*vistes* 'viste', *dijistes* 'dijiste', and *hicistes* 'hiciste') (Lapesa 1968:356-358), forms common in classical authors of the Siglo de Oro. Lexically, Latin American Spanish has an abundance of terms and meanings from earlier centuries, no longer used in Spain with their original senses. Some of these and their continental equivalents are:

Latin American:	Continental:
lindo	'*bonito*'/'*hermoso*'
liviano	'*lijero*'
pollera	'*falda*'
prometer	'*asegurar*'
esculcar	'*registrar*'
aguaitar	'*vigilar*'
peje	'*pez*'
lamber	'*lamer*'
fierro	'*hierro*'
pararse	'*estar de pie*' (Lapesa 1968:360-361)

Some common phrasal archaisms are:

Latin American:	Continental:
entrar a	'*entrar en*'
es muerto	'*ha muerto*'
es nacido	'*ha nacido*'
párese y camine	'*levántese y camine*' (Entwistle 1951:264)

This last, in Europe, would mean 'stop and walk', clearly a contradiction!

The rustic dialects of both Spain and Latin America are similar in many archaic practices. These are more widespread, however, in Hispanoamerica and more persistent as well, exemplifying the old rule that the natural conservatism of rural speakers increases with their distance from innovative metropolitan centers. Until the early 1700s, there was a tendency in the prestige dialect of both the Peninsula and Latin America to change vowels in hiatus into diphthongs. By this process, words such as *país*, *oído*, and *baúl* became *páis*, *óido*, and *bául*. In the Americas, however, country speech continued the older usage. Lost in Spain but preserved in American rustic Spanish were lexical items such as:

Latin American:	Continental:
agora	*'ahora'*
cuistión	*'cuestión'*
emprestar	*'prestar'*
muncho	*'mucho'*
ñublar	*'nublar'*
ñudo	*'nudo'*
anque	*'aunque'* (Lapesa 1968:362-363).

A number of sixteenth-century mariners' terms were adopted by emigrants to America and applied to different semantic areas by metonymy or metaphor, such as *amarrar*, 'to moor a ship' (to a sailor), which developed the meaning of 'tie in general' as in *'amarrar una corbata'*. *Caramanchel* 'hatchway' came to mean 'hut', *trincar* 'seize (an item aboard a ship)' to 'pin somebody down in a fight', and *canjilones* 'pleats in a ruff' to 'ruts in a road' (Entwistle 1951:264).

Naturally enough, not all of these emigrants were sterling characters. A number of them were rogues, who brought with them their *germanía*, much of it based on Gypsy speech, terms such as *jamar 'comer'*, *jando 'dinero'*, and *cho(n)ta 'policía'*. These became current in Latin American criminal circles and at times entered standard slang. Some are used today by Chicanos, who have no idea of their venerable antiquity.

Another trait of transplanted languages is their adaptation to new environments. Colonists find themselves confronted with the need to talk about new fauna and flora, new artifacts, and new social and economic conditions. Perhaps the most usual solution to this problem is the adoption of the concept together with its name in its culture of origin. For example, English settlers in North America were thus enabled to speak of strange animals such as *possums* and *raccoons*, shelters such as *wigwams*, weapons such as *tomahawks*, gatherings such as *powwows*, and appurtenances such as *moccasins* and *tom-toms*. Australian English acquired from the languages of the aborigines words such as *kangaroo*, *wallaby* 'small kangaroo', *koolabah* tree, *boomerang*, *billabong* 'water hole', and the metaphoric *jumbuck* from *jimba* 'white mist' for the sheep which were imported from Europe. Dutch immigrants in Africa added native

impala 'deer'
induna 'member of tribal council'

koejawel 'guava'
kraal 'native village'
malongo 'white man'
inyaya 'witch doctor' (Breyne 1956:219-239)

Incorporated into Portuguese from Tupí-Guaraní were hundreds of words such as *jururú* 'sad', *jaguar, jacarandá*, and *iça* 'toasted ant eaten by Indians'. A *pindaíba* is 'a rope made of palm fiber' and *andar na pindaíba* 'be within the rope' is 'to be broke', similar to English 'be on the ropes'. *Pacova* 'banana' was adopted as was the idiom, *ser pacova* 'to have no energy' (Silveira Bueno 1967:301).

Latin American Spanish has borrowed from many indigenous languages words for plants and animals such as *maíz* 'maize', *casabe* 'a food tuber', *aguacate* 'avocado', *zopilote* 'buzzard', *ñandú* 'ostrich', and *covacha* 'rodent'. New shelters were introduced from 'huts' *jacales* to 'temples' *teocal.li*. (In the printing of Nahuatl words containing geminate *l*, a dot often is inserted to distinguish it from Spanish *ll*.) Spaniards fought with Indians led by their *caciques* 'chiefs' and armed with *macanas* 'clubs imbedded with obsidian blades'. Loan words for native apparel included *huípil* 'blouse' and *usuta* 'sandal'. A new musical instrument which entered Hispanic culture was the *quena* 'flute'.

A final trait that Spanish shares with other colonial languages is the inevitable change due to isolation from an original source. An analogy can be drawn from the break-up of Vulgar Latin, once displaced, into a number of Romance dialects after the unifying force of the Roman Empire had disappeared. Every language is subject to drift, and when a group of speakers is cut off from a linguistic mainland, this tendency is increased. For example, a Briton can immediately identify a speaker of English from the United States by his accent, as can a Parisian a Québecois or a Spaniard a Colombiano. Lexicon also develops in new directions according to local cultural demands. A Briton had little need to refer to raccoons nor would a Hollander have been likely to summon his *inyaya* 'witch doctor'. To a Madrileño, the size and color of the horse pulling his hansom cab would have been irrelevant, but to a gaucho dependent upon his horse for his livelihood and social prestige, the characteristics of his mount were of primary importance. Hence, in Argentine Spanish more than 500 terms have developed to describe the horse in the minutest detail. Furthering the differentiation in lexicon was the slow pace of communication between Europe and its colonies before the advent of the twentieth century. There is some evidence that modern technology may not only arrest but perhaps even reverse this type of linguistic diversification.

Spanish in the New World thus parallels other colonial languages in that (1) disparate dialects of the homeland have been levelled and it is largely the prestige dialect which predominates, (2) traits of the mother tongue abandoned in Spain have lived on in Latin American usage, (3) accommodations have been made by the addition of countless loan words from indigenous languages which the Spaniards encountered in the course of their building a new civilization, and (4) the Spanish language in the Americas has diverged from that of the Peninsula as a result of centuries of separation and consequent language drift.

References

Breyne, Marcel R. 1956. Lehrbuch des Afrikaans. Munich: Pohl.

Entwistle, William J. 1951. The Spanish language together with Portuguese, Catalan and Basque. London: Faber and Faber.

Hasler, Juan. 1964. Étimos latinos, griegos, y nahuas. Xalapa, México: Universidad Veracruzana.

Lapesa, Rafael. 1968. Historia de la lengua española. 7th ed. Madrid: Escelicer.

Reed, Carroll E. 1977. Dialects of American English. Amherst: University of Massachusetts Press.

Silveira Bueno, Francisco da. 1967. A formação histórica da língua portuguêsa. São Paulo: Paraiva.

Chapter 6
The first Spanish-Amerindian
linguistic contact: The Taínos

One of the characteristics which most distinguishes Spanish (and its sister, Portuguese) from other Romance languages is the significant role played in its lexicon by non-Indo-European vocabulary. Before the discovery of America, Arabic had already contributed more than 4,000 words to Spanish; beginning in October, 1492, the indigenous tongues of America began to enrich the Hispanic word-stock with a veritable flood of new vocabulary. Many of these Amerindian terms—*chocolate*, for example—were subsequently borrowed from Spanish by other languages, not only in Europe but even in the Far East: to a Japanese, 'chocolate' is *chokoreto*.

Before the Discovery, the Western Hemisphere was the home of countless thousands of native languages—no one knows how many—a considerable proportion of which have since become extinct. Unlike the tongues of post-Roman Europe, which can be classified into three linguistic groups (Indo-European, Finno-Ugric, and Basque), the Amerindian languages fall into scores of seemingly unrelated 'families', some of which are represented by but a single member. Only a few of the indigenous languages of this continent have been found to belong to fairly extensive linguistic groups, such as Uto-Aztecan, which comprises several languages distributed between the U.S. Southwest and northern Central America. No valid generalization can be made about the characteristic traits of the native American tongues as a whole, many of which no more resemble one another than do English and Tibetan.

This seemingly chaotic linguistic diversity does not appear to have proven a serious barrier to intertribal trade, which was more extensive than generally realized. Natives of the Antilles, for example, who had no knowledge of metal working nonetheless wore tiny copper bells which they must have obtained by trade with the North American mainland, and the Pueblo Indians of New Mexico wore jewelry fashioned from sea shells. Some areas, such as the Caribbean, were occupied by tribes that spoke closely related dialects of the same language; in others, such as central Mexico and the Andes, a single ethnic group had achieved domination over its neighbors. In such cases, the language spoken by the culturally or militarily superior group became the lingua franca of many different tribes inhabiting a vast territory. It was these relatively few tongues, spoken over large geographical zones by many people, either as first or second language, that significantly influenced the Spanish implanted in each of these areas. The most important of these native languages are identified on Map 3. It is interesting to note (cf. Map 4) that with few exceptions the frontiers of these Amerindian zones correspond closely to the dialect boundaries of Latin American Spanish. In most cases, this correspondence can be attributed to geographic barriers that isolate a given region: e.g., the Amazon rain forests to the east and the Atacama desert to the south effectively cut off the Andean homeland of the Quechuas from the rest of South America.

The first of the major Indian tongues to leave a lasting imprint on Spanish was the Taíno dialect of Arawak, spoken by natives who had moved north from Brazil to occupy numerous islands in the Caribbean. Columbus, who landed in Guanahaní (Samana Cay) on October 12, 1492, described these people as very

Map 3 The major Amerindian languages.

Map 4 Dialect areas of Latin American Spanish.

handsome but extremely primitive, with no knowledge of clothing and only the most rudimentary of tools, spears used for fishing. When shown a Spanish sword, one of them in his innocence grasped it by the blade and cut his hand. Columbus's ships were shortly surrounded by dugout canoes, some large enough to hold 45 men, and the Taínos eagerly traded their spears, fruit, skeins of cotton thread, and, unfortunately for them, gold nuggets in exchange for Spanish trinkets. They showed no hostility toward the strange foreigners, whom they took for gods, and entertained them lavishly. Their only fear was the tribe of the Canibas, whence *caníbales*, who, they said, came with weapons on raids from Venezuela to capture them and eat them (Colón n.d.:41-44, 112).

Initial communication was carried on by *señas*. Once the Taínos discovered the Spaniards' fondness for gold, they indicated that to the west there was a king who ate from *vasos de oro*, and they were ingenious enough to express their desire for little bells by imitating their sound in *chuq chuq*. Since no help was available from the interpreters included in the expedition (speakers of Hebrew, Chaldean, and Arabic), the explorers evidently tried to teach the natives to speak in Spanish. Columbus noted that the Indians were quite successful in repeating Spanish words. Perhaps encouraged by this, Columbus decided early on to capture six or seven Taínos and take them to Spain 'so that they might learn to speak' and serve as interpreters in the future. And this he did, including at least one woman. What became of them is not known (Colón n.d.:42, 130, 42, 44).

What is known, however, is that less than three weeks after landfall, the Spaniards had begun to learn some Taíno. The earliest native words recorded, on November 3, were *canoa* 'canoe' and *hamaca* 'hammock'. These were followed by *niame* 'yam' and on December 26 by *axe*, spelled *aje* by Columbus, 'potato-like tuber', and *casave*, spelled *cazavi*, 'cassava', another tuber which was used to make bread, and still is, in Colombia. On January 2 are recorded *cacique* 'chief' and *bohío* 'conical hut', and on January 25, *tiburón* 'shark' (Colón n.d.:67, 106, 131, 138, 159). Columbus observed natives smoking tightly rolled dried leaves, which he called *tizones* 'firebrands' (Colón n.d.:70), and mistakenly assumed that these were for medicinal purposes like the *tabac* of Spanish Arabs. Contrary to popular impression, the term *tabaco* is thus not of Taíno origin but a European exportation (Corominas 1961:536).

Taíno has been the most successful of all indigenous languages in its extensive, widespread and lasting contributions to the Spanish lexicon. Nearly all of the words coming into Spanish before the conquest of Mexico were of Taíno origin with few exceptions such as *caribe* and *caníbal*, which are Caniba words. This number of borrowings is surprisingly large, considering the brief period of time during which they became established, from 1492 to 1519. All nouns, they may have entered early because the Spaniards had not yet found resources in their own or other languages to name aspects of their 'new reality' (Mejías 1980:25-26).

Naturally enough, Taíno was most influential in its area of origin, the Antilles.

Some Taíno regionalisms used in the Caribbean area are:

areito 'Indian powwow; disorderly assembly'
caimito 'tropical fruit tree', 'its fruit'
carato 'refreshing beverage of fruit juices, cornmeal, sugar' (Puerto Rico, Cuba, Venezuela)
coa 'sharpened stake or board used as shovel' (Venezuela)
coy 'canvas cot or cradle' (Puerto Rico, Colombia)

ditas 'vessel made of fruit shell or gourd' (Puerto Rico)

guanime 'roll of corn meal steamed in banana leaves, a sort of Puerto Rican *tamal*'

guanín 'thin plate of metal worn by Antillean chiefs as insignia', 'cheap gold alloy'

guásima 'a Cuban and Puerto Rican plant'

guayacán 'Antillean tree' (the wood is used for furniture; the fruit is edible; the sap has medicinal qualities)

güiro 'type of creeping gourd plant; musical instrument made from that plant'

jaiba 'crab', '(fig:) a crabby person'

juey 'land crab', metaphorically, 'greedy' or 'hypocritical person' (*cf. jaiba*)

majagua 'tropical tree: its fiber is used for rope and mats; its flowers and bark have medicinal properties', found also in Samoa (Santamaría 1942)

Two-thirds of the Taíno words attested in the sixteenth century reappear in texts of the seventeenth. Documentation shows that in the 1500s these lexical items appeared in Mexico, Ecuador, Peru, and what is now Venezuela and Colombia. In the 1600s, they spread as far south as present-day Bolivia, Paraguay, and Buenos Aires in Argentina (Mejías 1980:28-29). In short, they became part of the speech of North, Central, and South America.

Some Taíno words used both in and outside the Caribbean zone are:

ají 'chile'

aura 'vulture'

arepa 'roll made of cornmeal' (in Mexico, of fine wheat flour)

barbacoa 'barbecue'

batata 'sweet potato'

batea 'tray'

batey 'patio or yard adjoining farmhouse'

bejuco 'liana'

bohío 'hut (generally circular with conical roof) built of palm leaves'

cacique 'Indian chief', 'political boss' (fem. *cacica*)

canoa 'canoe'

caoba 'mahogany'

carey 'tortoise shell'

casabe 'edible tuber', 'bread made from its flour' (English 'cassava')

ceiba 'silk cotton-tree'

comején 'gnat'

enaguas 'petticoat'

guajiro 'Cuban peasant (originally name of a Taíno tribe in Cuba)'

guayaba 'guayaba'

hamaca 'hammock'

huracán 'hurricane'

iguana 'large lizard'

jíbaro 'Puerto Rican peasant (*cf. guajiro*, originally name of a Taíno tribe)'

macana 'club'
maguey 'century plant'
maíz 'Indian corn', 'maize'
mamey 'type of tropical fruit', 'tree that produces it'
maní 'peanut'
nigua 'chigger'
papaya 'tropical fruit (same in English)'
pulque 'alcohol drink fermented from juice of the *maguey*'
sabana 'plain'
tiburón 'shark'
tuna 'fruit of prickly pear'
yuca 'type of cassava' (see above)

Some of these, such as *caoba, carey, cacique, canoa, hamaca, maíz, maní*, and *tiburón*, have even gained currency in Peninsular Spanish.

The number of Taíno borrowings has been increased by morphological extension since, once Hispanized, they became subject to regular rules for inflection and derivation. For example, nouns are pluralized, verbs are conjugated, many words have been affixed with diminutives or pejoratives, and some bases have been subject to functional shift, not only once but several times:

bija 'red war paint' > *embije* 'act of putting on war paint' > *embijar* 'put on war paint'

cacique 'chief' > *cacica* 'female chief', 'wife of chief', or 'political boss' > *cacicazgo* 'position, area, or reign of *cacique*'

canoa 'canoe' > *canoero* 'person manning a canoe'

macana 'war club' > *macanazo* 'blow with a club' > *macanudo* 'terrific' > *macanudamente* 'terrifically' (Argentine slang) (Mejías 1980:26-27).

Lasting though the contributions of the Taínos have been, the Taínos themselves and with them their language became extinct only a few decades after the Discovery. Many succumbed to European diseases against which they had no immunity. Others were victims of wholesale massacre: Fray Bartolomé de las Casas describes the slaughter of an entire village by Pánfilo de Narváez's men 'because they thought the Indians were looking slyly at the horses' (Salas 1959:164). Countless thousands of natives, enslaved to labor on plantations, were literally worked to death or, in their despair, ended their sufferings by suicide (Picón-Salas 1958:36). At any rate, by 1550 the Taínos were extinct. Even by 1530, missionaries had given up learning the Taíno language, so few had its speakers become (Henríquez Ureña 1940:119-121).

References

Colón, Cristóbal. n.d. Diario de navegación. Buenos Aires: TOR.
Corominas, Joan. 1961. Breve diccionario etimológico de la lengua castellana. Madrid: Gredos.

Henríquez Ureña, Pedro. 1940. El español en Santo Domingo. Buenos Aires: Universidad de Buenos Aires.

Mejías, Hugo A. 1980. Préstamos de lenguas indígenas en el español americano del siglo XVII. México: Universidad Nacional Autónoma de México.

Picón-Salas, Mariano. 1958. De la Conquista a la Independencia. México: Fondo de Cultura Económica.

Salas, Alberto M. 1959. Tres cronistas de Indias. México: Fondo de Cultura Económica.

Santamaría, Francisco J. 1942. Diccionario general de americanismos. 3 vols. Méjico: Pedro Robredo.

Chapter 7
Spanish reaches the mainland:
The Aztecs and the Mayas

The experiences which the Spaniards had with the innocent primitives of the Caribbean hardly prepared them for what they were to discover in Mexico. In 1519, when Cortez sailed from Cuba to Cozumel, he was met by well-organized resistance from Mayans armed with obsidian swords and thick cotton armor which repelled Spanish missiles. His first encounter was almost his last, but after several days of battle, the Spaniards' guns were victorious. Here Cortez was joined by another Spaniard, Gerónimo de Aguilar, who had been shipwrecked 15 years earlier and, living with the Mayans, had learned their language (López de Escalera 1964:22).

From Yucatan, Cortez sailed to the west along the coast of Mexico. During this voyage, he came ashore at Tabasco, where frightened Indians presented him with many gifts, among them 20 female slaves, one of whom was a young woman of extraordinary beauty, the daughter of an Aztec chieftain who had sold her into slavery (López de Escalera 1964:645). Upon being baptized, she was given the name of Doña Marina, and since neither Mayan nor Nahuatl has an /r/, the Indians pronounced it [malín], adding to it the honorific suffix -tze because of her noble rank. This was then mispronounced by the Spaniards as 'Malinche' (Robelo n.d.:148), a name applied later to Cortez because of his constant association with her. Bilingual in both her native Nahuatl and in Mayan, she, together with Aguilar, provided Cortez a team of interpreters.

On arriving in Vera Cruz, Cortez burned his entire fleet to prevent his men from retreating to Cuba. Word of their arrival, with accurate drawings of the men and their horses, sped to Moctezuma in Tenochtitlan, thanks to couriers in the service of Aztec intelligence, and as the Spaniards advanced toward the Valley of Mexico, daily reports continued to reach the Emperor. As the invaders approached the capital, Bernal Díaz tells us:

> we were amazed and we said that it looked like something produced by magic in the book of Amadís because of the great towers and pyramids and buildings that they had in the water and all of masonry. Some of our soldiers wondered if they were dreaming what they were seeing (Díaz del Castillo 1943:1:257).

Continuing to the causeway, Cortez and his men were received by Moctezuma and his retinue dressed in ceremonial finery embroidered in gold and encrusted with jewels. La Malinche interpreted the flowery greetings exchanged by the two leaders. The ensuing conquest of the Aztec empire is a well-known story.

Once the Spanish came into possession of a land as rich and sophisticated as Mexico, governing it and converting its people to Christianity made establishment of ready communication with them urgently necessary. To this end, they felt a common language was required. Since Nahuatl was already a lingua franca spoken from coast to coast and since Carlos I had decreed that the Indians' morals were not to be corrupted by exposure to Spanish works and ways, the language chosen was that of the Aztecs. Missionaries took the lead in acquiring a practical command of the language so that they could both preach and teach. The church was the institution responsible for creating schools, the first of these being the Colegio de San Francisco de México, founded by Friar Pedro de Gante in 1536 (Picón-Salas 1944:70). These schools were attended by prominent Aztecs and their children, and classes were conducted in Nahuatl because it was thought important for the Indian leadership to be literate in their own language so that they could carry out the administrative tasks set by the Spaniards. Also taught were Latin and Greek, languages of the religious texts of the time. The Aztec students proved to be so adept that some of them even surpassed their teachers. On one occasion when a learned theologian from Spain delivered a lecture in Greek on abstruse points in theology, an Indian chieftain in the last row stood up and proceeded to correct the grammatical errors the distinguished visitor had committed (Bernal 1964).

The use of Nahuatl in education went hand in hand with the establishment of the first printing press in Mexico in 1530. The earliest publications were in Nahuatl, not Spanish, and consisted of religious tracts and textbooks. Somewhat later there appeared systematic studies of the Aztec language. The first of these was a grammar, *Arte para aprender la lengua mexicana*, by Fray Andrés de Olmos, completed in 1547. He also compiled two dictionaries, one of Huaxtecan and another of Totonacan, both of which have been lost (López de Escalera 1964:791). A lexicon, *Vocabulario en Lengua Castellana y Mexicana y Mexicana y Castellana*, was published in 1555 by Fray Alonso de Molina, who also wrote a grammar, *Arte de la lengua Mexicana*. The work of de Molina is still one of our most important sources of information about Classical Nahuatl.

Another grammar, *Arte Mexicana*, was published in 1595 by Padre Antonio del Rincón, a Texcocan Chichimec of royal blood, a graduate of one of the schools for Aztec noblemen and possibly the first native speaker to become a linguist. In his introduction he writes of the Mexican language (Nahuatl):

> no sólo porque es general en todas estas provincias de la Nueva España, sino porque ella misma es como madre de las demás lenguas bárbaras que en estos reinos se hallan, y así me parecía servía a todos en abrir y llanar [*sic*] el camino de la lengua mexicana, pues por este se entra a las demás (1595:9).

Rincón recognized the importance of Nahuatl both as a lingua franca and as a member of a major family of related languages (Uto-Aztecan). Further, he realized that a European who studied Nahuatl would thereby gain linguistic insights apt to help him master other native American tongues.

In the prologue, Rincón anticipated modern attitudes toward language. He spoke out against the traditional European idea that all languages must be described in terms of Latin and Greek. Different languages, he said, have different rules. At the same time, he was aware of the need to provide a systematic description: here he found useful the models provided by grammars of Latin and

Greek. Then he presented an outline of the contents of the book—he would discuss morphology, the syntactic peculiarities of a polysynthetic language, and, finally, phonology:[1]

No es possible guardarse en todo un mismo methodo y arte, en enseñar todas las lenguas, siendo ellas (como lo son) tan distantes y diferentes entre si; antes, la vniformidad en esto seria gran disformidad, y por consiguiente confussion y estoruo para quien las deprendiesse. Mas con todo esso no se puede negar sino que el camino mas llano y breue para aprouechar en qualquiera de las lenguas es el que an hallado la latina y griega, como se vee por el artificio con que se enseñan y aprenden: assi por hauer reduzido a cierto numero todas las partes de la oracion, poniendoles nombres conforme a sus officios y calidades, como tambien por hauer mostrado la variacion de las partes, que entre ellas son variables, enseñando el artificio de juntar, o construir las vnas con las otras, y finalmente dando reglas de la propia y buena pronunciacion. Por lo qual, hauiendo yo de escreuir Arte para deprender y enseñar la lengua mexicana, no me pareció apartarme del ordinario camino por donde procede la lengua latina, que es mas sabida entre nosotros, ni tampoco me he querido obligar a seguir del todo sus reglas, porque seria lleuar muy fuera de proposito (y como dizen) de los cabellos muchas cosas que aca piden muy diferentes preceptos. De manera que en aquello que me e podido aprouechar de la gramatica latina siempre me yre arrimando a ella, pero en las demas cosas, en [que esta] lengua se diferencia de la latina, por ser ellas nueuas, a sido forçoso reducirlas a nueuas reglas, con el nueuo estilo que se requiere. Va pues diuidida esta gramatica en cinco libros. En el primero se trata de la declinacion del nombre. En el II de la conjugacion del verbo. En el III se enseña el orden con que vnas partes de la oracion se deriuan de otras. En el quarto libro, en lugar de sintaxi, o construccion, porque en esta lengua no ay essa variacion de casos, se pone el arte que tienen en componer vnos vocablos con otros. El V y ultimo libro trata de la pronunciacion y acento, y aun en esto auiendonos aprouechado del latin en lo que el mexicano le es semejante: van juntamente puestas reglas para la pronunciacion y acentos nueuos que a esta lengua le son propios, y no se hallan en las demas (Rincón 1595:11-12).

At this time in their history, the Aztecs had just begun to develop a writing system, using a combination of their own pictographs plus two types of hieroglyphs borrowed from the Mayans: one type phonologic, in which a symbol represented a syllable, and the other logographic, in which a symbol represented an entire word (see Figure 6). Figure 6 depicts a section of a document named the Lienzo de Tlaxcala, which was painted by Indians at the order of the Viceroy of Mexico between 1550 and 1564, and which shows how the Aztecs kept historical records. The picture itself tells the essence of the story: Cortez, with the aid of his interpreter Doña Marina, is conferring with Moctezuma and his nobles, who have brought several animals as presents. The Aztec king is identified as such by the central logograph of the feather encircled by a headband, symbolic of a ruler. The symbols at the extreme upper right are phonologic: a stone *tetl*, bowl *co-mitl* which contains clay *zo-quitl*, with a hand *ma-itl*, the first elements combining to form *te-co-zo-ma*, which with the addition of the prefix *mo-* spells out the Emperor's name. To the left of these is a conventional symbol of an old man, *huehuetl*, showing that the leader here is the elder Moctezuma, not the younger (Chavero n.d.:29-30).

Even though the Nahoas were still in the first stages of writing their language, it is not to be thought that they lacked a literature. This consisted largely of poetry and folk tales, orally transmitted like the medieval Spanish *romances*. Fortunately, some of this literature has been preserved through the efforts of bilingual missionaries such as Fray Bernardino de Sahagún. Showing Aztec manuscripts to the Indians, he would ask them to recite for him the poems which they represented. Recording the version presented by one group of speakers, he would repeat it to another, and yet another. Collecting, combining, and editing led to three different versions in Nahuatl and, finally, one in Spanish, after almost 40 years of research (López de Escalera 1964:978-979).

The Aztecan poems were varied in their subject matter and their tone. Some, like *In Chichimeca*, were probably folk ballads intended to preserve the history of the group for future generations. This poem celebrates the arrival of the Chichimecan Nahoas in the Valley of Mexico in the year '5-Caña' 'five-reed' (like the Chinese, the Aztecs designated years by the names of animals and plants). The Indians had traveled for 374 years, says the poet, and he contrasts their earlier lives as hunters and food-gatherers with their later sophistication and power in Cuauhtitlan. The poem is doubtlessly very old. The sixteenth-century transcription is inconsistent in its spelling because of the exotic phonemes such as the glottal stops which the Spaniards transcribed in several different ways. Further, the Spanish translation, which has had its spelling modernized, is nonetheless archaic in tone.

LOS CHICHIMECAS	*IN CHICHIMECA*
En el año 5-Caña	Auh yn ipan macuilli acatl xihuitl
vinieron a acercarse los chichimecas:	acico yn chichimeca:
vivían como flechadores (cazadores),	tlamintenemia,
no tenían casas,	atle yncal,
no tenían tierras,	atle yntlal,
su vestido no eran tilmas tejidas,	atle yntlaquenyan manqui tilmatli,
solamente pieles de animal era su vestido,	zan ehuatlaquemitl,
sólo con yerba hacían su vestido.	zanpachtli yn quimoquentiaya.
Sus hijos sólo en redecillas	Auh yn inpilhuan zan chitaco
en "huacales" se criaban.	huacalco yn huapahuaya
Comían tunas grandes,	Quinquaya huey nochtli,
grandes cactos, maíz silvestre,	huey comitl, tzihuacxilotl,
tunas agrias.	xoconochtli.
Mucho se afanaban	Miec in quihiyohuiaya
con todo esto	yxquich yca
300 años	yn caxtolpohualxihuitl

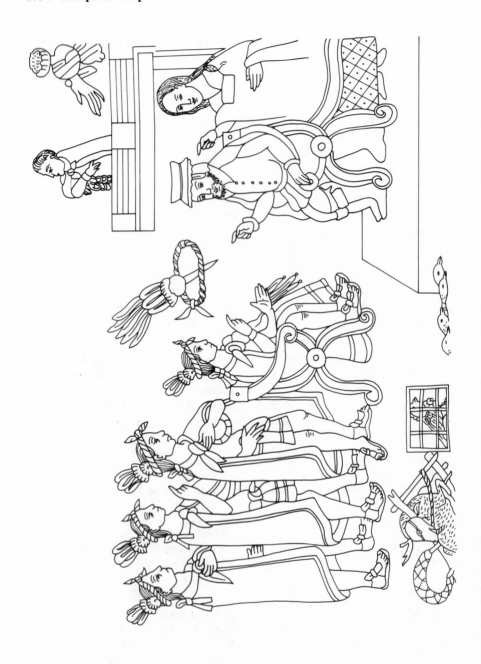

y sesenta y cuatro,
cuando vinieron a acercarse a la ciudad
de Cuauhtitlan.

Entonces comenzó, dio principio,
el señorío de los Chichimecas,
de los dueños de las casas en Cuauhtitlan.

ypan epohualli on nahui,
ynic acico ypan altepetl
Quauhtitlan.

Yn ipan peuh, tzintic,
intlatocayo chichimeca,
Quauhtitlan calque.

Another poem, *In Tlahcuilo*, contrasts good values with bad ones. The noble painter or scribe, God in his heart, works carefully and bestows divine inspiration. His opposite, with a shrouded heart, provokes indignation or boredom, and brings death.

EL PINTOR

El pintor:
la tinta negra y roja,
artista, creador de cosas con el agua negra
Diseña las cosas con el carbón, las dibuja,
prepara el color negro, lo muele, lo
aplica.
El buen pintor: entendido, dios en su
corazón.
diviniza con su corazón a las cosas,
dialoga con su propio corazón.

Conoce los colores, los aplica, sombrea;
dibuja los pies, las caras,
traza las sombras, logra un perfecto acabado.
Todos los colores aplica a las cosas,
como si fuera un tolteca,
pinta los colores de todas las flores.

El mal pintor: corazón amortajado,
indignación de la gente, provoca fastidio,
engañador, siempre anda engañando.
No muestra el rostro de las cosas,
da muerte a sus colores,
mete a las cosas en la noche.

Pinta las cosas en vano,
sus creaciones son torpes, las hace al
azar, desfigura el rostro de las cosas.

IN TLAHCUILO

In tlahcuilo:
tlilli tlapalli,
tlilatl yalvil toltecatl,
tlachichiuhque . . .
In qualli tlahcuilo: mihmati,

yolteutl,
tlayolteuiani,
moyolnonotzani.

Tlatlapalpoani, tlatlapalaquiani,
tlacevallotiani,
tlacxitiani, tlaxayacatiani,
tlatzontiani.
Xochitlahcuiloa,
tlaxochiicuiloa toltecati.

In amo qualli tlahcuilo:
yolloquihquimilli,
tequallani, texiuhtlati,
tenenco, tenehnenco.
Tlaticeua,
tlatlapalmictia,
tlatlayouallotia
tlanehnecuillolia.

Tlaxolopihcachiua, tlahciuhcahiua,
tlaixtomaua.

A third poem, *Tlayocoya In Ipalnemohua*, exalts the great poet-king Nezahualcóyotl, an example of the skill and divine inspiration praised in general terms in *El Pintor*.

EL DADOR DE LA VIDA INVENTA	*TLAYOCOYA IN IPALNEMOHUA*
Con flores hablas,	Xochitica on tlatoa,
dentro de ti vive,	mitec on nemia,
dentro de ti escribe,	mitec ya tlacuilohua,
inventa el Dador de la vida,	tlayocoya, in Ipalnemohua,
el que es Dios.	yehua teotl.
¡Oh príncipe chichimeca,	¡Chichimecatl yn tecpalli,
Nezahualcóyotl!	yn Nezahualcoyotl!

Another, *An Nochipa Tlalticpac*, asks the universal question about the brevity of life and gives the answer that nothing can resist the relentless pressure of time.

FUGACIDAD UNIVERSAL	*AN NOCHIPA TLALTICPAC*
¿Acaso de verdad se vive en la tierra?	¿Cuix oc nelli nemohua in tlalticpac Yhui ohuaye?
No para siempre en la tierra: sólo un poco aquí.	An nochipa tlalticpac: zan achica ye nican
Aunque sea jade se quiebra,	Tel ca chalchihuitl no xamani,
aunque sea oro se rompe,	no teocuitlatl in tlapani,
aunque sea plumaje de quetzal se desgarra.	no quetzalli poztequi.
No para siempre en la tierra: sólo un poco aquí.	An nochipa tlalticpac: zan achica ye nican.
(Tape 2, selection a.)	

Modern Nahuatl shows the influence of Spanish in its syntax, probably because it is largely spoken by bilinguals. This correspondence can be seen in the following passage, in word order if not morphology. The reader is invited to translate this sample, using the vocabulary and notes.

Nehuatl nicpia ce chantl huey ihuan cualtzin. Nicpia ce cuchitiloya zanpane; occe pa no hueltihuan ihuan no ta. No nan nechnotza pa nechteohuicalti tlacuilli, tlen huichihua pan tlacualchihualoyan; zantepan nipachaloa pan milli, campa huancatl miac xihuitl nepanpa xuchicualli ihuan nitequia miac xochizitzin (Ruvalcaba 1968:62).

Vocabulary (italicized forms with asterisks also appear in the Notes):

campa 'where'	*ni*-pachaloa* 'I walk'
ce 'a'/'an'	*ni*-*c*-pia* 'I have'
cual-*tzin** 'pretty'	*ni*-tequia* 'I cut'
cuchiti-loya 'bedroom'	no 'my'
cuchiti- 'sleep'	occe 'another'
loya 'room'	pa 'for'

chantl 'house'
huancatl 'there are'
huelti-*huan** 'brothers'
huey 'big'
huichihua 'cooked'
ihuan 'and'
miac 'many'/'much'
milli 'cornfields' ('*milpas*')
nan 'mother'
nech-notza* 'calls me'
nech-teohuicalti* 'feed me'
nehuatl 'I'
nepanpa 'different'

pan 'in'/'on'
ta 'father'
tlacualchihua-loya-*n** 'kitchen'
tlacual- 'eat'
chihua 'do something'
loya 'room'
tlacuilli 'dinner'
tlen 'which'
xihuitl 'trees'
xochizi-*tzin** 'little flowers'
xuchicualli 'fruit'/'banana'
*zan-pa-ne** 'only for me'
zantepan 'after'

Notes (on constituent morphemes):

-*c*-	(infix) indicates that the verb has a nominal object
-*huan*	(suffix) one of three plural markers
-*n*	(suffix) locative, 'place where'
-*ne*	(suffix) first person singular pronoun, objective case, 'me'
nech-	(verbal prefix) first person singular pronoun, objective case, 'me'
ni-	(verbal prefix) first person singular pronoun, nominative case, 'I'
-*pa*-	(infix) 'for'
-*tzin*	(suffix) diminutive
zan-	(prefix) 'only'

Phonological notes:

(1) Note that *c* before another consonant (as in *ni-c-pia* 'I have') is not [k] but a glottal stop [ʔ].
(2) Word stress is on the penultimate syllable.[2]

Nahuatl, as the dominant language of pre-Conquest Mexico, has left its imprint on Mexican Spanish. Three Aztecan traits have affected Mexican phonology. The phoneme /s/, unstable in much of Latin America, does not disappear when syllable-final but is very prominent and has a longer duration than elsewhere (Rosario 1970:99). If the objection be made that Nahuatl had no /s/ phoneme, it may be argued that, given this as true, the Indians learning Spanish probably substituted for /s/ their nearest native affricate /ts/, thus adding tenseness and length. The Peninsular phoneme /λ/ has disappeared in Mexico; some linguists, such as Amado Alonso, think that this is probably due to the fact that it did not exist in Nahuatl. However, since /λ/ was coalescing with /y/ in some parts of Spain during the sixteenth century, this opinion is not universally accepted (Alonso 1967b:210-212; Lope Blanch 1968:40). The third trait is suprasegmental. Alfonso Caso says that the substratum is reflected in the characteristic pitch contours of the Spanish spoken in central Mexico (Alonso 1948).

Nahuatl appears to have had no influence at all on Mexican Spanish syntax, but its lexical influence has been enormous. Of the 30,500 entries in Santamaría's *Diccionario de mejicanismos*, at least 20% are of Aztec origin. These lexical items encompass many spheres of existence, and some of these words have become international. Naturally, toponymic terms on the *altiplano* are largely Nahuatlisms—*Jalisco, Michoacán, Cuernavaca, Tlaxcala, México, Xochimilco*, and *Acapulco*, for example. Also surviving in Spanish are the terms referring to the native elements that became part of the new mestizo culture, such as native foods and drinks, indigenous plants and animals, agriculture, Aztec household equipment, clothing, and words applied to people.

The following list is a sample of Hispanized Nahuatl lexical items in common usage throughout Mexico. Those which are international are marked with an asterisk.

Food and beverages

*aguacate** 'avocado'
atole 'corn drink'
*cacahuate** 'peanut'
*cacao** 'chocolate bean'
camote 'yam'
cuitlacoche 'edible fungus'
*chicle** 'chicle'
chilaquiles 'dish of tortillas fried in chile'
*chile** 'chile'
*chocolate** 'chocolate'
ejote 'green bean'
elote 'corn on cob'
*enchilada** 'dish of tortillas and chile'

enjitomatadas 'dish prepared with tomatoes'
jícama 'tuber similar to turnip'
jitomate 'type of tomato'
*mescal** 'mescal'
mole 'chocolate chile sauce'
pinole 'corn drink'
pipián 'chicken stew'
posole 'corn drink'
quelite 'vegetable similar to spinach'
*tamal** 'tamale'
*tequila** 'tequila'
*tomate** 'tomato'

Plants and animals

ahuehuete 'cyprus tree'
cenzontle 'mocking bird'
cócono 'turkey'
*coyote** 'coyote'
chapulín 'grasshopper'
guajolote 'turkey'

*mezquite** 'mezquite'
nopal 'a cactus'
quetzal 'a bird'
tecolote 'owl'
zacate 'grass'
zopilote 'vulture'

Household equipment

comal 'tortilla warmer'
equipal 'woven or leather chair'
jacal 'house'
jícara 'type of cup'

metate 'grinder'
petaca 'suitcase'
petate 'straw mat'

Terms applied to people

ahuizote 'pest'

jacalear 'carry gossip'

apapachar 'pinch fruit'

cuate 'twin'

Clothing

cacles 'sandals'

*guarache** 'type of sandal'

huacal 'backpack'

huípil 'a blouse'

tilma 'a cloak'

Toys

canica 'marble'

papalote ' kite'

Miscellaneous

chueco 'crooked'

mecate 'lasso'

mitote 'powwow'

pilmama 'baby sitter'

Agriculture

chinampa 'earth-covered raft for growing food'

milpa 'cornfield'

pepenar 'pick a crop'

piscar 'pick a crop,' esp. cotton

Religion

copal 'incense'

nagual 'witch doctor' or 'werewolf'

hule 'rubber' (Santana 1960)

Some Nahuatl words have all but lost their original meanings and have taken on new ones through figurative extension. *Mitotear* 'powwow', for example, has come to mean a 'noisy party' and *cuate* 'twin', 'a close friend'. *Zoquete* 'clod of earth' has become, as in English, a disparaging term for a 'dullard'. *Totachar*, now 'speak unintelligibly', descends from Aztec *to tatli* 'Our Father', an allusion to the Latin used in Mass which the Indians did not understand. Two words refer to children, *chamaco*, originally 'fat', and *escuincle*, earlier 'a little dog'. *Apapachar*, once 'to pinch fruit', is 'to spoil a child'. A *coyote* is no longer merely an animal but also a 'shyster lawyer' or 'smuggler of illegal aliens'. One criminal term is *tecolote* 'owl', now 'night patrolman'. Another is *cuico*, from 'to sing', which has come to mean 'a person who tells on someone or confesses'.

These lexical items in Mexican Spanish were complemented by a lesser number from Taíno in the Antilles. Evidently, after the Spaniards had learned a new word from one indigenous group, they assumed that it was appropriate for another. And the members of the other group often adopted the new term, instead of using one of their own. For example, Nahuatl *acalli* 'boat' was replaced by Taíno *canoa* in the Aztecan Nahoas' Spanish. Some other Taíno words naturalized in Mexico are *aura* 'hawk', *enaguas* 'petticoat', and *tuna* 'prickly pear'.

In Yucatan and Guatemala, the dominant culture and language before the Conquest was that of the Mayans. However, the relationship between Mayan and Spanish has been very different from that between Spanish and Nahuatl. For one thing, Mayan has remained local. The Mayan lexicon that has been Hispanized has remained in its region of origin while Nahuatlismos have been fully incorporated into Mexican Spanish throughout, from the American Southwest to Costa Rica. There are perhaps three reasons for Mayan's limited influence. First, although Yucatan was the Conquistadors' first sighting of the Mexican mainland, they did not conquer nor occupy more than one-half of it during the sixteenth century, so that there was less contact between the two languages.

Second, the Mayans were comparatively sedentary and hence their contribution to Spanish outside their native area was relatively small. Within their native area, however, there have continued to be more native speakers of the indigenous language than there are in other regions of Mexico. At the present time, only 44.5% of the population of Yucatan speak Spanish as their first language. Some 46.7% are bilingual and 55.5% speak Mayan or a related dialect. According to Lope Blanch, there are reasons other than quantitative for Mayan's high level of maintenance. He notes that it is spoken not only by a majority of the rural population, marginal and lacking prestige, but also by the cultivated elite of the peninsula, and thus enjoys a higher status than that of other native tongues (Lope Blanch 1979:45-46).

Another difference between central Mexico and Yucatan lies in the contrast between missionaries such as Sahagún and Diego de Landa. The friar Sahagún learned Nahuatl and wrote his books in it, seeking to preserve both the language and the culture. The friar de Landa, on the other hand, spoke Mayan fluently but wrote in Spanish, and so far from trying to preserve the language and culture, is known chiefly for his 1562 burning of numerous Mayan statues and all but three of their books, which he claimed contained 'superstitions and falsehoods of the devil', although he also admitted that the Mayans had used them to record 'antiquities and their sciences' (Hammond 1982:34). After being recalled to Spain for oppressing the Indians, he wrote in his defense a description of the Mayans based on his experiences and the accounts of his native informants (*Relación de las cosas de Yucatán*). Today, de Landa is recognized as a leading expert on things Mayan. He is perhaps a unique example of a historian who has destroyed documents upon which he could have based his research (López de Escalera 1964:576).

Although nearly all of the Mayan manuscripts are lost to us, abundant inscriptions on their temples and other buildings are still extant and reveal that the Mayas had developed a true writing system. Its symbols were not all pictographs, like those of the Nahoas, but many were logograms (like the Chinese characters which represent entire words) and other signs which are syllabic and used to spell out words phonetically. Here the Mayas were unique:

> The natives of Yucatan are among all the inhabitants of New Spain especially deserving of praise. First, that before the Spaniards came they made use of characters and letters with which they wrote out their histories, their ceremonies, the order of sacrifices to their idols and their calendars in books made of the bark of a certain tree (Morley 1975:36).

The Mayan concern for time led to the creation of glyphs for years, months, and days, and, even more important, to the writing of numbers. Here they had two systems, one like the Arabic and one like the Roman. The one like the Arabic used a dot for one unit and a bar for five: for example, for 'twelve', there are two bars and two dots and for 'eighteen', three bars and three dots. For 'twenty' and over, up into the millions, the Roman type of symbols was employed, with a glyph representing a fixed numerical value, such as one sign for '100' and one for '2000', in a vigesimal system. These systems were combined to express numbers such as '103', a glyph and three dots (see Figure 7).

Classical Mayan is thought to have been a tone language (McQuown 1967:5:205), while other members of the family might not have been—*Quiché*, for example (Edmonson 1967:5:251). Further, the Mayas are said to have spoken slowly, with many pauses, and these characteristics mark the Spanish of their descendants. The stops /p/, /t/, and /k/ had glottalized counterparts which also occur in the Spanish of the region today. Some other traits of the Hispanic dialects of this part of Mexico which may be due to the Mayan substratum are the loss of intervocalic [ɣ] and the depalatalization of [ɲ] (as in [áwa] *'agua'* and [bánjo] *'baño'*). Mayan lacked these phonemes and also had no phonemic /f/, for which the natives substituted [p] and still do, in modern Spanish (as in [pamília] 'family'). The Mayan *x*, /ʃ/, has been maintained in native words incorporated into Spanish (as in [ʃtabai] *'xtabay'*, a 'ghost that torments lovers') (Lope Blanch 1979:60).

Especially problematic is the retroflex [R] which is common in the Spanish of Yucatan. Classical Mayan, like Nahuatl, lacked /r/, and in pre-Conquest times the nearest phoneme was velar /ɬ/. It is possible that in trying to reproduce Spanish [r], the Indians may have made a compromise between these two speech sounds. Or perhaps this pronunciation was brought to them by sixteenth-century Spaniards (Lope Blanch 1979:52).

In addition, there are two peculiarities in the treatment of the vowels in the

Figure 7 Mayan numerical notation.

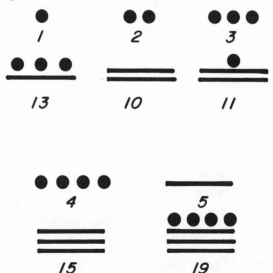

(Morley 1975: 88–90)

Spanish of this area which are thought to be due to Mayan. Words ending in a stressed vowel follow this vowel with a glottal stop, as in [sagúʔ] 'edible tuber'. By analogy, some Spanish words ending in a vowel, such as *hijo* and *niña*, have added the glottal stop while also shifting stress to the final syllable (Lope Blanch 1979:60). Another local vocalic phenomenon is the loss of any final vowel preceded by [č], a Mayan suffix which marked the second person singular of intransitive verbs (McQuown 1967:5:230).

Syntactically, Classical Mayan was polysynthetic and appears to have had little influence on Spanish syntax and morphology except in the case of *pasar a* plus infinitive 'to be about to do something', perhaps a calque of the corresponding Mayan construction (Lope Blanch 1979:60).

The most significant contribution of Mayan to Spanish has been lexical. The following sample is illustrative of Mayan loanwords in the Spanish of southern Mexico, a great many of which name local flora and fauna (these items are marked with an asterisk):

balá 'thing'
cu 'Mayan temple'
cucayo* 'firefly'
cutz* 'turkey'
cutzab 'five cent coin'

cha 'chewing gum'
chan 'small worthless object', if applied to people, a derogatory adjective: *chan Susana* 'no-good Susana'
chichitos 'crumbs'
chuto/chutito 'youngest son'
henequén* 'fiber'
kambul* 'pheasant'

lec 'water gourd'
nom* 'pheasant'
patí* 'animal' or 'blanket'
pepén* 'butterfly'
poch 'everything you see, you want'
quequeo* 'wild boar'
tauch* 'black zapote' ('bully-tree and its fruit')
tutupiche 'hairpin' or 'alopecia'
uixar 'urinate'
xix 'act of delousing' or 'leftovers'
xoy 'punch in the eye' (Santana 1960)

Notes

1. Some punctuation has been added to the original, but the spelling has been left intact with the exception of four instances of word division in accordance with modern usage.

2. The following is a translation of the Nahuatl passage on p. 102 (Ruvalcaba 1968:62):

I have a big and pretty house. I have a bedroom all to myself; (there is) another for my brothers and my father. My mother calls me to feed me dinner, which she has cooked in the kitchen; afterwards I go for a walk in the field, where there are many different fruit trees, and I cut many little flowers.

References

Alonso, Amado. 1948. Lecture. University of Chicago.

Alonso, Amado. 1967b. Estudios lingüísticos: Temas hispanoamericanos. 3rd ed. Madrid: Gredos.

Bernal, Ignacio. 1964. Lecture. Texas Western College, El Paso, Texas.

Chavero, Alfredo. n.d. Explicación del Lienzo de Tlaxcala, 1892. México, D.F.: Artes de México.

Díaz del Castillo, Bernal. 1943. Historia verdadera de la conquista de la Nueva España. Ed. Ramón Iglesias. vol. 1. México: Nuevo Mundo.

Edmonson, Munro S. Classical Quiche. In: Handbook of Middle American Indians. Ed. Robert Wauchope. Austin: The University of Texas Press. vol. 5. 249-310.

Hammond, Norman. 1982. Ancient Maya civilization. New Brunswick, New Jersey: Rutgers University Press.

Lope Blanch, Juan M. 1968. El español de América. Madrid: Ediciones Alcalá.

Lope Blanch, Juan M. 1979. Investigaciones sobre dialectología mexicana. México: Universidad Nacional Autónoma de México.

López de Escalera, Juan. 1964. Diccionario biográfico y de historia de México. México: Editorial del Magisterio.

McQuown, Norman A. 1967. Classical Yucatec (Maya). In: Handbook of Middle American Indians. Ed. Robert Wauchope. Austin: University of Texas Press. vol. 5. 201-247.

Morley, Silvanus Griswold. 1975. An introduction to the study of the Maya hieroglyphs. New York: Dover.

Picón-Salas, Mariano. 1958. De la Conquista a la Independencia. México: Fondo de Cultura Económica.

Rincón, Antonio del. 1885. Gramática y vocabulario mexicanos, 1595. México: Oficina Tipográfica de la Secretaría de Fomento.

Robelo, Cecilio de. n.d. Diccionario de aztequismos. México: Ediciones Fuente Cultural.

Rosario, Rubén del. 1970. El español de América. Sharon, Conn.: Troutman Press.

Ruvalcaba, J. Melquíades. 1968. Manual de gramática náhuatl. Guadalajara, Jalisco: n.p.

Santamaría, Francisco J. 1978. Diccionario de mejicanismos. Méjico: Porrúa.

Santana, Ruperto. 1960. Glossaries of Nahuatl and Mayan loanwords.

Chapter 8
The Inca empire: The Quechuas

The fourth of the great American Indian languages to exert a lasting influence on Spanish in this hemisphere is Quechua, still spoken by fifteen million people in the Andean highlands, which extend from southern Colombia through Ecuador, Peru, Bolivia, and as far as the northwest corner of Argentina (see Map 5) (Vela 1965:4). This area is comparable to those native to Taíno and Nahuatl, but Quechua differs from them in that it is relatively restricted to its homeland and thus has not affected the dialects of other regions but more often has been affected by them.

Andean Spanish was imposed on one of the most contradictory civilizations of the New World, extremely primitive in some respects and highly advanced in others. Ignorant of the wheel, the Quechuas nonetheless staged serious drama, they made drums from the skin of rebels but left conquered enemy chieftains in power after showering them with gifts; and with no knowledge of writing, they kept impeccable statistics (Hyams and Ordish 1963:267). They believed that their Incas, 'kings', were descended from the children of the Sun, Viracocha, and his sister-wife the Moon. Their son Manco and his sister-wife Ocllo were sent to an island in Lake Titicaca as emissaries from the gods to teach people how to live like human beings, how to build houses, cook food, and weave cloth (Garcilaso de la Vega 1950:28). Striking the ground with a golden staff, Manco and Ocllo traveled north to a high valley where the staff sank into the earth of its own accord; and here they founded Cuzco, their capital, and their dynasty, in which royalty, as demi-gods, continued to marry only royalty.

Though perhaps initially slow in its expansion, by the end of the fifteenth century the empire was burgeoning to an immense size. On its borders the Quechuas built forts, roads, and temples, and invited neighboring tribes to join them. When such invitations were rejected, as was usually the case, a military invasion followed, and the perimeter of the empire was extended still further. Into the conquered areas were sent colonists who brought Quechua law, economy, social customs, and language (Hyams and Ordish 1963:54).

Politically, the empire was governed by a highly organized system of legal requirements. There were laws concerning murder and robbery, adultery, inheritance, farming, hunting (Hyams and Ordish 1963:89-91), and even the activities to be performed by each age group at each social level. Among the lower classes, children in Group 3, ages one to nine, were subdivided into a younger group, 'Playing Children', and an older one age six and over, who had to help their parents with domestic chores. An adult male was subject to national service as a soldier or colonist, a farmer on his own and on state land, and was obliged to marry, within his caste, by the time that he was thirty. The state even regulated housekeeping:

Purics [commoners] were required to have their houses open at all times to

Map 5 The area of the Inca empire in 1500.

an inspector . . . who paid domiciliary visits to see that families were not only working according to the law, but even eating, dressing and washing in the manner prescribed. Thus, dirty housewives were punished by being made to eat the dirt of their unclean houses in public; the husband had to eat some dirt too, or to drink the dirty water in which face, hands and hair had been washed (Hyams and Ordish 1963:67-70).

These various laws were enforced by a pyramidal hierarchy of officers, from one in charge of 10,000 *purics* to a *chunca camayoc*, the chief of ten (Flornoy 1958:113).

The economic system of the empire, a very complex one, was also pyramidal. Its basic unit was the *ayllu*, a measure of land based on the fertility of the soil in relation to the number of villagers to be supported. This land was not privately owned, although each *puric* was granted a plot to cultivate for his own family. He had also to cultivate other land, some for the 'church' and some for the state, these crops to be stored in warehouses for distribution to the administrative and military personnel, to the aged and infirm, and to regions which had suffered crop failures (Hyams and Ordish 1963:61). The *ayllus* combined to form provinces, grouped into the four quarters of the empire, which converged at Cuzco, the capital (Bushnell 1958:124).

'Royal' Cuzco, as it was called by its Inca lords, was not only the seat of political and economic power, but also the center of religion and learning, a combination of Washington, New York, the Vatican, and Cambridge. Here lived the Inca and his nobles, high priests, and scholars, in mighty palaces of enormous stones fitted together with such precision that not even a knife blade could be inserted between them (Flornoy 1958:180). Their stern aspect was softened by flowering gardens and playing fountains provided with water by great municipal aqueducts (Brundage 1967:89-90). Everywhere were ornaments of silver and gold (Hyams and Ordish 1963:131).

The Quechuan splendor and wealth doubtless spurred on the Spaniards to further conquest which they undertook with Pizarro, in 1531. Their ventures were timely because they discovered a country in turmoil occasioned by a war of succession between the two sons of the late Inca, one of whom, Atahualpa, had just captured his half-brother Huáscar. Pizarro was well informed as to this struggle for power and determined to use it to his advantage. First he allied himself with the supporters of Huáscar and then sent word to Atahualpa to meet him in the great plaza of Caxamarca. The prince agreed, and came, unarmed, surrounded by thousands of his subjects. There he was approached by Father Valverde, who preached him a sermon on Christian doctrine and called upon him to acknowledge the sovereignty of Charles V and the Pope; this entreaty was translated, perhaps poorly, into Quechuan, by Pizarro's interpreter Felipillo. Atahualpa replied:

> I will be no man's tributary. I am greater than any prince upon earth. Your emperor may be a great prince: I do not doubt it, seeing that he has sent his subjects so far across the waters; and I am willing to hold him as my brother. As for the Pope of whom you speak, he must be mad to talk of giving away countries which do not belong to him. As for my faith, I will not change it. Your own god, as you tell me, was put to death by the very men he created. But my god still looks down upon his children (Hyams and Ordish 1963:222).

When he asked Valverde by what right he made these demands, the Father handed him a Bible. Turning over a few pages of this strange object, Atahualpa threw it to the ground and threatened the Spaniards with punishment for their criminal misdeeds (Hyams and Ordish 1963:222). In reply, the Spaniards cried 'Santiago y cierra España' and fell upon the Indians in the square, firing the cannons and muskets which they had secretly hidden there in advance, massacring the weaponless natives they had taken by surprise.

Atahualpa himself was taken hostage by Pizarro. Eager to gain his release, the Inca offered his captors gold: first, enough to cover the floor of the palace room in which he was held, 22 feet long and 17 feet wide, and then, enough to fill the room as high as he could reach (Hyams and Ordish 1963:231). The golden ornaments and vessels, according to Prescott, weighed over 13,000 pounds. A smaller room was filled with 26,000 pounds of silver (Prescott 1966:272). While the ransom was being gathered, Atahualpa covertly arranged for his prisoner Huáscar to be executed, to forestall the Spaniards' placing his rival on the throne (Brundage 1967:279).

Meanwhile, Atahualpa was becoming increasingly dangerous to the Spanish. His subjects were growing more and more restless, and his release would both free him to lead them against the Conquistadores and restore the state to its full power of wreaking vengeance for its humiliation. When his ransom had been paid and divided among the Spaniards, Pizarro probably decided to do away with the Inca under trumped up charges of inciting his people to insurrection. Atahualpa was found guilty—of twelve charges—and sentenced to be burned alive in the square of Caxamarca. At the last moment before the faggots were lighted, Father Valverde offered the Inca the 'more merciful' death by garroting if he would agree to become a Christian. So Juan Atahualpa was baptized and the 'Unique Inca, Son of the Sun, and Lord of the World . . . departed this life' (Hyams and Ordish 1963:245, 254).

With the loss of Atahualpa, the political and social organization of the kingdom crumbled into ruins. A major weakness of the Empire seems to have been its excessive centralization. Without the Inca, there was revolt among the provinces, some of which looked to the conqueror as the sole remaining authority. It was the Inca who had guaranteed the welfare of every citizen, in a delicately balanced structure which the Spanish did not comprehend. In assuming control of both the Aztec and Inca Empires, the Spaniards had replaced the leadership with their own administrators. The social machine of Mexico was enough like that of Spain so that it continued running, but that in the Andes could not. It may also be assumed that the Spanish would not have found a communal system profitable to maintain. Under the Inca, no man was asked to labor beyond his physical capacity. Under the Spaniard, however, the peasants were enslaved, tortured, and literally worked to death. Others died from European diseases (Hyams and Ordish 1963:261-262).

Despite the dissolution of their world, the Quechuas have maintained their identity and still regard the Hispanic as an interloper who will one day be expelled (Christian 1970). Hence, unlike the Indians in Mexico, a substantial proportion of the Quechuas, especially those in mountain areas, have resisted social and linguistic assimilation.

The language of the Quechuas, which they called *runasimi* 'man's mouth', gave rise to *topa simi* 'royal speech', the prestige dialect, which was mutually intelligible with the more common variety except for different taboos in lexical items and pronunciations. Much admired were elegance and exuberance in speaking, *hatun simi* 'high speech', often achieved through reduplication, onomatopoeia, frequent use of emphasis markers, and special positioning of morphemes. *Rimachic* 'one who speaks sententiously', a common name for boys, expresses this approbation. Conversely, a *mirccasimicta rimac* was looked down upon as a 'mixed-words speaker' (Brundage 1967:263-266).

Precision in speech must have been necessary to ensure accurate communication in this complicated culture, which, strangely enough, lacked a writing system. Even without written documents, the government maintained an official postal system which was operated by the *chasqui* 'he who carries the news' throughout the Empire. At three-mile intervals along the highways there were *chuklas* 'small stone houses' where three or more relay runners waited for messages (Flornoy 1958:15-16). Once a message was received, a courier would sprint with it to the next *chukla* and blow on his conch to alert the next *chasqui*. The average speed of transmission was about six miles an hour (Hyams and Ordish 1963:76). With him, the relay runner also carried a pot of *coca* leaves, a staff of authority, and a *quipu*. A *quipu* was a device for encoding information and figures. It consisted of a series of various sizes of cords, from ropes to fine threads, with knots of different kinds representing numerals according to the decimal system (Bushnell 1958:126). The cords were color-coded, as well, rose-purple for messages relating to the Inca, red for the army or war, and black for time, for example (Flornoy 1958:118). (See Figure 8.)

All Quechuan youths aged 20 to 25 were trained to serve as post-runners, whether they understood the messages they carried or not, while only the children of the nobility were schooled to 'read' and 'write' the *quipu*. This skill was taught them in the *yacha-huasi* 'house of teaching' in Cuzco. There the faculty consisted of the *amauta-cuna* 'sages', responsible for instruction in theology and philosophy, and the *haravec-cuna* 'poets', in literature and history (Hyams and Ordish 1963:112-114). The *quipu* assisted the fourth-year students in committing to memory the important texts of the past as well as the present and in serving the state as registers, *quipucamayus*, of all of the activities of the entire realm (Flornoy 1958:119).

Other historical records included boards covered with paintings based on research carried out by historiographers in the service of the government. These paintings depicted all of the significant events and traditions in the history and prehistory of the Empire, beginning with the creation of the world by Viracocha and including the Flood. Framed in gold, they were housed in a special building near the Temple of the Sun to which only the Incan nobility was admitted, where there was a staff of specialists whose duty it was to interpret and explain (Karsten 1949:139-140).

Figure 8 The chasqui and the quipu.

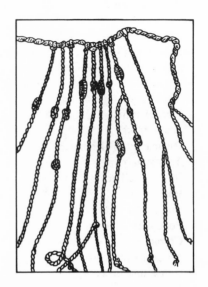

Father Cristóbal de Molina of Cuzco, a mestizo bilingual, wrote of the painted boards in 1575. He also preserved texts of hymns sung at high liturgical festivals, addressed to the pantheon of their gods, 'the Andean Olympus'.[1] In one of these, the Inca speaks to Viracocha, the Unseen Creator:

Ah Uiracochanticccicápac	O Uiracocha Señor del Universo:
Cay caricachon	(Ya sea éste varón,
Cay narmicachon	Ya sea hembra,
Uilca ulcoapu	El Señor del calor y de la generación):
Hinantima (na?)	Así como quien,
Achicchacamac	Hace sortilegio con saliva
Maypin canqui	¿Adónde estás?
Mana Choricayquiman	Ojalá no fuera tu hijo;
Hananpichum	Ya sea de arriba,
Harinpichum	Ya sea de abajo,
Quinraynimpichum	Ya del rededor de
Capacosnoyqui	Tu rico trono o cetro;
Haynillabay	Oyeme,
Hanancochamantarayac.	Desde el mar de arriba en que permaneces.
Harincocha	Desde el mar de abajo,
Tiyancayca	En que estás,
Pachacamac	Creador del mundo,
Ranahuallpa	Hacedor del hombre,

Apoynnayquicuna	Señor de todos los Señores,
Camman	A tí
Allcananiyuan (nauiy?)	Con mis ojos que desfallecen
Riacytam (Reesiytam?) munay [qui]	Por verte, o De pura gana de [conocerte]
Ricuptiy	Pues viéndote yo,
Yachaptiy	Conociéndote,
Unanchaptiy	Considerándote,
Hamuttaptiy	Entendiéndote
Ricucanquim (Ricuwankim?)	Tú me verás.
Yachauanquim	Me conocerás;
Intica, Quillaca	El Sol, la Luna,
Ppunchaoca	El día,
Tutaca	La noche,
Pocoyca	El Verano,
Chiraoca	El Invierno
Manam yancacho	No en balde
Camachiscam	Ordenados,
Purin	Caminan
Unanchasacaman	Al lugar señalado,
Tupuscamanmi	A su término
Chayan	Llegan
Maycanmi	Cualquiera que sea doquier
Topayauricta	Tu cetro real
Apachinaroanque	Llevas:
Haynillauay	Oyeme,
Oyarillauay	Escúchame
Manaracpas	No sea que
Saycoptiy	Me canse,
Uanuptiy	Me muera (Rojas 1937:416).

In words reminiscent of the Psalms, the Emperor praises God as the omnipotent and omnipresent creator of order in the universe and declares his desire to know Him and be known by Him.

In another hymn, the king of a lesser tribe, the Collas, congratulates Hatun Tupac who, on the death of his father, has succeeded to the throne, and, as the new Inca, has taken the name of his God, Viracocha.

Cam Cuzcocapaca,	Tú eres rey del Cuzco,
Nuca collacapaca,	Yo soy rey de Collas,
Upiasun,	Beberemos,
Micusun	Comeremos,
Rimasun,	Hablaremos,
Amapi rima (chun)	Que nadie hable ya.
Nuca collque tiyacani	Yo soy rico en plata,
Chuqui tiyac cani	Yo soy rico en oro

Viracocha Pachayachic	De Viracocha el Hacedor
Mucha	Yo soy adorador,
Nucac inti muchac, etc.	Yo del sol adorador, etc. (Rojas 1937:416).

Evidently a skilled politician, the subject monarch speaks to his ruler, king to king, and offers his support, which he feels to be substantial. He proposes an inaugural celebration where they will eat, drink, and be merry.

This poem was composed in Quechua, not surprisingly, since the Incas encouraged its use throughout the Empire, awarding political favors to conquered chieftains who adopted it. The linguistic unity fostered by the Incas proved of use to the Spaniards after the Conquest in their governing, evangelizing, and exploiting the labor of the Indians. These considerations were a powerful stimulus to the many studies of the Quechua language by Jesuit and Dominican missionaries between the late sixteenth and the early eighteenth centuries (Vela 1965:3). Most of these, however, were flawed in that the analysis was based on the grammar of Latin and hence failed to record many features peculiar to Quechua (Solá 1967:11). The importance of the language was considered by the rulers to be so great that in 1579 the Viceroy Francisco de Toledo established a chair of Quechua at the University of San Marcos in Lima, and he is said to have persecuted other native dialects which were in competition with it. Further, the government ruled that no clergyman could be ordained and no student could receive his degree without a fluent knowledge of Quechua (Vela 1965:3-4).

Modern Quechua is divided into three major dialects. The northernmost one is spoken in southern Colombia and in Ecuador. This variety has been less invaded by Spanish than have its counterparts. For instance, it has the archaic three vowels of the pre-Conquest era, /i/, /a/, and /u/; [e] occurs only as an allophone of /i/, and [o] as an allophone of /u/ except in Spanish loan words (Blansitt 1984). Among the consonant phonemes are two sets of four voiceless stops, one set unaspirated and one set aspirated: p,t,k,q and p^h,t^h,k^h,q^h (Lastra 1958:13). There are no glottalized stops (Muysken 1977:9).

In a central area around Cuzco there are the five vowel phonemes found in Spanish. The consonant phonemes include the four voiceless unaspirated stops /p/, /t/, /k/, /q/ but the aspirated stops /p^h/, /t^h/, /k^h/, /q^h/ have become fricative /ɸ/, /θ/, /x/, and /q/. There are four glottalized stops /$p^ʔ$/, /$t^ʔ$/, /$k^ʔ$/, and /$q^ʔ$/ (Blansitt 1984).

The dialect of the southern area near Cochabamba, Bolivia, has also adopted the five vowels of Spanish. It has the same four voiceless unaspirated stops as the other two dialects. Further, like the northern variant, it has four aspirated stops /p^h/, /t^h/, /k^h/, /q^h/ and like central Quechua it has the glottalized /$p^ʔ$/, /$t^ʔ$/, /$k^ʔ$/, and /$q^ʔ$/ (Blansitt 1984). (See Table 10.) The velars /k/, /g/, and /x/ are accompanied by a fourth, a velarized bilabial /f/, in the central area.

In other respects, the three varieties closely resemble one another. In all three, [b], [d] and [g] occur only in Spanish loanwords. All three share the palatals /ʃ/, /č/, /ɲ/, and /λ/. Quechua /r/ is retroflex (Lastra 1958:12-13; Muysken 1977:9;

Table 10 Voiceless stop phonemes, vowel phonemes in three Quechua dialects.

	Voiceless stops	Vowels
Northern	/p/ /t/ /k/ /q/ /pʰ/ /tʰ/ /kʰ/ /qʰ/	/a/ /i/ /u/
Central	/p/ /t/ /k/ /q/ /ɸ/ /θ/ /x/ /q/ /pˀ/ /tˀ/ /kˀ/ /qˀ/	/a/ /e/ /i/ /o/ /u/
Southern	/p/ /t/ /k/ /q/ /pʰ/ /tʰ/ /kʰ/ /qʰ/ /pˀ/ /tˀ/ /kˀ/ /qˀ/	/a/ /e/ /i/ /o/ /u/

Solá 1967:12). The three original Quechua vowel phonemes /i/, /a/, and /u/ may become devoiced when unaccented and followed by a voiceless consonant (Lastra 1958:12). Stress is usually but not invariably penultimate, depending upon a very complicated series of rules.

The phonology of Quechua has provoked widely different subjective reactions: Hyams calls attention to its wealth of consonants and says that 'the language is both guttural, sonorous and explosive' (Hyams and Ordish 1963:49), while Brundage states that 'because of constantly occurring liquid consonants and diphthongs ending in the semivowels *w* and *y*, it is a beautiful language, Italianate in sound and often poetic in mood' (Brundage 1967:267). (Listen to Tape 2, selection b and see Appendix 5.)

Morphologically, Quechua is polysynthetic and highly inflected. The verb base, for example, is suffixed not only for person, number, and tense, but also may receive numerous other particles which combine to express the complex ideas which other languages often take care of by syntactic means. This can be seen in the following forms of the verb meaning 'carry':

apa-ni	'I carry'	(-*ni* 'I')
apa-mu-ni	'I bring'	(-*mu* 'motion hither')
apa-chi-mu-ni	'I cause to be brought'	(-*chi* causative)
apa-chi-mu-pu-ni	'I cause someone to bring something for his advantage'	(-*pu* 'benefactive')
apa-chi-mu-pu-naya-ni	'I am very desirous of causing someone to bring something to me for his own advantage'	(-*naya* 'strong desire') (Brundage 1967:265)

Other suffixes which may be added to verb stems are frequentative, honorific, distributive, inceptive, reciprocal, reflexive, and continuative (Lastra 1958:30-

32). Still others indicate tense, usually, and some designate conditional, imperative, simultative, and validational (Lastra 1958:35-37). Some suffixes may be reduplicated for expressive emphasis as in [wasasasa] 'to roar with laughter' and [putututu] 'to stink to high heaven' (Hyams and Ordish 1963:29).

In contrast to these complexities, all verbs are conjugated according to a single model, with suffixes for three persons in the singular and four in the plural, where the first person plural form may be 'we' meaning 'you and I' or 'we' meaning 'someone else and I' (Hyams and Ordish 1963:50).

Like the verb, the noun also may be affixed with a number of postpositions. These may indicate plural, genitive, allative ('motion toward'), ablative ('motion away from'), purposive, locative, accusative, instrumental, and causative. When the personal suffixes of verbs are affixed to nouns, they serve as possessives:

go-n-ku 'they give' 3rd person plural
wasi-n-ku 'their house' 3rd person plural (Lastra 1958:24-25).

Most of the suffixes have allomorphs according to different phonological environments (Lastra 1958:27-29). Further, the suffixes can be detached and function as independent units of pronouns, adjectives, and other parts of speech (Hyams and Ordish 1963:30).

As to syntax, Quechua is an SOV language, as exemplified by the following sentence 'I have not yet told you that we went to the mountain':

noqa   manarase   rimaykichu
I   not-yet   to-tell-thee[objective]-not

monte-man
mountain [Spanish loan word] -toward

riska-yku-man-ta
to-go-we[exclusive]-toward [syllable for complement to object] (Hyams and
    Ordish 1963:30)

Adjectives may precede or follow the noun modified as in

yurak	*chu'uñu*	*hanaqpacha*	*g'ose*
white	frozen potato	sky	blue (Vela 1965:31)

There are no relative pronouns. An adjectival subordinate clause is simply placed in front of the modified noun.

The lexicon of Quechua offers several distinctive traits. Like Basque, it is rich in concrete terms and relatively poor in abstractions, which are therefore expressed concretely, giving the effect of metaphor. For example, 'to go swiftly' is 'to go windlike' *huayra huayralla* or 'to go like a hawk' *huaman huamanalla*. A speedy traveler is a 'windlike traveler', *huayrahina puric*. This elasticity of concrete words also led to the use of specifics in the formation of generic terms. *Llimpi* 'red' combined with *ñauray* 'all kinds of' to mean 'colors', and *anta* 'copper' with *ñauray* became 'metals'. One concrete word may include a cluster of related meanings. For example, *cocha* refers to a body of water of any size from 'a sea' to 'a pond'. *Pacha* means 'earth', 'time', 'epoch', 'place', or 'world', an extent of time or space. Quechua has no word for 'bad', and one must say 'not good'. Similarly, 'cruel' is 'not ever loving' (Brundage 1967:264-265). In contrast to this poverty is the abundance of terms for interpersonal relationships, especially kinship. For instance, there is a multiplicity of lexical items for 'brother' and 'sister', depending upon the sex of both the speaker and the subject (Hyams and Ordish 1963:30).

Quechua names of the pre-Conquest period reflected cultural values since they were chosen to confer prestige or bring good fortune. Men's names were honorific or drawn from the semantic areas of war, prosperity, luck, famous ancestors, tribes, or animals:

Yupanqui	'Esteemed'
Topa	'Royal'
Auqui	'Prince'
Lloque	'Dagger'
Chuqui	'Javelin'
Cusi	'Fortunate'
Huaman	'Hawk'

A boy of noble birth was given a name which related to some circumstance at the time he was born. When he was eight, in a ceremony celebrating his first haircut, he received another name, that which his father or grandfather was called at the same age or that of the Inca whom he was serving as a page. Later, when he became a knight, he took a man's name, often a family name or one which described his rank. If he became the Emperor, he could assume a fourth name, generally one from the religious realm, as did Hatun Tupac when he became *Viracocha Inca* 'God' 'Ruler' (Brundage 1967:268; Hyams and Ordish 1963:47).

Girls of noble families also had multiple names, one given at birth, another at puberty, and a third when they were ready for marriage. These last were such names as 'Golden', 'Lithe', 'Halo', 'Star', 'Pretty', 'Happy' or the name of a goddess such as *Ocllo* preceded by *Mama* 'Lady' (Brundage 1967:269).

There were two types of Quechua words which entered Spanish. Words of the first type, including terms for local flora and fauna, foods, and the like, have remained in their neighborhood of origin rather than spreading to other areas. Many of these have referents called by regional Amerindian names in other parts of Latin America as well, e.g., 'avocado' is *palta* in Peru while it is *aguacate* in Mexico. The same is true of Andean *choclo* 'ear of corn' which is Mexican *elote*. The widespread Taíno *cacique* 'chief' has never gained currency in the Andes where Quechuan *curaca* prevails. Some other local Quechua terms that have become an integral part of Andean Spanish are:

aco	'floury drink'
acuscambar	'to weary with questions'
achirarse	'to cloud over'
achucutar	'to humiliate'

atuga	'smelly lime water and corn'
carisina	'inefficient or masculine woman'
concho	'corn shuck' or 'dregs'
cuí	'guinea pig'
cuspi	'humming top' or 'small person who bustles about'
chacra	'cornfield'
chacarero	'owner of a *chacra*'
chasqui	'runner'
choclear	'strip kernels off ear of corn'
chompipe	'turkey'
chuño	'frozen dried potatoes'
guagua	'infant'
macolla	'plant sprout'
poroto	'black bean' or 'stupid person'
puna	'high plain'

A second type, Quechua words that have emigrated, is exemplified by these terms which have spread throughout Latin America (*) and in some cases to other parts of the world (**):

*coca***	'cocaine plant'
*cóndor***	'condor'
*Copacabano***	'Indian tribe' for whom the Copacabana Beach is named
*chamba**	'furrow' (Mex. 'job')
*chambear**	'dig a ditch' (Mex. 'work')
*chicha**	'beer made from corn'
*chirimoya**	'round mud-colored fruit'
*cholo***	'*mestizo*' or '*Pachuco*' (Southwestern U.S.)
*guano***	'seagull manure'
*Inca***	'Inca'
*llama***	'llama'
*mate**	'type of tea'
*pampa***	'level field' or 'treeless plain'
*papa***	'potato'
*pisco***	'a brandy'
*pita***	'century plant'
*soroche**	'altitude sickness'
*vicuña***	'vicuña'

Other words which have penetrated Andean Spanish, in spite of Quechuan resistance, were brought from Taíno and Nahuatl by Spaniards from the Caribbean and Mexico:

From Taíno:

ají	'chile'	*hamaca*	'hammock'
barbacoa	'barbecue'	*macana*	'club'

batea	'tray'	*maíz*	'corn'
bejuco	'liana'	*sabana*	'a plain'
bojío	'hut'	*yuca*	'edible tuber'
canoa	'canoe'		(Mejías 1980:28-29)

From Nahuatl:

copal	'incense'	*tianguis*	'market'
chocolate	'chocolate'	*zopilote*	'buzzard'
petaca	'suitcase'		(Mejías 1980:30)

Toponyms, or place names, in the Andean countries are usually of Quechua origin, such as *Lima* from *rimac* 'he who talks', an oracular idol in the valley where the capital now stands.

Quechua, in turn, was massively invaded by Spanish. An example of this is provided by Lastra's glossary of Cochabamba Quechua, in which more than 50% of the entries are Spanish loan words. Some of these have remained unchanged, such as *amistad, amor, and baño*. Others have been adapted to Quechua phonology, such as the nouns *Hwakundu* (*Facundo*), *kisu* (*queso*), *kweti* (*cohete*), and *prosesiyun* (*procesión*). A naturalized Spanish verb, affixed with Quechua particles, is *amontonar*, which has become *montona*—as in *montona-yku-y-ta-wan-tak*—'immediately after piling up' (Lastra 1958:71).

The combinatorial potential of Quechua morphemes, as well as the fact that many of these could also be used as free forms, gave this language a wealth and flexibility of expression well suited to become a general language of an empire, which it was, or a world language, if history had so decreed (Hyams and Ordish 1963:30-31). However, the destruction of the culture was accompanied by the impoverishment of its speech. No longer necessary were words for administration, technology, astronomy and learning; only subsistence vocabulary remains, 'a skeleton . . . of what must have existed originally' (Brundage 1967:263-264). But, over the long run, it may be seen that of the major Indian languages that have affected Spanish, Quechua has had the greatest staying power. Taíno died in the sixteenth century, and Nahuatl is not likely to survive the twenty-first (Hasler 1964:124), while Quechua does not show any signs of perishing. In fact, it recently achieved a status it has not enjoyed for hundreds of years when the Peruvian government decreed it should be a required subject in public schools.

Note

1. Rojas 1937:370. Rojas summarizes the commentaries of Molina, a Cuzco parish priest and mestizo bilingual, who wrote his *Relación de las fábulas y ritos de los Incas en el tiempo de su infidelidad* in 1575, not published until the nineteenth century.

References

Blansitt, Edward. 1984. Private conversation.

Brundage, Burr Cartwright. 1967. Lords of Cuzco. Norman: University of Oklahoma Press.

Bushnell, G. H. S. 1958. Peru. New York: Praeger.

Christian, Chester. ca. 1970. Private conversation.

Flornoy, Bertrand. 1958. The world of the Incas. Garden City, N.Y.: Doubleday.

Garcilaso de la Vega, El Inca. 1950. Comentarios reales. 3rd ed. Buenos Aires: Espasa-Calpe Argentina.

Hasler, Juan. 1964. Étimos latinos, griegos, y nahuas. Xalapa, México: Universidad Veracruzana.

Hyams, Edward, and George Ordish. 1963. The last of the Incas. New York: Simon and Schuster.

Karsten, Rafael. 1949. A totalitarian state of the past: The civilization of the Inca empire of ancient Peru. Helsingfors: Societas Scientarum Fennica.

Lastra, Yolanda. 1958. Cochabamba Quechua syntax. The Hague: Mouton.

Mejías, Hugo A. 1980. Préstamos de lenguas indígenas en el español americano del siglo XVII. México: Universidad Nacional Autónoma de México.

Muysken, Pieter. 1977. Syntactic development in the verb phrase of Ecuadorian Quechua. Lisse: Pieter de Ridder Press.

Prescott, William H. 1966. The conquest of Mexico, the conquest of Peru, and other selections. Ed. Roger Howell. New York: Twayne.

Rojas, Ricardo. 1937. Himnos quichuas. Buenos Aires: Imprenta de la Universidad.

Solá, Donald F. 1967. Gramática del quechua de Huánuco. Lima: Universidad Nacional Mayor de San Marcos.

Vela, A. Orlando. 1965. Gramática y diccionario Quechua. Lima: Studium.

Chapter 9
Chile: The Mapuche heritage

It is logical that once Peru had been conquered, the territory to the south would shortly thereafter fall under Spanish domination. Indeed, even before the Inca empire had been wholly subjugated, Diego Almagro, a henchman and rival of Francisco Pizarro, had already obtained from the Spanish crown permission to settle an *encomienda* extending from Cuzco two hundred leagues (758 miles) to the south. Almagro set out with high hopes, but was disappointed, having found fertile land and a good climate but not much gold. Since he felt he had as much right to the wealth of Cuzco as the Pizarro brothers did, he returned there from Chile to start a series of civil wars, in one of which Pizarro's brothers Gonzalo and Hernando became his prisoners. Gonzalo escaped, but Hernando was kept as a hostage until Francisco obtained his freedom by promising Almagro that he could occupy Cuzco until King Philip II had decided its rightful ruler. Once Hernando was released, Francisco marched on Cuzco, and in the ensuing battle, on April 6, 1538, Almagro was captured and executed (Munro 1942:51-53).

The second conquistador to try his hand at establishing a Spanish colony in Chile was Pedro de Valdivia. In 1540, two years after the death of Almagro, he received Pizarro's permission to head an expedition and he set out, with seeds, agricultural implements, domestic animals, and Indian women. Crossing the lifeless Atacama desert, he reached the Central Valley, where he founded the settlement of Santiago. Within a few months, the Indians living in that area became restive because of their mistreatment by the Spaniards, revolted, and burned Santiago. Valdivia was obliged to go back to Cuzco for reinforcements. When he returned to Chile, he continued south as far as the Bio Bio River, where in 1550 he established several colonies and came face to face with the Mapuches (Munro 1942:59-61).

The Mapuches were primitive and fiercely warlike tribes, only slightly less savage than their Pampero brothers on the other side of the Andes, this perhaps because of the influence of the nearby Inca civilization (Munro 1942:23-24). While the Mapuches were affected by the Quechuas, they never fell under their domination. The Mapuches fought well and continuously; when they were not at war they held intertribal athletic contests to sharpen their skill as combatants. In these, they wrestled, threw javelins, ran foot races, practiced archery, and fought with staves (Ercilla 1947:100-101, Canto X). Indeed, according to Ercilla, tests of strength were used to choose from among allied chieftains the *Toqui*, the 'chief of chiefs'. Every Chilean knows the tale of how Caupolicán won this exalted office by carrying on his shoulders a massive tree trunk for a day and a night, after which with a leap he flung it as if it were a spear (Ercilla 1947:37-39, Canto II). The Mapuches, thus, were ready for Valdivia and his soldiers. In 1553 the Mapuches attacked the Spaniards, provoking a battle in which Valdivia died. The Indians were exhorted by a young chief, Lautaro, a stable boy to Valdivia and a keen analyst of Spanish techniques. He trained his men, for example, how to take cover under fire and how to lure the Spanish cavalry into combat where horses were ineffective (Munro 1942:60-67). Moreover, the Mapuches gathered up the weapons and armor dropped by the Spaniards on the field of battle and used them against the invaders, to the latter's consternation and surprise (Ercilla 1947:80, Canto VIII). In fact, when Lautaro went to meet Valdivia's Captain Marcos, he wore a full suit of resplendent Spanish armor (Ercilla 1947:120, Canto XII). Under Lautaro, the Mapuches forced the Spaniards to withdraw to Santiago, almost three hundred miles to the north. Disease weakened the victorious warriors, however, and Lautaro himself was killed (Ercilla 1947:143, Canto XV) in 1557 in the battle of Talcahuano (Ercilla 1947:133, Canto XIV), and Caupolicán assumed the sole command. Little by little the Spaniards pushed the Indians southward toward the Bio Bio and captured their general as well (Ercilla 1945:297, Canto XXXIII). Caupolicán, like Atahualpa, was forcibly 'converted' to Christianity and sentenced to death by impalement (Ercilla 1945:302, Canto XXXIV). When his wife Fresia learned of this disgrace, she appeared before him to upbraid him for his cowardice in allowing himself to be taken alive and hurled his child at his feet (Ercilla 1945:299-300, Canto XXXIII). A galley slave was brought to be the executioner and Caupolicán remonstrated, saying that he was as noble as any Spaniard and deserved an honorable death. Then, although shackled, the Indian leader downed the slave with a mighty kick. At once, with stoic countenance, the emperor was executed—by impalement. And the Spaniards riddled his body with arrows (Ercilla 1945:303-304, Canto XXIV). Caupolicán is viewed today as one of Chile's great national heroes and his story is learned by every Chilean school child.

The heroic resistance of the Mapuches was chronicled by Alonso de Ercilla, a young Spanish nobleman who had left the court of Philip II and come to Chile with Valdivia. Inspired by the valor of the combatants on both sides, he composed an epic poem entitled *La Araucana* (probably the reason why the Mapuches are often miscalled Araucanians). Despite doubts as to the historical accuracy of Ercilla's account, stemming largely from its baroque style, one might suppose that his story is indeed sound. He was, after all, unlike his detractors, an eyewitness and participant. He describes the twofold difficulties of finding time to compose poetry when making war and of obtaining materials upon which to write. He complains that for want of paper he was forced to use bits of leather and playing cards which were often too small to hold six lines. Furthermore, many of the Mapuche names in his account are authentic, according to Undurraga: *Caupolicán* would seem to be based on *queupu* 'agate' and *licán* 'a crystal admired by witchdoctors' (Undurraga 1947:9-24); *Cayocópil*, based on *cayu* 'six' and *cupila* 'to cut', means 'manly', 'one who has had his hair cut six times', illustrating the Mapuche belief that bodily hair was effeminate (Ercilla 1945:17); *Galvarino* is based on *hualle*, 'oak', and *valín* 'worth'; *Lautaro* is derived from *Lav* 'extended' and *theru* 'type of hawk' (Undurraga 1947:18). It can hardly be questioned that Ercilla's description of Lautaro's death and Caupolicán's execution are genuine.

After withstanding the Spanish onslaught for 300 years, the Mapuches entered the period of independence with their culture intact; but, oddly enough, after Chile won her freedom, the indigenous culture began to decline. Now, of 300,000 Mapuches, 50,000 live on reservations (*reductos*) and even they must travel to neighboring towns to fulfill their needs. As a result, these Indians are rapidly becoming assimilated into the mainstream of Chilean life, and the outlook for their culture and language is not hopeful (Catrileo 1972a:1).

The Mapuche language is closely related to that of the extinct Pamperos of Argentina (Munro 1942:23). Like Quechua, its consonant stop phonemes are voiceless, but voicelessness is a feature of its fricatives and affricates as well. Its voiced consonants include five nasals, three laterals, and three semiconsonants. Dental [n] and alveolar [n], like dental [l] and alveolar [l], are in free variation. Also remarkable is the existence of [θ], spelled *th*, the alveolar affricate spelled *tr*, and the /r/ which is an alveolar retroflex. Like Castilian and Quechua, Mapuche has a palatal /λ/, spelled *lh*, as in Portuguese (Catrileo 1972b:5).

The vowels resemble those of Spanish except for a sixth one, /ɨ/, mid-front central, as in English *his fish*, spelled *ɨ* in modern Romanized Mapuche orthography (Catrileo 1972b:4). Suprasegmentally, stress is placed on the first vowel following the second consonant, *waká* 'cow' and *prófesor*, 'professor' (Blansitt 1984).

As to syntax, Mapuche is an SVO language, but word order for special effects is extremely flexible (Catrileo 1972b:1). Like Quechua, it is polysynthetic (Catrileo 1972b:33-34) and relator markers are postpositional (Catrileo 1972b:47). The verb is highly inflected, obligatorily for subject marker and optionally for tense, dual, plural, reflexive, benefactive, detrimental, imperative, cessation, pretense, passive, direction, surprise, place, and negation. These may all be added to the same stem at the same time since they are not mutually exclusive (Catrileo 1972b:9). An example of a Mapuche verb is

Kɨthawelngepaymi
'Someone came here and did some work for you'

Kɨthaw	'work'
el	benefactive
nge	passive
pa	'here'
ymi	subject relator marker (*y* = 3rd person, *mi* = 2nd person)[1]

Unlike the Mapuche verb, the noun is not inflected. Among unmodified nouns, only animates may be pluralized, through the use of a separate particle, *pu*, preceding the noun as in *pu che* 'people'. Among modified nouns, however, plurality may be indicated for both animates and inanimates. Plurality for animates is signaled by suffixing the adjective: *Kɨme che* 'kind person' becomes *kɨmeke che* or, redundantly, *pu kɨmeke che* 'kind people'. Modified inanimate nouns are also shown to be plural by adding -*ke* to the adjective: *fɨta ruka* 'big house' becomes *fɨtake ruka* 'big houses'. With the inanimates, again, *pu* may not occur. There are no other differentiations among nouns. Both the Mapuche noun and

verb enter into derivational processes. For example, both can accept the agentive
-fe, as in *kłthaw* 'work', which becomes *kłthawfe* 'worker'; *ruka* 'house', which
becomes *rukafe* 'housebuilder'; and *enseñachefe* 'teach-person-er' or 'teacher'
(Catrileo 1972b:35-37).

The Mapuche lexicon, like that of the Mayas, has remained predominantly
local, except for *malón* 'Indian raid', which spread throughout South America,
and *poncho* 'poncho', which is used internationally. A number of words have
been incorporated into Chilean Spanish, as the following sample illustrates. There
are many Mapuchismos for fauna, flora, and natural phenomena:

coligüe 'type of reed'
chepica 'weeds in farmer's field'
cheuque 'flamingo'
chungungo 'Chilean rodent'
hualve 'swampy ground'
huemul 'Chilean deer'
huillin 'beaver'
maque 'blackberry'
puelche 'cold west wind from Andes'
puñe 'potato'
puya 'type of bromeliad'[2]

There are also numerous terms for people:

che(y) 'concubine'
guaso 'peasant'
lolo/-a 'teenager'
pichicho 'small child'
pololo/-a 'boyfriend', 'girlfriend', 'date'
toqui 'principal chieftain'

Three refer to people in supernatural contexts:

calchona 'werewolf'
imbunche 'witch doctor'
pillan 'the devil', 'Satan'

Several designate artifacts:

canco 'flower pot'
cari 'cloth of light gray color'
chamanto 'striped poncho, used by farmers'
hualato 'wooden spade'
pilco 'opening in a poncho'
ruca 'Indian hut'
toqui 'axe'
trepuche 'whip'

Among these, *toqui* is of special interest, as not only an implement for a farmer but also as an emblem for the supreme ruler. And, oddly enough, the word is identical in form and meaning to its counterpart in Polynesian, suggesting contacts between the inhabitants of the Pacific coasts of South America and Polynesian seafarers (Blansitt 1984). Similar is *chauchau* 'food fed to peasants, soldiers, and sailors'. Two other words referring to food or drink are *chupilca* 'beverage made of corn meal and water', like Mexican *atole*, and *pilco* 'dish of beans and rice'. A miscellaneous group includes

maloca 'Indian raid'
pichi 'urine'
pichanga 'party'
pichín 'small quantity'
tinca 'hunch'

How fully many of these words have been incorporated is attested by their having served as bases for Spanish affixation and further semantic development. One of these is *imbunche* 'witch doctor', with the derived meaning of 'fouled up problem', which led to the neologistic *imbunchear* 'to make a problem worse'. Another is *pololo*, which is probably the plural marker *pu* plus *lolo*, 'teenagers', which underlies *pololear* 'to date'. A third is *puya* 'the prickly bromeliad', with its figurative extension *puyar* 'to insult', 'to quarrel' or 'incite others to keep quarreling'.

Mapuche, like Quechua, has been lexically invaded by Spanish, by entire words as well as by Spanish bases for use with Mapuche inflections, such as the verbs *enseña-* 'teach' and *ilkantu-* 'sing'. Many common nouns from Spanish have been adapted to Mapuche phonology:

kolekio 'school'
lifrú 'book'
papeltun 'paper'
plata 'money'
polhera 'dress', 'shirt'
prófesor 'teacher'
ufisá 'sheep' ('*oveja*')
waká 'cow'

The same is true of some proper names such as

Fránsiku '*Francisco*'
Kosé '*José*'
Kuan '*Juan*'
Pegró '*Pedro*'

As a result of cultural contact between the Mapuche and the Inca Empire, there have also been Quechua borrowings which have since become part of Chilean Spanish. Some of these are

cona 'housemaid'

chicha 'alcoholic drink'
chigua 'basket'
huincha 'wool or cotton ribbon or belt'
huiñapo 'ground corn, soaked and dried, used for making *chicha*'
palta 'avocado'
papa 'potato'

Chicha in Chile refers to a beverage made by fermenting the juice of grapes or apples, unlike the *chicha* of Peru, which is made from corn. It may be that the Spaniards took *chicha* to be a generic term for any mild alcoholic brew.

Notes

1. The gloss of *-nge-* as passive in this sample indicates an unnamed impersonal subject, like *se* in *se vino acá* in Spanish.
2. These and the other lexical items in this chapter are drawn from many different sources, predominantly the paper and the thesis by Catrileo (1972a, 1972b), Lagos-Sandoval (1980), Mejías (1980), Academia Chilena (1978).

References

Academia Chilena. 1978. Diccionario del habla chilena. Santiago de Chile: Editorial Universitaria.

Blansitt, Edward. 1984. Private conversation.

Catrileo, María Rayen. 1972a. Influencia del mapuche en el español de Chile. Unpublished paper, The University of Texas at El Paso.

Catrileo, María Rayen. 1972b. A tagmemic sketch of Mapuche grammar. M.A. thesis, The University of Texas at El Paso.

Ercilla y Zúñiga, Alonso de. 1945. The Araucaniad. Trans. Charles Maxwell Lancaster and Paul Thomas Manchester. Nashville, Tenn.: Vanderbilt University Press.

Ercilla y Zúñiga, Alonso de. 1947. La Araucana. Buenos Aires: Espasa-Calpe Argentina.

Lagos-Sandoval, Marcia. 1980. Non-standard lexical usage in the Spanish of Temuco, Chile: A case study. M.A. thesis, The University of Texas at El Paso.

Mejías, Hugo A. 1980. Préstamos de lenguas indígenas en el español americano del siglo XVII. México: Universidad Nacional Autónoma de México.

Munro, Dana Gardner. 1942. The Latin American republics: A history. New York: Appleton-Century.

Undurraga, Antonio de. 1947. Prólogo a Alonso de Ercilla y Zúñiga, La Araucana, 9-24. Buenos Aires: Espasa-Calpe Argentina.

Chapter 10
Indigenismos in Argentina, a different picture: Quechua, Pampero, Querandí, and Guaraní

The Spanish colonization of Argentina is different from that of the other areas in Latin America in nearly every respect. Spaniards, from the beginning, found no organized society with which they could attempt to communicate but only wild, primitive nomads, who were never subjugated during the colonial era. They provided no labor to be exploited, and whatever work was done was performed by the Spanish themselves. The invaders discovered no gold or silver, and the city they founded remained isolated and ignored for 200 years, unlike Lima and Mexico, which in this period were centers of wealth and power. Further, the nature and status of the native language or languages spoken there are virtually unknown. Since there was little social interaction between the aborigines and the newcomers, there was little linguistic interaction either. The Spaniards called the Indians *Pamperos*, but the term tells us little. Another puzzle lies in the fact that indigenous influences on Argentine Spanish seem not to come from speakers of this area but are largely importations from neighboring languages.

The first Spaniard to set foot on Argentine soil was Juan Díaz de Solís, in 1516, who was promptly eaten by the Indians (Ferns 1969:25). A second ill-fated expedition, in 1535, was led by Pedro de Mendoza, a recent Viceroy of Mexico, whose purpose was to establish a port on the Atlantic seaboard from which the riches of Peru could be shipped to Spain. Juan de Ayolas, one of Mendoza's officers, was sent to pick up the Quechuan booty, but on his return trip, he and his men were massacred by Indians in the jungle. In 1536, Nuestra Señora de Buen Ayre was established on the south bank of the river later called Río de la Plata, but in 1537 the unremitting attacks of the local Indians forced most of the Spanish to abandon their colony and return to Spain. A few of the survivors, in 1541, went up the Paraná River to join their fellow Spaniards who, making friends with the peaceful Guaraní, had founded the village of Asunción. Isolated from contact with the Spanish court, the colonists elected their own officials. The first governor, Diego Martínez de Irala, was succeeded in 1542 by Alvar Núñez Cabeza de Vaca. Alvar Núñez, stranded on the coast of Texas in 1529, had been exposed to native Americans before, and, since they had befriended him and helped him rejoin his compatriots in Mexico in 1536, he regarded them as human beings rather than as subhuman savages. On extending this favorable view to the natives near Asunción, however, he angered his fellow Spaniards to such an extent that they deposed him, put him in chains, and sent him to Spain for trial, where, fortunately, he was acquitted (Munro 1942:58-59).

Later, expeditions from Asunción gained control over much of the River Plate area and founded various frontier outposts which were well on their way to becoming cities even before the reestablishment of Buenos Aires in 1580. During the colonial period, therefore, many of the Spanish speakers in prominent urban areas were in contact with the native languages of the northwest and northeast, in Tucumán with Quechua, in Corrientes and Paraná with Guaraní (see Map 6) (Ferns 1959:26).

Meanwhile, the cattle and horses which had been brought to Argentina by Spanish colonists had roamed onto the pampas, where they found abundant pasture and few predators. They multiplied prodigiously into herds of millions of animals, and the nomadic Indians of these plains soon learned to ride them and became expert horsemen, attacking Spanish settlements and caravans, mur-

Map 6 Amerindian languages in the Río Plata area.

dering the men and carrying off the women. The resultant mestizo population was increased by the influx of city dwellers who had been displaced economically by black slaves imported from Africa. These newcomers to the pampa (*gauchos*, probably from Quechua *guacho* 'orphan') adapted to their new way of life very quickly by observing the Indians, adopting their artifacts, and imitating their activities (Torres-Rioseco 1946:136). Learning to use the *boleadora*, they became skilled hunters of cattle, the hides of which they sold to traders, especially those from England. These, in search of cheap leather, came inland with trade goods such as British gin, long lace underwear which the gauchos wore under their breechclouts, and big knives, *facones*, which were used in skinning animals, eating, and in dangerous sports such as dueling in which the aim of the contestant was to mark his opponent's face.

The Indians and the gauchos were the sole inhabitants of the pampa in a country which was still virtually empty except for the northwest and northeast until the middle of the nineteenth century. Then, Europeans for the first time became aware of the 12-foot-deep topsoil of the Argentine plains and began to immigrate, encouraged by the President, Domingo Faustino Sarmiento, who felt that an infusion from northern Europe was needed to develop the country. The success of this policy spelled the end of both Indians and gauchos, the Indians because they ravaged the new farming communities and inspired Sarmiento to call for their total extermination, and the gauchos because the open pampa, which had hitherto been public land, was now partitioned into individual holdings, and the free roaming livestock were confined by new fences and branded as private property. So, cattle hunters were deprived of their livelihood. They were forced to choose between two alternatives: to become *gauchos matreros* 'outlaws' or to hire out as *peones de estancia* 'ranch hands' to herd the cattle of the *patrón*.

Even though the Indian and the gaucho both became extinct, their linguistic inheritance lived on, preserved in literature written at that time by native speakers who faithfully recorded the current syntax and lexicon of their dialect. Thanks to these authors, called 'gauchesque', we can see the role of *indigenismos* in gaucho speech. What is most surprising about this role is the paucity of terms from the language(s) spoken by the *Pamperos* 'plains dwellers'. Even this descriptive comes not from a Pampero language but from Quechua *pampa* 'plain' plus a Spanish derivational suffix. Perhaps they called themselves Querandí, a word whose origin and meaning are and will remain unknown to us, most likely. Or they might have been Puelches, Tsonekas, or even Guaycurúes, even more unknown (Munro 1942:20-21). In other areas of Latin America we have seen that most of the loan words in Spanish have been borrowed from local languages, so the linguistic situation in Argentina must be considered unique. Instead of 'Pampero' words in rustic speech, we find that the majority of native loans come from Quechua in the northwest and Guaraní in the northeast. There are several possible explanations for this, and these are not mutually exclusive.

Before the Spaniards began to settle Argentina, the area of Tucumán in the northwest already had a substantial population of Quechua speakers, while the jungles of the northeast were inhabited by the Guaraní. Both of these areas were successfully colonized by the Spaniards well before the Río Plata region came under Spanish control. Quite possibly, some Spaniards from these two areas may have established themselves on the pampa in the sixteenth and seventeenth centuries, bringing with them native terms for South American fauna and flora. The men who were to become gauchos arrived during the eighteenth century and may have looked to these predecessors for vocabulary appropriate to their new environment. Or it may be that the forerunners of the gauchos did not come from the River Plate area—as is commonly assumed—but from the northwest or northeast. Or possibly the mutual hostility between the Spaniards and the indigenes precluded extensive borrowings, as it had when the Spanish encountered the cannibalistic Caribes. Perhaps this mystery will be solved by anthropologists and linguists in the future.

That the mystery exists is clearly evident in a sample of native Americanisms in Argentine rustic Spanish. This sample consists of every indigenous lexical item listed by the famous scholar Tiscornia in his glossaries to *Martín Fierro* and his tripartite *Poetas gauchescos*, as well as six more from Horacio Quiroga, 1943. The writers of these works, gauchos themselves, had spoken the dialect in which they wrote from childhood, and were proud of it. Of the total of 78 words, no fewer than 31, or 39.7%, are from Quechua. From Guaraní come 21, or 26.9%. Six words (7.6%) derive from Taíno in the Caribbean. Two each, 2.6%, are from Mapuche and from non-Indo-European languages in Brazil. Two are Africanisms, and only two, surprisingly enough, have been labeled as Pampero (Santamaría 1942). The etymology of ten others is uncertain, and it is not unlikely that some of these may also be Pampero. One last lexical item is from Aymara.

Quechua words used in Argentina are:
carancho 'type of hawk'
chacra 'vegetable or corn field' (cf. Mexican *milpa*)
cháguara 'rope'; 'whip'
chala 'corn shuck'
charqui 'jerky'; 'dried beef'
charquiar 'pull leather'
chasque 'pony express'
chilca 'resinous desert bush, used for fuel'
chilcal 'grove of *chilcas*'
china 'Pampa Indian woman'
chiripá 'breechclout worn by gauchos'
chucho 'malaria'; 'fear'
chuncaco 'type of leech'
chuspa 'tobacco pouch'
guacho 'orphan'; 'solitary man'
guanaco 'guanaco'
guasca 'strip of rawhide'
guayaca 'leather bag'

mate 'Paraguayan tea'
pampa 'pampa'
pampero 'strong cold wind from the pampa'; 'Indian of the Pampa tribe'
pilcha 'article of clothing'; 'any equipment of a cowboy'; 'beloved woman'
quincho 'woven reed mat, used as wall or roof of hut'
quirquincho 'type of armadillo'
totora 'dried reed used for constructing huts'
tucu 'firefly'
tupamaro (from *Túpac Amaru*) 'Uruguayan gauchos who joined the rebel-
    lion against Spanish rule'; (twentieth century) 'terrorist'
vizcacha 'rabbitlike rodent'
vizcachera 'hole in which *vizcacha* lives'
yapa (from *llapa*) 'tip'; 'small gift to customer who has made a purchase'
yuyo 'weed'; also, in other South American countries, 'various edible
    plants'

These items from the Tucumán region exemplify the Quechuan influence on
Argentine culture. That this influence should be strong is not surprising when
one recalls that northwestern Argentina was once a part of the Inca Empire and
is still the home of numerous Quechuas at the present time. An examination of
these words shows them to be not merely names of plants and animals in that
many designate artifacts which reflect a sophisticated culture, such as *chuspa*
'tobacco pouch' and *yapa* 'small gratuity to customer who has made a purchase'.

A much less developed culture underlies the words of the second largest group
of borrowings, those from Guaraní in the northeast:

biguá 'type of bird with metallic song'
caburé 'hawk'
chajá 'long-legged bird of Río Plata area'
chaná 'native of islands in mouth of Río Negro'
charabón 'ostrich chick'
isipó 'jungle liana'
mataco 'armadillo'
mensú 'peón'
ñacurutú 'big ugly owl'
ñandú 'ostrich'
ñandubay 'ironwood tree used for fence posts'
ñapindá '"cat's claw," type of bush with curved thorns'
ombú 'type of tree on pampa'
quiyapí 'cloak of beaver skins, used by Guaraní Indians'
saguaipe 'leech'
tacuara 'reed'
tape 'man of Indian characteristics'
tatú 'armadillo'
yaguané 'ugly'; 'black cow with white stripes'
yopará 'jungle liana'

Unlike the items from Quechua, only one of these refers to an article which has been manufactured, and most of the rest are names of animals and plants.

Four of the six Taíno terms are used throughout Latin America: *baquiano*, *cacique*, *hamaca*, and *hamacarse*. Here again we see how indigenous words were transplanted from one area to another in the Americas. The full list of Taíno lexical items in Tiscornia's glossaries is:

baquiano 'expert'; 'guide on pampa'
cacique 'Indian chief'
cotorra 'parrot' (uncertain origin, but probably Taíno)
hamaca 'hammock'
hamacarse 'swing'
jagüel '"tank" for watering cattle'

Only two Mapuche words appear in Tiscornia's lists:

chingolo 'type of small songbird'; (adj.) 'timid'
poncho 'poncho'

This small number might seem odd, given that the Mendoza and San Juan colonies were a part of and settled from Chile (Munro 1942:59). It may be that the Spaniards from Chile who had only been in contact with the Mapuches for about 20 years had not yet had time to acquire many native terms from them.

The two entries from non-Indo-European languages in Brazil are *naco* 'large hunk' of anything and *tamango* 'rustic leather sandal' and the two Africanisms are *malambo* 'a dance performed by two men' and *milonga* 'a dance introduced by blacks' and later 'a bawdy dance', often performed in bars and cafés of dubious fame in Buenos Aires.

The two which are thought to be Pampero are *bagual* and *quillango*. *Bagual* 'wild horse' is actually a corruption of the Spanish *caballo*, and, as such, reentered Spanish. *Quillango* 'guanaco robe worn by Pampa Indians' illustrates the process of borrowing an element from another culture together with its name.

The lexical items of uncertain origin are:

calamaco 'poncho of red wool'
chicholo 'guayaba candy wrapped in corn shuck'
guadal 'little pile of leaves and branches'
piche 'armadillo'
lulingo 'fool'
ruano 'roan horse with white mane and tail'
tararira 'large fish found in brooks and lakes'
tata/taita 'father' (general throughout Latin America)
teruteru 'noisy waterfowl' (used also in Bolivia)
tilingo 'crazy'; 'goofy' (used also in Mexico)

Some of these may be Pampero, such as *guadal*, *tararira*, and *teruteru*. On the other hand, some might not even be *indigenismos*, such as *calamaco*, *lulingo*, and *tilingo*. The one lexical item from Aymara in Bolivia is *chimango* 'hawk'.

In assessing these samples, it must be borne in mind that they are based on nineteenth-century gauchesque literature. Therefore, they may not accurately reflect rural usage at the present time. Since Argentina's excellent public school system has reduced illiteracy to about the same level as in the United States and Western Europe, it seems likely that country speech has become more standard, closer to the prestige dialect. These samples also fail to reflect usage in areas such as Tucumán, where Quechua loan words are probably far more numerous, or the northeast, where Guaraní borrowings would no doubt predominate.

References

Ferns, H. S. 1969. Argentina. New York: Praeger.

Hernández, José. 1941. Martín Fierro. 2nd ed. Ed. Eleuterio F. Tiscornia. Buenos Aires: Losada.

Munro, Dana Gardner. 1942. The Latin American republics: A history. New York: Appleton-Century.

Quiroga, Horacio. 1943. Sus mejores cuentos. Ed. John A. Crow. México: Editorial Cvltvra.

Santamaría, Francisco J. 1942. Diccionario general de americanismos, 3 vols. Méjico: Pedro Robredo.

Tiscornia, Eleuterio F. 1940. Poetas gauchescos: Hidalgo, Ascasubi, Del Campo. Buenos Aires: Losada.

Torres-Rioseco, Arturo. 1946. The epic of Latin American literature. New York: Oxford University Press.

Chapter 11
Paraguay: The triumph of an indigenous tongue: Guaraní

The Spanish colonization of Paraguay is as exceptional as that of Argentina but in an entirely different manner. Paraguay is the sole Latin American country in which an indigenous tongue enjoys equal status with that of its conquerors. Under Paraguayan law, Guaraní is the second official language and, as such, is used in courts of law, public education, scholarship, and the arts. In most Latin American countries, the native languages are spoken mainly by the downtrodden, but in bilingual Paraguay many university graduates speak and write in Guaraní by choice (The South American handbook 1979:557).

How did this come to pass? By the sixteenth century the Guaraní had spread to the foothills of the Andes, the coast of Brazil, the basin of the Amazon, and, by the middle of the century, in peaceful cooperation with the Spaniards, they founded Asunción, a major South American port (The South American handbook 1979:556). To this port came a body of Jesuit missionaries, who in 1609 were commissioned by King Philip II to convert the 'savages' to Christianity. The first Jesuit settlements were wiped out by slave hunters from Brazil, and the missionaries moved south with their charges, into an area which is now a part of three different countries: southeastern Paraguay, southern Brazil, and the province of Misiones in northeast Argentina. Here they established some 20 *reducciones* or communal villages, each under the supervision of two priests. With this administration, the 100,000 native inhabitants led highly regulated lives as farmers and profited greatly, especially from the sale of *yerba mate* 'Paraguayan tea'. Not only were the Jesuits efficient business managers but also excellent educators, bringing literacy in their own language to the Guaraní and providing a classical education to their superior students. Spanish was banned, thus creating the tradition of the native language as the vehicle for native thought (Munro 1942:99).

From the beginning, the friars had found the Indians gifted in art and had encouraged them in the building of magnificent churches adorned with impressive carvings and paintings, including a large wooden statue of God which had been hollowed out so that a priest could hide within it and speak 'with the resounding voice of the Eternal Father to impress the Indians of the mission' (The South American handbook 1979:566).

The Jesuits, under the command of their general in Rome, paid little heed to the Spanish civil rule and the local Catholic hierarchy. Further, their protection of the Indians and the economic competition of the *reducciones* soon aroused the envy and hostility of neighboring Hispanics. In the mid-seventeenth century, armed conflict broke out when Bishop Cárdenas, temporary governor, sought to continue in office and resist his replacement from Spain by organizing an army of *criollos* 'persons of Spanish blood born in the New World'. The Jesuits led

137

an army of Guaraní against him and defeated him. Again, in 1731, Jesuit-led forces quelled another *criollo* attack and yet another a few years later (Munro 1942:99-100).

Finally, in 1750, Spain decided to trade seven missions in exchange for the Portuguese town of Colonia, a notorious center for smuggling which the Spaniards wanted to curb. The mission Indians, who still thought of the Portuguese as slavers, rose in revolt, and there followed the long and bloody conflict of the War of the Seven Reductions. It was suspected, if never proved, that the Jesuits were behind this rebellion. The Guaraní, confronted by both Spaniards and *criollos*, were defeated, and the golden prosperity of the *reducciones* declined. A final blow was delivered by the court of Spain in 1767, when the king ordered the expulsion of the Jesuits from all Spanish territories. The missions were deserted, the churches decayed or were burned, and the Indians were pressed into peonage (The South American handbook 1979:556).

Three years after Paraguay became independent of Spain, in 1814 the self-styled 'enlightened despot' Gáspar Rodríguez de Francia became dictator and closed the borders to trade and immigration until 1840. The government was controlled by Francia and other members of his family for 57 years. His grand-nephew, in 1865, led the country into a disastrous war against Argentina, Brazil, and Uruguay, in which much Guaraní territory was lost and over half of the population was destroyed. Of the 221,000 who survived, only 28,000 were men. At the present time, there are only 40,000 pure Guaraní in Paraguay, but the importance of their culture and language continues (The South American handbook 1979:556-557). Poor in precious metals, Paraguay had attracted relatively few Spaniards in the colonial era, and there is less Spanish blood in the population there than in any place else in South America (Munro 1942:246). Trained by the Jesuits in economic survival, the Guaraní were not forced to assimilate into the culture of the conqueror. Their early education in literacy and their pride in their language endured. These cultural and linguistic traditions have been safe-guarded by several odd circumstances. One consists of the long periods of isolation which kept Paraguay free from the intrusion of other foreign elements which would have diluted the native stock. Another is that after the violent death of perhaps 88% of their men (The South American handbook 1979:557), the Guaraní women who remained must have produced a large number of progeny who continued the bicultural and bilingual development of the country.

The Guaraní language, still so prominent today, is unremarkable in its phonology, except for the six consonants /h/, /ʃ/, /ʔ/ (spelled with an apostrophe), [ǰ] (like English *j*), [r] (single flap, never trilled), and [v] (like English *v*). The unaspirated stops /p/, /t/, and /k/ have nasalized voiced allophones [mb], [nd], and [ŋg]. The role played here by phonological environments is extremely complex. As to vowels, there are no fewer than twelve. Five are like Spanish /a/, /e/, /i/, /o/, /u/, and there is a sixth, /ɨ/, a back unrounded vowel spelled *y*, similar to that of Russian or Polish. To each of these vowels corresponds a nasalized counterpart, also phonemic, the first five similar to those of Portuguese. The nasalized vowels can be written in four ways, with a tilde, two dots, a circumflex accent, or a macron. As to the suprasegmental of stress, most Guaraní words are accented on the last syllable, so written accent marks are used only to indicate exceptions to this rule (Guasch 1956:19-32). (Listen to Tape 2, selection c, and see Appendix 5.)

Morphologically, Guaraní is mildly polysynthetic, but its forms are less complex than those of Nahuatl, Maya, Quechua, or Mapuche. Verbs may be transitive, intransitive, reflexive, or reciprocal. The verb is prefixed for seven persons, three singular and four plural, including one for 'we' inclusive and another for 'we' exclusive. The 'we' inclusive marker, *ja-*, refers to both speaker and hearer and is used in sentences like *Japuka* 'We (you and I) are laughing'. The 'we' exclusive, *ro-*, refers to the speaker and anyone in his group as opposed to those whom he is addressing, as in *Ropuka* 'We (my associates and I) are laughing' ('and you are not') (Guasch 1956:113, 96-97).

Whether Guaraní has many tenses or a few tenses with a wealth of ways to express nuances is a moot point. The so-called present tense, for example, may express present time but can also be used of past events if a temporal occurs, such as *kuehe* 'yesterday', as in *kuehe ou* 'yesterday he comes'. Present progressive is indicated by a free morpheme following the verb and marked for person. A so-called imperfect, a suffix, is used for repeated past action, as in

upéramo	*ha'e*	*oúmi*	*xe*	*rógape*
'at that time'	3rd singular pronoun	'come'—repetitive past	'my'	'house-to'

'At that time he used to come to my house'.

Exclusive of the repetitive past are nine suffixes for other subtle variations such as recent past, recent past on the same day, past perfect with the idea of total cessation, indeterminate past used in proverbs, and past for subordinate clauses. The future is expressed in a similar way, with suffixes for near future ('I am about to ___'), remote future, future in subordinate clauses, and the equivalents of the English 'want to' and 'have to' (Guasch 1956:122-127).

Besides the indicative, Guaraní also has an imperative mood with both affirmative and negative forms. There is no subjunctive per se, but, like English, this language conveys notions of potential, conditional, exhortative, and the like by syntactic means (Guasch 1956:128-129, 137-138).

Other parts of speech, specifically nouns and adjectives, may function as *xendal* verbs by placing them in verb positions:

xe	*poxy*	*xe*	*rasy*
1st person pronoun	'anger'	1st person pronoun	'sick'
'I am angry'		'I am sick' (Guasch 1956:115)	

(Guaraní lacks a copulative verb.)

Subject pronouns are optional in Guaraní because, as in Spanish, the verbs are marked for person, as can be seen with the base *puka* 'laugh':

| *(xe) apuka* | 'I laugh' |

(*nde*) *repuka*	'you laugh'
(*ha'e*) *opuka*	'he/she/it laughs'
(*ñande*) *japuka*	'we laugh' (inclus.)
(*ore*) *ropuka*	'we laugh' (exclus.)
(*pee*) *pepuka*	'you laugh'
(*ha'e kuéra*) *opuka*	'they laugh' (Guasch 1956:114)

The optional subject pronouns and the direct object pronouns for first and second person have the same form and precede the verb. The use of these pronouns as objects is indicated by the deletion of the person marker on the verb, as can be seen with *juhu* 'find':

nde	*xe-*	*juhu*	*ha'e*	*ore-*	*juhu*
'you'	'I/me'	'find'	'he'	'we/us'	'find'
'You find me'			'He finds us'		

Third person direct object pronouns are *ixupe* for the singular and *ixupe kuéra* for plural; they follow the verb, and the person marker prefix is not deleted.

ha'e	*ojuhu*	*ixupe*	*ha'e*	*kuéra*	*ojuhu*	*ixupe*	*kuéra*
'he'	3rd person 'find'	'him'	'he/she'	pl.	3rd person 'find'	'he/she'	pl.
'He finds him'			'They find them' (Guasch 1956:97-99)				

Except for the third person *ixupe*, these same pronouns with the addition of the suffix *-ve* are used to express the indirect object. Thus, *xeve* means 'to me' and *oréve* 'to us'. When *ixupe* is used as indirect, it is not marked as such except by context (Guasch 1956:100).

These pronouns, again except for third person, can also be used as reflexives when the suffix *-jehe* is added. For example, *xe–jehe* is 'myself' and *oré–jehe* is 'ourselves'. Third singular or plural is expressed by *i jehe*, like Spanish *se*. These reflexive pronouns follow the verb (Guasch 1956:104).

These same basic forms, if followed by a noun or adjective, serve as possessives. For instance, *xe ru* is 'my father', *nde sy* 'your mother', and *ore kokue* 'our field'. The exceptional third person possessives are prefixed with *i-* as in *ipo* 'his/her hand' and *ikua* 'their finger' (Guasch 1956:100-101).

Neither the Guaraní noun nor the adjective which follows it is declined for gender, number, or case. Noun gender is indicated by separate words meaning 'male' or 'female', as in *ovexa kuimba'e* 'male sheep' or *ovexa kuña* 'female sheep'. When a speaker feels it necessary to indicate plurality, he can do so by placing after the noun a word such as *kuéra* and, after the adjective, *que*. For example, *mita kuéra* is 'children' and *kuña karai kuéra* is 'ladies'. The grammatical function of a noun in an utterance is shown by position and by a wide variety of suffixes (not case endings!), such as the dative *pe* and the locatives

me	'in'
pe	'in'/'into'

ári	'on top of'
rovái	'in front of'
kupépe	'behind'

and the directionals

goty	'toward'
vo	'to'
guivo	'from where'

There are also suffixes for temporal, comitative, instrumental, and agent, to name only a few, all of which function as prepositions do in English or in Spanish (Guasch 1956:52, 22, 211-212). These are invariable except for assimilation, which in Guaraní is very complex and widespread.

Although Guaraní relies heavily on postpositions, it is a subject-verb-object language and does have some other prepositional tendencies. Demonstratives, for instance, precede their nouns. There is no Guaraní article, but when a speaker wishes to express definiteness, he can use a demonstrative. Now, due to Spanish interference, many speakers use the singular *el, la,* or *lo* before a noun. When two nouns cooccur, the first limits or modifies the second:

Tu	+	*pasy*	=	*Tupasy*
'God'	+	'mother'	=	'God's mother'
óga	+	*jára*	=	*ogajara*
'house'	+	'owner'	=	'house's owner', or 'householder'
mita	+	*ao*	=	*mita–ao*
'child'	+	'dress'	=	'child's dress' (Guasch 1956:75-76, 50, 60)

Guaraní, like English, depends heavily on word order, and many syntactic relations are indicated by the position of a word or phrase in its clause. For example, the subject invariably precedes the verb, and a nominal direct object is marked as such by its position after the verb.

Questions in Guaraní may be indicated by any one of three interrogative particles: *pa* for a simple question, *piko* for a question expressing surprise, and *pipo* for one implying potentiality such as would be conveyed by a modal like *might* or *could* in English. These follow the verb or subject or a WH-form such as *who, what,* or *where*:

máva	*mba'asy*	*pipo*	*ou*
'what'	'epidemic'	interrog.	'come' (Guasch 1956:169-170)

While negation in Guaraní is extremely complex, the most common way to negate a verb is merely to prefix it with *nda-* and suffix it with *-i: jaha* 'we go' becomes 'we don't go' *nda-jaha-i* (Guasch 1956:164).

A sample of Guaraní words which have entered Spanish—in addition to those already listed in the previous chapter—is seen to consist mostly of names for local animals and plants:

ambayba 'type of pineapple'
ananá 'pineapple' (probably entered Spanish through Brazilian Portuguese
    and has spread internationally, cf. French, German, Russian *ananas*)
bacucu 'edible tuber' (called *jícama* in Mexico)
baypi 'beverage made of corn meal and water' (Mexican *atole*)
ca 'medicinal herb used against snakebite'
capibara 'large river rodent'
currucai 'type of rubber tree'
guambé 'small tropical tree and its fruit'
jacaranda 'rosewood tree'
jaguar 'jaguar'
jaguarete 'kind of wild cat'
macangua(y) 'bird of prey that feeds on snakes'
macanguaca 'herb used as antidote against snake venom'
mandioca 'tapioca'
maynimbí 'hummingbird'
pacoba 'banana'
patí 'type of river fish'
piquira 'shrimp'
piraña 'piranha'
surubí 'river fish similar to the pike'
tapioca 'tapioca'
vrundey 'type of wood used for fine furniture'
yacarete 'crocodile' (Mejías 1980:62-64; Santamaría 1942:2:134-135)

In view of the widespread bilingualism of Paraguayans, it is not surprising that many Spanish words have been incorporated into Guaraní without changing their forms. Some of these are:

arroyo 'gully'
asunto 'affair'
boleto 'ticket'
cada 'each'
carreta 'cart'
caso 'story'
católico 'Catholic'
comadre 'a woman's close friend'
compadre 'a man's close friend'
este día 'today'
factura 'invoice'
Jesucristo 'Jesus Christ'
jueves 'Thursday'
lección 'lesson'
mamá 'mama'
mostrador 'store counter'

soldado 'soldier'
sombrero 'hat'
vino 'wine' (Meliá Lliteras, Pérez Peñasco, and Farré Maluquer
    1960:passim)

Other Spanish loan words were borrowed with their rustic pronunciation or
have been adapted to Guaraní phonology, such as:

fóforo 'match'
gueí 'ox' (*buey*)
Helipe 'Philip'
kavaju 'horse'
ovexa 'sheep'
pa'i 'priest' (*padre*)
piola 'cowboy's rope' (*piala*)
voso 'purse' (*bolsa*)

In some cases, Spanish bases have been combined with Guaraní affixes, as in:

apagáne 'I will pay'
avende 'I sold'
bolichope 'in a store' (*boliche*)
carrerahápe 'in the races'
escuélape 'in school'
hi'áutope 'in his car'
igusto 'pleasing'
namigo 'your friend'
ndofaltái 'cannot be lacking'
ojecastiga 'are punished'
orequebranta 'drives us crazy' (*quebranta*)
oñemoseñoríta 'She's putting on a show of being a *señorita*'.
pecádogui 'from sin'
pacienciamíkena 'a little patience'
revendesépa 'Do you want to sell?'
roperdona 'I pardon you'.
xedisculpa 'Excuse me' (Meliá Lliteras, Pérez Peñasco and Farré Maluquer
    1960:passim)

Commenting on the attitude of modern Paraguayans toward their two languages, Father Guasch says that they are sad, they feel unschooled in both
tongues, and they lament the Hispanization of Guaraní and the Guaranization of
Spanish. The new generation is demanding better instruction and the use of
Guaraní in poetry, drama, and history, as it is 'the language of honor and intimacy,
of love and sorrow, of a legendary race which has sacrificed itself to the point
of heroism. . . . Such a language cannot die, shall not die' (Guasch 1956:10-
11).

References

Guasch, Antonio. 1956. El idioma guaraní: gramática y antología de prosa y verso. 3rd ed. Asunción: América-Moreno.

Mejías, Hugo A. 1980. Préstamos de lenguas indígenas en el español americano del siglo XVII. México: Universidad Nacional Autónoma de México.

Meliá Lliteras, Bartolomé, Alfonso Pérez Peñasco, and Luis Farré Maluquer. 1960. El guaraní a su alcance. Asunción: Ediciones Loyola.

Munro, Dana Gardner. 1942. The Latin American republics: A history. New York: Appleton-Century.

Santamaría, Francisco J. 1942. Diccionario general de americanismos, 3 vols. Méjico: Pedro Robredo.

The South American handbook. 1979. 55th ed. Eds. John Brooks and Joyce Candy. Bath, England: Trade and Travel Publications.

Part Three: Contemporary Spanish dialects in the Americas

Chapter 12
General differences between Peninsular and Latin American Spanish

What are some of the great general differences that distinguish the Spanish of Latin America, viewed as a whole, from that of Spain? One of the most important is the relative homogeneity of the language in the Western World. Alonso Zamora Vicente says that, over all,

> differences, within the vast territory of the Americas, are slight within the total structure of the language. There are far fewer differences between any two regions of enormous America, however far apart they may be, than between two neighboring valleys in Asturias, for example (1979:378).

This homogeneity is especially pronounced in the usage of the educated classes. While the speech of a Peruvian professor may differ but little from that of a colleague in Mexico City, the language of an Andean peasant may be very unlike that of his Mexican counterpart (Zamora Vicente 1979:379). Further, to a cultured Spaniard, the language of his South American peer may sound 'less refined' in its hospitality to popular (for him, 'substandard') characteristics. Moreover, while some areas in Latin America prefer one or another trait, all of these traits exist elsewhere in Latin America and, in addition, can be found in Spain as well. Some of these characteristics are:

1. Instability of unaccented vowels:
   [e] → [i] (*vistido, siguro*)
   [i] → [e] (*melitar, prencipal*)
   [e] → [j] (*tiatro, pior*)
   [o] → [w] (*cuete, tuavía 'todavía'*)
   [u] → [o] (*josticia, osté 'usted'*)
   [u] → [a] (*asté 'usted'*)

2. Change in diphthongs:
   [ej] → [aj] (*sais 'seis', raina 'reina'*)
   [aj] → [ej] (*agüeitar 'aguaitar', méiz 'maíz'*)

3. Excessive diphthongization or lack of diphthongization:
   [e] → [je] (*dientista, priesa 'prisa'*, an archaism from the sixteenth century)
   [je] → [e] (*apreta 'aprieta', quebras 'quiebras'*)

4. Reduction in consonant clusters:
   corrupción → *corrución*
   indigno → *indino*
   aspecto → *aspeito*
   doctor → *doutor*

5. Loss of intervocalic /d/:
   pedazo → *piaso*
   cuidado → *cuidao*

6. Hypercorrect insertion of /d/:
   vacío → *vacido*
   bacalao → *bacalado*

7. Change of accentuation:
   caído → *cáido*
   maestro → *máistro*
   maíz → *máiz*

Despite their present lack of status, many of these pronunciations are attested in the works of distinguished authors of the classical and preclassical periods (Zamora Vicente 1979:379-386).

The single most important distinction between Peninsular and Latin American speech is *seseo*. In Spain there are several areas in which *seseo* is predominant, including part of Andalucía. The Basques also pronounce *z* as [s] (but not *c* before *e* or *i* because these combinations do not exist in standard Spanish Basque orthography). Social class is at times a factor in some regions. In Castile everyone distinguishes between *z* and *c* before *e* and *i*, on the one hand, and *s*, on the other, but in adjacent regions, such distinction is often limited to the upper levels of society, as in Galicia. In Latin America, however, the distinction does not exist, and *seseo* is universal, in all areas and at all levels. Some speakers in Latin America use a dental [s] which may be taken for a [θ], but it is not. The only place where a true theta is in general use in the Americas is the Cuzco region of Peru, where the Indians pronounce *doce* as [doθe] and *trece* as [treθe] to distinguish them from *dos* and *tres* (Alonso 1967a:1:102, n. 35). Otherwise, with the tendency there to devoice a final unaccented vowel, these pairs would be homonyms, and transactions in the marketplace might well turn into altercations. This theta is not of Spanish origin, however, but a part of the Quechua phonemic stock.

In the stereotypic view of Ibero-American speech held by many Spaniards, it is supposed that all speakers are *yeístas*. This also is far from true. The entire Andean region distinguishes *ll* and *y* as the separate phonemes [λ] and [j]. Another misapprehension is that 'bilabial f', [φ], is a Latin Americanism, whereas in reality it was brought to Spain by Oscan legionnaires in the second century B.C. (Lapesa 1968:69-70; Palmer 1968:60).

In addition to these differences between the Spanish of the Peninsula and that of Latin America, there is a wide variety of intonational patterns in the New World, none of which correspond to those in Spain. As to the origin of these, linguists sharply disagree. Alfonso Caso in Mexico and Rodolfo Lenz in Chile held that the suprasegmentals had been affected by the indigenous substratum, but other linguists, like Amado Alonso, roundly dispute this theory (Lenz, Bello, and Oroz 1940:passim). However, even within individual countries, intonation differs enough from one area to another to suggest influence not only from one but from several Indian languages. A native of Chihuahua, Mexico, speaks with a relatively flat pitch contour and syllables of relatively equal stress and length, while his neighbor in Durango '*habla cantando*' (Lapesa 1968:344-346).

The morphology of Latin American Spanish is not significantly different from that of Spain except in a few respects. The most important of these is that in the New World the verb lacks a separate marker for the second person plural. In Spain there is *vosotros habláis* in contrast to *ustedes hablan*, but in Latin America only *ustedes hablan* for both familiar and formal address. Amado Alonso, as a refugee from Spain to Argentina, recalls his surprise at hearing a local farm wife shooing the chickens out of her kitchen with what to him was the stiffly polite '¡Vayansé!' (Alonso 1948).

Another morphological difference is *voseo*, the use of *vos* (where a Spaniard would say *tú*) together with a special verb form which varies from country to country. In Central America, Venezuela, Río Plata, and Colombia, for example, *tú hablas* has been replaced by *vos hablás*, *tú comes* by *vos comés*, and *tú vives* by *vos vivís*. In other areas, the Spanish second person plural endings (often without their final -*s*) are used as singular forms with *vos* (Zamora Vicente 1979:404). It is primarily the subject pronoun that has been affected, but *vos* may also serve as the object of a preposition. The direct or indirect objects and possessive forms correspond to those for *tú*.

In three countries, Argentina, Uruguay, and Costa Rica, *voseo* is characteristic of the speech of all social classes. In fact, Amado Alonso once quipped that in Buenos Aires children are taught that *vos* is spelled T-Ú so that they will not be startled when this form appears in literature from other parts of the Spanish-speaking world (Alonso 1948). *Voseo* in other Latin American countries is identified with uncultured speech. In some it has replaced *tú* altogether. In others, it coexists with *tú* where *tú* is characteristic of upper class usage. In the northernmost areas—Puerto Rico, Santo Domingo, and most of Mexico—there is no *vos* except in the Mayan south and in eastern Cuba.

The history of *vos* is similar to that of *you* in that both, originally second person plurals, came to be singular as well. In Spanish, however, *vos* became exclusively singular with the coining of a plural form of *vos* + *otros*, *vosotros*, in medieval Spain. In the *Poema del Cid* the King addressed a noble as *vos* and the nobles spoke to one another as *vos*, while *tú* was used for a person of a lower rank—a servant, a vassal, or a child. And in Gil Vicente's *La comedia do Viuvo* (1524), two peasant girls discover that the man whom they had taken for a shepherd and spoken to as *tú* was actually a prince, so, embarrassed, they stammer out some apologies, addressing him now with due respect:

Melicia—Y nos llamábamosle *tú*. Dezidnos, por Dios, señor, ¿quién sois *vos*?

By 1579, however, the high status of *vos* had slid so far that in the Spanish Court a gentleman who was called *vos* by a peer challenged the speaker to a duel. In 1626, Correas' *Arte grande de la lengua castellana* says, 'De *vos*, tratamos a los criados . . . y a los labradores y personas semejantes, y entre amigos a donde no hay gravedad ni cumplimiento se trata de *vos*' (Zamora Vicente 1979:407-409). Obviously, in the Americas *vos* would be used in speaking to Indians as they would be regarded as members of the lowest social caste. What of Mexico and Lima, where *vos* never took root? Both of these cities were seats of viceregal courts, where, as in Spain, the pejorative *vos* had been replaced with the now more acceptable *tú*.

As to the morphosyntax of the verb, periphrastic constructions are more popular in Latin America than in Spain. For instance, Spanish *¿Cómo le va?* frequently becomes *¿Cómo le va yendo?* The verb *ir* is also used as an intensifier of sorts in colloquialisms such as *Va y se cae* 'He goes and falls down'. In addition to the simple future (*hablaré, comeré*), there are two ways to form the future periphrastically (*he de hablar* and *voy a comer*). All of these exist as standard in Spain, but the analytical phrases are preferred in Latin America. Conversely, another morphosyntactic preference in Hispanoamerica is the use of the preterite where a Peninsular speaker would choose the analytic present perfect: *fui* rather than *he ido* and *hubo* instead of *ha habido*. Some verbs that are intransitive in Spain can be reflexive in the New World: *enfermar* may become *enfermarse* and *sanar, sanarse*. Another difference is that the archaism *dizque* is literary in Spain but casual in Latin America. Neologistic verbs in the Americas are often coined by adding -*ear* to a base (usually nouns) as in *chambear* ('dig a ditch' from Quechua *chamba* 'furrow'), *papalotear* ('to excel' from Nahuatl *papalotl* 'kite'), and *jinetear* ('ride a bronco' from Spanish *jinete* 'rider') (Álvar 1960:600).

Less important are morphosyntactic changes in the noun. Inflections for gender often produce an extra form: from *tigre* 'tiger' is derived *tigra* 'tigress', from *sapo* 'toad', *sapa* 'female toad', and *oveja* 'sheep', *ovejo* 'ram'. Similarly, from personal nouns ending in -*nte* are made feminine forms ending in -*nta*, such as *presidente* and *presidenta*, *asistente* and *asistenta*. Two apocopated nouns used as titles of respect for black females are *ña* from *señora* and *ma* from *mama*. Not the singular but the plural is preferred in expressions like ¿*Qué horas son*? and *Hace tiempos*. Diminutives and augmentatives appear frequently: *adiosito*, *ahorita*, *más acasito* 'just a tad closer', *amigaso* 'big buddy', and *huevón* 'a lazy lout'. Adjectives may double as adverbs: *Canta lindo* 'She sings pretty', *Cose bonito* 'She sews beautiful', *Corre rápido* 'He runs fast', and *Recién llegó* 'He arrived recently'. Latin American adverbial phrases include *no más* 'only', *si más* 'almost', and *a cada nada* 'for no reason at all' (Álvar 1960:612-613).

The greatest single difference between Latin American Spanish and that of the Peninsula is lexical. Whereas most of the phonological and morphosyntactic features of New World Spanish can be found in some corner of Spain, its lexicon is in many ways unique. The chief reason for this is the plethora of *indigenismos* used throughout Latin America even in countries where there are no longer any Indians, such as Puerto Rico or Uruguay. Native American vocabulary which has spread at home and abroad includes the following well-known terms:

Taíno:	Nahuatl:	Quechua:
alpaca	*cacahuate*	*coca*
barbacoa	*cacao*	*cóndor*
cacique	*chicle*	*Inca*
canoa	*chile*	*llama*
caray	*chocolate*	*pampa*
hamaca	*tequila*	*quina*
huracán	*tomate*	*vicuña*
iguana	*coyote*	
maíz	*mezquite*	
papaya		

Guaraní:	Mapuche:	Maya:
ananá	*poncho*	0
jaguar		
tapioca		

Other *indigenismos* are unknown to outsiders, having stayed at home, such as:

Taíno:
coa 'sharpened stake or board used as shovel'
coy 'canvas cot or cradle'
ditas 'vessel made of fruit shell or gourd'

Nahuatl:
ahuizote 'pest'
cuitlacoche 'edible fungus'
cócono 'turkey'

tiza 'chalk'

Maya:
cutz 'turkey'
lec 'water gourd'
xoy 'punch in the eye'

Quechua:
aco 'a floury drink'
carisina 'inefficient or masculine woman'

Mapuche:
chupilca 'a beverage made of corn meal'
hualato 'wooden spade'
ruca 'Indian hut'

Pampero:
quillango '*guanaco* robe worn by Indians'

Guaraní:
ambayba 'type of pineapple'
baypi 'a beverage made of corn meal'
maynimbí 'hummingbird'

Like other 'exported' languages, New World Spanish preserves many archaisms, such as:

altozano 'small plaza or church atrium' (northern South America)
arraiján 'myrtle'
esculcar 'frisk someone'
tiricia 'jaundice'
vegada 'time' (*vez*)

Also important in Latin American Spanish are the numerous *Andalucismos* which may support its descent from the speech of southern Spain, such as:

alcaso 'by chance'
amasijo 'farm'
cartucho 'paper bag'
chota 'police'
jamar 'eat'
jando 'money'
lejido 'tract of farmland owned by village' (a fusion of *el* + *ejido*)
pistear 'drink wine' (derived from *pisto* 'wine')
sardo 'soldier' (Álvar 1960:613).

The lexicon of Ibero-American Spanish contains many 'Occidentalisms' as well, words which stem from Leonese such as, for example:

andancio 'epidemic of a minor ailment' (literally 'that which goes around')

cangalla 'a skinny weakling' (used for both animals and people)
carozo 'large pit of a fruit'
columbiar 'to swing' (*columpiar* in Castilian)
chifle 'liquor bottle'
furnia 'a deep hole or pit'
lama 'mud'

In the Western world, some Peninsular words have acquired new meanings, such as:

	Old World:	New World:
álamo	'poplar'	'cottonwood'
boda	'wedding'	'party held at home'
carro	'cart'	'automobile'
ensenada	'small bay'	'fenced area for pregnant cows'
paramear	from *páramo*, 'bleak plain'	'drizzle'
tajamar	'prow of a ship'	'breakwater,' 'dam,' 'raft,' 'cistern' 'ne'er-do-well'

References

Alonso, Amado. 1967a. De la pronunciación medieval a la moderna en español, 2 vols. Madrid: Gredos.

Álvar, Manuel. 1960. Textos hispánicos dialectales: antología histórica. Madrid: Revista de Filología Española, Anejo XLLIII. 2 vols.

Lapesa, Rafael. 1968. Historia de la lengua española. 7th ed. Madrid: Escelicer.

Lenz, Rodolfo, Andrés Bello, and Rodolfo Oroz. 1940. El español en Chile. Eds. Amado Alonso and Raimundo Lida. Buenos Aires: Universidad de Buenos Aires.

Palmer, L. R. 1968. The Latin language. 6th ed. London: Faber and Faber.

Zamora Vicente, Alonso. 1979. Dialectología español. 2nd ed. Madrid: Gredos.

Chapter 13
Mexico

Latin American Spanish can be divided into five great regional variants: (1) Mexico and the adjacent areas of the southwestern United States and the republic of Guatemala; (2) the Caribbean, including both the coasts of Mexico, Colombia, Venezuela, and the islands of Puerto Rico, Cuba, and the half of Hispaniola known as Santo Domingo; (3) the Andes, extending from the highlands of Colombia through Ecuador, Peru, Bolivia, northwestern Argentina, and northern Chile, with the exception of Lima, which belongs to this area geographically but not linguistically; (4) Chile; and (5) the Río Plata, consisting of Argentina, Uruguay, and Paraguay. Each of these five zones, in turn, contains geographical subdialects. This is to say that the speech of a resident of Guatemala City differs considerably from that of a native of Santa Fe, New Mexico, yet both varieties have more traits in common than either has with the language of the other areas. The speech of the Mexican plateau, indeed, bears a closer resemblance to that of the Andes than does either one to those of the other three regions. And the three other regions, in turn, are like each other in many ways. Thus it can be seen that the five dialect areas fall naturally into two larger areas, one consisting of Highlands varieties and the other of the Lowlands. While the Highlands region comprises Mexico, the U.S. Southwest, Guatemala, and the Andes, the Lowlands include not only the Caribbean but also Chile and the three Río Plata countries, these four known collectively as the 'Cono Sur'. Central America may be viewed as a mixed or transitional zone in which usage is strongly influenced by Mexico to the north and the Caribbean on the east.

Our tour of Hispanic America will begin with the Highlands group, starting with Mexico.

A foreigner who has learned his Spanish from educated Mexicans will have no problem communicating when he gets to Madrid because of the strong phonological resemblance between the two varieties. In fact, Rubén del Rosario, a Puerto Rican linguist, declares:

La primera impresión de la pronunciación mexicana, por lo menos la del altiplano, es que está menos alejada del modelo castellano que la pronunciación de las Antillas (Rosario 1970:98).

He continues:

En general la pronunciación standard de México concuerda en muchos aspectos con el idioma normalizado de las clases superiores en otras naciones del hemisferio, destacándose en ella como particularmente diferencial el cuidado que se pone en la emisión de las eses y la firmeza de las *des* intervocálicas (Rosario 1970:102).

The care taken in pronouncing a firm intervocalic [ð] actually exceeds that taken in Castile itself and all of the Spanish high central plateau. It is almost as if Mexican speakers were trying to outdo the Castilians in this regard!

Indeed, the listener's impression of the similarity between Mexican and Castilian pronunciation is attributable to the treatment of many of the more frequent phonemes in the two. Both voiced and voiceless stops [b/p], [d/t], and [g/k] are produced in the same way in the two dialects, as is the fricative bilabial [β]. There is no distinction between *b* and *v* except orthographically. Perhaps the most striking resemblance is the maintenance of the prominent [s] not only intervocalically but also in preconsonantal position and before a pause. As in Castile, in Mexico there is actual contact between the tongue and the roof of the mouth in the articulation of [x], increasing the guttural nature of the sound. The affricates and the nasals are virtually identical, as are the laterals except for the absence of [λ] in Mexico. Like the other Highland varieties, and like Castile, Mexican Spanish has five vowel phonemes, unlike the Lowland systems which, according to some phonologists, have eight.

But despite the marked similarity between the Spanish of the Mexican *altiplano* and the Castilian *meseta*, there are many differences which sharply distinguish them. If someone accustomed to Mexican Spanish finds himself in a crowd in Madrid, perhaps in a large café or a hotel lobby, he is struck at once by the different acoustical effect. The general mingling of the sounds of Spanish in its homeland makes it seem more 'European', more like French or German, and the volume at which it is delivered intensifies this impression. One recalls the comment of Bernal Díaz, four and a half centuries ago, on the Spaniards' surprise at the quiet that reigned in the great central market on the Zócalo where thousands of Indians were engaged in trade.

Not only is Mexican Spanish characterized by traits that set it apart from other varieties, but it is also far from uniform in all parts of the country. Pedro Henríquez Ureña, the well-known Dominican linguist, feels that phonologically there are four major subdivisions (Henríquez Ureña 1938:334-335). The most influential is that spoken on the Central Plateau, dominant because this area is the most highly populated and the most important economically, politically, culturally, and in the fields of education and communications. Similar to the language of this area is that of the North, which was settled from the plateau and is growing rapidly in population and economic development. There are some minor differences which increase the farther one goes from Mexico City. For example, the intervocalic fricative [ð] and [ɣ] are pronounced with less tension and at times are lost (Rosario 1970:102-103). On the *altiplano*, consonants are more clearly articulated, not weakened or dropped, even in consonant clusters (Lope Blanch 1972:25). For example, *acción* is pronounced [aksjón], *experto* is [ekspérto], and *oxígeno* [oksíxeno]. In both regions, also maintained are consonant final [s], [l], [r], and [n]. In words of Nahuatl origin, final voiceless stops do not disappear (Rosario 1970:102). This is especially true in numerous toponyms such as *Tepic*, *Nayarit*, and *Tehuantepec*.

Spanish on the plateau and in the north contains at least three varieties of /s/. The one typical of the plateau is a dental produced with the tip of the tongue on the lower incisors, with a sound quite similar to [θ]; another, alveolar, is much like that of English; a third is postalveolar, like Castilian [ş]. All three of these occur in the north. One may be used in one community and yet another in a nearby area, depending upon the geographic or social origin of the settlers. Where [s] occurs before an initial trilled [r̄] as in *los ríos*, it is deleted in most varieties of Spanish but is retained on the *meseta* and in the north. A very special [s] is that of Jalisco and neighboring zones, where if it is word-final it is nasalized as in *adiós*ⁿ, *pues*ⁿ, and *tres*ⁿ (Lope Blanch 1972:15). The prominence of [s] in this variety of Mexican Spanish is attributed by Henríquez Ureña and Amado Alonso to Nahuatl [ts], which was a sibilant affricate, not a fricative, produced with the tip of the tongue on the lower front teeth. Lope Blanch hotly disagrees, calling attention to the fact that sixteenth-century Spanish possessed a similar dental sibilant which was written ç (Lope Blanch 1972:102-105). Thus, the dispute continues.

More commonplace in the central and northern areas is the bilabial fricative [ɸ], which is preferred to labiodental [f] by a majority of speakers of all social classes, 71% of the men and 57% of the women (Perissinotto 1975:100-103). The fricative [x] in these areas is similar to that of Castile except for the difference that its point of articulation is farther forward, and, if it is followed by a front vowel, this tendency is increased, and [x] comes to resemble [ç], similar to the German pronunciation of *-ch* in *ich*.

An apparently recent phenomenon is the treatment of vibrant [r̄] and flap [r]. Since about 1950, both have tended to become multiple, then voiceless, and then assibilated. In Mexico City one hears *un rato* as [un řáto], *tres* as [třés], and *calor* as [kalɔř] (Lope Blanch 1972:18).

All four dialect areas in Mexico are *yeísta*—that is, no distinction is made between *y* and *ll* except in two areas on the plateau. In the valley of Atotonilco, about 50 miles east of Guadalajara, [j] and [λ] are in contrast as in Castile. In Orizaba they contrast but *ll* is pronounced as a lengthened [ʒ]. In Puebla, Oaxaca, and Córdoba, they do not contrast and both are pronounced [ʒ] (Lope Blanch 1972:110-113). Whether spelled *y* or *ll*, in the north, [j] is often lost, especially in contact with a front vowel: thus, the final syllables of *río* and *amarillo, sea* and *estrella* are homonymic (Henríquez Ureña 1938:338).

Aspirate [h], which comes from Latin [f], is an archaism, having been used by all social classes in sixteenth-century Spain. It persists in the rustic speech of the plateau and the north, in words such as *juir* [xuír] 'flee', *jerrumbre* [xɛřúmbre] 'rust', and *jediondo* [xeðjóndo] 'stinking' (Boyd-Bowman 1960:65).

According to Lope Blanch, one of the most distinctive aspects of Mexican phonology is the treatment of the vowels. They tend to be closed and if unaccented are brief (Henríquez-Ureña 1938:336). On the plateau the vowels, unlike the consonants, which are maintained, are likely to be reduced and even lost. This is less true of the north, where vowels are strong and consonants weak. On the plateau, vowel weakening is conditioned by adjacent consonants. In 95% of these cases, the weakened vowels are in contact with [s]. In the remaining 5%, one-half of them are close to [č]. Environments in which this weakening or loss is most likely to occur are the following, in descending order:

(1) [s] + vowel + [s] as in *países*
(2) dental + vowel + [s] as in *partes* and *tardes*
(3) nasal + vowel + [s] as in *años* and *canciones*

This *debilitamiento* is less likely if the sibilant precedes the vowel rather than following it, as in *No se cuida* and *Va sin mirar*. While it is commonest in final unaccented syllables, it is not rare even in syllables which are stressed, as in *vista*, *chiste*, and *francés*. It occurs very often before a pause, as in *No vinieron todos*, as opposed to no weakening in *Estaban todos trabajando*. Linguists differ on the cause of this phenomenon. It might be due to a substratum influence from Nahuatl, but it can also be found in other dialect areas such as San Salvador, the Ecuadorian Andes, and Colombia. Very clearly attributable to substratum is the consonant cluster [tl] in word-initial and word-final position, as in *tlapalería*, *Náhuatl*, and *Tlahualilo*. If the cluster is in an intervocalic position, the syllable division is made before the [t] and not after: *a-tlas* as opposed to *at-las* for most Spanish speakers in other regions. Also from Nahuatl are the phonemes /ʃ/ and /ts/ which are found in plateau toponymics such as *Xochicalco* [ʃočikálko] and *Tzintzuntzan* [tsintsúntsan] (Lope Blanch 1972:24-25). In the northern state of Chihuahua, *ch* is pronounced [ʃ] by many speakers, as in Andalusia.

Patterns of intonation vary so widely from region to region in Mexico that valid generalizations applicable to the entire country are impossible to make. These patterns differ not only from Peninsular intonation, but also from those of any other Latin American country. Contrasting the intonation of Mexico City with that of Castile, Henríquez Ureña notes that in a Castilian sentence ending in a word stressed on the penult, the pitch begins to drop on the third syllable from the end and continues to fall until the final pause. The penult is brief, while the final unstressed syllable is long. In the Mexican capital, almost the opposite occurs: the pitch *rises* from the antepenultimate syllable to the penult. The penult is lengthened, while the final unaccented syllable is considerably shortened:

				1
				2
				3
Castile	Este	auto	es	nué-v-o.

				2
				1
				3
México	Este	auto	es	n-ue-vo.

(Henríquez Ureña 1938:335)

Henríquez Ureña describes the speech of the central plateau as having a relaxed articulation, a slow tempo, and a dominant high tone as compared to pronunciation in the north (1938:335). While Boyd-Bowman agrees that the pitch of the plateau is higher than elsewhere, he ascribes articulation and tempo to sociolect. The upper classes are careful to speak 'with precision and clarity', albeit rapidly. The lower classes 'make the least effort necessary to make themselves understood', dropping out segments and even syllables, substituting one fricative for another such as [ɣweno] for [βweno], and talking at a slower pace. The *rancheros* talk even more slowly. Semieducated speakers, between the upper and lower classes, adapt their articulation to the occasion, ranging from formal to casual style (Boyd-Bowman 1960:95).

Hispanic linguists quarrel as to indigenous influence on the suprasegmentals of the *altiplano*. Manuel Álvar flatly declares, 'Se encuentra en descrédito la acción fonética de las lenguas precolombinas en el español de America . . . (1960:611). Boyd-Bowman states with equal confidence: 'Este dulce sonsonete o "cancioncita," como lo llaman los mismos guanajuatenses, es el único rasgo fonético de cuyo origen indígena no cabe duda' (1960:95). Henríquez Ureña would agree, referring to the speech of the plateau, 'La entonación, en las clases populares, es idéntica a la que se emplea al hablar Náhuatl; en las clases cultas, el matiz local se atenúa' (1938:335).

In general, the morphosyntax of Mexican Spanish is very standard, highly similar to that of Castile. There are some differences, however, common to all social levels. The Mexican verb tends to be more 'analytical'. Where a Spaniard uses an inflected form, a Mexican is apt to express the same idea with a verb phrase. Sometimes this consists of a verb of motion, particularly *ir* and *andar*, plus a present participle to express tense and/or aspect. For example, *La luz se va yendo* 'The light is fading away' (Rosario 1970:104) refers to an action begun in the past, extending through the present into the future, with an imperfective aspect and a suggestion of gradually increasing degree. *¿Qué andas haciendo?*, 'What are you up to these days?', like the previous example, is also inclusive in tense, suggesting a habitual aspect. Curiously enough, *Voy llegando ahorita* 'I have just arrived' looks like a future, but in fact has a perfective sense. *Voy acabando ya* is a perfective future 'I'm just about through'. Castilian *Vamos a hacer una cosa* 'Let's do something' is at times in Mexico *Vamos haciendo una cosa*. The clause *Fulano se anda casando* suggests to the uninitiated that Fulano enjoys multiple marriages, but in Mexican usage means 'Fulano is getting ready to get married'. Another verb phrase heard in Spain, but more popular in Mexico, is composed of an auxiliary plus indefinite article plus a nominalized past participle in the feminine form, such as *meter una trompada* 'give a blow', *echar una platicada* 'chat', *poner una regañada* 'bawl out', *dar una planchada* 'iron' (Lope Blanch 1972:13-17). The verbs used as auxiliaries are in most cases semantically hollow and merely serve as carriers of tense, person, and number.

Yes-no questions in Mexico may be marked by a preposed *qué*, a construction unheard of in Spain. Lope Blanch comments that the *qué* here functions as a question marker much like *est-ce que* in French or *do* in English. An example is *¿Qué, no te lo dio a ti?* 'Didn't he give it to you?' (Lope Blanch 1972:14). Such expressions, with a rising intonation on *qué*, convey surprise, disappointment, or shock.

There are other phrases typical of Mexican Spanish. One reverses the order of constituents, if judged by Peninsular standards, so that *nada más* 'nothing else' becomes *más nada*, *nadie más* 'nobody else' becomes *más nadie*, and *nunca más* 'never again', *más nunca* (Rosario 1970:104). Another typical structure contains *con todo y*, a concessive conjunction like English *although*, as in *Se fue a trabajar con todo y estar agripado* 'He went to work although he had the flu' (Lope Blanch 1972:14). In other common phrases, a plural is used where in Spain a singular is preferred. Among verbs, *haber* with a plural subject is pluralized, as in *Habían varias personas* 'There were several people'; with both verb and noun *¿Qué horas son?* 'What time is it?' instead of *¿Qué hora es?*; the intensifier *medio* which is not inflected on the Peninsula becomes plural, substandard, in the presence of a plural adjective—e.g., in *medios muertos* 'half dead' (Rosario 1970:105).

Mexican Spanish is conservative in maintaining the reflexive passive in which the verb agrees with the subject, as in *Se venden botellas* 'Bottles for sale'. Seldom used is the impersonal *se* construction, *Se vende botellas* (Lope Blanch 1972:10). In the third person plural formal (*ustedes*) imperative of reflexive verbs, the *se* may be infixed between the stem and personal ending. Thus *váyanse* 'go away' = *váyansen*, *véngase* 'come' = *véngansen*, *espérense* 'wait' = *espérensen*, and *cállense* 'be quiet' = *cállensen*. This may come from a speaker's assumption that the *se* is part of the verb and therefore a plural ending must be added to it. This addition leaves the first -*n* with no significance, which often leads to its being dropped, so that *váyansen* becomes *váyasen*, *véngansen*, *véngasen*, *espérensen*, *espéresen*, *cállensen*, *cállesen*. Less frequent is the analogous process with the pronoun *me*, which presents optional forms such as *díganmen* 'give me', *dígamen*, and *démen*. Also by analogy are created personalized infinitives such as *irsen*. This is not an exclusively Mexican phenomenon, but exists in some parts of Spain, Costa Rica, and Colombia (Boyd-Bowman 1960:166-167).

In Mexico as in Spain and most of Peru, *tú* has not been replaced by *vos*. The Spanish verb in Mexico is conjugated approximately as in Castile. However, it lacks the familiar second person plural form. Hence no distinction can be made between the second person plural formal and informal. As in Spain and in many Latin American countries, an analogical -*s* is added to the second person singular of the preterite: *cantaste* becomes *cantastes* and *dijiste* becomes *dijistes*. Then, by dissimilation, in rustic speech the first *s* is lost, producing *cantates* and *dijites*. Both of these phenomena are especially widespread in the north. Another trait of rustic speech in Mexico and elsewhere is the use of -*nos* for -*mos* in the first person plural of the imperfect indicative (*comprábanos*), conditional (*diríanos*), present subjunctive (*váyanos*), and imperfect subjunctive (*creyéranos*). These also are analogical formations, based on the first person plural object pronoun *nos* (Boyd-Bowman 1960:165).

Some verb tenses are used differently in Mexico and Spain. Lope Blanch attributes this to independent development owing to geographical separation, and he cautions that Mexican usage should not be viewed as 'incorrect'. In Spain, both the simple preterite and the present perfect are perfective, distinguished only by temporal notions: the simple preterite refers to an act completed at any time in the past while the present perfect refers to a more recent past. Such at least is the theory to be found in prescriptive grammars; in practice, many Spaniards habitually use present perfect for any completed action. In Mexico, on the other hand, the distinction between the two is not temporal but aspectual. Preterite is primarily perfective and present perfect is durative or iterative. *Ya lo leí* is perfective and past. *Siempre lo he creído* is imperfective and durative, begun in the past and extending through the present: 'I have always believed it (and I continue believing it)'. *Durante estas vacaciones he ido al club muy seguido* 'On this vacation I've gone to the club quite often' is imperfective and iterative: presumably he has gone repeatedly and he will keep on going (Lope Blanch 1960:20-21).

Further, in Mexico the preterite has developed uses which do not exist in Spain. In popular speech it has replaced the pluperfect. *Apenas lo vio, salió corriendo* 'As soon as he saw it, he ran away'. It is also used as a perfective future: 'I'm going to start to do it, and by two I'll have finished it' is *Me pongo a hacerlo yo, y para las dos, ya lo acabé* (= *habré acabado*). The present perfect in Mexico has also acquired new senses. For one, it is used in exclamations as a historical present, to render more vivid a past event. For example, *Se me atravesó una viejita y le toqué el claxón . . . ¡qué susto se ha dado la pobre!* 'A little old lady crossed in front of me and I blew the horn at her . . . what a scare the poor woman had (= has had)'. The present perfect is also used as a substitute for the pluperfect subjunctive in 'if' clauses: *Si lo he sabido, claro que te lo traigo* (for *hubiese sabido* and *habría traido*) 'If I had known it (= have known it), of course I would have brought (= I bring) it to you' (Lope Blanch 1960:21-22).

In Mexico, the simple future is weakening, and in its place, several verb phrases are used. Lope Blanch attributes this preference to an original nuance of obligation (*to have to*) repugnant to the 'affable and courteous speech of Mexico'. Some of the phrases that replace the offending form are, instead of *cantaré*, *voy a cantar*, *he de cantar*, and *quiero cantar*. As in English, also acceptable for future time is a present form: *El año que viene nos vamos a Vera Cruz* 'Next year we go to Vera Cruz'. Since *haber de* in Mexico has become synonymous with the simple future, it has also taken on the latter's function as indicating probability: *Ha de ser su hermano* 'He's probably her brother'. Also weakening, by analogy, is the simple conditional: *Dijo que iba a venir más tarde* 'He said he was going to come later' instead of *Dijo que vendría más tarde* 'He said he would come later'. The conditional mood is also being replaced by the -*ra* imperfect subjunctive in the conclusion of conditional sentences: *Si hubieras venido, te hubieras divertido* (= *te habrías divertido*) 'If you had come, you would have had a good time' (Lope Blanch 1972:17-20).

The morphosyntax of the Mexican noun differs only slightly from Castilian. Some nouns have changed gender. Peninsular *bombilla* 'lamp chimney' in Mexican Spanish is *bombillo*, and *el muelle* in Spain is *la muelle* in Mexico. More important are formations of nouns marked by -*a* as feminine from etymons which previously showed no formal gender marker.

Peninsular:	Mexican:
el/la director	*la directora*
el/la doctor	*la doctora*
el/la huésped	*la huéspeda*
el/la presidente	*la presidenta*
el/la jefe	*la jefa*
el/la carnal	*la carnala*
el/la testigo	*la testiga*

Such neologisms are gaining currency in Spain at present but are quite old in Mexico (Lope Blanch 1972:18).

Since the Mexican verb lacks a familiar second person plural, naturally enough it also lacks the corresponding pronoun. Instead of *vosotros*, in Mexico there is *ustedes*, as in all of Hispanoamerica. Instead of *os*, Mexicans use third person plural pronouns.

One of the problems of the Spanish language is the ambiguity of the pronoun *se* as to person, number, and gender in constructions such as *Ya se lo dije*, which could mean 'I already told it to him', 'to her', 'to them (masc.)', 'to them (fem.)', or 'to you (singular or plural)'. On the continent and in cultured Mexican Spanish, this problem is solved by the addition of a prepositional phrase such as *a él, a ella, a ellos, a ellas, a usted, a ustedes*. But in popular speech in Mexico some speakers, aware of the ambiguity, indicate that *se* is plural by adding an *-s* to *lo/la*, producing sentences like *Ya se los dije* 'I already told it to them' (Lope Blanch 1972:22). Still unresolved is the problem of gender! The sentence *Se las venden a los americanos* means 'They sell it (*la tierra*) to the Americans' and not 'They sell them to the Americans', nor does it specify whether the American buyers are male or female (Rosario 1970:104).

Ordinarily in the Hispanic world, when an indirect object pronoun is present to indicate who or what is concerned (a dative of interest), a definite article is used before the subject when it refers to a part of the body, an article of clothing, or something closely related to a person:

Me duele la cabeza 'My head aches'
Le duele la cabeza 'His/her head aches'
Tómate la leche 'Drink your milk'

Occasionally in Mexico, a possessive pronoun replaces the definite article:

Me duele mi cabeza.
Le duele su cabeza.
Tómate tu leche.

Some linguists think this redundancy is caused by influence from Nahuatl in which possessives are more frequent than in Spanish. Lope Blanch disagrees, however, pointing out that the same construction is not uncommon in the *Cid* (Lope Blanch 1972:23).

Spanish possessive pronouns that precede the noun are by definition unstressed proclitics. If a speaker adds emphasis, a possessive from a different set must follow the noun. Consider the difference in:

Esa es su idea 'That's his idea'
Esa es una idea suya 'That's *his* idea (and I don't agree with it)'

The changes in the pronominal form and syntactic order are accompanied by greater stress and higher pitch on the possessive. In Mexico, however, an alternative structure has arisen, as in *Ese es tu problema*, where heavy stress and highest pitch do appear on the preceding possessive, probably a calque of English 'That is *your* problem! (Not mine!)' (Lope Blanch 1972:27).

Another anomaly of Mexican Spanish is the suffixation of a noun or adjective with -*eco*, which in Nahuatl has a number of uses. It is primarily a locative and as such, when affixed to a toponym, designates an inhabitant of a certain area, for example, *Yucateco, Tamaulipeco, Guatemalteco*, and *Chiapaneco*. Less commonly, -*eco* may be added to roots referring to persons, in which case it plays a despective role, pointing out people's shortcomings, as in *cacareco* 'pockmarked', *chapaneco* 'a runt', and *caneco* 'a drunk'. In this use it may not be a derivative from Nahuatl but a deformation of the Spanish diminutive -*ico* (Lope Blanch 1972:22-23).

Another hallmark of Mexican Spanish is the frequency of adverbializing adjectives, as in *Canta suave* 'He sings swell', *Huele feo* 'It smells ugly', and *Corre rápido* 'He runs fast'. While these forms are found in Spain as well, they are far more popular in Mexico (Lope Blanch 1972:18).

As to the Mexican word stock, the single greatest influence has been that of the substratum languages, especially Nahuatl (see Chapter 7). There are several other lexical characteristics that differentiate Mexican from Peninsular Spanish. Lope Blanch, himself a Castilian, comments that to the ear of a Spaniard, Mexican vocabulary has an archaic ring. Many Peninsular words and phrases have retained in Mexico their sixteenth-century meanings, while in Spain they have acquired new semantic contents that have replaced their traditional senses. The following sample glossary illustrates the semantic conservatism of the Mexican lexicon:

Mexico:	Spain:
Lexical items retaining old meanings:	Terms that have replaced traditional lexical items:
cómo (+ adjective)	*qué* (+ adjective)
se me hace	*me parece*
también no	*tampoco*
¿qué tanto?	*¿cuánto?*
mucho muy	*muchísimo*
dizque	*según dice/dicen*
de que	*cuando*
cada que	*siempre que*
cada y cuando	*de vez en cuando*
otro día	*al día siguiente*

lindo/-a	*bonito/-a*
pararse	*ponerse de pie*
prieto	*negro*
liviano	*ligero*
bravo	*valiente*
demorarse/dilatarse	*tardar*
esculcar	*espiar, registrar*
recibirse	*graduarse*
luego	*inmediatamente*
cristianar	*bautizar* (Lope Blanch 1972:10-12)

Of course, it must not be imagined that Mexican speakers are unaware of the meanings of the items in the 'Spain' column. In fact, most of these terms, in Mexico, are in free variation with the so-called 'archaisms' in the Mexican list.

As a result of nearly five centuries of geographical separation, the lexicons of Spain and Mexico have, naturally enough, diverged considerably in the area of terms introduced into the language since the Conquest and colonization. In this respect, the differences between Peninsular and Mexican usage resemble those existing in British and U.S. speech. The following is a brief sample of different lexical usage in Mexico and in Spain:

Mexico:	Spain:	Meaning:
(la) sobrecargo	*(la) azafata*	'stewardess'
estufa	*cocina/fogón*	'kitchen stove'
necio/-a	*testarudo/-a*	'stubborn person'
aparador	*escaparate*	'store counter'
sombrilla	*paraguas*	'umbrella'
charola	*bandeja*	'tray'
pasto/zacate	*césped*	'lawn'
pena	*vergüenza*	'shame'
de repente	*por casualidad*	'unexpectedly'
panteón	*cementerio*	'cemetery' (Lope Blanch 1972:15)
plomero	*fontanero*	'plumber'
frijoles	*judías*	'beans'
saco	*americana*	'jacket'
tahona	*panificadora*	'baker' (f.)
cigarro	*pitillo*	'cigarette'
cerro	*otero*	'hill'/'mountain' (Lope Blanch 1972:20)

Both Mexican and Peninsular Spanish have accepted numerous loanwords from English. Some of these borrowings that are common to both varieties are:

estándar	*club*
snob	*coctel*
pedigree	*cheque*

filmar   *líder*
fútbol   *sándwich*
interviú   *hall* (Lope Blanch 1972:27)

However, because of the proximity of Mexico to the United States, the Mexican vocabulary contains many Anglicisms unknown in Spain. For example:

carro ('auto')   *réferi*
checar   *lonchería*
hobby   *clóset*
fólder   *registrado (certificado)*
overol   *emergencia*
suéter   *elevador*
cloch ('clutch')   *yonque* ('junk')
suiche ('switch') (Lope Blanch 1972:27)

Despite the enormous economic and cultural influence of the United States in Mexico, English loanwords in Mexican Spanish are not appreciably more numerous than in other Latin American dialects, according to Lope Blanch, who writes:

> . . . teniendo en cuenta que México es país limítrofe de los Estados Unidos y que gran parte de su población—inclusive en estratos semicultos—habla inglés, deberemos admitir que la influencia ejercida por esta última lengua sobre la lengua española es mucho menor de lo que cabría esperarse (1972:27).

In another study, 'Anglicismos en la norma lingüística culta de México', he adds:

> Todo . . . permite imaginar que la influencia de la lengua inglesa sobre el español mexicano debe de ser extraordinariamente amplia y profunda. Sin embargo, es muy posible que la fisionomía del español hablado en México no difiera, a este respecto, de la de otros países de lengua castellana mucho más alejados—geográfica, histórica y económicamente—de los Estados Unidos (1979:184).

In the northern border states, Rubén del Rosario observes, the proportion of English loanwords is understandably greater. Many of these northern anglicisms, such as those listed here, never have made their way into the Spanish of the interior:

chain 'shine'   *marqueta* 'market'
daime 'dime'   *mecha* 'match'
jaigüey 'highway'   *traque* 'track'

Surprisingly enough, Rosario notes, in Central America and in the Antilles, English loanwords play a far greater role than in Mexico City (Rosario 1970:109).

While all varieties of Spanish make use of numerous figures of speech, the word stock of Mexico seems to be exceptionally rich in these terms. Quite a few of them are humorous and serve the useful social purpose of correcting disapproved conduct. Among these are numerous neologistic verbs formed by adding *-ear* conjugational endings to a stem, usually a noun. Many of these deride men who are not manly:

cachuquear 'double-cross'
chaquetear 'betray' ('be a turncoat')
rajolear 'back down'
chivear 'quail'

Others express contempt for a man whose behavior is slothful or animalistic or whose appearance is ridiculous:

huevonear 'be lazy'
gusjear 'eat like a vulture'
changuear 'ape another'
laquear 'plaster one's hair with goo'

Verbs of this kind stereotype women as garrulous, inconsequential, and constantly complaining:

cacaraquear 'cackle'
periquear 'chatter like a parrot'
chismolear 'gossip around'
pedorrear 'raise a stink'
pintorreguear 'put on war paint'

Verbs with children as agents are equally satirical. Children have sticky fingers (*pegostear*), they pout (*jetear*), and whine (*jirimiquear*) as women do, and tattle on each other (*capear*). Often they sass adults (*pirfantear, retobear*). As the objects of the four verbs meaning 'to spoil' (*apapachar, chiplear, chiquear, chulear*), they reflect the annoyance of the macho males with whom they are associated. Punishing children is made light of in *nalguear* and *sonajear* 'spank'.

Some derisive verbs are multivalent in that they convey criticism ranging from harsh, satiric reproof to tolerant amusement or appreciation, depending upon the speaker's estimation of the person(s) to whom he is referring. *Garrotear*, for example, derived from *garrote* 'cudgel', means 'to thrash': sports fans would appreciate their own team's thrashing an opponent but condemn their team if defeated at the hands of an inferior group.

Closely akin to these verbs are bivalent in-group terms, sometimes called 'counter-words', which form a part of the jargon of a social subgroup to express the mutual solidarity of its members. These may be exemplified most vividly by criminal cant, in which they convey humorous appreciation when referring to lawless acts committed with professional skill but ridicule when referring to a victim or to the police:

colear 'tail someone'
coyotear 'be a shrewd lawbreaker'/'steal'

cusquear 'solicit as prostitute'
chulear 'pimp'

A subcategory of these concerns bodily injury inflicted with a weapon, usually a knife:

cuetear 'shoot'
macanear 'blackjack'
plomear 'fill someone with lead'
alfilear 'stab'
canalear 'slash'
filetear 'slice'
navajear 'knife' (Cotton and Sharp 1985:211-212)

Some of this criminal cant referring to violence is characterized by a grim sort of 'gallows humor' that may come from a desire to make light of a heinous crime. Further shrouding of a black reality with jocosity is exemplified in countless verbs and nouns associated with death. Some verbs and verb phrases for *morir*, with their literal translations, are:

azotar 'whip'
petatearse 'lie down on your sleeping mat'
dar el changazo 'take a big noisy fall'
llevárselo candinga 'be carried off by the devil'
ponerse la pijama de madera 'put on one's wooden pajamas'

Colorful phrases for *matar* are:

amolar 'grind down'
bailarse a uno 'flirt'
madrugar 'get the jump on' ('ambush')
matanciar 'massacre'
muraguear 'make dead'
quemar 'burn'

Some metaphoric nouns synonymous with death are:

la canica 'the skinny one'
la dientona 'the big-toothed one'
la güera 'the blonde'
la igualadora 'the leveler'
la mocha 'the sly hypocrite'
las patas de catre 'the cot legs'
la tembleque 'the trembler'
la tilica 'the skinny one' (Rosario 1970:107)

While the subdialects of the *meseta* and the north almost imperceptibly merge into one another, so that no well-defined boundary may be established between them, the same is not true of speech of the Gulf Coast. While a thorough description of this variant must await further investigation, some valid generalizations can be made in regard to its salient traits. The language of the Caribbean coast can be termed a 'transitional' dialect which forms, as it were, a 'bridge' between the Spanish of central Mexico and that of the Antilles (Cuba, in particular) (Lope Blanch 1979:143).

Pedro Henríquez Ureña writes that in the speech of the Gulf Coast far fewer indigenous loanwords are to be found than in the interior. Articulation is more vigorous than in Mexico City and the tempo of speech more rapid. As on the plateau, however, the language is spoken at a relatively high pitch. In coastal Spanish, the vowels are not reduced or deleted as they are on the *meseta*. Many of the phonological characteristics of the speech of the eastern coast are reminiscent of those of Andalusian and Antillean Spanish. Syllable-final consonants (especially [s]) are weakened and often disappear. The intervocalic [ð] of the past participial suffix -*ado* usually is deleted. The same is true of intervocalic [r] and final [-n], producing forms such as *quieo* (*quiero*) and *tie* (*tiene*), frequent in rustic speech in both Andalusia and Castile. Between vowels [x] is relaxed to a simple aspirate [h] (Henríquez Ureña 1938:339). As in other Andalusian-based varieties of Spanish, syllable-final [r] and [l] are frequently interchanged (Zamora Vicente 1979:415-416). In the state of Tabasco, initial [f] is replaced by a velarized [φ], resulting in a sound intermediate between [φ] and [x] (Henríquez Ureña 1938:339). (This same phenomenon has been observed also in the Colombian, Ecuadorian, and Peruvian highlands) (Boyd-Bowman 1960:69-70, n. 33).

Lope Blanch believes that investigation now in progress will show not one, but at least four, coastal variants in Mexican Spanish. He tentatively delimits them, from north to south, as follows: (1) the coast of Tamaulipas to the region just north of Veracruz (at about the latitude of Tamazunchale); (2) the central stretch of the coast of Veracruz; (3) the southern coast of Veracruz; and (4) the coast of Tabasco, linguistically and culturally a transitional area as, indeed, it was before the coming of the Spaniards (recall that the bilingual Malinche came from there) (Lope Blanch 1979:143).

Yucatan, until well past the mid-twentieth century, was so isolated from the rest of Mexico that linguistically it has constituted an entirely separate area. Indeed, the highway connecting Yucatan with the capital was not completed until the 1950s. Cultural and political factors contributed significantly to this isolation. During the colonial period, Yucatan formed part of the Capitanía General de Guatemala, from whence it was governed. Its Amerindian substratum was (and is) Mayan, not Nahuatl. Spanish never succeeded in displacing Mayan as the first language of the majority of *Yucatecos*—today, more than 50% of its people (including members of the educated classes) are bilingual in Mayan and Spanish. It remains to be seen whether modern lines of communication by highway and air, established in the mid-twentieth century, will eventually modify the cultural and linguistic situation of Yucatan and incorporate the peninsula into the mainstream of Mexico.

Lope Blanch states that the northern half of the state of Campeche should be included in this dialectal area, but since fieldwork on the speech of Yucatan has not been completed, a full description of this variant is not yet feasible. However, it is possible to point out some of the well-known peculiarities of Yucatecan speech (Lope Blanch 1979:142). For example, the phonology of Yucatan Spanish differs so greatly from that of any other area of Mexico that a *Yucateco* can be identified at once by his 'accent'. The most striking characteristic of his pronunciation consists in the so-called *consonantes heridas*, that is, the stops [p'], [t'], [k'], followed by a glottal stop. The phoneme /g/, nonexistent in Mayan, is usually omitted before [w]: thus, *agua* is pronounced [áwa]. Mayan has no /ɲ/; hence, some Spanish words containing this phoneme, such as *baño*, are pronounced with an alveolar [n] followed by a [j], i.e., [bánjo]. In the case of many other words, like *albañil* or *pequeñito*, the difficulty is avoided by simply eliminating the [ɲ] and substituting an [n]: [albaníl, pekeníto]. In Mayan, a glottal stop is added to words ending in a stressed vowel. As a result, many speakers have extended this pronunciation to Spanish words, moving the stress to the final syllable at the same time, so that *hijo, niña*, become [xixóʔ], [niɲáʔ] (initial [x] derived from Latin [f] is retained, as in rustic Spanish elsewhere). Words beginning with [f] (a phoneme lacking in Mayan) are articulated with [p]: thus *familia = pamilia* and *fresco = presco*. Final unstressed [-e] after [č] is often deleted, perhaps because [-č] in Mayan is a conjugational suffix: accordingly, *coche = coch* and *cambalache = cambalach*. In the lexicon of Yucatan Spanish there are many Mayan loanwords that begin with consonant clusters consisting of [ʃ] + [t] (spelled *xt-*), a combination common enough in German, but most exotic in Spanish! An example is *xtabay* 'a spirit that haunts lovers' [ʃtabáy]. There is no [r] or multiple [r̄] in the Mayan phonemic inventory. As a result, in the Yucatan dialect [l] and [r] tend to be in free variation; and when [r] *is* pronounced, it is retroflex [R], sounding much like its counterpart in Midwestern U.S. English! Many speakers make no distinction between multiple and single-flap *r* ([r̄] and [r]), rendering both as [R]. As in the rustic Spanish of New Mexico, intervocalic [j] following a stressed vowel is often dropped, so that, for example, *cuchillo* is [kučío]; perhaps as a hypercorrection a [j] is sometimes heard in words such as *sandía* 'watermelon' [sandíja] (Lope Blanch 1979:60).

In the area of morphosyntax, Yucatan Spanish deviates less. Indeed, most of its traits appear more attributable to archaism than to a Mayan substratum. As in sixteenth-century Spanish, *tener* and *estar* are today used as auxiliary verbs with the past participle in forming the present perfect indicative. For example, *Tengo trabajado mucho* 'I have worked a lot', or *Está ido a cortar leña* 'He has gone to cut firewood'. Neither of these sentences would have been viewed as 'abnormal' in the 1500s. In Yucatan *ha* (for *hace* 'ago') is another archaism, still common in Standard Spanish poetry: though *¿Cuánto ha que llegó?* 'How long ago did he arrive?' may sound 'literary' to an outsider, it is normal usage among the common folk of Yucatan. However, a Mayan calque is probably responsible for the construction, *pasar a* + infinitive 'to be about to . . .' as in, for instance, *Me pasé a caer* which means '*Estuve a punto de caer*' ('I was about to fall') (Lope Blanch 1979:60).

The lexicon of Yucatan differs not only from that of Spain but also from that of the rest of Mexico. This is due both to the Mayan substratum discussed earlier and to the fact that here many Spanish terms have different referents. Consider the following:

Yucatan Spanish:	Standard Spanish:	Meaning:
papagayo	*cometa*	'kite'
volantines	*voltereta*	'somersault'
nené	*criatura*	'baby'
menudo	*monedas sueltas*	'change'
encima	*adehala*	'lagniappe'
vereda	*raya del pelo*	'part in hair'
gancho	*horquilla*	'hairpin'
chupaflor	*colibrí*	'hummingbird'
filarmónica	*armónica*	'harmonica'
tirahule	*tirador*	'slingshot'
brincar la soga	*saltar a la cuerda*	'jumping rope'
lascar	*desportillar*	'chip'
enhilar	*enhebrar*	'thread needle'
costurar	*coser*	'sew'
hilera	*hilo*	'thread'
charros	*tirabuzón*	'corkscrew' (Lope Blanch 1979:59-132 passim)

Central American Spanish is a transitional dialect, strongly influenced by Mexico from the north and the Caribbean from the east. It is spoken in the Mexican states of Chiapas and parts of Tabasco, Guatemala, El Salvador, Honduras, Nicaragua, and Costa Rica, which serve as a bridge between Central and South America. Panama, although geographically a part of Central America, linguistically belongs to its southern neighbor Colombia (Henríquez Ureña 1938:341). The phonology of Central America resembles that of Caribbean Spanish, strongly influenced by Andalusian, in several respects: syllable-final consonants are frequently weakened or lost. This is particularly true of [s], which either becomes [h] or drops out entirely. In Nicaragua, [s] before a pause or a following consonant often is pronounced as a glottal stop. Thus, *está* becomes [ɛʔtá]. Syllable-final [n] (pronounced [m] in Castilian before a bilabial, as in *cambiar*) becomes velar [ŋ] [kaŋbjár], [eŋtrár], and [iŋpeðír], another Andalusian trait (Zamora Vicente 1979:416).

As in Yucatan, and probably for the same reason, *f* is realized as [p], there being no [f] in Mayan, and Mayan [ʃ] is maintained especially in numerous toponyms. In Costa Rica, as in New Mexico, oddly enough, [r] or multiple [ř] assibilates or becomes retroflex, especially in the cluster [tř]. When [i] is in contact with a retroflex [R], it opens to [ɨ]. In the numerous Aztec words, [tl] is reduced to [t].

As in Galicia and Asturias, final unstressed [o] is pronounced [u], as in [líbru]. As in Yucatan and New Mexico, /j/ is unstable: often it is omitted in words like *silla*, which becomes [sía], and often it is inserted epenthetically in words like *sangría*, which becomes [saŋgríja]. Two-syllable words like *país* and *maíz* have retained the archaic diphthong and are pronounced as one syllable, [pájs] and [májs]. The diphthongs [aj] and [ej], at least in Guatemala, vary freely: [aséjte] or [asájte].

Central America, including parts of Yucatan and the states bordering on Guatemala, is a *voseo* zone, in contrast to nearly all of Mexico. (Its absence in Mexico is attributable to the presence there of one of the two viceroyalties that ruled Latin America during the sixteenth century; *vos* had by this time become a despective form in Spain and therefore was avoided by groups of high prestige.) In the middle part of Central America, there are three forms for 'you', ranging in formality from *usted* and *vos* down to *tú*. As a result, the verb has two forms for second person singular: *vos sabés* and *tú sabes*. It has been reported that refugees who have recently settled in the Southwest of the United States sound odd to oldtimers because of their importation of *vos*. The prestige of this pronoun varies—it is chiefly used by the uneducated in Guatemala, Honduras, El Salvador, and Nicaragua, while Costa Rica to the south, like Argentina and Uruguay, finds it acceptable in the highest social levels.

Except for *voseo*, the verb in Central America behaves much as in Mexico. The preterite is used where Peninsular Spanish would choose present perfect, and the future is often expressed by verb phrases rather than inflections:

He de contar rather than *Contaré*
Va a decir rather than *Dirá*

In Central America the construction *va y* plus a present tense form also substitutes for future:

No se levante, porque va y se cae (Lapesa 1968:359)

Costa Ricans are often called *ticos* because of their habitual use of diminutives. *Tico* itself appears very frequently, as in *poquitico*, and *-ico* occurs in *nietecico*, *pajarico*, and *angelico*. Other simple diminutives are *-ito/a* and *-illo/a*, and, at times, they are compounded, as in *manecita* and *piececico*, 'little hand' and 'little foot'. Nouns and adjectives in Central America are intensified by the suffix *-azo/a* or *-uso/a*, as in *amigazo* 'good friend', *paisanazo* 'country hick', and *cansadazo* 'worn out'.

An excellent example of two levels of Costa Rican speech is presented in the following humorous tale by the *costumbrista* Magón (Manuel González), in a conversation between the author, an educated journalist from San José, and an ingenuous, probably illiterate, peasant, *ñor* Cornelio (González Zeledón 1920a:157-162). Words and phrases underlined in the text illustrate popular usage and will be discussed.

EL *CLIS* DE SOL

No es cuento, es una historia que sale de mi pluma como ha ido brotando de los labios de *ñor* Cornelio Cacheda, que es un buen amigo de tantos como tengo por esos campos de Dios.

Ñor Cornelio vino a verme y trajo consigo un par de niñas de dos años y medio de edad, nacidas de una sola "*camada*", como él dice, llamadas María de los Dolores y María del Pilar, ambas rubias como una espiga, blancas y rosadas como durazno maduro y lindas como si fueran "*imágenes*", según la expresión de *ñor* Cornelio. Contrastaba notablemente la belleza infantil de las gemelas con la sincera incorrección de los rasgos fisionómicos de ñor Cornelio, feo si los hay, moreno subido y tosco hasta lo sucio de las uñas y lo rajado de los talones. Naturalmente, se me ocurrió en el acto preguntarle por el progenitor feliz de aquel par de boqui-rubias. El viejo se chilló de orgullo, retorció la *jetaza* de *pejibaye* rayado, se limpió las babas con el revés de la peluda mano y contestó:

—¡*Pos* yo soy el *tata*, *más que* sea feo el *decilo*! ¡No se parecen *a yo*, pero es que la mamá no es *tan pior*, y *pal* gran poder de mi Dios no hay nada imposible!

—Pero dígame, *ñor* Cornelio, ¿su mujer es rubia, o alguno de los abuelos era así como las chiquitas?

—No, señor; en toda la familia no ha habido ninguno *gato* ni *canelo*; todos hemos sido *acholaos*.

—Y entonces, ¿cómo se explica usted que las niñas hayan nacido con ese pelo y esos colores?

El viejo soltó una estrepitosa carcajada, se enjarró y me lanzó una mirada de soberano desdén.

—¿De qué se ríe, ñor Cornelio?

—¿*Pos* no *había de rirme*, don Magón, cuando veo que un *probe inorante* como yo, un *campiruso pión*, sabe más que un hombre como *usté*, que todos dicen que es tan *sabido*, tan leído y que hasta hace leyes *onde* el Presidente con los *menistros*?

—A ver, explíqueme eso.

—*Hora* verá lo que *jué*.

Ñor Cornelio sacó de las *alforjas* un buen pedazo de *sobao*, dió un trozo a cada chiquilla, arrimó un taburete en el que se dejó caer satisfecho de su próximo triunfo, se sonó estrepitosamente las narices, tapando cada una de las ventanas con el índice respectivo y soplando con violencia por la otra, restregó con la planta de la *pataza* derecha limpiando el piso, se enjugó con el revés de la chaqueta y principió su explicación en estos términos:

"*Usté* sabe que *hora* en marzo hizo tres años que hubo un *clis* de sol, en que se *escureció* el sol en todo el medio: bueno, pues como unos veinte días antes, Lina, mi mujer, salió *habelitada* de esas chiquillas. *Dende* ese *entonce*, le cogió un desasosiego tan grande, que aquello era *cajeta*; no había como *atajala*, se salía de la casa de día y de noche, siempre *ispiando pal* cielo; se iba al solar, a la *quebrada*, al *charralillo* del cerco, y siempre con aquel capricho y aquel mal que no había descanso ni más remedio que *dejala* a gusto. Ella siempre había sido muy antojada en todos los partos. Vea, cuando nació el mayor, *jue* lo *mesmo*; con que una noche me *dispertó* tarde de la noche y *m'izo* ir a *buscale cojoyos* de *cirgüelo* macho. *Pior* era que *juera* a nacer la criatura con la boca abierta. Le *truje* los *cojoyos*; *endespués jueron* otros antojos, pero nunca la llegué a ver tan desasosegada como con estas chiquitas. *Pos hora* verá, como le iba diciendo, *le cogió por ver pal* cielo día y noche y el día del *clis* de sol, que estaba yo en la montaña *apiando* un *palo pa* un *eleje*, es que se estuvo *ispiando* el sol en el breñalillo del cerco *dende* buena mañana.

"*Pa* no *cansalo* con el cuento, así siguió hasta que nacieron las muchachillas estas. No le niego que *a yo se me hizo cuesta arriba* el *velas* tan *canelas* y tan *gatas*, pero *dende* entonces parece que hubieran traido la bendición de Dios. La *mestra* me las quiere y les *cuese* la ropa, el Político les da sus cincos, el cura me las pide *pa paralas* con *naguas* de puros *linoses* y *antejuelas* en el altar *pal* Corpus, y *pa* los días de la Semana Santa, las sacan en la procesión arrimadas al Nazareno y al Santo Sepulcro; *pa* la Nochebuena, las mudan con muy bonitos vestidos y las ponen en el portal junto a las Tres Divinas. Y todos los costos son de bolsa de los mantenedores y siempre les dan su medio *escudo*, *gu* bien su papel de a peso, *gu* otra buena regalía. ¡Bendito sea mi Dios que las *jue* a sacar *pa* su servicio de un *tata* tan feo como yo!. . . Lina hasta que está *culeca* con sus chiquillas y *dionde* que aguanta que no se las *alabanceen*. Ya ha tenido sus buenos pleitos con *curtidas* del *vecinduario* por las malvadas *gatas*.

Interrumpí a *ñor* Cornelio, temeroso de que el panegírico no tuviera fin y lo hice volver al carril abandonado.

—Bien, ¿pero *idiai*?

—¿*Idiai* que? ¿*pos* no ve que *jue* por *ber ispiao* la mamá el *clis* de sol por lo que son *canelas*? ¿*Usté* no sabía eso?

—No lo sabía, y me sorprende que usted lo hubiera adivinado sin tener ninguna instrucción.

—*Pa qu'es engañalo*, don Magón. Yo no *juí* el que *adevinó* el *busiles*. ¿Ud. conoce a un *mestro* italiano que hizo la torre de la iglesia de la villa? ¿Un hombre *gato*, pelo *colorao*, muy blanco y muy macizo que come en casa *dende* hace cuatro años?

—No, *ñor* Cornelio.

—*Pos* él *jue* el que me explicó la cosa del *clis* de sol.

In Magón's representation of ñor Cornelio's pronunciation, it can be seen that intervocalic [ð] is deleted in the past participle of -*ar* verbs (*acholaos*, *sobao*, and *colorao*) and in word-final position (*usté*). *Cojoyos* shows the intervocalic devoicing of [ɣ] to [x] and also indicates that Costa Rican Spanish is *yeísta*. The spelling of *fue* and *fuera* as *jué* and *juera* probably demonstrates the use of a bilabial velarized fricative [ɸʷ]. The loss of the final *r* of the infinitive when followed by a pronoun beginning with *l* is seen in *decilo* (*decirlo*), *velas* (*verlas*), and *dejala* (*dejarla*) and is an archaism, possibly of Leonese origin (Lapesa 1968). Magón does not indicate the aspiration of syllable-final [s] in the peasant's speech—probably because it is normal in his own as well. As usual in rustic Spanish, consonant clusters are often reduced: *clis* for *eclipse*, *inorante* for *ignorante*.

The vowels [i] and [e], if unstressed, frequently substitute for one another:

[i] to [e]:   [e] to [i]:
menistros   *ispiando*
habelitada   *dispertó*
adevinó

Vowels in hiatus are reduced to a single syllable:

para el → *pa el* → *pal*
reirme → *rirme*
maestro/a → *mestro/a*

If the first vowel in hiatus is [e], it becomes [j]:

peor → *pior*
peón → *pión*
apeando → *apiando*
de onde → *dionde*
y de ahí → *idiai*

The metathesis common to rustic Spanish everywhere appears in *probe* for *pobre* and *culeca* for *clueca*. There is apocope in *ber* for *haber*, *clis* for *eclipse*, and *ñor* for *señor*. Popular etymology may be responsible for ñor Cornelio's mangling of *lentejuelas*, *lente* 'lens' suffixed with *juela*, a diminutive, to produce 'little lenses' or 'sequins'. He evidently is unfamiliar with the word *lente* and substitutes *ante* for it. Perhaps he thinks that sequins are sewed only on the front, *ante*, of a dress.

In general, the morphology of ñor Cornelio's speech differs from that of academic modern Spanish only in its use of some archaic forms such as *truje* 'I brought' and *escureció* 'it got dark', widespread in rural usage in many areas. There is no *voseo* here because of the social relationship of the speakers. Cornelio respects Magón as an educated man from the city and Magón respects Cornelio as his senior.

Other archaisms include:

pos 'pues'
onde 'donde'
dende 'desde'
mesmo 'mismo'
palo 'árbol'
masque 'aunque'
escudo ('a coin')
endespués 'después'

Another phrasal archaism is *se me hizo*, which today would be *me pareció* except in Mexico and other northern areas. *Tan pior* is 'so bad', literally 'so worse', for emphasis, also common in Mexico. *Le cogió por ver* 'it occurred to her' would never be used in Mexico because there *coger* has a sexual meaning which makes it semi-taboo.

The morphology of the pronoun in this sample is standard except for the use of *yo* as object of the preposition, as in *a yo*.

Typical of Central America are certain lexical items created from Spanish bases:

> *imágenes 'retratos'*
> *gato/canelo 'rubio'*
> *campiruso 'rústico'*
> *sabido 'sabio'*
> *sobao 'azúcar semi-refinado'*
> *cajeta 'notable'*
> *quebrada 'arroyo'*
> *eleje 'eje'*
> *alabancear 'alabar'* (but from the base of *alabanza* plus *-ear*)
> *curtida 'desvergonzada'*
> *vecinduario 'vecindario'*
> *idiai 'entonces'*

The use of *imágenes* for 'portraits', like *santos* in Spain, is probably attributable to the peasants' experience with pictures being limited to church. *Campiruso*, spelled *campiruzo* in Spain, is possibly derived from *campero* plus the despective augmentative *-uzo*. In *sabido*, for *sabio*, an intrusive *d* has been introduced, perhaps a hypercorrection. *Sobao* is a past participle of the Spanish verb *sobar* 'to rub soft'—presumably the sugar has been coarsely ground. *Cajeta* 'candy' meaning 'nice', 'sweet', 'something to notice' is metaphoric, as is *quebrada* 'broken' for 'a cleft in the earth' (a meaning it has in Colombia as well). *Un eleje* shows the fusion of the article *el* with the standard noun *eje* 'axle'. *Alabancear* and *vecinduario* are probably evidence of the tendency of the uneducated to use big words and 'improve' upon the language in order to achieve self-importance. *Curtida* is a Standard Spanish word which usually refers to tanned leather but here seems to satirize 'thick-skinned women' who are impervious to criticism. Probably the most typical Central Americanism from Spanish is *idiai*, from the interrogative '*¿Y de ahí?*' 'And from there?' or 'What is your conclusion?' or 'So what?'

In 'Clis de sol' there are very few *indigenismos* and with good reason: most Central American terms of Indian origin have as their referents native flora and fauna, a characteristic common to other dialects of Latin American Spanish. The context of the story makes these words inappropriate. In another story, however, 'Un día de mercado en la Plaza Principal' (Gonzaléz Zeledón 1920b:36-49), in which a young boy is sent to the market to buy groceries, *indigenismos* are plentiful as he tells what he sees as well as what he buys. More than two-thirds of these words are from native American languages. From Nahuatl come 14 words, 58.5% of the total of Indian items:

achiote/achote 'red paste made of fruit from achote tree, used as condiment or dye'
aguacate 'avocado'
ayote 'gourd-shaped fruit of a palm tree'
coyol/coyolito 'bell-shaped fruit of a palm tree'
chayote/chayotillo 'green vegetable with a thorny exterior'
chichigua 'nursemaid'
chile 'chile'
elote 'ear of corn'
nance 'cherry-sized fruit of tropical tree of Tabasco and Central America'
tacaco 'green vegetable with a thorny exterior'
tiliche 'notion'
tilichero 'peddlar of *tiliches*'
tuna 'fruit of the prickly pear'
zapote 'black-skinned fruit with greenish flesh'

Following Nahuatlismos in number are terms taken from Taíno, four and a half or 18.8% (one of these is a blend of Taíno *batata* and Quechua *papa*):

cacique 'chief'
maíz 'corn'
papa 'potato'
pejiballe/pejibaye 'gourd-shaped fruit of a palm tree'
yuca 'edible tuber'

Three terms, 12.5%, come from Mayan:

agüío 'black and yellow songbird'
cacao 'cacao'
pita 'century plant'

Only two and a half, 10.4%, are derived from Quechua:

chompipe 'turkey'
papa 'potato'
zapallo 'gourd'

Of these 24 lexical items, all but five are, predictably, names of fruits and vegetables and the one meat mentioned, the turkey.

A minority of the terms from the little boy's account are of Spanish origin, most of which have been adapted semantically to the Central American environment:

chonete 'battered straw hat' (used in Costa Rica only)

güesilla 'a fruit' (similar to a *guayaba* or passion fruit, like a canteloupe or *huesina*)

jaboncillo 'candy made from milk, often with a pecan atop or inside' (in Mexico, *jamoncillo*)

marañón 'a tropical fruit used for wine to cure dysentery'

matasanos 'tree that produces a fruit similar to the *mamey*, with a black shell and orange pulp' (Does it cure or kill?)

mozotillo 'a type of caged songbird'

plátano 'banana'

rey de picudo 'a type of caged songbird'

setillero 'small black and white bird that eats seeds of the *saetilla*, *sagittaria*' (used in Costa Rica only)

vainicas 'bean pods'

viuda 'a type of caged songbird'

Of these 11 terms, five refer to fruits or vegetables and four to birds. These adapted Spanish words are outnumbered more than two to one by those which are indigenous in origin.

In summary, the Spanish of Mexico and Central America is characterized by its 'archaic' flavor and its large number of *indigenismos* which have affected not only the lexicon but also regional intonation. Further, critics agree that it bears witness to the lively imagination and linguistic creativity of its speakers. Despite the proximity of the 'Colossus of the North', it is both holding its own and playing a role in what a Mexican columnist has termed 'la Mexicanización de los Estados Unidos'. It is also one of the three zones whose dialects are most familiar to people elsewhere, doubtless because of the popularity of its music, movies, and television. It is the medium of expression in the works of distinguished authors such as Manuel Azuela, Octavio Paz, and Carlos Fuentes in Mexico and in Central America Rubén Darío, writers held in high esteem throughout the Hispanic world, even in Spain.

References

Álvar, Manuel. 1960. Textos hispánicos dialectales: antología histórica. Madrid: Revista de Filología Hispánica, Anejo LXXIII. 2 vols.

Boyd-Bowman, Peter. 1960. El habla de Guanajuato. México: Universidad Autónoma de México.

Cotton, Eleanor Greet, and John M. Sharp. 1985. The social function of humorous figures in Mexican speech. Paper read at The Western Humor and Irony Membership and excerpted in Whimsy III: Contemporary Humor. Eds. Don L. F. Nilson and Alleen Pace Nilson. Tempe: Arizona State University. 211-212.

González Zeledón (Magón), Manuel. 1920a. El clis de sol. In: La propia. San José de Costa Rica: García Monge y Cía. 157-162.

González Zeledón (Magón), Manuel. 1920b. Un día de mercado en la Plaza Principal. In: La propia. San José de Costa Rica: García Monge y Cía. 36-49.

Henríquez Ureña, Pedro. 1938. El español en Méjico, los Estados Unidos y la América Central. Buenos Aires: La Universidad de Buenos Aires.

Lapesa, Rafael. 1968. Historia de la lengua española. 7th ed. Madrid: Escelicer.

Lope Blanch, Juan M. 1972. Estudios sobre el español de México. México: Universidad Nacional Autónoma de México.

Lope Blanch, Juan M. 1979. Investigaciones sobre dialectología mexicana. México: Universidad Nacional Autónoma de México.

Perissinotto, Giorgio Sabino Antonio. 1975. Fonología del español hablado en la Ciudad de México. México: El Colegio de México.

Rosario, Rubén del. 1970. El español de América. Sharon, Connecticut: Troutman Press.

Zamora Vicente, Alonso. 1979. Dialectología española. Madrid: Gredos.

Chapter 14
The Andean countries

Linguistically, the Andean zone extends from southern Colombia in the north to northwestern Argentina and the northern tip of Chile in the south; it includes Ecuador, Peru, and the western highlands of Bolivia, the area once occupied by the Inca Empire (see Map 7). Present-day dialect boundaries within this vast territory do not coincide with political boundaries, which have changed several times since the independence of these nations was achieved in the 1820s.

Stereotypically, the three northernmost of the Andean countries, Colombia,

Map 7 The Inca Empire in 1550 and concentrations of modern Quechua speakers.

The Inca Empire in 1500

Concentrations of Modern Quechua Speakers

176

Ecuador, and Peru, have been divided by linguists into three zones: coastal, highland, and lowland jungle (Escobar 1976:86). The jungle areas, however, are sparsely inhabited by primitive Indians of various tribes who have little contact with outsiders and are ignorant of Spanish. Coastal Spanish does differ from highland Spanish in many ways which are analogous to the contrasts between Andalusian and Castilian in Spain. It is as though the Spanish settlers from the cool *meseta* preferred the Andes while those from subtropical southern Spain liked the warmer climate of the coast (Zamora Vicente 1979:422).

The Andean region has a strong Quechua substratum which has influenced the phonology, morphosyntax, and lexicon of Spanish, especially among the many bilinguals who make up a large proportion of the population there. The substratum of Quechua varies from one locale to another, producing variations in different areas. The linguistic situation is becoming even more complicated today in view of the massive migration of highlanders to the urban centers on the coast. Escobar states that two-thirds of the population of Lima—a city of six million—is made up of newcomers from the Sierra (Escobar 1976:88), who surely will affect urban speech in years to come, perhaps leveling some of the differences that exist today.

Another sharp contrast is between rural and urban usage; the former is extremely archaic, like rustic Spanish everywhere, even in Spain. Cultured city dwellers are more likely to speak a Spanish relatively free of localisms. The uneducated in the cities speak more like country folk in their use of archaisms, analogical verb forms, and substandard phonology.

Historically, there is some similarity between the development of Spanish in Mexico and in the Andes. In central Mexico and central Peru, the presence of the Spanish viceregal court promoted a normative usage, strongly influenced by Castilian standards. Hence, many regional traits found elsewhere in the Andean countries are lacking there. For example, *voseo*, a general feature of Andean, is alien to the speech of all social classes, in both cities and countryside, highland and lowland, in central Peru, no doubt because it had become offensive to the ears of Spaniards. Other areas of the Andes distant from Lima were not affected by courtly practices and there *voseo* has continued to prevail (Lapesa 1969:356). In Mexico as well, regions far from the capital, in the south, close to Guatemala, have preserved *voseo* for the same reason.

One generalization applicable to the Andean countries is that in the highlands the tempo of speech, like that of Castile, is relatively slow compared with that of the coast, which is much more rapid and comparable to Andalusian. On the Altiplano, pronunciation has been and continues to be strongly influenced by Quechua while the speech of the lowlands differs little from that of southern Spain. In the Sierra, consonants are very clearly articulated, almost to an exaggerated degree while the vowels are pronounced 'with an uncertain timbre' (Toscano Mateus 1953:37; Escobar 1976:94). The contrary is true in the lowlands, where vowels are well enunciated and consonants slighted.

The lack of voiced stops in Quechua—or perhaps, of any phonemic distinction between voiced and voiceless occlusives—has occasioned considerable confusion. Speakers in different areas have reached different solutions to this problem. In Colombia and Ecuador, /p/, /t/, and /k/ are frequently voiced, except in Bogotá, where Quechua influence is absent (Toscano Mateus 1953:110-115), producing *chamba* (*champa*), *qué dal* (*qué tal*), and *golumpio* (*columpio*). By contrast, in Bolivia, /d/ is replaced by /t/ after a preceding /s/ and *desde* becomes *deste* (Kany 1947:205). As elsewhere in the Hispanic world, the stops /b/, /d/, and /g/ have fricative allophones. In most of the Andean countries, the graphemes *b* and *v* are pronounced identically as [β]. In Colombia, however, research now in progress indicates that at least 30% of Bogotanos make a phonemic distinction between [b] and [v] (Amastae 1983). Moreover, Colombians pronounce /b/, /d/, and /g/ as stops rather than fricatives when preceded by any other consonant. The absence of voice as distinctive extends to the fricatives as well, where /f/ and /s/ are frequently voiced to [v] and [z] (Flórez 1963:7). In Ecuador, Peru, and Colombia, /f/, which did not exist in Quechua, is interchangeable with [β] and a number of other sounds such as [x] and [h]. Thus *foto* becomes *boto*; *elefante* goes to *elebante*; *función*, *junción*; *bufón*, *bujón*; and *fumo*, *jumo* (Flórez 1963:8; Toscano Mateus 1953:83-84). When /f/ is pronounced, it is a bilabial [φ] in the popular speech of Peru and Ecuador, as in *juamilia* (*familia*) and *enjuermo* (*enfermo*) (Boyd-Bowman 1960:70). In the prestige dialect of Peru, [φ] is avoided (Zamora Vicente 1979:413). Fricative [ð], a consonant lacking in Quechua, is maintained in the highlands even in illiterate speech but is lost on the coast, even among the educated, resulting in forms such as *tuavía* (*todavía*), *criao* (*criado*), and *hei bistío* in Ecuador, Peru, and Argentina (Toscano Mateus 1953:113); at times, this sound occurs epenthetically, as in *dentrar* (*entrar*) and *dir* (*ir*). Alternatively, it may replace /l/ or /r/, as in *alfider* for *alfiler* and *sombredero* for *sombrerero* (Toscano Mateus 1953:50).

The pronunciation of /s/ is one of three traits by which an Andean lowlander can immediately identify a highlander, and vice-versa. In the mountains /s/, frequently described as strident and high-pitched, is invariably maintained throughout. On the coast, /s/ in an intervocalic position may become [x], as in *nojotros* for *nosotros*. If syllable-final on the coast, it becomes an aspiration or is lost: 'Hunt for it', *búscalo* in normal Spanish, on the coastal lowland will become *bújcalo* or *búcalo* (Flórez 1963:9). The vowel preceding a deleted [s] is opened, as elsewhere in lowland Spanish (Lapesa 1968:349). In general, a predorsal Andalusian [s] rather than a concave apical Castilian [ṣ] has been observed in parts of Colombia, Ecuador, Chile, and Argentina. The apical [ṣ] has been attested in Colombia, Bolivia, and Peru (Zamora Vicente 1979:416). It is probable that the Andalusian [s] is lowland, since coastal inhabitants twit highland speakers for their '*s chicheante*', which suggests a palatal sibilant (Toscano Mateus 1953:77). In some coastal areas the predorsal [s] becomes interdental, producing *ceceo* as in southern Spain. The highland [ṣ], word-final, may become [z] in Quito and Loja, where its voicing marks a word boundary, disambiguating phrases such as [asíðo] (*ha sido* or *has ido*) which become [aṣíðo] and [azíðo] (Robinson 1979:140). In Ecuador, as in many other Latin American countries, words spelled with the letter *x* are pronounced as spelled, i.e., with

[ks] and not [s] or [ɣs] as in Spain (Toscano Mateus 1953:80-81).

The second trait which identifies the speech of Andean highlanders is the pronunciation of /r/ and /rr/ as assibilated fricatives, general in the popular speech of Chile, Bolivia, Peru, Ecuador, and southern Colombia (Zamora Vicente 1979:414-415). In the Ecuadorian Sierra, [ř] and [ř̃] are in free variation, resulting in mispronunciations such as *rurral* for *rural* and *resurrección* for *resurrección* (Toscano Mateus 1953:96). An assibilated /r/ after a /t/, as in *tranvía* 'streetcar', sounds to outsiders like [č], *chanvía* (Toscano Mateus 1953:97). Further, assibilation is no doubt responsible for *r* becoming *s* in a few Spanish words such as *sospresa* instead of *sorpresa* and *despostillar* instead of *desportillar* 'to chip' (Toscano Mateus 1953:89). While it was once thought that the Andean assibilated /r/ was attributable to Quechua, more recent investigations have revealed its presence in Spain among Spanish speakers in the Basque country, Aragon, and Navarre (Zamora Vicente 1979:415). As opposed to these highland characteristics, coastal /r/ and /rr/ are standard Spanish and regularly contrast. If syllable-final, /r/ on the coast may disappear as in Andalusia and the Caribbean. In the highlands of Colombia, some speakers use an aspirate vibrant [r̃] and in the mountains of Ecuador an aspirate single [r]. Zamora Vicente describes the [r̃] as being similar to that of standard Spanish but preceded by a *jota*, producing words such as *cajrro* instead of *carro* and *pejrro* instead of *perro* (Zamora Vicente 1979:415). The Ecuadorian aspiration occurs in words like *gritajle*, *buhla*, and *Cahlos* for *gritarle*, *burla*, and *Carlos*. This phenomenon is not limited to Ecuador but also occurs in regions in Andalusia, New Mexico, Central America, and the Antilles (Toscano Mateus 1953:92).

Among uneducated people on the coast, [r] and [l], when final in a word stressed on the last syllable, tend to disappear, just as in Andalusia. Thus *peor* → *peó*, *señor* → *señó*, *trabajar* → *trabajá*, *animal* → *animá*, and *papel* → *papé*. Another *Andalucismo* in this area is that [r] and [l] are in free variation if they occur syllable-finally in an unaccented syllable or are followed by another consonant. Accordingly, *porque sí* → *polque si*, *por mi madre* → *pol mi mare* and *alma* → *arma*, *alguno* → *arguno*, and *el polvo* → *er polvo* (Boyd-Bowman 1953:226-227).

In the Sierra, /r/ and /l/ in syllable-final position are regularly distinguished, but there are isolated words in which they may vary: *solprender*, *Almendáriz*, and *sarsa*, *cormillo* (*colmillo* 'eyetooth'). In even fewer words, /r/ may become [l] intervocalically as in *celebro* for *cerebro*, *pelegrino* for *peregrino*. These archaisms are attested in sixteenth-century Spanish and may have been imported into Latin America at that time (Toscano Mateus 1953:87-88).

The third important trait that identifies highland speech in the Andean countries is the general preservation of the phonemic distinction between /j/ and /λ/ at all social levels. In the central and northern Ecuadorian highlands, /λ/ is realized as [ʒ] but remains in phonemic contrast with /j/ (Boyd-Bowman 1953:224). Most scholars agree that this maintenance and its realization are due to the Quechua inventory, which also contrasts *y* and *ll* (Boyd-Bowman 1960:82, 1953:225; Lapesa 1968:345-349; Toscano Mateus 1953:99; Zamora Vicente 1979:76-77).

Quechua also held as phonemic /ʎ/ and /ʒ/, but, as spoken in central and northern Ecuador today, has merged both of these into one phoneme /ʒ/. In short, in both Spanish and Quechua, this phenomenon occurred, probably at the same time (Toscano Mateus 1953:101).

In contrast to the Andean highlands, the coasts and lowlands are *yeísta* (Boyd-Bowman 1953:224; Escobar 1976:94; Zamora Vicente 1979:76-77). Indeed, most of Latin America lacks /ʎ/ altogether. Further, /j/, the descendant of /ʎ/, if intervocalic and in contact with high front /i/ or /e/ often weakens and disappears (Escobar 1976:94; Lapesa 1968:356; Zamora Vicente 1979:80). So *novillo* → *novío*, *billete* → *biete*, *silla* → *sía*, and *capilla* → *capía* (Boyd-Bowman 1960:82).

The pre-Conquest Quechua phoneme /ʃ/, now lost in Bolivia and Peru, has survived in Ecuador. It flourishes there in numerous words, many of which were indigenous and then adopted into Spanish, such as *oxota* 'sandal', *shigra* 'type of tree' or 'net to carry things in', *chushig* 'owl', and *munashca* 'beloved' (Toscano Mateus 1953:79-81). In some Spanish words, /s/ followed by /j/ palatalizes to [ʃ]: *siete* → *shete*, *dieciocho* → *dieshocho*, *cielo* → *shelu*. In some other words, /s/ followed by a stop becomes [ʃ] in popular speech in the highlands: the archaic *cascar* → *cashcar*, and *peste* → *peshte* if used as an interjection meaning 'A plague on you!' Humorously, *costumbre* → *coshtumbre*. Many nicknames change Spanish [s] to *sh*: *Pacífico* → *Pashi*, *Soledad* → *Shuli*, and *Casimiro* → *Cashi*. These hypocorisms also occur in child language in words like *zapato*, which becomes *shapato*. Foreign words and proper nouns with [ʃ] which enter the Spanish of the Sierra preserve this sound unchanged: *shutar* from English 'to shoot' (a sports term), *pelush* from French *peluche* 'plush', *Hiroshima*, and *Wáshington*, but on the coast, where the phoneme /ʃ/ is unknown, *Guásinton* (Toscano Mateus 1953:81-82). In uncultured speech in Quito, [ʃ] is also pronounced in place of [ʒ] for /ʎ/ (Toscano Mateus 1953:102). Highlands speakers also have no trouble with imported words with [ʒ] which was a phoneme in Quechua: [piʒáma] from Spanish *pijama*, [garáʒ] from the French *garage*, and [ʒérsi] from English *jersey* (Toscano Mateus 1953:86).

In both the Colombian and Ecuadorian highlands, the fricative *jota* is less scrapy and more relaxed than in Castile (Flórez 1963:5; Toscano Mateus 1953:85). On the coast it becomes a mere aspiration [h], as in [dího] instead of [díxo], [muhé] instead of [muxér], and [méhiko] instead of [méxico], just as in Andalusia, the Antilles, and Vera Cruz (Boyd-Bowman 1953:229). Also, in sixteenth-century Spanish, Latin words beginning with [f] were pronounced with an initial aspirate [h] in all varieties of peninsular Spanish. This archaic pronunciation persists in rustic speech in Colombia and Ecuador, among other Latin American countries, perhaps reinforced by the existence of aspirate /h/ as a phoneme in Quechua (Boyd-Bowman 1960:67-68; Flórez 1963:8; Toscano Mateus 1953:84).

In the Andean countries, the nasals behave very much as in other regions of the Hispanic world, with a few minor differences. As elsewhere, they tend to assimilate to the point of articulation of a following consonant, but in Ecuador they are less clearly enunciated and almost disappear in the nasalization of the preceding vowel (Toscano Mateus 1953:108). Further, assimilation is hampered in that /n/ → [ŋ] in word final position, regardless of the environment of the following speech sound:

[uŋ óɣro] 'an ogre'
[coŋ léče] 'with milk'
[coŋ náðie] 'with no one'
[eŋ mi tjéřa] 'in my land'

This is common in the coastal regions of Colombia and Peru and throughout Ecuador. Areas that do not velarize /n/ are the highlands of Colombia, Peru, and, perhaps, Bolivia (Boyd-Bowman 1960:84; Flórez 1963:9; Toscano Mateus 1953:108). Velar [ŋ] may even occur within a word, syllable-final, in Peru and the coasts and south of Colombia (Zamora Vicente 1979:416). This *Andalucismo* may be illustrated by the pronunciations [eŋláse] '*enlace*' [kaŋsáðo], and [óŋra] '*honra*'. Assimilation, however, is allowed in Ecuador before a bilabial, as in [um pán] 'a loaf of bread', [um bořégo] 'a lamb', [um ɸusíl] 'a rifle' (where /f/ is bilabial) (Toscano Mateus 1953:108). Toward the Pacific coast in Colombia, word-final /n/ is pronounced [m] by all social classes; *pan* becomes [pám], *tren* [trém], and the phrase *a la orden* [a la órdem] (Flórez 1963:9). In the Ecuadorian highlands, *ni* followed by a vowel is palatalized to [ɲ], as in [ɲébe] 'snow', [antóɲo], and [matrimóɲo], in the speech of all social classes. In the same area, the uncultured palatalize even further with [ɲíɲɔ], [ɲúɲes], and [ɲivél]. The opposite tendency, depalatalization, may also be observed in this region, where *pestañear* becomes *pestanear*, *compañía* becomes *companía*, and *albañil* becomes *albanil* (Toscano Mateus 1953:106-107), as in Yucatan.

Spanish consonants occurring in clusters have traditionally tended to be reduced in popular speech on the continent and in the New World. For example, in Colombia:

doctor → [dotór]
acción → [asión]
columna → [kolúna]
examen → [esámen] (Flórez 1963:7)

In Colombian cultured speech, however, it is almost compulsive to articulate *x* as [ks], as in [eksámen] and [téksto] (Flórez 1963:6). Analogously, in the common usage of Ecuador and coastal Peru, reduction occurs in words such as

conscripto → [konskríto]
indigno → [indíno]
significar → [sinifikár]
victrola → [vitróla] (Boyd-Bowman 1960:63; Toscano Mateus 1953:118)

This tendency has caused schools to insist on the pronunciation of all consonants in these groups, and speakers who do not know the written forms at times insert an erroneous consonant (Flórez 1963:7).

séptimo → [séktimo]

espontáneo → [ekspontáneo]
aritmética → [arismétika]
insecto → [insépto]
alumno → [alúgno]
calumnia → [kalúbnja] (Toscano Mateus 1953:119)

Another general tendency in popular usage is metathesis, which involves transposition not only of a pair of phonemes, but even of entire syllables:

nadie → [nájde]
níquel → [níkle]
Gabriel → [grabiél]
pusilánime → [pusilámine]
murciélago → [mursiéjalo]
polvareda → [polvaðéra] (Toscano Mateus 1953:120)

Unlike the pronunciation of the consonants (clear in the highlands and diffuse in the lowlands), the vowels are produced with an 'uncertain timbre' in the Sierra, but precisely on the coast (Toscano Mateus 1953:52). From southern Colombia down through Peru, speakers continually confuse /e/ with /i/ and /o/ with /u/ because of substratal Quechua, which has only the three phonemes /i/, /a/, and /u/, with [e] and [o] as allophones. As a result, minimal pairs can coalesce:

trébol → [tríbul]
dulzura → [dolsóra]
mi vida 'my darling' → [me véða] ('he forbids me'?)
manteca 'lard' → [mantíka] ('small blanket'?) (Escobar 1976:90-91; Lapesa 1968:345; Zamora Vicente 1979:390)

When Quechua-dominant bilinguals are advanced enough to add two vowel phonemes to their repertoire, /e/ is pronounced [ɨ] and /o/ is pronounced [ʋ]:

escuela → [ɨskwɨ́la]
bandera → [bandɨ́ra]
iglesia → [ɨglɨ́sja]
roto → [rʋ́tʋ]
frota → [frʋ́ta] (Escobar 1976:90-91)

Toscano Mateus comments that a cultured gentleman from Quito was taken for Portuguese because of his pronunciation of unstressed /o/ as *u* (1953:50).

Just as in Mexico, in the Andean highlands of Colombia, Ecuador, Peru, and Bolivia, vowels tend to be relaxed, devoiced, and even lost, particularly when in contact with a sibilant. Some examples are:

váyase as [bájase]
lapiz as [láps]
pues as [ps]
viejecito as [βjexsíto]

Vowels may also be lost if unaccented and syllable-final before a pause where even whole syllables may be deleted:

gracias as [grs]
precioso as [psióso]
balazos as [balás]

Entire phrases may syncopate:

se platicaba as [splatikáβa]
por se as [péso]
quién sabe qué as [kjénsβeké]

Indeed, this phenomenon may characterize structures of some length:

siempre está cerrado as [sjémpstsȓáðo]
pues entonces cuando escapó as [psntonskwanskapó]

Toscano Mateus points out that one possible reason for this loss of vowels may be the 'instability' of the vowel in Quechua. However, both he and Zamora Vicente comment on the close similarity of this Andean trait with the highland speech of Mexico, and both refer the reader to Henríquez Ureña's *El español en Méjico, los Estados Unidos y la América Central* for a full discussion of this peculiarity. Zamora Vicente predicts that further research may throw light on this vowel loss (Flórez 1963:8; Toscano Mateus 1953:50; Zamora Vicente 1979:411).

Spanish diphthongs and vowels in hiatus are problems for Quechua-dominant speakers in the highlands. Where Spanish diphthongs do not correspond to Quechua syllabic structure, they are made into two syllables. For example, *jaula* is pronounced [xáola] and *iglesia* becomes [eglésea] (Escobar 1976:91). Conversely, a hiatus in a Spanish word is dealt with in any one of three ways: (1) by shifting the accent and/or reducing the two vowels to a diphthong [tráe] → [tráj], [baúles] → [báwles], and [sandía] → [sándja]; (2) by inserting between the two vowels a [j] or [w] ([sandía] becomes [sandíja], [día] becomes [díja], and [baúles] becomes [bawúles]); (3) by separating the two vowels with a glottal stop ([baúl] is pronounced [baʔól], [día] becomes [déʔa], and [fidéos] is articulated as [fedéʔos]). 'Initial bilinguals' prefer solution (1), while 'advanced bilinguals' regularly opt for solution (2) (Flórez 1963:8; Escobar 1976:92-93; Toscano Mateus 1953:248).

The last and most difficult Spanish diphthongs for the Quechua-dominant speaker to master are [je] and [ej]. One solution is the elimination of one of the two components as in *piedras* → [pé:ðras], *peine* → [pé:ne]. Equally difficult is [we]: *huevo* becomes [wíβo] (Escobar 1976:91-92). As a result of this phonological problem in the highlands, many people, including the well educated, have trouble with radical-changing verbs, which they often regularize:

aprieta → [apréta]
cimienta → [siménta]

fuerza → [fórza]
rueda → [r̄óða]

Because of uncertainty as to which verbs change their stem vowels in this way, at other times speakers diphthongize regular forms such as:

corre → [kwér̄e]
ofende → [ofjénde]

Some of these forms, such as [ofjénde], are archaisms (Toscano Mateus 1953:238-239). Thus, not all of the peculiarities of the vowels in the Andean dialect are due to Quechua. Escobar suspects that various influences are working simultaneously and that the future will see the phonology of the native speakers of Spanish and that of the Quechua-dominant fuse into a new 'creolization' (Escobar 1976:95).

Suprasegmentals in the Andean countries are major features in distinguishing the speech of this region from other varieties of Spanish. A visitor from Castile immediately notices that, in general, people speak with a pitch higher than his, as in Mexico. There are variations, however, in different areas; the intonation of the coastal lowlands is like that of the Caribbean while that of the highlands is similar to the local Quechua substrata (Toscano Mateus 1953:41-42). This is true not only of the speech of local Indians and *mestizos*, but also of the prestige class (Kany 1947:194). The novelist Jorge Icaza has described highland contours as '*aquella voz en perpetuo trance de pedir perdón*' (Toscano Mateus 1953:42).

Another distinguishing difference of suprasegmentals in Andean concerns stress. Since accent is not phonemic in Quechua, bilinguals tend to misplace it (Escobar 1976:92). Often, primary stress is not placed on the verb but on another word deemed important for emotion or emphasis. *¡Ay nó se!* functions as an interjection showing impatience at someone's failure to do what is expected of him (Toscano Mateus 1953:254). Some common emphatic command forms switch the accent to the final vowel, as in *¡Vamós!* 'Let's go', *¡Andé!* 'Hurry!', and *¡Callé!* (to order someone to hush or to express incredulity or disgust, as in 'Oh, come on now!'). *Oyé* is used with an interrogative tone to demand attention, 'Do you hear me!' Quechua-dominant speakers often regularize the stress on Spanish words by shifting it to the penultimate syllable, as in *platáno*, *corázon*, *arbóles*, and *fabríca* (Escobar 1976:92). Secondary stress often occurs in polysyllabic words and phrases, such as *ácáso* and *cáfesíto* in Ecuador and *en séguída* and *el almuércíto* in Colombia (Flórez 1963:10; Toscano Mateus 1953:42). Edward Blansitt disputes the idea of secondary stress, however, and says that it only seems to occur because the speaker has raised the pitch on a given pretonic syllable. As a result, listeners feel that he is accenting the wrong syllable (Blansitt 1983).

The tempo of speech on the coast is rapid and comparable to that of Andalusia. In the highlands, the rate is much slower and like that of Castile (Flórez 1963:10; Toscano Mateus 1953:44).

The morphosyntax of Andean Spanish varies more widely than that of most other Latin American areas, depending on the degree of Hispanization of the speakers. In general, people who are Spanish-dominant use Standard Spanish. In Bogotá and Lima, eloquence is prized by all social classes. (For cultivated Colombian Andean, listen to Tape 2, selection d, and for cultivated Peruvian Andean, Tape 2, selection e, and see Appendix 5). Two well-known *Bogotano* sayings are that this city is the 'Athens' of America and that here even the bootblacks speak Greek. But in regions where Quechua plays a greater role, usage is more deviant.

For example, an outstanding difference is the Andean structure of a verb used as an auxiliary, plus a present participle, as in the very common *dar + -ndo*:

Yo y mis hermanos le damos vendiendo . . . . = *'Yo y mis hermanos le vendemos . . .'* (Escobar 1976:94; Flórez 1963:17; Toscano Mateus 1953:266; Zamora Vicente 1979:435)

Several other common verbs are often used in this unique construction: *poner, dejar, botar,* and *mandar.* For instance,

De rabia puso rompiendo la olla = *'De rabia rompió la olla'.*
Antes de cenar, dejarás apagando el fuego = *'Antes de cenar, apaga el fuego'*
El botó dañando mi juguete = *'El tiró mi juguete y lo dañó'*
Me mandó sacando mi patrón = *'Me despidió mi patrón'* Toscano Mateus 1953:284-285)

This deep penetration of a Quechua structure has many uses, one of the most common the expression of a polite imperative, as in *Dame haciendo. . .* for *Hágame, por favor. . .* (Toscano Mateus 1953:33). Such use of the participle is acceptable now in informal cultured speech though more frequently heard in Indian Spanish. In these expressions, even the word order can be altered through Quechua influence, as in

Hablando mandó = *'Mandó hablar'*
Pegando mandó = *'Mandó pegar'* (Toscano Mateus 1953:285)

Evidently, when these Indians learned Spanish, they also fastened upon the present participle as a simple verb form because of its lack of inflections:

Tú, compadre chiquito, gustándome. Tú sabiendo números, ¿no? Yo necesitándote aquí (Toscano Mateus 1953:272)

Another Andean deviation is disregard of agreement among Quechua-dominant bilinguals. In Quechua, in a subject-verb relationship with a plural subject, the marking of plurality may occur only once, either on the subject or on the verb, and this practice has been extended into the Spanish of Ecuador:

Nosotros estaba pinsandu
Ahí llegó p's ladrones (Toscano Mateus 1953:299)

And in Peru the number of the noun may not be expressed in sentences such as:

La señora vende huevo = *'La señora vende huevos'*
Lleva piedra = *'Lleva piedras'* (Escobar 1976:95)

Syntactic influence of Quechua can also be seen in the placement of the verb at the end of clauses, as in

El alma de taita amo grande creo que está penando = 'The soul of father big boss I think is in pain (in Hades)' (Zamora Vicente 1979:304)

Some of the traits that Andean Spanish shares with other varieties are periphrasis, *voseo*, analogical and archaic forms, the treatment of *haber* and *estar*, and problems with reflexives and prefixes. Many periphrastic forms are preferred to simple forms throughout. In Colombia, for example, there are:

Se manda cambiar = '*Se marcha*'
Va y se cae = '*Se caerá*'
He de contar = '*Contaré*'
Va a decir = '*Dirá*'
Es entonces que llegó = '*Llegó entonces*' (Lapesa 1968:359)

In Ecuador there are:

Hace de molestar = '*Molesta*'
Hacía de estudiar = '*Estudiaba*'
Hizo de hacer de trair = '*Trajo*' (Toscano Mateus 1953:278-280)

In Bolivia there may be heard:

Si me hace recuerdo a vos cuando eras más joven = '*Si me recuerda a ti cuando eras más joven*'
Vaya usted a hacerse la burla de otras = '*Vaya usted a burlarse de otras*'
¡Andá! Dale encuentro a la Felipita = '*Anda, encuentra a la Felipita*' (Kany 1947:201)

Periphrastic locutions in Peru include:

Agarró y se murió la nina = '*Se murió la niña*' (Kany 1945:199)

Although *vos* is a low prestige form avoided by the educated except in casual speech, it is characteristic of popular usage throughout the Andean countries except for central Peru (Lapesa 1968:357). Different verb forms are used with this pronoun in different regions (see Table 11). In Colombia appear the suffixes which are most generally used elsewhere in Latin America (Flórez 1963:13). *Vos* in Ecuador predominates in both the lowlands (where it coexists with *tú*) and the highlands. In the lowlands, the usual Latin American suffixes occur, but in the highlands they differ (Toscano Mateus 1953:37). Where *vos* is used in the northwest and south of Peru, inflection of the verb varies according to the area. In the northwest, *vos* is used with the Standard Spanish second person singular suffixes. In the south, the suffixes used also in the Ecuadorian highlands reappear. In southern Peru, with -*ar* verbs the final -*s* is usually deleted and with the -*er* and -*ir* verbs it is pronounced as an aspiration (Kany 1945:68, 73-74).

Table 11 Andean Spanish verb forms with *vos*.

	Present Indicative	Future	Imperative
Colombia, Ecuador	vos hablás	vos hablarás	hablá
Lowlands (General	vos comés	vos comerás	comé
L.A. *voseo* usage)	vos vivís	vos vivirás	viví
Ecuador Highlands,	vos hablái(s)	vos hablarís	habla/hablá
Southern Peru	vos comís	vos comerís	come/comé
	vos vivís	vos vivirís	vive/viví

It seems probable that the substitution of *-ís* for Standard *-éis* in the present indicative comes from the use of *i* for *e* by Quechua-dominant speakers. Future forms such as *hablarís* are probably the result of analogy with first person singulars such as *comerí* and *vivirí*.

Analogy also plays a role in the regularization of irregular verb forms. This occurs at all social levels, in popular speech in both Spain and the Americas, was found in the cultured speech of the sixteenth century, and is still found in child language. In the preterite it is responsible for forms such as:

traducí (*traduje*)
cabí (*cupe*)
andé (*anduve*)
satisfací (*satisfice*)

In the future, there are:

contradeciré (*contradiré*)
deshaceré (*desharé*)

and in the singular imperative:

pone (*pon*)
sale (*sal*)
dice (*di*)
hace (*haz*) (Toscano Mateus 1953:244-245)

Analogy, as well as archaism, plays a role in an epenthetic *-s* in the second person singular of the preterite. After this additional *-s*, often the first *-s* of the suffix is lost by dissimilation. Thus:

comiste → *comistes* → *comites*
cantaste → *cantastes* → *cantates*
llevaste → *llevastes* → *llevates*

Analogy and archaism also operate in widespread conjugational switches such as *traíba* (*traía*), *cáiba* (*caía*), and *réiba* (*reía*) (Toscano Mateus 1953:232).

Oddly enough, the forms with -ba- are etymologically correct, descending from the Latin imperfects *trahebat, cadebat*, and *ridebat*.

The archaic preterite *vide* for *vi* resembles closely its Latin etymon *vidi*. *Vido* may descend from the hypothetical Vulgar Latin **vidaut*, according to Menéndez Pidal, though such a form may be challenged as wholly unattested (Menéndez Pidal 1941:312, 320). The imperfects such as *vía* are of more recent origin, going back to the sixteenth century, and were used by Cervantes in *Don Quixote* (Toscano Mateus 1953:242). Another archaism also used by Golden Age authors is *truje* for *traje*, general in Andean rustic speech as in the rest of Latin America and Spain (Toscano Mateus 1953:244). *Ser* is ancient also when used in place of *haber* to form the perfect tense as in *si yo no me llamaría así, no se lo juera dicho*. *Ser* also substitutes for *estar* in expressions of location, producing archaisms such as *Valencia es en España* (Toscano Mateus 1953:287). Another archaic practice, historically legitimate, is the use of the imperfect subjunctive in -ra as a pluperfect indicative: *cantara* stems from Latin *cantaveram* ('I had sung'). This usage is not only popular but also literary, in the Andes as in Argentina and Uruguay (Toscano Mateus 1953:264-265).

Haber is of interest in its present subjunctive form *haiga*, archaic but popular in the Andes highlands and lowlands and elsewhere (Toscano Mateus 1953:241). Generally, when *hay* occurs in inflected tenses, there is agreement with the subject, frowned upon by academicians. To them, 'There were many men in the street' should be *Había muchos hombres en la calle*, but often *había* is replaced by *habían*. Another shared trait is the apocopation of *estar* by the loss of the first syllable as in *Ta bueno* and *¿Onde tará?* (Toscano Mateus 1953:241).

In the Andean countries, as in other regions, many verbs are made reflexive which are not reflexive in Spain, such as *enfermarse, recordarse*, and *regresarse*. Often the addition of -se implies that performing this act will be of interest or importance to the person addressed, as in *Véase esa película* 'You really should see that film' (Flórez 1963:17). The converse is also true, though less common, as in *desayunar* for Standard *desayunarse* and *embarcar* for *embarcarse* (Toscano Mateus 1953:293).

A final shared characteristic of Andean Spanish, which is also to be found in popular speech in other countries, is confusion of prefixes. There are a number of reasons for this. One is that lower classes sometimes adopt prestige forms mistakenly because of near homonomy. *Antecristo* 'before Christ' appears in place of *Anticristo* 'anti-Christ'. This vacillation changes the meaning of *antediluviano* 'before the Flood' to *antidiluviano* 'against the Flood'. A second reason is the persistence of archaisms. In popular speech *oscuro* 'dark' becomes *escuro* (Toscano Mateus 1953:57-59). This is the spelling which occurs in medieval and Renaissance Spanish classics such as the *Cantar de Mío Cid* and the *Lazarillo de Tormes*.

With reference to the parts of speech, in the Andes the uses of the verb tenses closely resemble those of Mexico but with some important local differences. As elsewhere in the Hispanic world, the present may express future time, as in *Mañana se instala* 'He's moving in tomorrow' (Flórez 1963:15). Present may also function as a vivid perfect tense, as in *Todavía no me devuelven los pesos* 'They still haven't returned my money' (Kany 1945:156). The imperfect is used instead of a present in the Andes, as elsewhere in Latin America, in sentences such as *Hace mucho tiempo que no le veía* (*veo*) (Kany 1945:157). It is often used as a courteous present, as in *¿Qué deseaba?* and in a conditional sense, as in 'If I had money I would buy a house' *Si tuviera dinero, compraba una casa* (Flórez 1963:16). The imperfect replaces the pluperfect in sentences like *Todavía no venía* (*había venido*) *mi tío cuando yo salí* 'My uncle had not arrived when I left'.

Very generally in Latin America, the preterite is preferred to the present perfect. In Colombia, for example, one may hear *Esta mañana compramos* = '*Esta mañana hemos comprado*' (Flórez 1963:16); in Ecuador, *¿Ya trajeron el pan?* = '*¿Ya han traído el pan?*'; in Peru, *¿En dónde compraste hoy los huevos?* = '*has comprado*' (Kany 1945:163). This tendency is less pronounced, however, in more puristic areas and in regions where schoolbook Spanish is spoken on formal occasions in contrast to informal ones calling for the native Indian tongue. In Bolivia, for instance, present perfect in these situations is like that of Spain, as in *Yo le he conocido en el pueblo cuando era juez* (Kany 1947:197). But Bolivia is exceptional. Elsewhere, the preterite is often used in place of the present or future for emphasis on suddenness or total completion of an action or state (as in Mexico).

¡Ya se acabó! 'It's all over!'
¡Nos fuimos! 'Let's go!' (Kany 1945:164)

This is like Russian *pošlí*, literally 'We went' but colloquially 'Let's go right now!' In both cases, tense has given way to aspect.

While the preterite is preferred to the present perfect for the expression of action completed in the past, the present perfect has acquired in the Andean countries an application unknown elsewhere. Present perfect may be used in Standard Spanish to express an act begun in the past and continuing into the present. In the Andes, the present connotation of this tense has been strengthened at the expense of its reference to the past. This is particularly true of the present perfect of *ser* and *tener*. Thus, *ha sido* may be equivalent to *es* and *ha tenido* to *tiene* (Kany 1945:167). This equivalence of present perfect to present is probably responsible for the use of the pluperfect as a simple past. So *había sido* may mean *era* and by extension even refer to the present or to the future:

> *Mañana ha sido* (*será*) *día de asueto, ¿no?* 'Tomorrow is/will be a holiday, right?'
> *El año que viene ha sido* (*será*) *bisiesto* 'Next year is/will be leap year' (Toscano Mateus 1953:260)

Another Andean oddity in this tense is the existence of some non-Standard forms of *haber* as an auxiliary (due to Quechua phonology):

yo hi/hei   *nosotros himos/mos/habemos*

tú has
vos *habís/habés*
él, ella ha   *ustedes, ellos han* (Toscano Mateus 1953:234)

Further, *haber* may fuse with a preceding or following vowel sound or disappear altogether:

Mi atrasadu '*Me he atrasado*' 'I am late'
Yo, niña heicho (*he hecho*) *todo lo cristianamente posible* 'I as a girl have done everything humanly possible'
Yo stado esperando (*he estado*) 'I have been waiting'

Another shortened form is *bía* for *había*, the imperfect indicative (Toscano Mateus 1953:235).

Sequence of tenses is also avoided in the subjunctive when the subordinate clause expresses an idea that is timeless or still valid:

No quería que la manden (*mandaran*) 'She didn't (and doesn't) want people to boss her'
Siguió hablando sin que nadie le haga (*hiciera*) *caso* 'He kept on talking without anyone paying attention to him'

Toscano Mateus points out that this disregard for sequence of tenses was characteristic of sixteenth-century Spanish, but may have been reinforced by analogous structures in Quechua (1953:263).

Another archaic tendency in Andean and Río Plata Spanish is the Latinate *-ra* subjunctive as a preterite or pluperfect indicative. This is not unknown in other parts of the Hispanic world, but in these two dialects this usage by the press, radio, and literati is far more frequent and deliberate than it is elsewhere:

Se cumple en el día de hoy el aniversario de la muerte de don A.V., quien fuera (había sido/fue) personaje de importancia 'Today is the anniversary of the death of Mr. A.V., who was a man of importance' (Flórez 1963:16).

One stylist considers this *-ra* practice 'sickly sweet', another calls it an affectation, but in the Andes it is viewed as an elegant form (Kany 1945:171). The suffix *-se*, which occurs far less frequently, is thought because of its rarity to be even more prestigious and is reserved for the language of literature (Kany 1945:183).

Passive voice with *ser* is avoided in the Andes, as elsewhere. The *se* passive construction in Colombia and Ecuador behaves as in Spain: if the subject is plural, the verb may be pluralized, as in *se venden adobes*. Or the *se* may be used as a singular impersonal subject, as in *se vende adobes* (Flórez 1963:17; Toscano Mateus 1953:294). In Ecuador, the recognition of *se* as impersonal subject apparently has weakened so much that speakers bolster it with a redundant *uno*, as in *Uno se trabaja* (Toscano Mateus 1953:294).

In southern Colombia and Ecuador, especially in the highlands, another archaic form that has been reinforced by Quechua is the use of the future indicative as a 'softened' imperative, as in the English 'Thou shalt love thy neighbor as thyself'. Thus, *Esperará un momentico* is equivalent to Standard Spanish *Espere un momentito, por favor* (Flórez 1963:17; Kany 1945:157; Toscano Mateus 1953:258). When the command is affirmative, the object pronouns may be suffixed to the verb, but when it is negative, they may precede, as in Standard Spanish: *Daráme (Déme) unos diez sucres* and *No te harás (No te hagas) el chistosito* (Kany 1945:158). At times, as in rustic Spanish everywhere, these object pronouns are infixed between the verb stem and the ending, as in *digálemos* in place of *digámosle*. In other imperatives, the object pronoun sometimes occurs before the personal suffix of the verb:

> *cálle(n)sen 'cállense'*
> *díga(n)men 'díganme'*
> *díga(n)len 'díganle'*

In forms such as *cállensen*, we see an epenthetic *n* following the suffixed pronoun, and in those like *cállesen*, metathesis (Toscano Mateus 1953:234). Such forms are also common in the Spanish of northern Mexico and New Mexico, as are the structures containing a hollow auxiliary verb and a nominalized participle in *-ada*:

> *Echémonos una bañada 'Vamos a bañarnos'*
> *Me he tirado una gran dormida 'He dormido mucho'*
> *Vamos a echarnos una nadadita 'Vamos a nadar'* (Toscano Mateus 1953:285)

Such constructions are not unknown in Spain, but there the auxiliary is almost invariably *dar*.

A number of verbs that are transitive in Standard Spanish seem to be intransitives in Ecuador. Their objects—which have been deleted—are, however, well known to both speaker and listener. Some of these are:

> *ostentar 'ostentar riqueza'*
> *dar 'dar golpes'*
> *tener 'tener dinero'*
> *merecer 'lograr alcanzar'*
> *amontonar 'amontonar insultos'* (Toscano Mateus 1953:203)

Other verbs customarily followed by a preposition when construed with a noun phrase may lose the preposition in Ecuadorian Spanish, giving the impression that the object of the preposition has become the direct object, whether this is the fact or not. These may be exemplified by:

> *Fíjate esto 'Fíjate en esto'*
> *Te he pensado mucho 'He pensado mucho en ti'*
> *Te he soñado anoche 'He soñado contigo anoche'*
> *Juan me invitó un café 'Juan me invitó a un café'*
> *Me has chismeado 'Has chismeado de mí'* (Toscano Mateus 1953:299-300)

Still other verbs that are intransitive in Standard Spanish are used as transitives in Ecuador. For instance, *soberbiar*, usually reflexive in Spain with the meaning 'act arrogantly', appears transitively with the sense of *'rechazar por soberbia'*, 'to refuse something through arrogance'. *Sestear*, from *siesta*, is all too transitive in:

Al que es flojo, el tigre lo conoce por la pisada. Pone su mano sobre la huella, y si le tiembla, es porque el tal cristiano tiene miedo. Entonces lo sigue y lo *sestea* (Toscano Mateus 1953:302).

The Andean noun does not differ greatly in its morphology and syntax from general Latin American usage. Some nouns are not of the same gender as that assigned them by the Royal Academy, such as Colombian *la pus* 'the pus', *la pijama* 'the pajamas', *el chinche* 'the bedbug', *el lagartijo* 'the lizard', and *el mugre* 'the filth' (Flórez 1963:11). In Ecuador, forms with different gender are *la azucarera* 'the sugarbowl', *la cuchilla* 'the knife', and *el mosco* 'the fly', among others (Toscano Mateus 1953:158-160). In both Colombia and Ecuador, gender endings may be assigned to nouns that are invariable in Standard Spanish to indicate the sex of the referent, producing forms such as *testiga* 'witness', *ayudanta* 'aide', *negocianta* 'businesswoman', *abogada* 'lawyer', and *presidenta* 'president'. In the animal world there are *el ovejo*, *la tigra*, and *la lora* (Flórez 1963:11; Toscano Mateus 1953:163). In both countries, as elsewhere in the Hispanic world, feminine proper names may be applied to men by changing the suffix *-a* to *-o*, as in *Cecilio* and *Inocencio*, and reversing the process gives *Fernanda*, *Jesusa*, and *Rosenda* for women (Flórez 1963:12). There is no gender in Quechua, and substratum loan words going into Spanish are given gender according to their form, such as *la papa*, *el cóndor*, *la mashca* ('barley meal'), and *el morocho* ('white corn') (Toscano Mateus 1953:166).

As to number, Colombia and Ecuador vary from Spain in assigning plural where the Standard is singular as in:

¿Qué horas son?
Hace tiempos 'some time ago'
Las onces 'happy hour'
Los bajos 'ground floor'
Los altos 'upper story'
Las vueltas 'small change' (Flórez 1963:12; Toscano Mateus 1953:188)

And Ecuadorian Spanish may delete the final *-s* on compounds to create singular forms like *el paragua*, *el sacapunta*, *pararrayo* 'lightning rod'. Words that end in [s], such as *lápiz*, are thought by some speakers to lack a plural form and hence 'the pencils' becomes *los lápiz*. Popular Spanish everywhere pluralizes nouns ending in a stressed vowel by adding *-ses*, producing forms such as *cafeses*, *mamases*, and *papases*. On the Ecuadorian coast, back formation then creates new singulars such as *mamás* and *papás*. Some Standard Spanish nouns which are invariably plural are also made singular in Ecuador:

pantalones → *pantalón*

tijeras → *tijera*
calzones → *calzón*
anteojos → *anteojo* (Toscano Mateus 1953:169-171)

New truncated nouns have also been created in the Andes through problems with articles and syllable division:

Standard Spanish:	Andean:	Gloss:
la hamaca	*la maca*	'the hammock'
la acequia	*la cequia*	'the ditch'
la azotea	*la zotea*	'the flat roof'
la alacena	*la lacena*	'the cupboard' (Toscano Mateus 1953:139)

In Colombia and Ecuador, the number of noun suffixes has been greatly reduced. The only diminutives are *-ito/-a* and *-ico/-a* (*una comidita, un ratico*). These are widely used as is the augmentative *-ón*, as in the despectives *mujerón*, *hembrón*, and *señorón*. Peculiar to Colombia is *-ero* to designate an inhabitant of a particular region: if from Cartagena, then *Cartagenero*, or from Palenque, *Palenquero*. Ecuadorians often change the suffix *-ista* to *-isto* for male referents, in describing people with a habitual attitude or activity: *egoísto, pensionisto, pleitisto* 'shyster lawyer' (Flórez 1963:12-13; Toscano Mateus 1953:163-164).

The morphology of the adjective in the Andes differs little from that of popular Spanish elsewhere. A number of common adjectives undergo apocopations not recognized by normative Spanish grammar; *primer* and *tercer* lack *-a* before a feminine noun, as in *la primer victoria*. *Ciento* becomes *cien* in all environments: *la casa número cien, cien por cien*. Also general in uncultured Spanish are double comparatives like *más mejor* and *más peor*. And, as in many other varieties of Spanish, *-azo/-a* and *-ote/-a* may be affixed to form superlatives (*grandazo, grandote, grandotote*). Two common prefixes also form superlatives, *re-* and *requete-*, but *rete-*, frequent in Mexico, is unknown here. In the highlands there is a third way to express the superlative: reduplication of the adjective (*bueno bueno* and *ocioso ocioso*), which may be due to the influence of Quechua although it is not unknown in Spain. On the coast the suffix *-ísimo/-a*, usually reserved for adjectives, may be affixed to nouns as an intensifier. For example, *alacransísimo* is 'a very big scorpion', *tiempísimo* is 'a very long time', and *añísimos* 'very many years' (Toscano Mateus 1953:175-178).

Most of the adverbial uses in Andean Spanish are the same as in Mexico: *ahorita* 'right away', *siempre* 'definitely', *recién* 'recently' (in place of *recientemente*), and *no más* 'only' (instead of *solamente*) (Flórez 1963:18-19). Adjectives in the Andes are often used as adverbs, a widespread practice in the Americas: *Canta lindo* 'he sings well', *tocan bueno* 'they play well', *yo le pago los intereses puntual* 'I'll pay him the interest punctually', *camina rápido* 'he walks fast', and *lo hago fácil* 'I do it easily' (Flórez 1963:20; Toscano Mateus 1953:337). Almost the reverse occurs when words expressing degree, usually invariable, are made to agree with an adjective or verb being modified: *medio muerto* → *medios muertos* 'half dead', *de puro tonta* → *de pura tonta* 'so stupid that', and *son los que mejor se portan* → *son los que mejores se portan* 'they're the ones that behave best' (Toscano Mateus 1953:339).

Bilingual speakers in the Andean countries frequently have difficulty with the article, which does not exist in many Indian tongues. These speakers often omit the article where it would normally occur, resulting in Ecuadorian sentences such as *Voy a hacienda* and *Alza sombrero*. Even among Hispanics the article disappears in some common expressions such as *todo mundo* (considered elegant in Colombia), *segunda vez* (in Bolivia), and *darle a uno gana* (Kany 1945:21; Toscano Mateus 1953:151-152). At times the article appears when it should not. Standard Spanish *Voy a casa* becomes Ecuadorian *Voy a la casa* 'I'm going home', and, by analogy, *El arzobispo está en palacio* changes to . . . *está en el palacio* 'the archbishop is in his palace' (Toscano Mateus 1953:152). In Peru: *A la voz de 'aura' nos trenzamos a los puñales* 'At the cry of 'Now!' we grappled, stabbing at one another' (Kany 1945:20). In Colombia, Ecuador, and Peru, an article often precedes either a person's given name or surname. This usage is archaic, having occurred in sixteenth-century literature, but is now viewed as rustic (Kany 1945:22). At times despective in Spain, it is neutral in the Americas (Toscano Mateus 1953:153). There is also confusion as to gender, so that Quechua-dominant bilinguals may say *el mujer* and *la hombre* or simply use the masculine article across the board (Kany 1945:19).

Pronoun usage in the Andean area is quite similar to that of Spain, with a few exceptions. In Ecuadorian cities, children address their parents as *usted* or *tú*, the *tú* form gaining in acceptability. Parents' pronouns vary from family to family. Some call their children *usted* and some call them *tú*. Mothers may use the *usted* form while fathers use *tú*. Parents who customarily use *tú* (or *vos*) may reserve *usted* for scolding or to show extreme affection. The ancient *su mercé* is the customary term for blacks on the coast and Indians in the highlands when they address a member of the elite (Toscano Mateus 1953:210).

Andean direct object pronouns are generally Standard, *lo* preferred in Colombia and in the coastal lowlands of Ecuador. The highlands, however, opt for *le*. Another substandard form is *mos* for *nos* (Flórez 1963:13; Toscano Mateus 1953:202-204). The use of two proclitic pronouns in different cases is avoided. In the Ecuadorian highlands, a direct object pronoun may be omitted if there is also an indirect object:

Pedro me ha pedido el libro, ¿le doy?
Dale (Toscano Mateus 1953:202)

If both coexist, they may be separated by a verb: *No me vuelvas a nombrarle.* In Standard Spanish, enclitic pronouns are unstressed. But in the Andes, as in Argentina, it is usual to say *digalé*, *vamonós*, and *dejelés* (Toscano Mateus 1953:206-208).

Another difference between continental Spanish and American Spanish pronouns concerns the possessives. *Su* 'your'/'his'/'her'/'its'/'their' tends to be replaced by a prepositional phrase with *de*, as in *de ella*, disambiguating the referent, in Ecuador and Colombia (Flórez 1963:13). An even greater difference is the widespread use of the Quechua possessives *-y*, *-la*, and *-za*, especially in direct address, to express affection:

viditay 'vidita mía'
vidala 'vida mía'
mi guaguaza 'mi querido bebé' (Zamora Vicente 1979:391)

Another Americanism in the Andes is the virtual loss of the demonstrative *aquel*, for which the speaker substitutes either *ese* or *de más allá*. The relative pronouns differ in that *quien*, *el cual*, and *cuyo* have vanished from common speech, in which forms like *que* and *el que* are substitutes:

Era un hombre que (= *a quien*) *le gustaba mucho divertirse*
El padre, que su (= *cuyo*) *hijo trabaja en el campo* (Flórez 1963:13; Kany 1945:133)

Questions beginning with an interrogative pronoun in Ecuador are often reinforced by a redundant element such as *mucho*, *más*, or *no más*:

¿Qué mucho es p's?
Majadero. ¡Qué más te quisieras vivir en una casa decente!
¿Dónde no más estuviste?

Other Ecuadorian questions show the influence of Quechuan word order:

¿Qué para hacer? '*¿Para hacer qué?*' (Toscano Mateus 1953:193-194)

Cúyo, which has disappeared in Standard Spanish everywhere, still exists in the highlands of the Andes as an interrogative pronoun: *¿Cúyo es ese libro?* (Kany 1945:133).

Prepositional usage in the Andean countries is similar to that of Mexico, more so than to Spain. In Spain, for example, *desde* plus a preterite refers to the beginning of an action which has continued to the present moment. In Mexico, Central America, and the Andes, however, this construction refers to a completed action, the results of which extend to the present: *Desde ayer llegó* 'He arrived yesterday (and is still here)'; *Se rasuró desde temprano* 'He shaved early (and is still clean-shaven)' (Kany 1945:362-363). The preposition *hasta* in Spain means 'until'. In Mexico, Cuba, Puerto Rico, Venezuela, and the Andean countries, though, it may have a negative sense: *Hasta las tres iré* 'I won't go until three'. A classic example of noncommunication occurred in a doctor's office with an interchange between a patient and the nurse. The patient asked *¿Estará el doctor hasta las ocho?* 'Will the doctor stay in his office until eight?' The nurse replied *No, llega mucho antes* 'No, he will get here long before then!' (Kany 1945:371)

Standard Spanish has many compound prepositions with *de* as their obligatory final element (*dentro de*, *cerca de*). In the Andes, however, *de* may be omitted, creating structures like the following.

Son cerca las doce 'It is near to twelve'

Formamos tres veces al día delante las celdas 'We lined up three times a day in front of the cells'
Dentro la acequia estaba el sapo 'In the irrigation ditch was the toad'

The presence of *de* in Standard compounds at times has led to the use of an intrusive *de*, as in *sobre de* (in place of *sobre*) and *entre de* (instead of *entre*). It also occurs in phrases like *dicen de que*, probably through analogy with verbs such as *acordarse de*, *olvidarse de*, and *gustar de*.

Me dijo de que vendrá 'He said that he would come' (Bolivia)
Ya él sabrá de que a Luis nadie le pisaba el poncho 'He'll soon find out that no one pushes Luis around' (Peru)
Puede de que no 'Maybe not' (Ecuador) (Kany 1945:351-354)

Standard Spanish *de* is often replaced by *en*, especially in the Colombian press and on the radio: *las ocho en la noche, muebles en madera*. In turn, *en* is often replaced by *entre*: *entre el bolsillo, entre el agua* (Flórez 1963:21). In all of the Andean countries, a preposition has been derived from *donde* with the same sense as the French *chez*, 'the place where a person usually is to be found':

Anda cuando quieras ande (donde) doña Brígida 'Go whenever you want to doña Brígida's' (Bolivia)
Me acerqué donde el director 'I approached the director's office' (Peru)
Se refugió a la noche donde su querida 'He took refuge at night at his girlfriend's' (Ecuador)
Voy donde mi tío 'I am going to my uncle's' (Colombia)

Donde as a preposition is also attested in Spain and has caused a bitter controversy as to its acceptability. Cuervo did not find it offensive but later prescriptive grammarians did. One called it an *abuso*, another a *barbarismo*, and a third a *viciosa construcción* (Kany 1945:363-365).

Lexical usage varies widely in the Andean region, not only from country to country but also from area to area within the same country. The only traits shared are the preservation of an abundance of words which have been lost in Castile and the massive borrowing from local Indian languages, principally Quechua, among other linguistic sources.

In Colombia, many lexical items have the same meanings as in Mexico in contrast to Spain, where these meanings are expressed by other words:

Colombia and Mexico:	Spain:
apartamento	*piso*
automotriz	*de vehículos automotores*
carro	*coche*
dirección	*señas*
estampilla	*sello de correos*
flaco	*delgado*
manejar (un coche)	*conducir*
mesero	*mozo*

prender	*encender*
quedar	*estar*
salón de belleza	*peluquería de señoras*
tarea	*deber escolar*
verdura	*legumbre* (Flórez
	1963:23-28)

However, many Colombian usages are different from those of Mexico.

Colombia:	Mexico:	Spain:
andén	*acera*	*acera*
a ver	*buenó*	*dígame*
bomba	*gasolinera*	*gasolinera*
caucho	*hule*	*goma*
coger (*un bus*)	*agarrar*	*tomar*
charro	*de mal gusto*	*de mal gusto*
chusco	*simpático*	*atractivo*
embolador	*bolero*	*limpiabotas*
habano	*plátano*	*plátano*
medias (*para hombre*)	*calcetines*	*calcetines*
mono	*güero*	*rubio*
pelado	*muchacho*	*muchacho*
perico	*café con leche*	*café con leche*
pisco	*guajolote*	*pavo*
tinto	*café solo*	*café solo*
vaina	*cosa/molestia*	*cosa/molestia*
vestido (*de hombre*)	*traje*	*traje* (Flórez 1963:23-28)

Some forms of address that are common in Colombian speech are:

Term:	Person addressed:
don	anyone without special distinction
doctor	anyone with any university degree
profesor	any teacher, even in primary schools
maestro	intellectual, author, artist, skilled artisan
señor	one who is respected and well-liked (used with first name, as *Don* is in Spain)

More intimate and colloquial are:

Term:	Person addressed:
mijo	husband, boyfriend
mija	wife, girlfriend
misia	(contraction of *mi señora*, used with first name)
niña	an elderly lady, to show respect and affection
seño	a superior (contraction of *señora* or *señorita*)
su merced	*patrón* of the farm/member of one's family, in Bogotá

The forms *madre* and *abuela* are avoided because they have offensive connotations (Flórez 1963:14-15). Also intimate and colloquial are hypocoristic given names such as *Pati* (*Patricia*), *Susi* (*Susana*), *Beti* (*Isabel*), *Mari* (*María*), and *Yoni* (*Juanito*) (Flórez 1963:33).

Many marine terms have entered the Spanish of Colombia, as they have in Mexico and Argentina. Some examples are:

Term:	Sailors' meaning:	Extended meaning:
aferrarse	'grapple'/'cast anchor'	'seize'
amarrar	'moor a boat'	'tie'
botar	'launch a ship'/'steer a ship'	'throw away'/'waste'
chusma	'common sailor'	'rabble'
embarcarse	'embark'	'enter a vehicle'
rancho	'sailors' ration'	'pickled fish'
vararse	'dock a ship'	'park a car' (Flórez 1963:29)

Colombian Spanish is rich in regionalisms, many of them Standard items which have been given new meanings:

Location:	Term:	Meaning:
Tolima/Huila	*barqueta*	'canoe'
Santander	*bolera*	'nuisance'
Atlantic Coast	*aguantar*	'await'
Antioquia	*el algo*	'snack' (Flórez 1963:29)

Other semantic changes, as in Mexico, concern figurative language. Here, however, the tendency toward extension is less important than toward limitation or restriction of meaning. For example:

Word:	Spanish gloss:	Colombian gloss:
orejón	'big-eared'	'suspicious'
bogar	'to row'	'to toss off alcohol beverage'
cepillar	'to brush'	'to flatter'
moreno	'swarthy'	'black'
amarga	'bitter'	'beer'
dulce	'sweet'	'soda'
culebra	'snake'	'debt' (Flórez 1963:30)

Another linguistic source for the Colombian lexicon has been English, especially popular with urban youth: *blue-jeans*, *chequear*, *drive-in*, *folder*, *guachimán*, *guaya* ('wire'), *hamburguesa*, *motel*, *parqueadero* ('parking lot'), *perro caliente* ('hot dog'), *strapless* (Flórez 1963:32).

The lexicons of Ecuador, Peru, and Bolivia are principally characterized by the adoption of hundreds of words from Quechua and Aymara, and the preservation of numerous archaisms. Country folk use Quechua words in everyday speech, and city dwellers less so, for informal situations in order to joke or to entertain. Spanish-Quechua blends have been created, such as *caballo chupa* 'horsetail plant', *sachamédico* 'quack doctor', and *hacer achi* 'sneeze'. In the mountains, popular songs reflect this mixture of the two languages:

De frío, amor mío,
Chugchucunguimí ('Estás temblando')
Y abres tus bracitos
Buscándome a mí (Toscano Mateus 1953:32-34).

The semantic value of many Spanish words and phrases has been affected by Quechua in another way. Where an Indian word has several meanings, all of these may be transferred to its Hispanic calque. For example, the Quechua word for 'know' also means 'be accustomed to', and *saber* has thus acquired this secondary meaning in Ecuador, Bolivia, Peru, and Argentina (Kany 1945:206). Similarly, *hablar* has come to mean not only 'talk' but also 'scold'; *llevar* 'to carry' and 'to bring'; *papa grande* signifies 'grandfather'. Quechua *mama* 'mother' also means 'thumb' and by extension an important member of a class such as a *mama cuchara* 'a large spoon' (Toscano Mateus 1953:33). The phrase *meter breque* 'put on the brakes' analogously combines Spanish with English (Toscano Mateus 1953:133). Popular etymology has been responsible for the birth of many malformations:

Word:	Meaning:	Source:
alrevesado	*'enrevesado'*	*al revés*
campapé	*'canapé'*	*cama*
dentrar	*'entrar'*	*dentro*
friambre	*'fiambre'*	*frío* (Toscano Mateus 1953:133-134)

Quechua has also influenced numerous verb phrases peculiar to Ecuador. *Para* plus infinitive, for instance, forms a delicate proposal or invitation in sentences such as *Ois ve, para irnos el domingo al cine, ¿ha?* '¿Quieres venir conmigo al cine el domingo?' In Ecuador, Colombia, Peru, and northern Argentina, *como* + the infinitive *ser* is often used in place of *como son* or *como es* to mean 'for example': *En el Ecuador hay muchos volcanes, como ser el Cotopaxi, el Pichincha* (Kany 1945:257; Toscano Mateus 1953:268). In Peru and Ecuador, *ser* is also used in an elliptical construction where the complement, always derogatory, is omitted out of consideration for the listener: *No seas . . .* or *Tú sí eres . . .* (where the deleted adjective is similar in sense to *tonto, bruto, perezoso,* or *descuidado*). An analogous phrase is *No te hagas . . .* , 'Don't pretend to be. . .' (Kany 1945:234-235). In Ecuador, *es* has lost its identity when suffixed to *mejor*, producing phrases such as *Es mejores que vengas* 'It is better that you come' (Toscano Mateus 1953:289). *Es* has also been absorbed into its surroundings in *quierde* for *que es de*, probably as a result of the resemblance of [s] and assibilated [ř]. The meaning of *quierde* is not always clear even to native speakers, but it is always interrogative: *¿Quierde el dinero?* 'What has happened to the money?' *¿Quierde Antonio?* 'Where is Antonio?' In Bolivia this same fusion is pronounced *quiste*: *¿Quiste mi sombrero?* (Kany 1945:260) Another Ecuadorian fusion is the archaism *dizque*, which may mean 'I say that', 'he says that', or 'you say that' (Toscano Mateus 1953:296). Still another Ecuadorian oddity is *estar de* + infinitive, a periphrastic form used impersonally to express suitability: *Está de irse* 'It's time to go' and *El niño está de comerle* 'The child is cute enough to eat' (Toscano Mateus 1953:282-283).

Even more interesting is the unusual application of several terms of address. *Don* in Standard Spanish may only precede a given name, unless an insult is intended, as in *Don Gonzales*, which implies that the referent is illegitimate. In both Ecuador and Colombia, however, *Don* may precede a surname as a term of respect. It is also a common noun meaning 'Indian' or '*mestizo*'. *Doña* also means 'Indian' or '*mestiza*' but occurs only with the woman's given name. Another term of address is *amigo*, for one who is not a close friend but an acquaintance. More intimacy is expressed by *cholo* or *cholito* and for one's best friend *guate* (from Mexican *cuate*?) (Toscano Mateus 1953:217-218).

Unlike Mexico, in Ecuador the majority of Indians keep their native surnames, such as *Vilcarima* 'speaking idol'. Many first names, on the other hand, are hypocoristic forms from Spanish:

Andi 'Andrés'
Bili 'Belisario'
Cunshi 'Concepción'
Chipi 'José'
Gugu 'Gregorio'
Ishaku 'Isabel'
Luchu 'Luis'
Shishi 'Cecilia'

When a child is named for his Spanish patron saint, at times there is a change in the word's gender, as in *Genovevo* and *Margarito*. Given names on the coast are often allusive:

Demóstenes	*Matusalén*
Alcibíades	*Lenín*
Guasintón	*Stalín*
Salomón	*Hitler*

Segundo Napoleón Bonaparte
Eterno Redentor del Mundo (Toscano Mateus 1953:219-222)

Many Ecuadorian nicknames come from Quechua and often refer to negative qualities:

Alcurrucu 'old dog'
Chuno 'wrinkled by the sun'
Chuspi 'small eyed like a fly'
Güisto 'crooked mouth'
Mapahuira 'dirty lard'
Pimi 'gaptoothed'
Pondo 'fat as a pot'

A political party once called its opposition *Cucuchupa* 'worm tail'. *Papaya, mamey*, and *aguacate* are all slang terms for 'dummy', and *boca de cajeta* is 'sweet mouth' (Toscano Mateus 1953:223-224).

Some Standard Spanish past participles have become derisive Ecuadorian adjectives which sometimes have wildly different meanings:

Term:	Ecuadorian meaning:	Spanish meaning:
aguado	'foolish'	'soggy'/'abstemious'
apurismado	'sad'/'sickly'	'tumorous'
arreado	'lazy'	(from *arrear* 'to herd')
entumido	'cowardly'	'swollen'
quebrado	'dark-skinned'	'broken'
salado	'accident victim'	'witty'
tupido	'dim-witted'	'thick' (Toscano Mateus 1953:270-271)

Thus, it can be seen that Andean Spanish in phonology, morphosyntax, and lexicon resembles that of Mexico in many respects but is different enough to be viewed as a distinct dialect. Both variants have been influenced by the substratum in a parallel fashion but Nahuatl and Quechua have little in common. Both offer the same kinds of phonological contrasts between the highlands and the coasts. Perhaps the most striking similarities are to be found in morphosyntax and the greatest differences in lexicon.

References

Amastae, Jon. 1983. An investigation of the phonemic distinction between /b/ and /v/ in Bogotá. Colloquium Series lecture, University of Texas at El Paso.

Blansitt, Edward. 1984. Private conversation.

Boyd-Bowman, Peter. 1953. Sobre la pronunciación del español en el Ecuador. Nueva Revista de Filología Hispánica 7. 221-233.

Boyd-Bowman, Peter. 1960. El habla de Guanajuato. México: Universidad Nacional Autónoma de México.

Escobar, Alberto. 1976. Bilingualism and dialectology in Peru. The International Journal of the Sociology of Language 9. 85-96.

Flórez, Luis. 1963. El español hablado en Colombia y su atlas lingüístico. Bogotá: Caro y Cuervo.

Kany, Charles E. 1945. American-Spanish syntax. Chicago: The University of Chicago Press.

Kany, Charles E. 1947. Some aspects of Bolivian popular speech. Hispanic Review 15. 193-205.

Lapesa, Rafael. 1968. Historia de la lengua española. 7th ed. Madrid: Escelicer.

Menéndez Pidal, Ramón. 1941. Manual de gramática histórica española. 6th ed. Madrid: Espasa-Calpe.

Robinson, Kimball L. 1979. On the voicing of intervocalic *s* in the Ecuadorean highlands. Romance Philology 33. 1.137-143.

Toscano Mateus, Humberto. 1953. El español en el Ecuador. Madrid: Revista de Filología Española, Anejo LXI.

Zamora Vicente, Alonso. 1979. Dialectología española. 2nd ed. Madrid: Gredos.

Chapter 15
The Caribbean

Just as the Spanish variants of Mexico and the Andean highlands have many traits in common which are reminiscent of the Castilian meseta, so the dialects of the islands and coastal regions share features which recall the speech of Andalusia. As Lapesa notes:

> . . . las semejanzas [del español en América] . . . con el habla de Andalucía son más estrechas . . . en las Antillas y costa del Caribe, sin duda como consecuencia del inicial predominio migratorio andaluz y de la continua relación con Canarias. En el Continente el habla de las altiplanicies se aproxima a la de Castilla mucho más que la de los llanos y costas, donde están más acentuadas las semejanzas con Andalucía. . . (1968:355).

While one may not care to argue for or against the highland-lowland position versus the Andalucista, it is true that certain generalizations may be made that characterize the lowland Spanish of the Caribbean basin, Chile, and the three countries of the Río Plata. In phonology, especially among the segmentals, the treatment of many sounds is not only similar in these areas but is also like that of southern Spain. The morphosyntax does not differ significantly from that of Spanish elsewhere, and, like Spanish elsewhere, it varies widely from country to country and class to class. For example, Spanish as written by an educated *Puertorriqueño* is indistinguishable from that composed by a peer in Mexico City or Madrid. But, if the Puertorriqueño reads aloud, he at once identifies his origin. (Listen to the 'disappearing Caribbean *s*', tape 2, selection f, and see Appendix 5.) The dialects of these areas are perhaps farthest apart in their lexicons, because of two reasons, one geographical and one historical. Their physical environments differ—from temperate Chile to tropical Cuba—as do the substratum languages from which they borrowed. And, with the arrival of thousands of Africans in the Caribbean, Spanish was enriched by yet a new source.

The phonology of lowland Spanish has several general characteristics. Its sounds fall roughly into three groups: (1) those which are the same as in general Spanish, (2) those which are characteristic of the lowland group as opposed to Castilian, and (3) those which are local. Among the consonants, the stops are standard. Most of the fricatives are standard as well, even if pronounced with less tension and therefore less clarity. There is no phonemic distinction between *b* and *v* (Henríquez Ureña 1940:137), and both are realized as [β]. The voiceless counterpart, *f*, is the bilabial fricative [ɸ] for the majority of speakers (Zamora Vicente 1979:413), although it is sometimes avoided by the elite, as in the rest of the Spanish-speaking world.

More limited to lowland, even in cultured speech, is a relaxed [ð], which is often deleted (Zamora Vicente 1979:412). Fricative [ɣ] is the same as elsewhere.

However, its unvoiced counterpart [x] is more typical of lowland articulation. It is pronounced in two ways, which are in free variation. It can be a very weak velar in which the tongue does not touch the velum, producing a sound acoustically similar to [h], or it may be an actual [h], laryngeal or pharyngeal. These also are Andalusian in nature (Navarro Tomás 1948:66). Also lowland and Andalusian is /s/ (Zamora Vicente 1979:288). When it occurs syllable-final either before a pause or another consonant, it reduces to an aspiration or is simply deleted (Navarro Tomás 1948:71-74). As opposed to highland speech, /s/ has no [z] allophone. The tongue approaches the point of articulation of a following consonant, giving the air audible friction but allowing it to pass through the oral cavity without voicing. If the following consonant is a nasal, an odd phenomenon occurs—a preceding vowel is nasalized and /s/ becomes the appropriate nasal, but devoiced. Thus, for instance, [mismo] becomes [mĩm̥mo].

Of the two affricates, one is Andaluz and the other is not. The first, /č/, in some places becomes [ʃ] as in Seville (Canfield 1981:42). The other, [ǰ], is the realization of the semivowel phoneme /j/, like an English j in juice, in Puerto Rico and Santo Domingo (Saciuk 1980:16-17). In the River Plate countries, however, ll and y are pronounced as a palatal fricative [ʒ]. The other semivowel, /w/, is pronounced as in general Spanish.

The Caribbean lateral /l/ is also that of general Spanish, and throughout the lowlands implosive /l/ and /r/ are in free variation, another Andalusian trait (Navarro Tomás 1948:81). Castilian /ʎ/ is nonexistent. The vibrants /r/ and /rr/, which vary in the highlands, are pronounced as in general Spanish in the lowlands, except for some parts of Puerto Rico. In many areas, syllable-final /r/ disappears before a pause or a following consonant (Navarro Tomás 1948:87).

Nasals in the lowlands are not only peculiar when they follow an /s/. The phoneme /n/ before a pause when word-final or when syllable-final before another consonant becomes the velar [ŋ], especially when its syllable is a prefix that corresponds to an independent preposition like en or con. Since the speaker produces en and con with word-final [ŋ], he continues to insert [ŋ] even when n is word-medial. Thus, entrar becomes [eŋtrár] and convenir [koŋbenír]. This practice is also Andalusian (Zamora Vicente 1979:416).

Vowels in the lowlands behave somewhat differently from their highland equivalents. In Standard Spanish, /e/, /a/, and /o/ have as allophones [ɛ], [ɑ], and [ɔ] in certain environments: e.g., when in contact with [ř], [řéɣla]; or when preceding /x/, [káxa]; or in a syllable closed by any consonant except m, n, s, d, x, [sɑl] (Navarro Tomás 1932:52-53). These environmental changes also occur in the lowlands with an additional rule: when syllable-final /s/ is aspirated or lost, again a preceding /e/ → [ɛ], /a/ → [ɑ], and /o/ → [ɔ]. Further, if the /s/ is deleted, the opening of the vowel may serve to supply an absent morpheme or identify a part of speech:

[pjé] 'pie'   [pjɛ́] 'pies'
[bé] 've'   [bɛ́] 'ves'
[djó] 'dio'   [djɔ́] 'Dios' (Navarro Tomás 1948:46)

Here again may be seen a resemblance to Andaluz.

As to suprasegmentals, the lowland dialects in general are delivered at a more rapid pace than in the highlands, and, as in the highlands, they differ from one another substantially. The tempo of speech in Cuba is faster than in Santo Domingo, where it is relatively slow. Pitch is higher in Cuba while in Santo Domingo it is fairly low, as in Castile (Henríquez Ureña 1940:150-151). The pitch range of Puerto Rico is much narrower than elsewhere (Navarro Tomás 1948:112-113). An accented syllable lengthens in Santo Domingo, while in Puerto Rico it shortens, and the lengthening occurs in the previous syllable.

The lowland dialect spoken in the Caribbean Islands is relatively uniform. These islands, the Antilles, were dominated by shipping from Andalusia, for which they served as a staging area during the colonial period. Further, although other Latin American countries had broken away from Spain by the 1820s, the future Caribbean island nations continued to be colonies until 1898. These factors in the history of the Antilles had a twofold effect on their language. First, the Andalusian dialect was firmly implanted and maintained there, and, second, the normative influence of Peninsular institutions, both administrative and educational, continued to prevail long after mainland countries such as Mexico had severed their ties with Spain. (Listen to Tape 2, selection g, and see Appendix 5.)

Accordingly, the morphosyntax of the Spanish of the islands differs but little from that of southern Spain: upper class speech is similar in both areas, as is the speech of the semi-educated and that of the rustic population. In the Antilles, as in Spain, *voseo* is virtually unknown, except for two small areas in eastern Cuba. Rustic usage in both areas includes plurals such as *sofases* and *manises*, the past tense form *truje*, the subjunctive *haiga* for *haya*, and the adverb *asina* for *así*.

Characteristics which Caribbean shares with other Latin American dialects include gender and number assignments which differ from those of Spain (*el sartén, la tijera*), the use of the present tense for the future (*El sábado vamos a compras*), the preference for the preterite over the present perfect (*Lo vi esta mañana*), and the reflexivization of verbs (*recordarse*) (Rosario 1970:86-87). Also, Caribbean is like the rest of Latin America in its lack of *vosotros* and corresponding verb forms, for which it substitutes *ustedes* and a third person plural verbal suffix. As in Mexico and the Andes, the accent in the first person plural of the subjunctive tends to remain on the stem, as in *váyamos*, and the *m* may change to *n* by analogy with *nos* to produce *váyanos*. As elsewhere, *compraste* may become *comprastes*, which in turn may dissimilate to *comprates*. *Somos* may be realized as *semos*, and the auxiliaries *he* and *hemos* may become *ha* and *hamos*. As elsewhere, forms such as *siéntense* may be altered to *siéntesen* and some verbs that are radical-changing in Spain lose this feature, as in *escrebir*, *recebir*, and *aprevar* (Navarro Tomás 1948:125-129; Henríquez Ureña 1940:175). Most of these characteristics are true of rustic Spanish in general.

The few morphosyntactic localisms which Caribbean does not share with other variants include the odd Cuban and Puerto Rican placement of a subject pronoun before the verb in a question, as in ¿*Qué tú dices*? There, *su* with no qualification is taken to mean second person formal 'your'. Santo Domingo, like most varieties of Latin American Spanish, is *loísta* in that the third person direct object pronouns are always *lo* and *los* while *le* and *les* are always indirect objects. *Se lo* in Santo Domingo may become *ge lo*; *ti* and *tigo* serve as subject pronouns when the subject is compound: *Yo y ti no semo na* or *Yo y tigo no semo na*. In Puerto Rico, a noun is often derived from a present tense verb, indicative or subjunctive, as in *bofeteo*, 'a blow', *atoro* 'stubbornness', *acabe* 'the finishing', and *amanesca* 'the dawning'. At times the Puerto Rican present participle agrees with the subject, as in *La mujer está muriéndase* (Navarro Tomás 1948:130). African influence in Puerto Rico can be seen in formations such as the despective suffix *-ngo/a* in *matungo* 'nag' and in the stem in *bembudo* 'thick lipped' (Navarro Tomás 1948:118).

Although the pronunciation of the segmental phonemes in the Antilles is more or less uniform throughout the islands, there are some local characteristics. A distinguishing trait of Puerto Rican pronunciation is the treatment of vibrant /r̄/: 59% of the speakers prefer a weakly voiced velar articulation, 23% an alveolar, as in Castilian, and 18% a 'mixed' [r̄], either velar or alveolar, but aspirated, sounding like a Castilian [r̄] preceded by a weak [x] (Navarro Tomás 1948:89-91). In both Puerto Rico and Santo Domingo, syllable-final /r/ either becomes [j] or assimilates to a following consonant: *porque* becomes *poique* and *carne* becomes *canne* (Navarro Tomás 1948:86; Henríquez Ureña 1940:175). This same phenomenon is common in the Canary Islands (Lapesa 1968:333). In Cuba, /r̄/ tends to be voiceless, and /č/ weakens to [ʃ], as in Santo Domingo, especially in the speech of women (Canfield 1981:42), while in southwest Puerto Rico /č/ tends to be prepalatal (Canfield 1981:77).

By and large, where these Caribbean dialects correspond to each other they resemble Andalusian as well. However, phonologically, they share a number of traits from West African languages which are also found in Brazilian Portuguese, Black English, and French creoles (some of these traits will be illustrated in the course of this discussion). As a result, there are two schools of thought. One emphasizes the close similarity of Antillean pronunciation to that of southern Spain and points out that on the Caribbean islands the speech of blacks does not differ from that of whites of the same economic status. The other group notes that some of these shared traits are attributable to the vast number of African slaves brought to these regions from the middle of the sixteenth century well into the nineteenth. Some of these slaves were transplanted from estates in Spain, where they had become speakers of rustic Spanish. The majority, however, were imported directly from West Africa, by traders from Spain and especially from Portugal. Brought to Curaçao and Aruba in the southern Antilles, these blacks were held for resale and, while there, developed a pidgin which may have served as a substratum for further development in whatever linguistic locale they were later to find themselves—where their second language was to be Portuguese, Spanish, English, or French, or a creole such as Papiamentu or Palenquero.

Most interestingly, some of the characteristics which are supposedly Anda-lusian are also supposedly African, such as the disappearance of syllable-final

/s/, which occurs not only in southern Spain but also in the slave speech of the sixteenth and seventeenth centuries and in the Palenquero of Colombia:

ponemos [ponémɔ]
se espanta [se pánta]
juez [hwé]
mosca [mók:a] (Nathan 1978:50)

Also in Palenquero is the aspiration of /s/, as in:

escoba [ehkóba]
fósforos [ɸɔ́ɸoroh] (Nathan 1978:41)

Another cluster of traits which might derive from either Andalusian or African concerns the behavior of /l/ and /r/. They are often in free variation:

Andalusian:	Creoles/popular usage:
mujer [muxél]	*call* Eng. [kár]
	desculpa (B. Port.) [deʃkúrpa]
	castigar (B. Port.) [kaʃtigál] (Nathan 1978:23-24)

And /r/, in a final syllable, may assimilate to a following consonant, causing it to geminate, or simply to disappear:

Andalusian:	Creoles/popular usage:
(*carne*) ([kánne])	*verdad* (Pal.) [beddá]
cuerno [kwénno]	*Puerto Rico* (Fr.) [pótto ríko]
	shark (Eng.) [ʃá:k] (Nathan 1978:33-34)

Or /r/, in syllable-final position, may become [j]:

Andalusian:	Creoles/popular usage:
(*porque*) ([pojké])	*madrina* (Pal.) [maína]
ladrón [lajrón]	*ladrillo* (P.R.) [lajrío]
padre [pájre]	*compadre* (Cuba) [kompáj] (Nathan 1978:44-45)

Another characteristic which may be African, though there is dispute among linguists, is the velarized /r̄/—not Andalusian—which exists in Puerto Rico, Santo Domingo, and northern Brazil. Álvarez Nazario believes this sound is due to an African substratum because it is also common in French and English creoles as well as Black Portuguese. Rubén del Rosario and Navarro Tomás doubt this theory and feel that velar /r̄/ may be attributable to mistaken attempts of Taínos or Africans to produce Spanish /r/, which was nonexistent in their native languages (Nathan 1978:55).

Some of these phonological features can be observed in texts in which writers have exploited dialectal differences for a humorous purpose. One of these is a dialogue between a *criollo*, a white Cuban, and an *africano*, a black:

Criollo:

Venga *uté* a *tomai seivesa* y *búquese* un compañero, que hoy me sobra *ei* dinero. En medio de la grandesa, *Dio*, mirando mi *probesa*, me ha dado una lotería, y en mi *randiante* alegría me ha convertido en poeta; y aquí está mi papeleta, que no he *cobrao entuavía*.

Criollo:

Venga usted a tomar cerveza y búsquese un compañero, que hoy me sobra el dinero. En medio de la grandeza, Dios, mirando mi pobreza, me ha dado una lotería, y en mi radiante alegría me ha convertido en poeta; y aquí está mi papeleta, que no he cobrado todavía.

Africano:

¡Ah! si *oté* no lo *cubra*, si oté *tovía* no fue, *¿pa* qué *buca* que *bebé*? ¿Con qué oté lo va *pagá*? Cuando oté lo *cubra anjá, antonsí ma qui te* muere bebe oté como oté quiere, come oté como dan *gana*, y *durmi* oté una semana *ma que lan* tempo *si piere*.

Africano:

¡Ah! si usted no lo cobra, si usted todavía no fue, ¿para qué busca que beber? ¿Con qué usted lo va a pagar? Cuando usted lo cobra, ajá, entonces sí aunque tu mueras bebe usted como usted quiere, come usted como (le) dan ganas, y duerme usted una semana aunque el tiempo se pierde.

(Bachiller y Morales 1883:100-101; López Morales 1971:64).

In this passage from Cuba, the *criollo*'s speech is slightly closer to Standard Spanish than that of the *africano*. Nevertheless, there are some common characteristics. For instance, /s/ and /d/ disappear for the *criollo* in *uté*, *búquese*, *Dio*, *cobrao* and *entuavía* (loss of intervocalic /d/, which is a general trait of lowland Spanish) as they do for the *africano* in *oté*, *tovía*, *buca*, *gana*, and, finally, *piere* where [rd] becomes [r], supposedly an African tendency (Nathan 1978:40). The speech of both contains intrusive nasals in *randiante* and *anjá*, and archaisms in *entuavía* and *ma que* which is *manque* with the loss of syllable-final [ŋ]. Some differences are that, for the *criollo*, syllable-final /r/ and /l/ often become [j], as in *tomai*, *seivesa*, and *ei*, while the *africano*'s /r/, syllable-final, is deleted. The *criollo* metathesizes in *probesa* while the *africano* syncopates in *tovía* and *antonsí*. Vowels alternate only in the speech of the *africano*, where /u/ becomes [o] in *oté*, /o/ becomes [u] in *cubra*, [we] becomes [u] in *durmi*, and /e/ becomes [i] in, for example, *qui*, *ti*, and *si*. *Lan*, in the last line, is an undifferentiated article in Black speech in the Caribbean (Nathan 1978:94). In assessing this sample, one must keep in mind that its author is only an amateur linguist burlesquing popular speech and may have exaggerated the contrast between the two speakers.

An even greater contrast is to be observed in a conversation from 'La juega de gallos, o el negro bozal', a skit published in Puerto Rico in 1852. One of the speakers is José, a *bozal* slave (one born in Africa), whose language recalls Pichardo's description of Black Spanish in Cuba in 1836:

un lenguaje relajado y confuso se oye diariamente en toda la isla, por donde quiera, entre los negros bozales o naturales de Africa (. . .): este lenguaje es común e idéntico en los negros, sean de la nación que fuesen, y que conservan eternamente, a menos que hayan venido mui niños: es un castellano desfigurado, chapurrado, sin concordancia, número, declinación ni conjugación, sin *r* fuerte, *s* ni *d* final; frecuentemente trocadas la *ll* por la *ñ*, la *e* por la *i*, la *g* por la *v*. . . (López Morales 1971:66)

The other speaker is Nazaria, also a slave, but one born in Puerto Rico, and whose Spanish is standard, bearing out Pichardo's comment that 'los negros criollos hablan como los blancos del país de su nacimiento o vecindad. . .' (López Morales 1971:167). Nazaria is scolding José for not doing his work, and she is also ridiculing his amorous advances. The arrival of their master, Don Antolín, puts an end to their interchange:

Escena 1.
José y Nazaria.

José.—¡Ja! . . . Nazaria . . . *¿Tú mirá* señorita anoche cómo taba miringando? . . . y niña Fererica tambié . . . ¡Ja! . . . *¡qué duce!* . . .

Naz.—Déjate, José, de estar mirando cosas que no te importan. ¿Quién mete un negro bozal como tú estar pensando en merengue y en amoríos? Acaba de limpiar las botas y vete a hacer tus oficios. Ahorita el amo se levanta, y no tienes nada hecho por estar charlando toda la mañana. ¿Qué haces aquí en la sala metido?

José.—¡Ah, Nazaria . . . *no son tu corazoná!* . . . Tú siempre *ta jablando* a mí con *grandísima rigó*. Yo *ta queré* mucho a ti; *grande, grande* así *(Señalando con las manos.) son* mi *sufrimienta* . . . Aquí . . . *(Poniendo la mano sobre el corazón.) yari, yari* mucho . . . si tú ta queré mi corazó . . .

Naz.—¡Siaa! . . . qué voy yo a hacer con tu corazón ni tu cariño! . . . ¿Piensas que yo voy a querer un negro tan feo como tú, cuando no faltan niños blancos que me estén haciendo señas y no les digo que sí, porque me quiero guardar para uno que me dé la libertad?

José.—Yo *ba libetá a ti* Nazaria . . . Yo *ta trabajando*, y *ta juntando* dinero pa ti . . .

Naz.—La paciencia me vas a acabar . . . si no te vas, se lo digo a la señorita en cuanto se levante.

José.—No, Nazaria; *no ta gritando* así *hombe, ¡bróngaman* Dio! . . . *Mirá*; *yo tiene* uno becero en *casa ño* Juan de Dio, *yo tiene* dinero juntando y niña Fererica *ba a da a mí pa comprá uno llegua.*

Naz.—Si, para alcahuete nada más sirves tú. Si el amo lo llega a saber . . .

José.—Nazaria, no; *ése no son cagüetería; yo jase* lo que señorita me *mandá* . . . ¡Ja! niña *Fererica son bueno amo!* . . . siempre *ta regalá* dinero *a mi,* y *to son* pa ti Nazaria si *tú ra* tu pechita y *tú queré* mucho a mí . . . Yo te *ba jasé uno baile* con música ño Juaniné *pa bailá* hupanene contigo. *(Canta la contradanza del "Vapor" y va como a querer bailar con Nazaria; ésta lo rechaza y amenaza con el plumero.)* ¡Ah! *¡Dio mía Señore!* . . .

Escena 2.
Don Antolín, José y Nazaria

Ant.—¡Negro del demonio! . . . ¿Ese es el modo que tienes de hacer los
oficios?, ¿bailando un estafermo como tú, sin estar el comedor barrido?
Anda, quítate de mi presencia. Te voy a vender para La Habana, o
mandarte otra vez para una hacienda para que tengas trabajo y te den
mucho foete, que es lo que tú mereces, bribón . . . Mira, di a Señor
Epifanio, mi gallero, que si ha pesado los gallos, que venga acá.
José.—Gallo *ta nan so, mi amo*.
Ant.—Hablador infernal, anda ve (Caballero 1961:387-393).

Again, this sample is not to be taken as truly representative of *bozal* Spanish,
but recent studies of creolized language in the Caribbean confirm the existence
of many of these features. The most numerous *desfiguraciones* are found in the
simplification of the verb. In no tense are suffixes for person or number used.
The infinitive—minus *r*—is used to express the present tense: *tú queré, ella
mandá*. Or it may, in fact, indicate past: *Tú mirá señorita anoche*. It may also
be used as a true infinitive:

pa comprá uno llegua
pa bailá hupanene contigo

In the case of some very common verbs, present tense may be realized for all
persons by the third singular:

yo tiene uno becero
yo jase

Or, as in *yari, yari mucho*, from '*llore, llore mucho*', a verb form may be
distorted almost beyond recognition.

The infinitive may also be used, with *ta* (from *estar*), to signify habitual
present:

ta queré
ta regalá

Habitual and/or progressive in the present may be realized as:

Tú siempre ta jablando a mí
Yo ta trabajando y ta juntando dinero

Slightly more complex is *taba miringando*, a past progressive. *Ta* may also serve
as a copula:

Gallo ta nan so, mi amo
'*Los gallos están en el sol, mi amo*'

Son, or *sa*, is another copulative for any person.

Ah, Nazaria . . . no son tu corazoná
grande, grande son mi sufrimienta
ése no son cagüetería

and, later in the same play:

Yo no son negro nan casa qui son negro no conuco
'*Yo no soy negro de casa, que soy negro del conuco*'
'I am not a house servant but a field hand'

Futurity is expressed by *ba* plus the infinitive:

Yo ba libetá a ti
Yo te ba jasé
Niña Fererica ba a da a mí

Two imperatives, one compound and one simple, are seen in:

no ta gritando así . . . Mirá

An ambiguous verbal structure is *yo tiene dinero juntando*, which may have one of two senses, either '*yo tengo dinero juntado*' or '*yo he estado juntando dinero*'.

The morphology of the noun as portrayed in this passage shows that the *bozal* speaker has several problems with substantives and their accompanying modifiers. As to number, all of José's nouns are singular in form, even where the context clearly calls for a plural, as in line one:

¿Tú mirá señorita anoche cómo taba miringando?
'Did you see the young ladies last night, how they were dancing the *merengue*?'

In Scene 2, José says *Gallo ta nan so, mi amo* in spite of the fact that the *amo* has just asked him about *los gallos*, plural.

The *bozal* speaker also has problems with Spanish gender: *pechito* becomes *pechita*; *sufrimiento, sufrimienta*; *Dios mi Señor, Dio mía Señore*; and *amo* is used to refer to a woman. Concordance between noun, adjective, article, and demonstrative is ignored:

grandísimo rigor → *grandísima rigó*
una yegua → *uno llegua*
esas no son alcahueterías → *ése no son cagüetería*

Bozal *uno* fails to drop the *o* before a masculine noun, as in *uno becero* and *uno baile*. In all of his lines except one, José omits an obligatory definite article, and where it is supplied he uses the creole form *nan*.

There are both grammatical and phonological reasons for these nonstandard features. In the Bantu and Sudanese languages, notions of number are often expressed not by suffixes but by prefixes. Some nouns are invariant and only an attendant adjective is affixed to show plurality. Moreover, in these languages syllable-final sounds other than nasals do not occur, and /s/ as a phoneme is rare. Gender as a grammatical feature based on sex is unknown in these two families of languages, and, instead, there are numerous different classes of nouns categorized originally according to semantic characteristics such as animateness, size, agentivity, and abstractness (Bodmer 1944:205).

Some minor morphosyntactic anomalies include reduplication (*grande grande*, *yari yari*), the omission of the paratactic *de* (*uno becero en casa ño Juan de Dio*), and the tendency to express a pronominal object, direct or indirect, with *a* plus a stressed pronoun instead of an unstressed form:

> *Yo ba libetá a ti 'Yo voy a libertarte'*
> *ba a da a mí 'va a darme'*

A good example of rustic Puerto Rican at the present time can be seen in the following passage from the drama *La carreta* by René Marqués. (Listen to Tape 2, selection h and see Appendix 5.) Doña Gabriela's family are about to leave their native countryside to live in the city. Don Chago, her father, has refused to move with them but has come to say goodbye:

Don Chago.—*Eh* que aquí siempre *pueo jasél* alguna *chiripita*. Allá no habría *ná* pa *ehte cahco e* viejo.

Doña Gabriela.—Déjese e cuentoh, padre. *Uhté* eh un viejo ñoño con el corasón *mu* flojo. Eso eh lo que pasa. Le *tié* miedo al cambio.

Don Chago.—(*Siempre de buen talante.*) ¿*Mieo*? *Pué* ser. Loh añoh noh van poniendo miedosoh.

Doña Gabriela.—¿Y qué dijo mi hermano Tomá?

Don Chago.—¡Qué *diba* a dicil! Que ehtaba bien.

Doña Gabriela.—Entonce, ¿ehtá tó *arreglao*? ¿Se va uhté a vivil con el-loh?

Don Chago.—Sí.

Doña Gabriela.—Cualquiera lo entiende. Se fue *antiér* y ya ehtá aquí otra ves. ¿*Pa* qué uhté volvió si no se viene con *nojotroh*?

Don Chago.—Pueh . . . pa ná. Pa ehtar con uhtedeh hoy.

Doña Gabriela.—Y pa eso ha andao mah e quince quilómetroh con esa *ahma*.

Don Chago.—El ahma no se usa pa *caminal*. Tengo lah piernah durah.

Doña Gabriela.—(*Señalando el lío de ropa que trae* Don Chago.) Y pa *venil* a dehpedirnoh se trajo uhté la ropa.

Don Chago.—(*Fingiendo.*) ¿Qué ropa? Ah sí. Eh que no quería *dejala* allá sola. No me guhta que me traqueteen mih cosah.

Doña Gabriela.—Y se cree que allá le van a aguantál toah suh maníah. La mujé e Tomá no lah va a aguantál. ¿Cómo lo recibió?

Don Chago.—Bien . . . (Marquéz 1971:8)

The speech of these two characters is typical of Caribbean. Syllable- or word-final /s/ is represented as an aspiration, as in *Eh* for *Es*, *cahco* for *casco* and *ahma* for *asma*. *Nojotroh* may be an archaism, since it is treated as *nos* plus *otros* instead of a unitary lexical item. Final /r/ becomes [l] (*jasél, caminál, veníl, aguantál*) or disappears (*dejala, mujé*). *Chiripita* is a general Latin Americanism with different meanings in different countries. Here it means '*trabajo de poca importancia*'. Intervocalic /d/ is lost, as in *pueo, mieo, arreglao*, and in final position in *uhté*. Initial /d/ is deleted on the unstressed *de*, as in *cahco e viejo* and *la mujé e Tomá*. There is an intrusive [ð] in *diba*, another general Latin Americanism, which Lapesa terms an Andalusian trait of Leonese origin (Lapesa 1968:329). Also Andalusian are numerous apocopes, such as *mu* (for *muy*) *tie* (for *tiene*), *pué* (for *puede*) as well as *pa*, a usage which is general uneducated Spanish. Syllable-final /n/ is probably [ŋ] and /r̄/ is probably velar as well, but these are not represented in this dialogue, doubtless due to the orthographic difficulty of recording these sounds. (Another illustration of Jíbaro speech can be heard on Tape 2, selection i. See Appendix 5.)

Like English and French, Spanish has served as the basis for the creation of creoles in the Caribbean. The most important of these is Papiamento, spoken on the islands of Curaçao, Aruba, and Bonaire—islands which now belong to Holland but which were under the Spanish crown from 1499 to 1634. During these 135 years, the language of the conquerors was increasingly imposed upon the Indians, and there developed a pidgin, based on Spanish, without inflections and with numerous indigenous items in the lexicon. The islands were conquered by the Dutch in 1634 and continued in their possession until 1800. The Dutch made profitable use of these newly acquired territories as a market for wholesale trade in African slaves, with whom they were abundantly supplied by the Portuguese. In the period between 1650 and 1750, 20,000 were imported annually, and after 1750, this figure was increased to 100,000 a year. Most of the West Africans spoke a Portuguese pidgin which overlaid the Spanish pidgin, resulting in a fusion which was to become a creole language called Papiamento—with some admixture of Dutch (Zamora Vicente 1979:441).

In 1795 these territories were taken over by the French but in 1802 they were returned to Holland, which continued to rule them until 1986. The official language of the government and of education was Dutch. In order to teach Dutch, however, it had to be translated into Papiamento, the spoken language of everyone in the country except for a few officials from Holland. With the cessation of legal slave trade, the influence of Portuguese diminished, and with the arrival of many immigrants from Venezuela and Colombia, that of Spanish increased. As a result, 85% of the lexicon of Papiamento is Spanish, 5% is Dutch, and the rest is of Portuguese or African origin, with a sprinkling of English (Zamora Vicente 1979:442-446).

In Papiamento phonology, the effect of Spanish can be seen in the present-day fricative pronunciation of the once occlusive /b/, /d/, and /g/. In final position, /d/ either becomes [t] or is lost and initial /f/ turns into [h]: *Mi a humá un cigaría* '*Yo he fumado un cigarillo*'. Labiodental /v/ becomes [β]: *Mi ruman a bini 'Mi hermano ha venido*'. Final /s/ is often lost and before /j/ palatalizes to [ʃ]: *atención* becomes [atenʃó]. Also realized as [ʃ] is Spanish /č/. Among educated speakers, /z/ is preserved in loan words from Dutch. Papiamento, like Latin American Spanish, has no [θ]. Initial *h* is aspirated as in [hómber] ('*hombre*') and /x/ is realized as [h] as in [hóβen] ('*joven*'). Syllable-final /l/ and /r/ are often deleted: *el* becomes *e*, *mujer* [muhé], and *cerca* [séka]. Vibrant [r̄] is replaced by simple [r]. Syllable-final /n/ is velarized to [ŋ] as in the Antilles, an Andalusian trait. An intrusive [n] frequently appears syllable-final, as in [mansa] for *masa*. Nasalization of /j/ frequently produces an [ɲ], as in [ɲáma] '*llama*' and [áɲa] '*haya*'. This tendency to nasalize, inherited from Portuguese, is diminishing at the present time (Zamora Vicente 1979:442-443).

Vowels in Papiamento are similar to those of Portuguese in Brazil and Spanish in the Andes, in that unstressed /e/ may become [i] and unstressed /o/, [u]:

[dilánti] '*delante*'
[múʃu] '*mucho*'

Also worthy of note is the tendency to shorten words of several syllables:

[ríba] '*arriba*'
[múʃa] '*muchacho*'
[βíspa] '*víspera*'

Suprasegmentally, it does not make much difference which syllable receives heavy stress, and meaning is not affected: [ténde] and [tendé] both mean *tender* (Zamora Vicente 1979:443).

The morphology of Papiamento represents an extreme and highly functional simplification of that of Spanish (and occasionally Portuguese). The verb is not inflected for person and number, which are supplied by context or by pronouns. There is, as a result, only one verb form for each tense. All tenses are signalled by verb phrases made up of an auxiliary verb plus the verb stem. The stem itself usually is an apocopated Spanish infinitive, with the accent shifted to the penult.

comprar → *cumpra*
comer → *come*
escribir → *skirbi*

The present tense consists of *ta* (from Spanish or Portuguese *está*) + the verb stem: for example, *ta skirbi* 'write(s)' 'is/are writing'. The imperfect is formed by the auxiliary *tábata* (from *[es]taba* + *[es]tá*) before the stem: thus, *tábata skirbi* is 'was/were writing' or 'used to write'. The preterite consists of the auxiliary *a* (from *ha*) plus the stem:

El a contestá '*El contestó*'
Mi a come '*Yo comí*'
No a caba '*Nosotros acabamos*' (Goilo 1962:54)

The future is formed by placing *lo* (from Portuguese *logo* 'immediately') before the subject pronoun. The final vowel of the stem is accented:

Lo mí cantá '*Yo cantaré*'
Lo bo murí '*Tú morirás*' (Zamora Vicente 1979:445)

The verb without any auxiliaries serves as a singular and plural imperative:

Muchanan, bini 'Come, boys'
Duná mi un florin 'Give me a guilder' (Goilo 1962:66)

There are three ways to form a Papiamento passive. One is *ta* + *ser* or *worde* + past participle (the verb stem, accented on the final syllable) as in:

E carta ta ser/worde skirbí 'The letter is written'
E carta a ser/worde skirbí 'The letter was written'
E carta lo ser/worde skirbí 'The letter will be written'
E carta lo a ser/worde skirbí 'The letter would be written' (Goilo 1962:108)

Some anomalous verbs are derived from the forms heard most frequently, such as *bai* (Port. *vai*, 3rd sg.) and *ban/bam* (Sp. *vamos*, 'let's go'). *Sea*, as in *Sea un bon mucha* 'Be a good child', comes directly from Spanish and is used as the imperative form of *ta* (Goilo 1962:66). The several forms of *tener* (*tene, tini, tin*) combine with *taba* (Sp. *estaba*): *E tabatín hopi placa* 'He had a lot of money'. Without a subject, *taba* is the equivalent of Spanish *había* 'there was/were' (Zamora Vicente 1979:445). *Ta* does not occur with a few common verbs, most of which are modals:

Lexical item:	Meaning:	Source:
ta	'to be'	*estar*
tin cu	'to have to'	Port. *tem* or Sp. *tiene* + *que*
por	'to be able to'	*poder*
sa/sabi	'to know how to'	*saber*
conocé	'to know a person'	*conocer*
ke/kier/quier	'to want'	*quiere*
mester	'must'	*menester* (Sp. n. or adj.)

A few other verbs may or may not require *ta*: *debe* ('*deber*'), *gusta* ('*gustar*'), *costa* ('*costar*'), *bal* ('*valer*'), *stima* ('*estimar*'), *merecé* ('*merecer*'), *parce* ('*parecer*'), and *nificá* ('*significar*') (Goilo 1962:22).

The Papiamento noun is also simplified. Normally, it is not inflected to show gender, with a few exceptions, all of which refer to people:

Masculine:	Feminine:
primu	*prima*
sobrinu	*sobrina*
amigu	*amiga*
conde	*condesa*
rey	*reina*
bailarín	*bailarina*
actor	*actrís*
señor	*señora*
maestro	*maestra*
autor	*autora*
esposo	*esposa*
novio	*novia*

suegro	*suegra*
viudo	*viuda* (Goilo 1962:74)

The noun is also infrequently inflected for number. Pluralization is optional but may be indicated by the particle *-nan* which can be attached not to the noun, but to a final element in a noun phrase instead:

e casnan bunita   '*las casas bonitas*'
e cas bunitanan   '*las casas bonitas*'
e buki akinan   '*los libros aqui*'

Nan may also be suffixed to demonstratives, personal pronouns, and numerals:

Unda esunnan di mi ta?   '¿*Donde están los mios?*'
Unda bosonan ta bai?   '¿*A dónde van ustedes?*'
E dosnan riba mesa   '*Los dos en la mesa*' (Goilo 1962:75-76)

The personal pronouns are as follows:

mi	*nos*
bo	*boso/bosonan*
ele/el/e	*nan*

These serve both as nominative and objective as well as possessive, which has the additional *su* 'his', 'her', 'its'. *E* serves as singular or plural definite article, and the indefinite is the invariable *un*. Adjectives are also invariable, with final *-o* or *-a* endings, which do not show gender (Goilo 1962:12-14).

The phonology and morphosyntax of Papiamento can be seen in the following reading selection:

Mi ta Señor B. Mi nomber ta Antonio Francisco Bernardo. Mi ta biba na Otrobanda, den Klipstraat number 2. Mi ta traha na Punda, na oficina. Mi ta skirbi carta, dies carta pa día. Mi ta haci hopi trabou. Mi amigu ta traha na Isla. É ta traha tur día. Señor Jansen no trabaja. É tin placa. É tin hopi placa. Cu placa nos ta cumpra hopi cos; buki, skrif, potlood, pen, ink, i hopi otro cos. Mi tin un pen i un potlood. Cu un pen i un potlood mi ta skirbi. Mi ta skirbi carta i mi ta skirbi mi les. Mi ta skirbi den un skrif. Mi ta skirbi carta riba papel. Mi no ta skirbi carta cu potlood, ma cu pen. Nos ta drumi tur día. Nos ta drumi ocho ora. Mi amigu ta traha ocho ora

Yo soy el señor B. Mi nombre es Antonio Francisco Bernardo. Yo vivo en Otrobanda, en Klipstraat número 2. Trabajo en Punda, en una oficina. Escribo cartas, diez cartas por día. Yo hago mucho trabajo. Mi amigo trabaja en la Isla. Él trabaja todos los días. El señor Jansen no trabaja. El tiene dinero. Él tiene mucho dinero. Con dinero compramos muchas cosas; libros, cuadernos, lápices, plumas, tinta, y muchas otras cosas. Yo tengo una pluma y un lápiz. Con una pluma y un lápiz yo escribo. Yo escribo cartas y yo escribo mis lecciones. Yo escribo en un cuaderno. Yo escribo cartas en papel. Yo no escribo cartas con lápiz, sino con pluma. Dormimos i é ta drumi diesseis ora. É ta come hopi, ma é no ta bebe hopi.

cada día. Dormimos ocho horas. Mi amigo trabaja ocho horas y él duerme dieciséis horas. Él come mucho, pero él no bebe mucho (Goilo 1962:15).

The largest number of lexical items here (20) are from Spanish:

Señor	traha	tur
mi (poss.)	oficina	no
nomber	dies	placa
Antonio	pa	riba
Francisco	haci	ocho
Bernardo	é	diesseis
Otrobanda	Isla	

The next largest group (18) is composed of items which come either from Spanish or from Portuguese:

mi (subject)	trabou	les
ta	amigu	ora
biba	tin	come
skirbi	nos	papel
carta	cumpra	drumi
día	cos	bebe

Definitely from Portuguese are *na*, *cu*, and *ma*. From Dutch come *Klipstraat*, *hopi* ('heap'), *skrif* ('notebook'), and *potlood* ('pencil'). From English are *pen* and *ink*. *Number* and *les* 'lessons' may be derived from Spanish, Portuguese, Dutch, or English and *buki* from either Dutch or English; *den* is of uncertain origin. Metathesis may be observed in *nomber*, *skirbi*, and *drumi*. Otherwise, the spelling conventions are similar to Spanish, as is the word order.

It is interesting to compare the speech of José in 'La juega de gallos . . .' with that of Antonio Francisco Bernardo. Both use *ta* as an auxiliary with the verb stem to form verb phrases. Neither José nor Antonio shows regard for the person or number of the verb: *yo tiene*, *gallo ta nan so* and *mi tin*, *nos ta drumi*. Agreement in gender or number in the noun phrase is also ignored: *grande . . . son mi sufrimienta* and *otro cos*, *otrobanda*, *dies carta*.

In none of these four selections from Puerto Rican Spanish, Cuban Spanish, or Papiamento is there much evidence of lexical influence from Africa, which is curious. The Taínos had become extinct by 1550, and shortly thereafter native-born Africans began to be imported at the rate of many thousands per year. Yet, at the present time, *Africanismos* are outnumbered by *Tainismos* by a margin of three to one (López Morales 1971:81), probably because of the diverse nature of the languages the blacks brought with them (López Morales 1971:68-69). In a recent study, López Morales found that African lexical items account for about 1% of the vocabulary used by his informants. He notes that this figure fails to take into account the frequency with which these words occur (1979:81). Some of them, however, are not only in general use in the Antilles but also have become widespread in Latin America (these have been starred once) or internationally known (these have been starred twice). The largest group includes terms for food and drink; the second largest concerns people, their appearance, clothing, and behavior; the third largest, animals and plants; and the fourth, amusements.

I. Food and drink (12):
    A. Food in general:
        1. *fufú* 'mashed fruits and yams'
        2. *ñame*** 'yam' (etymon of *yam*)
    B. Types of bananas:
        1. *banana***
        2. *congo*
        3. *chongo** (in Mexico, 'head')
        4. *chumbo*
        5. *güimbo*
        6. *guineo/-a*
        7. *mafafo*
        8. *malango*
    C. Drink:
        1. *champola* 'nonalcoholic beverage made of *guanábana* (a fruit), water, and sugar'
        2. *quimbombó* 'beverage from fermented pulp of *yuca* root'

II. People, their appearance, and behavior (9):
        1. *bembo/-a, bembe, bembó/-á* 'large-lipped person'
        2. *cachimba* 'loose woman'
        3. *chango** 'person looking or acting like a monkey'
        4. *cheche* 'bully'
        5. *congo* 'Black'
        6. *jelengue* 'row'/'rumpus'
        7. *malanga* 'loafer'
        8. *malanga* 'rustic straw hat'
        9. *sanaco/-a* 'fool'/'foolish'

III. Animals and plants (7):
        1. *conga** 'large tropical rodent'
        2. *chango** 'monkey'
        3. *chimpancé*** 'chimpanzee'
        4. *jubo* 'long, thin snake'
        5. *mozambique/mazambique* 'black thrush'
        6. *quimbombó* 'acrid fruit and its tree'
        7. *yaya* 'pliant tropical tree'

IV. Amusements (6):
        1. *bachata* 'drunken spree or party'
        2. *bongó*** 'bongo drum'

3. *cachimba** 'a pipe to smoke'
4. *conga*** 'conga dance'
5. *mambo*** 'mambo dance'
6. *marimba*** 'xylophone'

V. Other (2):

1. *quimbamba* 'distant or unknown place'
2. *tonga* 'a neat pile of things'

Most of the words in the category of food and drink predictably refer to tropical fruits brought in from Africa or similar to those in the homelands of the blacks. The same is probably true of the names of plants and animals. Of the nine terms referring to people, their appearance or behavior, six are pejorative. Some are metaphoric, such as the comparison of a person to a monkey (*chango*) and to a big banana (*malango*), to which is also compared the curved, high-crowned hat of the Caribbean peasant. One wonders if the dance, the *conga*, derives from the darting movement of the rodent of the same name, or perhaps from a long tail. More likely, since *conga* was associated with black culture, it came to mean a black dance. The lexical items associated with entertainment reflect the contribution of the blacks to Caribbean music which, in turn, influenced music heard all over the world.

References

Bachiller y Morales, Antonio. 1883. Desfiguración a que está expuesto el idioma castellano al contacto y mezcla de las razas. Revista de Cuba 14. 97-104.

Bodmer, Frederick. 1944. The loom of language. New York: Norton.

Caballero, Ramón C. F. 1961. La juega de gallos o el negro bozal. In: El elemento afronegroide en el español de Puerto Rico. Ed. Manual Álvarez Nazario. San Juan: Instituto de Cultura Puertorriqueña. 387-393.

Canfield, D. Lincoln. 1981. Spanish pronunciation in the Americas. Chicago: The University of Chicago Press.

Goilo, E. R. 1962. Papiamentu textbook. Aruba, Netherlands Antilles: D. J. de Wit.

Henríquez Ureña, Pedro. 1940. El español en Santo Domingo. Buenos Aires: La Universidad de Buenos Aires.

Lapesa, Rafael. 1968. Historia de la lengua española. 7th ed. Madrid: Escelicer.

López Morales, Humberto. 1971. Estudios sobre el español de Cuba. Long Island City, N.Y.: Las Américas Publishing Company.

Marqués, René. 1971. La carreta. 8th ed. Río Piedras, Puerto Rico: Editorial Cultural.

Nathan, Deborah Ruth. 1978. The influence of African slave speech on the phonology of Caribbean and coastal Latin American Spanish. M.A. thesis, The University of Texas at El Paso.

Navarro Tomás, Tomás. 1932. Manual de pronunciación española. 4th ed. Madrid: Centro de Estudios Históricos.

Navarro Tomás, Tomás. 1948. El español en Puerto Rico. Río Piedras, Puerto Rico: Universidad de Puerto Rico.

Rosario, Rubén del. 1970. El español de América. Sharon, Connecticut: Troutman Press.

Saciuk, Bohdan. 1980. Estudio comparativo de las realizaciones fonéticas de /y/ en dos dialectos del Caribe Hispánico. In: Dialectología hispanoamericana. Ed. Gary E. Scavnicky. Washington, D.C.: Georgetown University Press. 16-31.

Zamora Vicente, Alonso. 1979. Dialectología española. 2nd ed. Madrid: Gredos.

Chapter 16
Chile

Unlike the other dialects of Latin America discussed so far, all of which are spoken in more than a single country, Chilean Spanish is limited to only one. Why is Chile a separate dialect area? There are several reasons. Two are geographical. Chile is partitioned from the rest of South America by mountains second in formidability only to the Himalayas. These, the Andes, in centuries past formed a barrier along the entire eastern border with Argentina. Further, most of the northern third of the country is occupied by the uninhabitable Atacama desert, which effectively banned any influence from Bolivia and Peru (except for the ore-rich northern tip, which belongs to the Andean dialect area and has changed hands several times since the mid-nineteenth century) (see Map 8). Another marked difference lies in the presence of many indigenous languages, chief among them Mapuche, spoken by the native Araucanians.

As a rule, Chile has been divided into three principal linguistic zones, northern, middle, and southern, with Chiloé as a subdialect in the south. With the migration of settlers from the Central Valley, however, traits from this mid area have been established in both the north and the south. The cultured speak like their peers elsewhere in the lowland regions of Latin America and Andalusia, with a conscious attempt to conform to literary standards. Their language differs little from one part of the country to another (Oroz 1966:193). The speech of the less educated, however, is not homogeneous. One possible reason is the lack of schooling (education promotes uniformity), while another may be differences in substrate tongues which underlie it. Rodolfo Lenz believed this speech to be 'principally Spanish with Araucan sounds' (1940a:249). This thesis has been refuted by several learned linguists, among them Amado Alonso, who pointed out that the supposed peculiarities 'alien to the nature of the Spanish language' were equally attributable to one part or another of Spain. He found this especially true of the segmentals (1940a:284-289).

Although upper-class speech in Chile is very close to upper-class usage in other areas of Latin America, it does offer a few distinctive traits. The point of articulation of the consonants /k/, /g/, and /x/ before /i/ and /e/ is farther forward than in other countries. The point of articulation of /č/ is also advanced to a postalveolar position. Geminate vowels are reduced to one, as in *cooperativa*, which becomes [koperatíβa], as in many other dialects. Suprasegmentally, the upper-class pronunciation of consonants is accompanied by less muscular tension than in Spain or on the Mexican *altiplano*, and a syllable which contains a stressed vowel is lengthened (Oroz 1966:192-195).

These tendencies are magnified in the speech of the uneducated and it is there that one finds the characteristics that most clearly distinguish Chilean Spanish from that of other dialects. In general, the segmentals resemble those of Andalusia and, consequently, of the Caribbean (Oroz 1966:194). The fricative allophones

Map 8: Dialect areas of Chile.

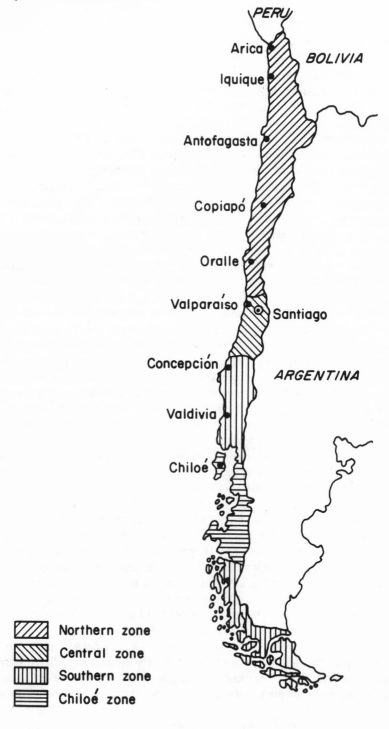

PERU

Arica

BOLIVIA

Iquique

Antofagasta

Copiapó

Oralle

Valparaíso

Santiago

Concepción

ARGENTINA

Valdivia

Chiloé

▨ Northern zone
▧ Central zone
▥ Southern zone
▤ Chiloé zone

of /b/, /d/, and /g/ are weakened and often lost, if intervocalic: *caballero* → [kaajéro], *pedazo* → [peáso], and *aguja* → [aúxa]. Usually, [ð] disappears in word-final position and, in some words, even initially: [berðá], [ónde], and, for *dijo*, [íxo]. And, at times, [ð before [r] may become [j]: *padre* → [pájre] (Oroz 1966:195). Initial or medial /f/ often becomes [x] when occurring before a back vowel or semivowel, as in *fumar* → [xumár], *fogata* → [xogáta], *fuerte* → [xwérte], *difunto* → [dixúnto], and *afuera* → [axwéra]. Medial /f/ may also be realized as [θ] intervocalically: *café* → [kaθé], *enchufe* → [enčúθe] (Oroz 1966:137).

In popular speech in Chile, syllable-final or intervocalic /s/ is aspirated, becomes a glottal stop, or is deleted, with the last-mentioned process occurring with the greatest frequency:

> *nosotros* → [noxótřoh]
> [noʔótřoʔ]
> [noótřo]
> *casa* → [káha]
> [káʔa]
> [káa]
> *mesa* → [méha] (Oroz 1966:101-103)

And /s/ inside of a sentence, if intervocalic, even though word-initial, may become an aspiration or be lost:

> '*Como se pide*' [kómohepíe]
> '*Esa pampa verde ¿qué significa?*' [esa pámpa βerðe ke inifíka] (Oroz 1966:136-137)

The aspirated [s]—which Lenz thought to be an Indian characteristic—is commonest in Chile, Argentina, Venezuela, and the Antilles. It is widespread, as well, in all coastal areas of Hispanic America, from Mexico to Argentina, and is considered by Amado Alonso to be an Andalusian trait (Alonso 1940a:284). Also Andalusian is the tendency to front the point of articulation of /x/ to a prepalatal position before a front vowel, producing a sound that closely approaches [ç], as in German *ich* (Alonso 1940a:286). As opposed to aspirated [s], this fronted palatal /x/ is peculiar in the Americas to Chile. Also fronted, as in Puerto Rico, is /č/, from a palatal to an alveolar position.

The liquids /l/ and /r/ are similar to Antilles usage also. For some speakers they are in free variation, word final: *olor* → [olól], *hacer* → [asél], *mujer* → [muxél] (Oroz 1966:110). For other speakers, they are acoustically equivalent (Canfield 1981:31). The segment [r] syllable-final may assimilate totally to a following consonant, causing it to geminate, as in *carne* → [kánne]. Or it may become an aspiration, [káhne], or it may simply disappear: *soltarle* → [soltále]. In both popular and informal cultured speech /r/ may be assibilated or fused. It may be assibilated under several conditions: (1) in intervocalic position, (2) syllable-final before /s/ (*fuerza* → [fwérsa]), and (3) in some clusters: [dř], [ndř], and [ldř] (*podré* → [podřé/pořé], *vendré* → [bendřé/benřé], and *saldré* →

[saldřé/salřé]. As an assibilated [ř], it fuses with a preceding /t/ into a single prepalatal voiceless affricate [tř] which sounds to the uninitiated like a forwarded [č] (Oroz 1966:110-112).

Since Chilean phonology is so similar to that of the Caribbean and Andalusia, it is surprising that syllable-final /n/ does not become a velar but assimilates to the point of articulation of a following consonant, as in Castile (Oroz 1966:109).

Cultured speakers differ from the less privileged in their treatment of consonant clusters. The cultured maintain both consonants but assimilate the first to the second: *atlas* → [áðlas] and *absoluto* → [apsolúto]. The uncultured simply drop the first consonant: *absoluto* → [asolúto] and *eructo* → [erúto]. In popular speech *bue-* and *hue-* are customarily pronounced as [ɣwe]: *bueno* → [ɣwéno] and *hueco* → [ɣwéko] (Oroz 1966:194-195).

The upper classes also differ from the lower in their articulation of vowels. Educated speakers produce vowels with less tension than in Spain, and this trait is even more obvious in the speech of the uncultured, especially with vowels that receive little stress, and, as a result, the phonemic distinction between /e/ and /i/ as well as that between /o/ and /u/ is partially lost. As in Mexico, popular speakers in Chile reduce the diphthong [ew] to [u], as in *Eusebio* → [uséβjo] (Oroz 1966:193-195).

Chilean Spanish is generally *yeísta* although there are a few small areas south of Santiago in which /j/ is still distinguished from /ʎ/. For some speakers, /j/ is realized as [ǰ], an affricate similar to English *j*, as occurs in Puerto Rico (Oroz 1966:114-119; Canfield 1981:31).

Although contemporary linguists are unanimous in their disagreement with Lenz's thesis that Chileans speak 'Spanish with Mapuche sounds', they would endorse his statement as applied to suprasegmentals. Amado Alonso writes:

> no hay que descartar la probabilidad de que el araucano, ya como sustrato, ya como adstrato, haya dejado alguna huella en el chileno, sobre todo en las melodías, y en los rasgos rítmicos. . . (1940a:289).

Oroz adds that the differences between Chilean and Peninsular intonation are probably due to indigenous influences. He feels that there are four different intonational zones, not thoroughly studied as yet. The northernmost of these, adjacent to Peru, has Quechua as its substratum and is characterized by what sounds like an accentual displacement. The secondary accent is not one of stress, however, but of higher tone, and the hearer who is unfamiliar with this phenomenon interprets it to be a shift. In the Central Valley, which has the greatest prestige and is the most populous zone, intonational features are uniform for all social classes. In the southern zone there is a difference in pitch which Chileans from other areas describe as *canto*, and the tone tends to rise at the end of a phrase. In the fourth zone, the Island of Chiloé, the standard is similar to that of the center of the country for speakers of European origin, but for natives there exist many different patterns which depend upon the indigenous group from which the speaker descends, e.g., the Mapuches, Huilliches, or Veliches. The Europeans begin with a low tone at the beginning of a clause which then gradually rises to descend again in the final syllable. The Indians, on the other hand, begin lower, do not rise as high, and fall more suddenly. The intonation of the inhabitants of the island town of Chonchi does not resemble either of these. It begins with a high tone, goes up even higher, and does not descend much, word-final. Because of this peculiarity, outsiders often misinterpret statements by Chonchinos as questions. The islanders, in general, speak rapidly, while those in the other zones speak more slowly, especially in the rural areas (Oroz 1966:188-191).

The morphosyntax of Chile is that of Standard Spanish, for cultured speakers; for the unlettered it is similar to rustic Spanish in other parts of Latin America and the continent. These similarities are especially prominent in the category of the verb. Periphrastic verb phrases are in general preferred to inflected forms for expression of the future: *Voy a comer* for *Comeré*, and even the simple future of probability: *Han de ser las diez* or *Deben ser las diez* in place of *Serán las diez*. Hortatory subjunctive phrases almost invariably replace simple present subjunctives. Where a Spaniard has a choice between *veamos* and *vamos a ver*, a Chilean prefers the latter (Oroz 1966:384). Also periphrastic are the structures which make use of an auxiliary verb such as *echar*, *pegar*, *dar*, and *hacer* plus a nominalized past participle or noun: *echar una mirada* for *mirar*, *dar una leída* for *leer*, and *pegar un grito* for *gritar*. Other verb phrases consist of a verb of motion such as *venir* or *andar* with a present participle: *Vengo buscando mi perro* for *Vengo a buscar mi perro* (Oroz 1966:388-390). Like Andean usage, Chilean popular speech in some areas employs the present participle as a finite verb in sentences such as *¿Qué haciendo se cayó el niño?* '*¿Por qué causa se cayó el niño?*'

Some tense forms may have different semantic values. At times, a shorter form is preferred to a longer: the preterite is used instead of the present perfect in referring to a recent past: *Esta mañana volvimos tarde* instead of *Hemos vuelto*. The present perfect, in turn, commonly expresses an event that began in the past and continues to the present: *Este verano no ha hecho calor*, said while the summer has not yet ended. And the verbal sense of *hubo* in *¿Qué hubo?* ([kjúβo]) is entirely lost and replaced by the meaning of 'Hi!'(Oroz 1966:383-384). The preterite *Nos fuimos* has the meaning of 'Let's go right now!' In popular speech -*s* is added to the preterite second person singular, as in *comprastes* and *cantastes* (Oroz 1966:303). Instead of a conditional, an imperfect indicative frequently occurs in the conclusion of a conditional sentence: *Si tuviera plata, lo compraba* for *compraría*. And the Chilotes substitute a conditional for the imperfect subjunctive in the if-clause:

Si yo sería el Presidente, negaba el indulto
'If I were President, I would deny the reprieve' (Oroz 1966:385)

There is a tendency not to use the subjunctive in a subordinate noun clause after a verb of desire:

No quería que yo iba a ser su compaire

'*No quería que yo fuera su compadre*' (Oroz 1966:391)

Chilean impersonal verbs also have characteristics which are common to rustic Spanish in the Americas. *Hay* will be made to agree with an apparent subject when personal endings permit, as in *Habían tantos niños*. The same is true of *hacer* 'ago', as in *Ya hacían dos noches que no había puesto la fuente* (Oroz 1966:381-382).

There are also many similarities among adverbial constructions. Forms which are invariable in Standard Spanish, such as *medio*, *puro*, *mejor*, and *peor*, are made to agree with a noun or a pronoun as if they were adjectives:

Anda media enferma
Son los que mejores se portan

Hasta 'until' is used to mean 'not until': *Lo supe hasta hoy* 'I did not learn it until today'. Conversely, *hasta que no* means 'until', emphatically:

No estaré tranquilo hasta que no me digas que estás bién
'I will not feel calm until you tell me that you are well'

As elsewhere, *recientemente* is shortened to *recién*, and *cuánto* is replaced by *qué tanto*. In Chile, as in the Río Plata area and in Ecuador, *lo que* may be used as a temporal conjunction meaning '*cuando*' (Kany 1945:374): *Lo que llegó allá, le dijo a la niña* (Oroz 1966:398). The supposed Central Americanism *idiái*, from *¿Y de ahí?* 'So what?', is used in popular speech in Chile and also in Argentina and Peru (Oroz 1966:392-396).

Chile is a *loísta* country: *lo* is used rather than *le* as a direct object pronoun, as in many regions of Spain and Latin America. In constructions like *se lo* and *se la*, an *-s* is added to *lo/la* to indicate that *se* is plural, as in *Los niños pidieron pan y no había quién se los partiese*. At times there is a redundant invariable *le* to indicate the presence of an indirect object: *Pedro le dió el dinero a los otros*. Rustics often make *yo* a prepositional object, as in *Ese vestido para yo es bonito* 'That dress seems pretty to me'. Pronouns in plural command forms, as elsewhere, are infixed, resulting in structures such as *déjemen tranquilo* for *déjenme tranquilo*, *traigalón* for *tráiganlo*, and *comanselón* for *cómanselo*. In other command forms, pronominal *le* has become an intensifier:

Ándale	¡*Épale!*	*Camínele*
Córrale	*Apúrele*	¡*Ópale!* (Oroz 1966:374-378)

Chilean Spanish is also in the general current of Latin American rural usage in its treatment of the noun. Often, there is confusion as to prefixes:

Espirina	*ensamen*
prefasora	*aspargatas*
almediatamente	(for '*alpargatas*', 'sandals') (Oroz 1966:363)

Frequently, there is adaptation of nouns to indicate more clearly the gender of the referent:

la cliente → *la clienta*
la testigo → *la testiga*
la juez → *la jueza*
el carrerista → *el carreristo*
el pesimista → *el pesimisto*

At times, there are gender changes due to false analogies. *El paraguas* loses *-s* to become *el paragua* which in turn is assumed to be feminine because of the *-a* ending. *El micrófono* apocopates to *el micro* and through analogy with *la foto* changes to *la micro*. A noun ending in an accented vowel is pluralized by *-ses*: *ají/ajises* and *maní/manises*. *¿Qué hora es?* becomes *¿Qué horas son?* (Oroz 1966:366-367)

Prepositional usage in Chile also differs from that of Spain in that unexpected forms appear or at times prepositions are lost altogether:

Spain:	Chile:
entró en el teatro	*entró al teatro*
ir a la consulta del médico	*ir al médico*
dice que viene	*dice de que viene*
recuerda a su familia	*se recuerda de su familia*
visitaron a sus hermanos	*visitaron sus hermanos*
conozco a Los Andes	*conozco Los Andes* (Oroz 1966:399-401)

Although Chilean popular speech most closely resembles the rustic speech of all of Latin America, it does have a few local traits. Again, the largest number of these can be seen in the category of the verb. Some intransitive verbs are made transitive:

A esta niña la creció la tía   'La tía crió a esta niña'
El niño cayó su libro   'Al niño se le cayó el libro' (Oroz 1966:390)

In Chile both *tú* and *vos* coexist and are conditioned by geographical and social factors. In general, *tú* is predominantly found in the speech of the middle and upper classes while the working classes of the city, farmers, and miners use *vos*. As a result, second person singular verb forms are, at times, nonstandard (see Table 12).

In the perfect tense system, some of the forms of the auxiliary *haber* are anomalous (see Table 13).

Indicative forms of *haber* in tenses other than present are normal except for the second singular:

Imperfect:	*vos/tú habíais*
Preterite:	*vos/tú hubistes*
Future:	*vos/tú habrís*

The preterite *hubistes* is seldom used in forming the perfect tense in Chilean

Table 12 Second person singular verb suffixes in Chile.

	-ar	-er	-ir
Indicative:			
Present	-ái/-ás/-as	-ís/-es	-ís/-es
Imperfect	-abáis	-íais	-íais
Preterite	-astes	-istes/-isteis	-istes
Future	-arís	-erís	-irís
Subjunctive:			
Present	-ís	-áis	-áis
Imperfect	(-ra) -árais	-iérais	-iérais

Table 13 Present indicative of *haber*.

yo	hei/hai/hey/hay	nosotros	habimos/habemos/hamos
vos/tú	habís/(h)ai/(h)ais/habés	ustedes	han
él/ella	ha	ellos/ellas	han (Oroz 1966:315)

popular speech. The conditional future *habríais* is also rare. In the present perfect subjunctive, the auxiliary is *haiga* with *haigáis* as the second singular. The pluperfect subjunctive auxiliary is normal except for the second singular, which is *hubiérais* (Oroz 1966:302-305).

Another local trait in Chilean rustic speech is the morphologic or semantic alteration of pronouns. A respectful term for 'you' is the extremely archaic *su merced*, which peasants use in addressing the *patrón*. A respectful 'you' on the island of Chiloé is *ustedes* or *ustés*, terms which are plural in form but may be singular in meaning: ¿*Ustés es familia de Barrientos*? was directed to one *señorita*. Pronominal *yo* may be used in place of *a mí*:

> *Yo me gusta pasear mucho* 'A mí me gusta pasear mucho'
> *Yo me duele mi muela* 'A mí me duele la muela'
> *Yo me tocó la mala* 'A mí me tocó la mala'

Because of this equivalence of *yo* to *a mí*, *a mí* is sometimes used as a subject:

> *A mí no quise ir* 'Yo no quise ir'

In popular speech throughout Chile, *nos* is regularly replaced by *los*:

> *Lo juimo* 'Nos fuimos'
> *Vámolo* 'Vámonos'
> *Enséñeloh onde los tiene nuestra madre* 'Enséñenos donde los tiene nuestra
>   madre' (Oroz 1966:374-375)

Consigo, third person singular or plural, may also refer to first or second *conmigo* and *contigo*, as in *No las tengo todas consigo (conmigo)*. Likewise, *sí* may be used to mean any person, as in *Señor, yo estaba en sí misma y Dios en sí mismo estaba.* 'I was engrossed in my thoughts and God was engrossed in his.' (Oroz 1966:379). Very frequent in educated Chilean is the use of an indefinite redundant *le*, as in *Se me le cayó*. This shows emotional involvement of the speaker in the event being described (Kany 1945:139). Three unstressed pronouns in succession are extremely rare in Spanish.

A few Chilean adverbs differ from standard Latin American. Very popular on Chiloé is *desta* 'from now on', as in *Papá, desta ya no voy hasta el mes próximo.* Another Chilote temporal is *contra más*, meaning '*mientras más*': *Contra más tarde lleguemos, peor será.* A general Chilean locative is *lo de* '*casa de*': *Voy a lo de Pedro.* Some speakers may omit *de* in this expression: *Se fué pa lo el capitán.* Another locative is *en*, for '*en casa de*': *Alojé en un amigo* (Oroz 1966:392-393).

Prepositional usage in Chile occasionally differs from that of other dialectal areas of Latin America. In some locative expressions, *en* is used in place of *a*:

Pasé en el mercado 'Pasé a . . .'
Llegué en un viejito que estaba haciendo carbón 'Llegué a . . .'

En may also be used for *con*: *¿Qué sacan en llorar?* And *con* may be used for *de*: *Me dejé con la hiladura 'Dejé de hilar'.* *De* may also be replaced by *a*, a Gallicism: *cocina a gas.* Standard Spanish *estar para* plus an infinitive 'to be about to' or 'on the point of' in Chilean *lengua vulgar* is *estar por*: *Está por caer.* Locative prepositions are sometimes omitted:

Llegamo Tocopilla (a Tocopilla)
Comí la casa de ella (Comí en)

Prepositions are frequently deleted before the relative *que*:

Yo no visito la casa que él vive (en que)
Me fuí a Europa con la familia que vivo (con que) (Oroz 1966:399-402)

The lexicon of Chilean Spanish, while relatively Standard, contains a number of local items which may be differentiated on two axes, the age of the speaker and his socioeconomic status. The older people (over 30) are more conservative while the youngsters (13-20) are more creative, and it is they who coin neologisms, the majority of which fall into the semantic areas of social life and people's traits, conditions, and feelings. These terms tend to be derogatory, unlike those used by the more mature, who generally are positive. Younger people also use more varied figures of speech and the intensifiers *híper*, *súper*, and *más*. The older groups use fewer figures and employ affixes for diminutives and augmentatives, twice as often as the younger speakers. The language of the two older groups is more differentiated than that of the younger people, which is more homogeneous, probably because of the greater educational opportunities available today (Lagos-Sandoval 1980:94-95).

These local lexical items in the following glossary—which is by no means exhaustive—belong to the five categories of school, work, home, social interaction, and physical or emotional characteristics. They will be labeled Y for the younger speakers, O for their elders, 1 for the upper class, and 2 for the laboring class.

Table 14 A sample of Chilean colloquialisms.

I. School category (25)

User	Term	Meaning	Comment
Y1,2	*correrse*	'cut class'	(St.Sp. 'be embarrassed')
O1,2	*hacer la cimarra*	'cut class'	(*cimarra* 'maverick')
Y1	*no cachar ni cobre*	'not understand'	('not even a penny')
Y2	*no cachar la onda*	'not understand'	('be tuned out')
O2	*quedar colgado*	'not understand'	('be hung up')
Y1,2	*torpedo*	'crib notes'	
O1,2	*torpedo*	'crib notes'	
O2	*sapear*	'copy on exam'	
Y1	*luquiar*	'copy on exam'	(< Engl. *look*?)
Y1	*irme como el ajo*	'flunk exam'	
Y1	*irme híper mal*	'flunk exam'	
Y2	*irme como la mona*	'flunk exam'	
Y1	*sacar la mugre a*	'punish'	
O2	*sacar la mugre a*	'punish'	
O2	*aforrar*	'punish'	(St.Sp. 'bind a book'/'line clothing')
O2	*atrincar*	'punish'	(St.Sp. 'subdue')
Y2	*lumear*	'punish'	(Map. *luma* 'policeman's club')
O1	*retárselo*	'punish'	
Y1,2	*mateo*	'A+ student'	(St.Sp. 'checkmate')
O1,2	*mateo*	'A+ student'	(St.Sp. 'checkmate')
Y1	*irme super bien*	'get A on exam'	
Y1	*irme a la pinta*	'get A on exam'	(card game with betting?)
Y2	*irme capísimo*	'get A on exam'	
O1	*irme regio*	'get A on exam'	
O2	*irme flor*	'get A on exam'	
Y1,2	¡*córtala*!	'stop bothering me'	(cf. Engl. 'cut it out')
Y2	*cabréate*	'stop bothering me'	('go bore yourself')
O2	*cabréate*	'stop bothering me'	('go bore yourself')

II. Work category (9)

User	Term	Meaning	Comment
O2	*billete*	'monthly salary'	('paycheck'/'banknote')
Y1,2	*estar pato*	'be broke'	(from *empatado*?)
O2	*estar pato*	'be broke'	(from *empatado*?)
Y1	*empatado*	'be broke'	('tied score' > 'income and outgo are equal'?)
Y1	*estar pelado*	'be broke'	('skinned')
Y2	*estar sin chaucha*	'be broke'	(Mapuche 'new potato kept for seed' > 'small, worthless coin')
O1	*andar afligido*	'be broke'	
Y1	*súper cansado*	'very tired'	(< Engl.?)
O2	*choreado*	'very tired'	(*choro* 'clam')
Y1,2	*se me fué la onda*	'be forgetful'	('be tuned out')
O2	*se me fué la onda*	'be forgetful'	('be tuned out')

III. Home category (17)

User	Term	Meaning	Comment
Y1	*tú*	'you'	(always when addressing parent)
Y2	*tú*	'you'	(sometimes when addressing parent)
O1	*tú*	'you'	(sometimes when addressing parent)
O1	*usted*	'you'	
O2	*usted*	'you'	(always when addressing parent)
Y1,2	*once-comida*	'snack'	(with a drink usually, at 5 or 6 p.m.)
O1,2	*once-comida*	'snack'	
Y1,2	*living*	'living room'	(has displaced *sala*)
O1,2	*living*	'living room'	(has displaced *sala*)
Y1,2	*pieza del cachureo*	'storeroom'	(*cachureo*: 'cosas abandonadas')
O1,2	*pieza del cachureo*	'storeroom'	
Y2	*pilchas*	'clothing'	(Argentina: 'cowboy's whole outfit, including his equipment')
O2	*pilchas*	'clothing'	
Y1,2	*polera*	'T shirt'	(< *polo*)
O1,2	*polera*	'T shirt'	(< *polo*)

User	Term	Meaning	Comment
Y1,2	*chomba*	'sweater'	(Mapuche? Quechua?)
O1,2	*chomba*	'sweater'	(Mapuche? Quechua?)
Y1	*suéter*	'sweater'	(Engl.)
O1	*suéter*	'sweater'	(Engl.)
Y1,2	*chalas*	'sandals'	(Quechua)
O1,2	*chalas*	'sandals'	(Quechua)
Y1,2	*bototos*	'military boots'	(humorously despective)
O1,2	*bototos*	'military boots'	(humorously despective)
Y2	*calamorros*	'workboots'	(< 'miners' or soldiers' boots')
Y1	*rasco*	'ill dressed person'	(< *rasca* 'drunkenness')
Y1	*peliento*	'ill dressed person'	(< *piel* 'skin'? <*pelería* 'shedding' <*pelo* 'hair'?)
O2	*destartalado*	'ill dressed person'	(In St.Sp. used only for inanimate objects)
Y1	*en pelotas*	'naked'	(< *piel* 'skin' + -*ot*- despective)
Y2	*pilucho*	'naked'	(< *piel* + -*uch*-
O2	*pilucho*	'naked'	despective)

IV. Interpersonal category (41)

User	Term	Meaning	Comment
Y1	*salir a lesiarla*	'fool around'	(< *leso* 'fool')
O2	*pichanga*	'small party for friends and family'	(< Mapuche *pichi* 'small'?)
Y1	*malón*	'pot luck dinner'	(< Mapuche 'Indian raid')
O1	*malón*	'pot luck dinner'	(< Mapuche 'Indian raid')
Y2	*pichanga*	'pot luck dinner'	(< Mapuche *pichi* 'small')
O2	*pichanga*	'pot luck dinner'	(< Mapuche *pichi* 'small')
Y2	*fiestoca*	'large party'	(fiesta + despective suffix)

User	Term	Meaning	Comment
O2	*fiestoca*	'large party'	
Y1	*chamullear*	'haggle'	(< Chilean *chamullar* 'talk wildly/lie/cheat')
Y2	*meter chamullo*	'haggle'	(same as above)
Y1,2	*micro*	'small city bus'	(< *microbús*?)
O1,2	*micro*	'small city bus'	(< *microbús*?)
Y1,2	*liebre*	'minibus'	('rabbit' in St.Sp.
O1,2	*liebre*	'minibus'	Perhaps a Volkswagen Rabbit?)
Y1	*lata de sardinas*	'minibus'	('can of sardines')
Y1,2	*vereda*	'sidewalk'	(< *vereda* 'path,'
O1,2	*vereda*	'sidewalk'	also Arg.)
Y1,2	*está más rayado/-a*	'out of date'	('like a scratched record')
Y2	*fuera de onda*	'out of date'	('be tuned out')
Y1,2	*fome*	'displeasing'	(< Brazilian Port.
O1	*fome*	'displeasing'	'hunger' as in Engl. 'strictly from hunger')
Y1	*latoso*	'displeasing'	(< *lata* 'tin' > 'nonsense')
Y2	*penca*	'displeasing'	('thorny leaf of
O2	*penca*	'displeasing'	century plant or cactus')
O2	*me cae penca*	'I dislike him/her'	
Y1	*choro*	'something entertaining'	(< Mapuche?)
Y2	*cualquier onda*	'something entertaining'	
O2	*salvaje de bueno*	'something entertaining'	(cf. 'terribly good')
Y2	*socia*	'esteemed friend'	(< *socio* 'partner')
Y1	*bastante choro/-a*	'helpful'	(< Mapuche?)
O2	*paleteado*	'helpful friend'	(St.Sp. 'row hard but badly' > Chilean 'slap a friend on back')
O1	*afuerino*	'outsider'	(cf. Arg. *pafuerano*)
O2	*afuerino*	'outsider'	(cf. Arg. *pafuerano*)
Y1	*choreado*	'feel out of place'	
Y1	*fuera de órbita*	'feel out of place'	('out of orbit')
Y2	*fuera de onda*	'feel out of place'	('out of tune')

User	Term	Meaning	Comment
O2	*como pollo/gallo en corral ajeno*	'feel out of place'	
Y2	*puchos*	'cigarettes'	(< Mapuche 'cigarette butt'/ 'youngest child in family')
O2	*pitillos*	'cigarettes'	(Andalusian slang, lit., 'little whistle')
Y1	*pitear*	'smoke'	(< *pitillos*)
O2	*pitar*	'smoke'	(< *pitillos*)
Y1	*verde*	'cop'	(color of uniform)
Y1,2	*paco*	'cop'	(< *Francisco*?)
O2	*paco*	'cop'	(< *Francisco*?)
Y2	*carabinero*	'cop'	(< Ital. *carabiniere*?)
O1,2	*carabinero*	'cop'	(< Ital. *carabiniere*?)
Y1,2	*tira*	'detective'	(< *tirar* 'pull in'?)
Y2	*juanita*	'patrol car'	(< *Juan el gordo*
O2	*juanita*	'patrol car'	'child's game of tag' in Chile?)
Y1,2	*cuca*	'paddy wagon'	(< *cucaracha*?)
O1	*cuca*	'paddy wagon'	(< *cucaracha*?)
O1,2	*furgón*	'paddy wagon'	('boxcar')
Y2	*para cantar*	'to squeal'	(cf. Engl. 'squeal'/
O2	*para cantar*	'to squeal'	'sing'

V. Human characteristics and conditions (44)

User	Term	Meaning	Comment
Y1,2	*guagua*	'baby'	(Quechua)
O1,2	*guagua*	'baby'	(Quechua)
Y1	*cabrita*	'grade school girl'	(cf. Engl. 'kid')
Y1	*lola chiquilla*	'adolescent girl'	(< diminutive of *Dolores*? or Mapuche *pololo* 'boyfriend'?)
Y2	*lola*	'adolescent girl'	(same as above)
O1,2	*lola*	'adolescent girl'	(same as above)
Y1,2	*súper bonita*	'attractive, sexy girl'	
Y1,2	*súper buena*	'attractive, sexy girl'	

User	Term	Meaning	Comment
Y2	*encachado*	'attractive male'	(< Rogue slang *la*
O2	*encachado*	'attractive male'	*de cachas* 'small knife'?)
O1	*estupendo*	'handsome man'	
Y1	*pinchar*	'feel mutual sexual	(St.Sp 'puncture')
Y2,O1	*estar pinchando*	attraction'/'succeed in amorous relationships'	
O2	*estar colocado*	same as above	
Y1	*pololear*	'to date formally'	(< Mapuche *pololo*)
O1	*pololear*	'to date formally'	(< Mapuche *pololo*)
Y2	*pololeo*	'dating formally'	(< Mapuche *pololo*)
O2	*pololeo*	'dating formally'	(< Mapuche *pololo*)
O2	*se mejora*	'have a baby'	
Y1	*andar como los/las tristes*	'feel ill'	
O1	*no valer un peso*	'feel ill'	(cf. Engl. 'not worth a cent')
Y2	*como la mona*	'feel ill'	(< St.Sp. 'feel ill'/ 'have a hangover')
O2	*como la mona*	'feel ill'	
Y2	*como pollo*	'feel cold'	
Y1	*parar las chalas*	'die'	(*chalas* 'sandals')
Y2	*parar las patas*	'die'	
O2	*irse cortado*	'die'	
Y1	*piña*	'head'	(< St.Sp. 'pineapple')
Y1	*pensadora*	'head'	
Y2	*coco*	'head'	(< St.Sp. 'coconut')
Y2	*nuca*	'head'	(< St.Sp. 'nape of neck')
O1,2	*el mate*	'head'	(St. Cono Sur 'gourd')
Y2	*patas*	'feet'/'legs'	(General informal Spanish, humorous)
Y1,2	*cuatrojos*	'bespectacled person'	(cf. Engl. 'four eyes')
O1,2	*cuatrojos*	'bespectacled person'	
Y1	*piticiego/-a*	'bespectacled person'	(Quechua prefix *piti-* '*poco*,' 'a little blind'

User	Term	Meaning	Comment
Y2	*piti*	'bespectacled person'	(apocopated form of *piticiego*)
Y1	*chancha*	'fat person'	(St.Sp. *chancho/-a* 'hog'; cf. Engl. 'pig')
Y2	*ballena*	'fat person'	(St.Sp. 'whale')
Y2	*penca*	'ugly person'	('thorny leaf of century plant or cactus')
O2	*federico*	'ugly person'	(wordplay on *feo*, similar to Australians or cockneys)
Y1	*lateado*	'bored'	(< Sp. slang *lata* 'boring talk' < 'tin can noise')
O1	*lateado*	'bored'	
O2	*choreado*	'bored'	(< *choro*)
Y1	*le patina*	'stupid'	(< L.A. idiom 'Le patinan las moscas en la cabeza' 'Flies skate on his head')
Y1,2	*rayado*	'stupid'	(like 'a scratched record')
O2	*rayado*	'stupid'	(like 'a scratched record')
Y1	*cocido*	'drunk'	(St.Sp. 'boiled')
O2	*curado*	'drunk'	(cf. Engl. 'pickled')
Y1	*p'al gato*	'beaten'/'wounded'	('for the cat'; cf. Engl. 'something the cat dragged in')
Y1	*apaleado*	'beaten'/'wounded'	(beaten with a *palo* 'stick')
O1	*apaleado*	'beaten'/'wounded'	
Y2	*machacado*	'beaten'/'wounded'	('mashed')
O2	*machacado*	'beaten'/'wounded'	('mashed') (Lagos-Sandoval 1980:13-31)

Of these 135 lexical items, 102 (75.5%) descend from Spanish; 14 come from Mapuche (10.4%). Quechua and English have each contributed five bases (3.7%), Italian two (1.48%), and Portuguese one (.7%). The history of six terms is unknown. Almost two-thirds of the total are figurative in nature, for the most part metaphoric. The frequency of figures of speech in each of the five categories can be seen in Table 15:

Table 15 Percentages of figurative items per category.

	Category	Total no. of items	No. of fig. of sp.	Percentage
I.	School	24	16	66.7
II.	Work	9	6	66.7
III.	Home	17	5	29.4
IV.	Interpersonal	41	29	70.7
V.	Human Traits and Conditions	44	28	63.6
	Totals	135	84	62.2 (Average)

Predictably, the categories with numerous figures of speech refer to those subjects in life which arouse emotion. In contrast, the household category, III, contains many neutral terms such as those referring to 'living room', 'storage room', or to 'clothing', 'sweater', and 'T shirt'.

Of the 84 figurative items, one-fourth, 21, refer to 14 different animals:

ballena 'whale	*gato* 'cat'
cabrita 'kid'	*liebre* 'rabbit'
cimarra 'maverick'	*mona* 'monkey'
cuca 'cockroach'	*pato* 'duck'
chancha 'sow'	*pollo* 'chicken'
choro 'mussel'	*sapo* 'toad'
gallo 'rooster'	*sardina* 'sardine'

Of the 21 animalian figures, seven, or 33%, refer to marine creatures, one to a whale, one to a sardine, and five to mussels, *choros*. The older members of the uneducated class associate *choreado* with negative meanings, 'to be very tired' or 'bored'. The younger members of the upper class also attribute a negative meaning to *choreado*: 'to feel out of place'. But to these youngsters, the base, *choro*, has positive connotations: *choro/-a* is 'something entertaining' and *bastante choro* is 'helpful'. One may suspect that the past participle formed from *choro* is an older figure and the adjectival newer, used mainly by the youth.

Throughout Latin America, young people refer to themselves as *la onda nueva*, 'the new wave'. It is not surprising, therefore, that *onda* in the sense of 'dial reading when tuning in a radio or TV station' should be strengthened among the young and, as an 'in-word', serve as fruitful ground for breeding new metaphors. For a young person to be 'off the beam', for whatever reason, is negative:

fuera de onda 'out of tune'	*no cachar la onda* 'not understand'
fuera de onda 'out of date'	*se me fue la onda* 'forget'

The meanings 'out of tune' and 'out of date' may combine the generational and the technical senses. *Cualquier onda* on the other hand is affirmative —'whatever channel' one tunes in is likely to be 'something entertaining'.

Also notable in this sample is the high number of despectives, 86 out of 135 or 63.7% (see Table 16). Again, the most numerous despectives are to be found in the semantic areas involving subjective reactions: work, school, human traits, and interpersonal relations. The household category with its neutral terms is once again of little interest. Some of the despectives are figurative and some are not. Metaphoric and despective are most of those with animalian referents, such as *cimarra* 'truant' and *chancha* 'fatso'. There are three despective metaphors with the base *penca* 'thorny leaf of a century plant or cactus', and these mean 'something displeasing', 'an ugly person', or 'a person I don't like'. Literal despectives include *luquiar* 'copy on an exam', and *apaleado* 'beaten with a stick'.

Table 16 Percentage of despective items per category.

	Category	Total no. of items	No. of fig. of sp.	Percentage
I.	School	24	18	75.0
II.	Work	9	8	88.9
III.	Home	17	5	29.4
IV.	Interpersonal	41	26	63.4
V.	Human Traits and Conditions	44	29	65.9
	Totals	135	86	63.7 (Average)

Samples of popular speech in Chile were first collected by Rodolfo Lenz, who arrived there from Germany in 1890. What little Spanish he knew had been acquired in university classes in his homeland, and he lacked training in the dialects of Spain. As a result, whatever he heard that was different from his school-boy Spanish he supposed to be peculiar to Chile (Alonso 1940a:281). This seeming disadvantage, however, enabled him to view Chilean pronunciation in an objective way. A skilled phonetician, he transcribed the speech of Chileans exactly as he heard it, so well that Amado Alonso said that in 'la historia de la fonética española, Lenz ha de figurar siempre en lugar de honor' (1940b).

One of his phonetic transcriptions showing the pronunciation of a cultured Chilean is extracted here (and followed by a version in standard orthography):

uŋ gránde ᵈe 'pána-abandonába   kon frekuénsia su palásio ᵈe ma-
drí i se-ibᾶ-alχéte ¿a ke nó sáben u'tée(s) a ké íba? pue-síbᾶ sakál la
trípa   ᵈe máláno, porke le suseᵈiᵥ-una kósa muí řára : no poᵈia-atra-
besár bokáɔ-en su kása, auŋke su kosinéro e'tuᵈiába kon el mi'mísimo
demónio para-abrílle lapetíto, y en alχéte komía kom(ɔ) un saᵇanón
del bódrio kargáo ᵈe pimentón y asafrán koŋ ke sɔ-alimentáᵇan, tumbáo'
kon él en lo-súrko', lo'trabaxa(ᵈ)óre ðɔ-úna posesión ke tení-ayí...

pepíyo sɔ-apresuró-a baxár de lo-sěřo', saliéndɔ-al eŋkuéntro dɔakél
señór kon el líbro baxo-ɔl bráso y el sombréro, góřa o lo ke ɸ(u)éseɔn
la máno.

Un Grande de España abandonaba con frecuencia su palacio de Madrid y se iba a Algete. ¿A que no saben Vds. a qué iba? Pues iba a sacar la tripa de mal año, porque le sucedía una cosa muy rara: no podía atravesar bocado en su casa, aunque su cocinero estudiaba con el mismísimo demonio para abrirle el apetito, y en Algete comía como un sabañón del bodrio cargado de pimentón y azafrán con que se alimentaban, tumbados con él en los surcos, los trabajadores de una posesión que tenía allí . . .

Pepillo se apresuró a bajar de los cerros, saliendo al encuentro de aquel señor con el libro bajo el brazo y el sombrero, gorra o lo que fuese, en la mano (Lenz 1940a:198-199).

It is interesting to compare this passage with an illustration of the pronunciation of an uneducated peasant:

la kalcóna

é'to' éraŋ dó' kasáo ke bibían en eɹ saɹto, teníaŋ kínta, slémbra' i tɾe' niŋíto. er marío salí-a tɾa(ᵇ)axál. lo kel marío salí-a tra(ᵇ)axál benía éya i s-ecába únosúŋto ke tenía debáxo el katɾe i salía éya, pué', éc-obéxa e'koŋdíer marío i dexába lon niŋíto sólo. yúna bé' yegól marío i no layó. i preguŋtó por éya. leixéron lo' niŋíto kə abía salío i se ɸé él pa su tɾabáxo. kuáŋdo yegó, senoxó kon éya i le preguŋtó óŋdə aŋdába i le íxo ke abía éido. asér únɐ elixénsia. yəl ótɾo día kuando se ɸé lómbre pal tɾabáxo le íxo ke nó ɸéra asél lo ke íso ayél. eŋtóⁿse éya le dió ɾábia i lo íso airér. yel ómbre le' abía exáo díco a lon niŋíto ke lawoitáran. lo ke salió él, eŋtɾó éya paéŋtɾo e la kása i lo' niŋíto la ɸéron awoitál, i la bíeroŋ ke sakó úna' oyíta ke tenía ebáxo əl kátɾe i secó poɹ tò er kuérpo i salió éca obéxa i salió. se ɸé; yeɹ niŋíto ke lawoitó, no lo bió éya. ɸé er niŋíto ke lawoitó i le díxo a lo' ótɾo: mi mamíta salió éc-obéxa. yeɹ der médio le íxo: bámo' a ecállo' losótɾo tamién, pa seyír a mi mamíta, a ber óŋde bá. i secáron i kiáron a loríya er ɸégo éco soɾíto. en é'to yéga ər páire i lo' ayó eco sóɾo. yéɹ taŋ. enoxáo le' preguŋtó: i tu mamíta ¿óŋde 'tá? yer mayól le koŋte'tó: salió éc-obéxa. yel ómbre le preguŋtó: i los úŋto, ¿óŋde lo éxa? yeɹ niŋíto se lo ɸé a entɾegál. el páire lecó úŋto a lo' cikíyo i lo' íso kri'tiáno yeŋtóⁿse agaɾó la' óya i la' e'paró pa ɸéra. íso tíra los úŋto i lo ecó ar ɸégo. kuaŋdo yegó éya taŋ· enoxá i leíxo: yá nó me berí'má', i salió aŋdáɾ yen lo' peasíto ke keábaŋ de la' oyíta er pegaíto secó éya a'ta mitá er kuérpo; keó la mitá éca kri'tiána i la mitá éca obéxa; i se salió aŋdáɾ i se ɸé ar kombéŋto e la domínika i déi la koɾiéron i se ɸé éya. i yá éɹ se ɸé a koⁿɸesál der pekáo ke kometió i niŋgúm páire lo iⁿsorbió [1]; i lo maŋdáron pa ɾóma i puayá keó él, yéya keó éc-obéxa akí. la koɾetiáron lo' niŋo, i la macukáron múco a'ta ke se murió. i sə akabó ər kuéŋto.

La calchona

Éstos eran dos casados que vivían en el Salto; tenían quinta, siembras y tres niñitos. El marido salía a trabajar. Lo que el marido salía a trabajar, venía ella y se echaba unos untos, que tenía debajo del catre, y salía ella, pues, hecha oveja escondida del marido y dejaba los niñitos solos. Y una vez llegó el marido y no la halló. Y preguntó por ella. Le dijeron los niñitos que había salido y se fué él para su trabajo. Cuando llegó, se enojó con ella y le preguntó dónde andaba, y le dijo que había ido a hacer una diligencia. Y al otro día, cuando se fué el hombre para el trabajo, le dijo que no fuera a hacer lo que hizo ayer. Entonces ella le dió rabia y lo hizo adrede. Y el hombre les había dejado dicho a los niñitos que la aguaitaran. Lo que salió él, entró ella para adentro de la casa y los niñitos la fueron a aguaitar, y la vieron que sacó unas ollitas que tenía debajo del catre y se echó por todo el cuerpo y salió hecha oveja y salió. Se fué; y el niñito que la aguaitó no lo vió ella. Fué el niñito que la aguaitó y les dijo a los otros: "Mi mamita salió hecha oveja". Y el del medio le dijo: "Vamos a echarlos nosotros también para seguir a mi mamita, a ver dónde va." Y se echaron y quedaron a la orilla del fuego hechos zorritos. En esto llega el padre y los halló hechos zorros. Y él tan enojado les preguntó: "Y tu mamita ¿dónde está?" Y el mayor le contestó: "Salió hecha oveja." Y el hombre le preguntó: "Y los untos, ¿dónde los deja?" Y el niñito se los fué a entregar. El padre les echó untos a los chiquillos y los hizo cristianos y entonces agarró las ollas y las disparó para afuera. Hizo tira los untos y los echó al fuego. Cuando llegó ella tan enojada y le dijo: "¡Ya no me veréis más!" y salió a andar y en los pedacitos que quedaban de las ollitas, el pegadito se echó ella hasta mitad del cuerpo; quedó la mitad hecha cristiana y la mitad hecha oveja; y se salió a andar y se fué al convento de la Domínica y de ahí la corrieron y se fué ella. Y ya él se fué a confesar del pecado que cometió y ningún padre lo absolvió; y lo mandaron para Roma y por allá quedó él, y ella quedó hecha oveja aquí. La corretearon los niños, y la machucaron mucho, hasta que se murió. Y se acabó el cuento (Lenz 1940a:204-207).

(Listen to Tape 2, selection j, which records this second passage.) These two transcriptions illustrate the principal characteristics of Chilean Spanish at two social levels, their similarities and their differences. The shared traits outnumber those which are unique:

(1) Word-initial or intervocalic /d/ weakens in cultured and often disappears entirely in uncultured speech ([ðe] and [bokáo] for *bocado*; [íxo] for *dijo* and [marío] for *marido*).

(2) The same is true of intervocalic /b/ ([alimentáβan]; [tra(β)axál]).

(3) Word-initial /f/ tends to go to [ɸ] for both groups ([ɸ(u)ése]; [ɸéra]).

(4) Syllable-final /r/ and /l/ are in free variation for both groups ([aβrílle] for *abrirle*; [sárto] for *Salto*).

(5) Vibrant /r̃/ is assibilated for both groups ([r̃ára]; [r̃áβja]).

(6) The cluster [tr̃] is usually assibilated for both groups. (It does not appear in the transcription of the cultured speaker here but does in that of the uneducated in [entr̃ó] 'entró'.)

(7) An /x/ becomes a front palatal [ç] for both groups ([alçéte]; [lejçéron]).

(8) Syllable-final /s/ tends to become a glottal stop or disappear ([lo-súrkoʔ] for *los surcos*; [siémbraʔ] for *siembras*).

Lenz's transcriptions, of course, do not show the important differences in these informants' patterns of intonation.

References

Alonso, Amado. 1940a. La interpretación araucana de Lenz para la pronunciación chilena. In: El español en Chile. Eds. Amado Alonso and Raimundo Lida. Buenos Aires: Universidad de Buenos Aires. 279-289.

Alonso, Amado. 1940b. Rodolfo Lenz y la dialectología hispanoamericana. In: El español en Chile. Eds. Amado Alonso and Raimundo Lida. Buenos Aires: Universidad de Buenos Aires. 269-278.

Canfield, D. Lincoln. 1981. Spanish pronunciation in the Americas. Chicago: The University of Chicago Press.

Kany, Charles E. 1945. American-Spanish syntax. Chicago: The University of Chicago Press.

Lagos-Sandoval, Marcia. 1980. Non-standard lexical usage in the Spanish of Temuco, Chile: A case study. M.A. thesis, The University of Texas at El Paso.

Lenz, Rodolfo. 1940a. Estudios chilenos (Fonética del castellano de Chile). In: El español en Chile. Eds. Amado Alonso and Raimundo Lida. Buenos Aires: Universidad de Buenos Aires. 197-208.

Lenz, Rodolfo. 1940b. Para el conocimiento del español de América. In: El español en Chile. Eds. Amado Alonso and Raimundo Lida. Buenos Aires: Universidad de Buenos Aires. 209-268.

Oroz, Rodolfo. 1966. La lengua castellana en Chile. Santiago: Universidad de Chile.

Chapter 17
The Río Plata

The Río Plata area is unlike the rest of Latin America in several ways. For one, it has a very cosmopolitan population, as it was settled by people from the Andes, from Spain, and from non-Spanish-speaking countries of Europe, especially Italy. Further, this area has no single substratum language but instead has been influenced by a multitude of different linguistic groups: the Incas in the northwest, the Guaraní in the northeast, and others such as the Diaguitas, Querandíes, Pampas, Kénaken, Patagones, and Onas (Rosario 1970:113). Also, its inhabitants are spread over an enormous territory, the giant Argentina and the smaller Uruguay and Paraguay. As a result, there have developed a great number of subdialects which differ substantially from those of Spain, especially in phonology and lexicon.

Phonologically, Buenos Aires dominates most of Uruguay as well as the entire eastern half of Argentina, from 300 miles to the north all the way down to the southernmost tip. The segmental phonemes in this vast area do not in general differ from those of other varieties of Latin American Spanish, but there are a few that characterize the speech of this region for all social classes. Not only is no distinction made between /ʎ/ and /y/, but both are realized as [ʒ]. Moreover, many speakers devoice [ʒ] to [ʃ]:

mayo → [máʃo]
calle → [káʃe]
caballo → [kaβáʃo]
la calle Lavalle → [la káʃe laβáʃe] (Rosario 1970:115)

Unlike its neighbors to the northeast and northwest, it has no assibilated vibrant /r̄/. Syllable-final /s/, as in other lowland areas, is deleted or represented by an allophone, and, depending on the speaker, *busca* may become [búka], [búhka], or even [búxka], before a velar consonant (Canfield 1981:23). Finally, for some descendants of immigrant families, /ɲ/ is pronounced [nj] (Alonso 1948).

As for the treatment of segmentals by the less educated speakers, one finds it to be typical of substandard Spanish in general:

(1) Loss of intervocalic /d/ and syllable-final /s/ (*cansado* → [kansáo], *los panes* → [lopáne]).
(2) Reduction of consonant clusters (*examen* → [esámen], *disgusto* → [dixúhto]).
(3) Confusion of fricatives (*bueno* → [ɣuéno], *admirar* → [almirár], *fuerza* → [xwérsa]).
(4) Metathesis (*objeto* → [oxéβto], *derramar* → [r̄edamár], *vereda* → [βeðéra]).
(5) Raising of final unaccented vowels (*frente* → [frénti], *poco* → [póku]).
(6) Alteration of diphthongs (*baile* → [béjle], *veinte* → [bájnte], *jaula* → [xáβla]).

(7) Elimination of hiatus (*maíz* → [májs], *peor* → [pjór], *teatro* → [tjátro]).
(8) Misplacement of accent (*vayamos* → [báʒamos], *telegrama* → [telé-ɣrama]) (Rosario 1970:116-117).

The suprasegmentals which typify the eastern speaker include the shifting of accent to the final syllable on a structure of verb plus personal pronoun, *digamé*, as in Chile. An accented syllable is lengthened, as in Italian. Italian influence has been said to underlie the intonation contours of the urban centers of Buenos Aires and Montevideo (Rosario 1970:116-117).

The phonology of regions other than the Argentine *litoral* varies widely. In the northwest, it is Andean, with a Quechua substratum, and in the northeast it is Paraguayan, with a substratum of Guaraní. In the Andean northwest, syllable-final /s/ is not deleted, but in the northeast it is. Northwestern speakers in a rectangular patch around Santiago del Estero distinguish between /λ/ and /y/ but realize /λ/ as [ʒ], while in the northeast /λ/ is pronounced as in Castile. The entire northern one-third of Argentina has an assibilated vibrant [ř] (Canfield 1981:25-26).

In the morphosyntax of the Río Plata dialects, there is little differentiation according to geography. The greatest deviation from Latin American Spanish in general is the high degree of prestige enjoyed by *voseo*, which may be heard over the whole gamut of conversations, from the street to the professional office to the arts (Rosario 1970:118). Unlike Chile, with its plethora of special *vos* forms, the Río Plata *voseo* affects only the second person singular in the present indicative, present subjunctive, and the singular imperative. In the indicative and subjunctive, the accent is shifted to the personal ending: *vos tomás* and *vos tomés*, with the exception of the *-ir* verbs whose ending is *-ís* in the indicative. In the imperative the final [ð] is omitted, producing *tomá*, *comé* and *viví*. Radical-changing verbs maintain their stem vowel: *vos te acostás*. The second singular of *ser* is *sos* (Kany 1945:64-65).

Exclusive of *voseo*, the general traits of Río Plata resemble those of the rest of Latin America:

(1) Change of gender (*la calor, el sartén, el porción*).
(2) Apocope of *recientemente* to *recién* (*Vino recién*).
(3) Use of *lo de* in place of *casa de*.
(4) *No más* as an intensifier (*hací no más* 'just exactly that way'; *diga no más* 'just tell' (me); *lindo no más* 'very, very nice').

One strange expression is *desde ya* 'right now!' (Rosario 1970:125), probably from Brazilian Portuguese. Hypocoristic usage is responsible for *vesre 'revés'*, a language like Pig Latin in which constituent syllables of a word are scrambled. Supposedly invented by fourth-grade children, it is used by adults as well, to be funny:

gotán 'tango'
tabo 'bota'
rope 'perro'

feca con chele '*cafe con leche*'
jotraba chorede '*trabajo derecho*' (Muro 1980:3; Borges and Clemente 1968:59)

Popular and rustic Río Plata is also similar to uneducated usage elsewhere:

(1) Anomalous plurals in -*ses* for nouns which end in a stressed vowel (*sofases*, *ñanduses* 'ostriches').
(2) Use of *los* for *nos* (*los vamos* instead of *nos vamos*).
(3) Infixation of object pronouns in imperatives (*sientensén*, *diganmén*).
(4) Pluralization of the impersonal verbs *haber* and *hacer* (*habían personas*, *hacen muchos años*).
(5) Preference for periphrastic verbal constructions (*venga a ver si compra* '*vea si compra*', *aplaudir la cara* 'cachetear') (Rosario 1970:117-118).

It is axiomatic that large urban centers are major sources of innovation in language. It is not surprising, therefore, that the lexicon developed in Buenos Aires and Montevideo has been and continues to be lively and imaginative. Old words, in Spanish, have received new shapes or new meanings. Moreover, the non-Hispanics, who account for more than half of the urban population, have contributed to the Río Plata vocabulary most generously. Besides the numerous additions from Italian there are imports from French and Brazilian Portuguese, sister languages, from which it is easy to accept lexical items as loans. Further, the long and close economic relationship between Argentina and Great Britain has insured the introduction and maintenance of borrowings from British English, and American English has played a part, too, as has Irish.

Lexical growth has also prospered because of the high standard of living in this area and the resulting abundance of consumer products and diversions, in addition to the highest level of literacy in Hispanic America. Furthermore, Buenos Aires, with Mexico City and Madrid, forms the triumvirate of powerful centers for telecommunications and movies, thus spreading the urban language abroad and importing elements of rural usage into the larger centers of population.

Because of the number of inhabitants in the cities and their diversity, there are diverse sorts of social dialects as well. Teenage speech is characterized by many terms which come from Cocoliche, a Spanish-Italian patois. Members of the upper classes show a strong tendency to ignore a Standard Spanish expression in favor of affecting a modern cant derided by Bioy Casares as 'el argentino exquisito'. For example, pretentious speakers and writers use words and phrases such as

actualizado 'actualized' for '*moderno*'
aglutinarse for '*unirse*'
buceador for '*el que profundiza*'
dialogar for '*pelearse con*'
fundacional for '*fundamental*'
efectivizar for '*llevar a cabo*'
microexperiencias for '*pequeñas experiencias*'
movilizarse for '*moverse*'

óptica for '*punto de vista*'
promocionar for '*promover*'
el guáter for British 'w.c.' (Bioy Casares 1978:passim)

A brief sample of popular terms in general usage is presented below. Gathered from Muro and Borges/Clemente, it consists of 159 items. Sixty-seven (42.1%) have Spanish bases with altered meanings, most of which are not neutral, especially if they refer to people. Those which are positive or commendatory are marked ' + ', the numerous despectives are marked ' − ', and a few, which have to do with human activities, including crime and violence, are bivalent, ' ± ', depending on the speaker, listener, and their attitudes. Those which express neither approval nor disapproval are marked '0'. Those which are humorous are marked 'H', and the absence of humor is indicated by ' − H'. Some of these terms are literal (signalled by 'lit') and those which are figurative have been labeled with the following abbreviations: 'met' (for metaphor), 'an. met' (for animalian metaphor), 'meton' (for metonymy), 'onom' (for primary or secondary onomatopoeia), 'irony', or 'hypocor' (for hypocoristic, that is, either shortened forms or baby talk).

A sample of Argentinean and Uruguayan words of Spanish origin (66).

I. Human appearances, attitudes, and emotions (20)

Lexical item:	Meaning:	Affect, humor, and figure:	Literal meaning:
azotea	'head'	−, H, met	'flat roof'
pensadora	'head'	0, H, meton	'thinker'
fosforera	'head'	−, H, met	'matchbox'
mate	'head'	−, H, met	'gourd'
jeta	'face'	−, H, an. met	'snout'
jetón	'ugly face'	−, H, an. met	'big snout'
pinta	'good looks'	+, H, met	'paint'
tarro	'good luck'	+, H, met	'stein'
metejón	'amorous passion', 'crush'	0, H, meton	'big push'
podrido/-a	'bored', 'impatient'	−, H, met	'rotten'
seco/-a	'bored', 'impatient'	−, H, met	'dry'
opio	'something boring'	−, H, met	'opium'
bodrio	'something boring, unpleasant'	−, H, met	'soup kitchen food'

Lexical item:	Meaning:	Affect, humor, and figure:	Literal meaning:
la muerte en carroza	'something boring or unpleasant'	−, H, met	'death in a cart'
la muerte en bicicleta	'something boring or unpleasant'	−, H, met	'death on a bicycle'
colorinche	'screamingly bright color'	−, H, blend? onom?	'color' + 'bellow'?
amarrete	'stingy'	−, H, met	'tie yourself up!'
crudo/-a	'inexperienced'	−, H, met	'raw'
jabón	'fright'	−, H, met	'soap'
palmado/-a	'exhausted'	−, H, met	'decked with funereal palm fronds'

II. Human activities (17)

Lexical item:	Meaning:	Affect, humor, and figure:	Literal meaning:
largar el rollo	'tell everything you know'	−, H, met	'hand over the roll'
llorar la carta	'try to arouse sympathy'	−, H, met	'bewail the letter'
garronear	'beg', 'cadge'	−, H, an. met	'to spur'
meter el perro	'try to cheat'	−, H, an. met	'sic the dog on'
engrupir	'deceive'	−, H, met	'to group'
grupo	'gossip or lie'	−, H, met	'group'
un corso de contramano	'exaggerate'	−, H, an. met	'rub against the nap'
no te mandés la parte	'don't exaggerate!'	−, H, met	'don't send in an official report'
andá a cantarle a Gardel	'don't exaggerate!' 'don't give me that baloney!'	−, H, met	'go sing to Gardel'.
cachar	'kid someone'	±, H, met	'smash'; Engl. 'catch'
yugar	'to work'	−, H, an. met	'to yoke'
piolar	'be a showoff'	−, H, met	'twirl the rope'
empilcharse	'dress up'	+, H, irony	'put on one's rags'
picárselas	'go away', 'leave'	±, H, an. met	'spur a horse'

Lexical item:	Meaning:	Affect, humor, and figure:	Literal meaning:
tomárselas	'go away', 'leave'	±, H, met	'take one's bags'
borrarse	'go away', 'leave'	±, H, met	'erase oneself'

III. Types of people (14)

Lexical item:	Meaning:	Affect, humor, and figure:	Literal meaning:
gallego/-a	'(any) Spaniard'	−, H, met	'Galician'
tano/-a	'Italian'	−, H, hypocor	'Italian'
gringo/-a	'Italian or other foreigner'	−, H, met	'Greek'
mina	'girl', 'woman'	0, H, met	'mine'
diarero	'newspaper boy'	0, −H, meton	'daylier'
hincha	'football fan'	+, H, met	'inflate'
amigazo	'good friend'	+, −H, lit	'big friend'
gil	'credulous person'	−, H, met	(from Gil Blas)
orejero	'gossiper'	−, H, meton	'ear-er'
garronero	'cadger', 'sponger'	−, H, an. met	'spurrer'
poligrillo	'tramp'	−, H, an. met	(blend of *polilla* + *grillo*?)
boludo/-a	'stupid'	−, H, met	'large-testicled'
bienudo	'snob'	−, H, onom	(aug. of 'well')
fiambre	'corpse'	−, H, met	'cold cut'

IV. Crime and violence (4)

Lexical item:	Meaning:	Affect, humor, and figure:	Literal meaning:
adornar	'tip or bribe'	±, H, met	'adorn'
afanar	'steal'	±, H, met	'long for'
hacer pomada	'kill'	±, H, met	'make into hairoil'
hacer bolsa	'kill'	±, H, met	'make into a bag'

V. Objects and possessions (11)

Lexical item:	Meaning:	Affect, humor, and figure:	Literal meaning:
guita	'money'	+, H, met	'thin cord of hemp'

Lexical item:	Meaning:	Affect, humor, and figure:	Literal meaning:
palo	'money'	+, H, met	'the numeral '1' on a 1,000,000-peso banknote'
faso	'cigarette'	+, H, hypocor	(from *fajar* 'roll a cigarette'? cf. Pachuco *frajo*)
pilchas	'clothes'	+, H, irony	'rags, cowboy's outfit'
tapado	'shawl', 'cape'	0, −H, lit	'covered up'
catrera	'bed'	−, H, lit	'cot'
bañadera	'bathtub'	0, −H, lit	(nominalized participle)
heladera	'fridge'	0, −H, lit	'freezer'
pava	'tea kettle'	+, H, an. met	'turkey'
conventillo	'tenement house'	−, H, irony	'small convent'
loquero	'insane asylum'	−, H, lit	(from *loco*)

VI. Miscellaneous (1)

Lexical item:	Meaning:	Affect, humor, and figure:	Literal meaning:
che	'hey you!'	0, −H, lit	(Probably from Valencia *che* 'you') (Muro 1980:passim; Borges and Clemente 1986:passim)

Most of these words or phrases, of course (59 of 67, or 88%), are affectively charged. Those with positive affect refer to concepts which Argentinians find pleasing, such as having good looks, good luck, or a close friend. Those which are negative fall into several categories. One group has to do with one's subjective reaction to an unpleasant situation. Eight of these decry boredom, exhaustion, or fright. Another group criticizes types of behavior generally disapproved of in Argentine society, such as being a blabbermouth, exaggerating, showing off, gossiping, cadging, and practicing various kinds of deception. Still another group shows contempt for foreigners and those who imitate them. Three words concern poverty and/or refer to places where one would scarcely like to be ('tramp', 'tenement house', and 'insane asylum'). The four terms which have to do with crime or violence are ±, which is to say that if used by the underworld they might be commendatory of professional skill, but if by the law-abiding would be critical in the extreme. These, with four other bivalent terms, must be counted, thus, as potentially favorable, +, and potentially deprecatory, −. Added to those words which are simply either plus or minus, we find that the total of the words with favorable connotations is 18 (of the 59 which are subjective) or 30.5%, while the total of the negative or potentially negative words is 48 or 81.4%. The eight neutral terms refer, for the most part, to elements which have little affective value, one way or the other, such as 'newsboy', 'bathtub', and 'refrigerator'.

An even greater number of these lexical items, 60 of 67 (89.5%) have humorous overtones. A few of these reflect jocular approval, such as *pilchas* 'glad rags' and *empilcharse* 'dress up'. Most of the terms that express humor, however, scoff at human weaknesses or follies.

A similar number in this sample—59, or 88%—are figurative. The most frequent figure is the metaphor, accounting for 47, nine of which are animalian, all but one negative. These refer to animal snouts, rooster spurs, fierce dogs, and with *poligrillo*, a possible blend of *polilla* 'moth' plus *grillo* 'cricket'. There are five metonymies, three ironies, two hypocoristic forms, and two instances of secondary or linguistic onomatopoeia. One of these is *colorinche* 'screamingly bright color', which may consist of *color* plus the despective diminutive *-inche* or may be a blend of *color* and *berrinche* 'bellowing'.

Many social standards, of course, are well-nigh universal, and, as Ullmann has pointed out, many of the figures in which they occur are shared by different languages as well (Ullmann 1966:238). In this sample, consider, for instance, *podrido* and *seco* 'bored', analogous to English 'have a rotten time' or 'read a dry book'. *Jabón* 'fright' is similar to English 'be in a lather'. *Crudo* 'inexperienced' is like English 'a raw recruit', and *borrarse* 'erase oneself' has independently come to mean 'leave' in the Spanish of both Argentina and the southwestern United States.

The results of this analysis are summarized in Table 17.

Table 17 Spanish-based lexicon in general use in Argentina (67).

Characteristic:	Total number:	Percentage:
Neutral	8	11.9
Emotionally charged	59	88.0
Favorable (+)	18 (of 59)	31.0
Critical (−)	48 (of 59)	81.4
Humorous (H)	60	89.5
Literal (lit)	7	10.4
Figurative	59	88.0
Metaphor	47 (of 59)	79.7
Metonymy	5 (of 59)	8.5
Onomatopoeia	2 (of 59)	3.4
Irony	3 (of 59)	5.1
Hypocoristic	2 (of 59)	3.4

The sample contains 26 terms (16.5%) with Italian bases.

Argentinean and Uruguayan words of Italian origin (26).

I. Human appearances, attitudes, and emotions (6)

Lexical item:	Meaning:	Affect, humor, and figure:	Literal meaning:
yeta	'bad luck'	−, H, met	(from *iettatore* 'possessor of evil eye'?)
facha	'untidy appearance'	−, H, met	*faccia* 'face'
batifonda	'loud, unpleasant noise'	−, H, met	*battifondo* 'beat the base'
estrilar	'be enraged'	−, H, met	*strillare* 'scream'
berretín	'fit of rage'	−, H, met	*berretino*, 'child's cap'
piantao	'crazy'	−, H, met	(from *piantare* 'forsake' or *spiantare* 'demolish')

II. Human activities (8)

Lexical item:	Meaning:	Affect, humor, and figure:	Literal meaning:
morfar	'eat gluttonously'	−, H, meton	*morfire* 'to mouthe'
escarpir	'to walk'	±, H, meton	*scarpe* 'shoes'
yirar	'run around'	±, H, meton	*girare* 'turn', 'rotate'
guardar	'watch out'	±, −H, lit	*guardare* 'watch'
laburar	'to work'	±, −H, lit	*lavorare* 'work'
fato	'date', 'appointment'	0, −H, lit	*fatto* 'done'
tener fiaca	'feel lazy'	±, H, meton	*fiacca* 'indolence'
matufia	'deceptiveness'	−, H, met	(*mato* 'checkmate' + *fia* 'become'?)

III. Types of people (5)

Lexical item:	Meaning:	Affect, humor, and figure:	Literal meaning:
capo	'boss', 'expert'	±, −H, met	*capo* 'head'
vermicheli	'boss'	±, H, met	*vermicelli*

Lexical item:	Meaning:	Affect, humor, and figure:	Literal meaning:
bacán	'rich man'; 'pimp'	−, H, met	*baccano* 'big noise'
linyera	'tramp'	−, H, met	*legnera* 'woodpile'
salame	'stupid person'	−, H, met	*salami*

IV. Crime and violence (3)

Lexical item:	Meaning:	Affect, humor, and figure:	Literal meaning:
biaba	'beating'	−, H, met	*biavol-a* 'faded'
lunfa	'thief'	±, H, met	(perhaps from Greek *louphazo* 'lie still'?)
cana	'cop'	±, H, met	*canna* 'cane', 'policeman's billy'

V. Objects and possessions (3)

Lexical item:	Meaning:	Affect, humor, and figure:	Literal meaning:
berreta	'anything cheap'	−, H, met	*berretta* 'beret'
fungi	'hats'	−, H, met	*funghi* 'mushrooms'
pastasciuta	'dough'	0, −H, lit	*pastasciutta*

VI. Miscellaneous (1)

Lexical item:	Meaning:	Affect, humor, and figure:	Literal meaning:
chau	'hello!' 'goodbye!'	+, −H, met	(from Venetian Italian *sciavo* 'slave', 'servant') (Muro 1980:passim; Borges and Clemente 1968:passim)

In some cases the morphology or meaning of an item has been altered while in others the original signification and/or form has remained intact. At times it is extremely difficult to determine whether a meaning, especially a slang meaning, has originated in Argentina, or earlier in Italy. *Lunfa* 'thief' may or may not come from South Italian rogue slang. It is certain, however, that its derivative *Lunfardo* denotes the subdialect of Cocoliche used by the underworld. *Vermicheli* 'boss' may or may not reflect Italian argot. It is probable that *capo* 'boss' had this meaning on the continent, as did *batifonda* 'loud, unpleasant noise', which has changed only in its morphology.

The Italianate lexicon in the sample is very similar to that with Spanish bases, predictably. These terms are used by Spanish speakers of recent Italian origin who presumably share the same values as their fellow Argentinians, as well as a comparable cultural and linguistic history. The five most important features of the Spanish sample are also the five most important for the Italian items: emotionally charged, critical, humorous, figurative, and metaphoric. Unimportant in both lists are the neutral and literal. Relatively small for both is the category of favorable affect, and bivalent ± terms for both occur in the categories of human activities and crime and violence. The findings of the analysis are given in Table 18.

Table 18 Italian-based lexicon in general use in Argentina (26).

Characteristic:	Total number:	Percentage:
Neutral	2	7.7
Emotionally charged	24	92.3
Favorable (+)	10 (of 24)	41.6
Critical (−)	23 (of 24)	95.8
Humorous (H)	20	76.9
Literal (lit)	4	15.4
Figurative	22	84.6
Metaphor	17 (of 22)	77.3
Metonymy	5 (of 22)	22.7

The Portuguese-based terms in the sample, compared to those from Spanish and Italian, are relatively few in number: 12, or 7.6%.

A sample of Argentinean and Uruguayan words of Portuguese origin (12).

I. Human appearances, attitudes, and emotions (3)

Lexical item:	Meaning:	Affect, humor, and figure:	Literal meaning:
caradura	'cheeky'	− , H, met	'hard face'

Lexical item:	Meaning:	Affect, humor, and figure:	Literal meaning:
fulo/-a	'angry'	−, H, met	(from Port. noun *fula* 'haste', 'large quantity', 'type of felt for hat', 'an African people and its language', 'the act of pounding cloth in a machine to make it pliant')
bife	'slap in the face'	±, H, met	'beef'

II. Human activities (2)

Lexical item:	Meaning:	Affect, humor, and figure:	Literal meaning:
vichar	'spy on'	±, H, meton	*vigiar* 'watch'
farra	'drunken spree'	±, H, meton	*farra* 'frolic', 'get together'

III. Objects and possessions (7)

Lexical item:	Meaning:	Affect, humor, and figure:	Literal meaning:
mango	'money'	+, H, met	(from *mango* Brazilian slang for *milréis* coin, in turn from *mango* 'mango' [fruit])
tamangos	'very big shoes'	−, H, meton	*tamancos* 'rough shoe with wooden sole'
facón	'machete'	0, −H, lit	(*faca* 'knife' + aug. *-ão*)
buraco	'hole'	0, −H, lit	*buraco* 'hole'
cafúa	'jail'	−, H, met	*cafua* 'cave'
matungo	'old horse'	−, H, met	(from *matadura* 'saddle sore' + despective *-ungo*)
galpón	'shed'	0, −H, lit	*galpão* 'shed'

Since Argentina and Brazil share a common border, one might expect these loans from Portuguese to be more numerous. However, not many Brazilians have immigrated, and Hispanics have never shown much inclination to borrow from Lusitanian culture. Even so, the same five categories are the largest and the same two categories are the smallest. The words referring to objects and possessions account for over 50% of the list, and these words are tinged with a rural or workaday cast: *tamangos* 'heavy working shoes', *facón* 'machete', *matungo* 'broken-down horse', and *galpón* 'shed'. This last, oddly enough, comes from Portuguese *galpão* 'shed' which in turn derives from Nahuatl *calpulli* 'a large palatial room'. The figures for Portuguese may be seen in Table 19.

Table 19 Portuguese-based lexicon in general use in Argentina (12).

Characteristic:	Total number:	Percentage:
Neutral	3	25.0
Emotionally charged	9	75.0
Favorable (+)	4 (of 9)	44.4
Critical (−)	8 (of 9)	88.9
Humorous (H)	9	75.0
Literal (lit)	3	25.0
Figurative	9	75.0
Metaphor	6 (of 9)	66.7
Metonymy	3 (of 9)	33.3 (Muro 1980: passim; Borges and Clemente 1968:passim)

French-based words in the sample number only six, 3.7%.

A sample of Argentinean and Uruguayan words of French origin (6).

I. Human appearances, attitudes, and emotions (2)

Lexical item:	Meaning:	Affect, humor, and figure:	Literal meaning:
escracho	'face'	−, H, met	*crache* 'saliva'? *crache* 'similar'?
ragú	'hunger'	−, H, irony	*ragoût* 'stew'

II. Crime and violence (2)

Lexical item:	Meaning:	Affect, humor, and figure:	Literal meaning:
macró	'white slaver'	−, H, met	*maquereau* 'mackerel', 'madam of brothel'

Lexical item:	Meaning:	Affect, humor, and figure:	Literal meaning:
enfriar	'murder'	±, H, meton	*enfroidir* 'chill', 'murder'

III. Objects and possessions (2)

Lexical item:	Meaning:	Affect, humor, and figure:	Literal meaning:
biyuya	'money'	+, H, met	*bijou* 'jewel'
bulín	'cheap room in tenement'	−, H, met	*boulin* 'pigeon hole' (Muro 1980:passim; Borges and Clemente 1968: passim)

At least four of these six items refer to aspects of life of the underprivileged and/or criminal. Again, the predominant five categories prevail: emotionally charged, critical, humorous, figurative, and metaphor. But the humor here is hardly carefree and seems even sardonic. Surely these terms which have been incorporated into Argentine popular speech contrast with the French affected by the upper classes until just recently, when it became modish to sprinkle one's conversation with English. The figures for French-based words are given in Table 20.

Table 20 French-based lexicon in general use in Argentina (6).

Characteristic:	Total number:	Percentage:
Neutral	0	0
Emotionally charged	6	100.0
Favorable (+)	2	33.3
Critical (−)	5	83.3
Humorous (H)	6	100.0
Literal (lit)	0	0
Figurative	6	100.0
Metaphor	4 (of 6)	66.6
Metonymy	1 (of 6)	16.7
Irony	1 (of 6)	16.7

The Amerindian bases in the sample—ten or 6.3%—are three from Taíno and seven from Quechua:

A sample of Argentinean and Uruguayan words of Amerindian origin (10).

I. Human appearances, attitudes, and emotions (3)

Lexical item:	Meaning:	Affect, humor, and figure:	Literal meaning:
macanudo/-a	'wonderful'	+, H, irony	Taíno *macana* 'war club'

Lexical item:	Meaning:	Affect, humor, and figure:	Literal meaning:
batata	'timidity', 'embarrassment'	−, H, met	Taíno *batata* 'yam'
guarango/-a	'rude', 'indelicate'	−, H, meton	Quechua *huaránac* 'disastrous'

II. Human activities (3)

Lexical item:	Meaning:	Affect, humor, and figure:	Literal meaning:
tener cancha	'to be an expert'	+, H, met	Quechua *cancha* 'court for games'
macana	'lie'	−, H, met	Taíno *macana* 'war club'
sobre el pucho	'immediately'	±, H, met	Quechua *pucho* 'stub'

III. Types of people (2)

Lexical item:	Meaning:	Affect, humor, and figure:	Literal meaning:
opa	'idiot'	−, H, meton	Quechua *upa* 'deaf mute'
canchero	'expert'	+, H, met	Quechua *cancha* 'court for games'

IV. Miscellaneous (2)

Lexical item:	Meaning:	Affect, humor, and figure:	Literal meaning:
pampa	'pampa'	0, −H, lit	Quechua *pampa*
tuco/-a	'firefly'	+, −H, meton	Quechua *tuco* 'brilliant' (Muro 1980: passim; Borges and Clemente 1968:passim)

All but two of these are quite subjective in nature, referring to people, their activities, and emotions. The five categories again prevail with the difference that, among the emotionally charged, the favorable and the critical are equal in number, as opposed to all the other lists, in which the critical (−) averages 87.7%. Three of these terms are so widespread as to be general Latin American: *macana, cancha,* and *pampa, cancha* in Spain as well, and *pampa* in international usage. It is probable that most speakers who use these words have no idea of their Indian origin. The analysis is presented in Table 21.

Table 21 Amerindian-based lexicon in general use in Argentina (10).

Characteristic:	Total number:	Percentage:
Neutral	1	10.0
Emotionally charged	9	90.0
Favorable (+)	5	55.0
Critical (−)	5	55.0
Humorous (H)	8	80.0
Literal (lit)	1	10.0
Figurative	9	90.0
Metaphor	5 (of 9)	55.5
Metonymy	3 (of 9)	33.3
Irony	1 (of 9)	11.1

Excluding words with unidentified bases and those of English origin, a summary is given in Table 22.

Table 22 Summary.

Characteristic:	Span-ish (67)	Ital-ian (26)	Portu-guese (13)	French (6)	Amer-indian (10)	Aver-age
Neutral	11.9%	7.7%	25.0%	0%	10.0%	10.9%
Emotionally charged	88.0%	92.3%	75.0%	100.0%	90.0%	89.1%
Favorable (+)	31.0%	41.6%	44.4%	33.3%	55.5%	33.0%
Critical (−)	81.4%	95.8%	88.9%	83.3%	55.5%	81.0%
Humorous (H)	89.5%	76.9%	75.0%	100.0%	80.0%	84.0%
Literal (lit)	10.4%	15.4%	25.0%	0%	10.0%	12.2%
Figurative	88.0%	84.6%	75.0%	100.0%	90.0%	87.5%
Metaphor	79.7%	77.3%	66.7%	66.7%	55.5%	69.2%
Metonymy	8.5%	22.7%	33.3%	16.7%	33.3%	22.9%
Onomatopoeia	3.4%	—	—	—	—	—
Irony	5.1%	—	—	16.7%	11.1%	11.0%
Hypocoristic	3.4%	—	—	—	—	

Four lexical items in this glossary are of unknown origin.

A sample of Argentinean and Uruguayan words of unidentified sources (4).

I. Human appearances, attitudes, and emotions (2)

Lexical item:	Meaning:	Affect, humor, and figure:	Literal meaning:
mersa	'vulgar'; 'inferior'	?	?
colifa/colifato/-a	'crazy'	?	?

II. Types of people (2)

pibe	'boy'	?	?
piba/pibeta	'girl'	?	? (Muro 1980: passim; Borges and Clemente 1968:passim)

Colifa looks Italianate and may be related to *collera* 'anger, rage, passion' plus *-fato*, the Italian past participle of *fare* 'to make'. *Pibe* and its derivatives are attributed to Italian by Rosario but suggest an Indian source perhaps akin to Mapuche *piti* 'small' (Rosario 1970:12).

The words and phrases in the Río Plata lexicon discussed so far come from different sources but have similar characteristics and fall into similar categories. Neither one of these remarks can be made of the loanwords which come from English, the traits of which are almost diametrically opposed.

A sample of Argentinean and Uruguayan words of English origin (35).

I. Sports, physical activities, and games (14)

fútbol/fóbal	*ski*
handball	*tenis*
básquetbol	*gol*
béisbol	*jockey*
hockey	*hacer el footing* 'take a walk'
cricket	*bridge*
rugby	*póker*

II. Clothing, fabrics, and style (8)

jumper	*nilon/nailon*
pullóver	*wash and wear*
suéter	*stretch*
cardigan	*estar in/out*

III. Food and drink (7)

sandwich [saŋgwíče]	*cocktail/coctail/cóctel*
lunch	*gin tonic*

chinchibirra 'ginger beer' *whisky*
five o'clock 'tea'/'happy hour'

IV. Human appearances, attitudes, and emotions (1)

orsai 'out of place' – , H, met (from *offside*)

V. Types of people (1)

Johnnie 'U.S. citizen' ± , H, met

VI. Objects and possessions (1)

living room

VII. Miscellaneous (3)

night club
mitin 'meeting'
service (Muro 1980:passim; Borges and Clemente 1968:passim)

As has been seen, the items in the other samples are emotionally charged rather than neutral, humorous rather than flat, and figurative rather than literal. Among the English borrowings just the reverse is true, as Table 23 shows. Of the total of 35, only two with English bases are emotionally charged, and only these two are humorous or figurative (both are metaphoric). Why are the English terms so different? Because most of them have nonhuman, inanimate referents and hence lack affective potential, much like the 'objects and possessions' category in the other linguistic sources. The words of English origin merely name objects, diversions, and activities that have been adopted outright. Surely a term such as *wash and wear* is recognized as 'foreign' and as yet not fully Hispanized. Of the two variants which refer to football, *fútbol*, used by the upper class, contrasts with *fóbal*, used by the uneducated, showing that the process of Hispanization is under way.

Among the borrowings, the largest category has to do with sports, physical activity and games, with 14 terms (40%). Eleven of these show the Argentinians' love of sports and racing. One, *hacer el footing*, is 'take a walk', analogous to the Peninsular *flanear* from French. The second largest group consists of lexical

Table 23 Contrasting traits of English-based loanwords.

Characteristic:	Other languages:	English:
Neutral	11.0%	94.3%
Emotionally charged	89.0%	5.7%
Favorable (+)	33.0%	2.9%
Critical (–)	81.0%	5.7%
Humorous (H)	84.0%	5.7%
Literal (lit)	12.2%	94.3%
Figurative	87.5%	5.7%

items that name different kinds of clothes, fabrics, and matters of style (eight terms, 22.9%). Three refer to sweaters, filling a void that is curious in Spanish—which has no native designation for this much-worn article of clothing. *Nailon*, *wash and wear*, and *stretch* refer to modish fabrics that are considered *in* at the present time, while *minifaldas* are *out*.

The third largest category contains elements that refer to food and drink. Both *sandwich* and *lunch* fill a lexical void as *sweater* did. In Spain there is the term *emparedado* 'walled in' for a food similar to a poorboy sandwich, but not like the school children's peanut butter and jelly. *Lunch* refers to a concept hitherto alien to Hispanic culture, in which the midday meal traditionally takes hours and consists of several generous courses rather than a quick *sandwich*. *Five o'clock* may signify 'afternoon tea' or 'the happy hour', depending upon the participants. All of the terms referring to beverages reflect a British influence and may be considered upper class—the gaucho drank gin, but neat, not with tonic! *Chinchibirra*, British for 'ginger ale', exemplifies total Hispanization, like *fóbal*, and cocktail (spelled in three different ways) shows different stages in this process. *Whisky* also has variant spellings, but it always means 'Scotch', which is *in* for the wealthy.

The categories which are the largest for loans from other languages are the smallest for loans from English. For human appearances, attitudes, and emotions we have only the one word *orsai*, probably derived from sports. For types of people we have the only other figurative term, *Johnnie*, for 'a citizen of the United States' in place of *gringo*, which in Argentina is reserved for Italians. *Living room* is similar to *living*, used in Chile, and *mitin* is shared with the rest of the Hispanic world. *Night club* is replacing *cabaret*, providing another example of the present trend to borrow from English rather than French.

As English loanwords become increasingly Hispanized, they frequently receive an orthography more in accordance with Spanish. And surely they are pronounced in accord with Spanish morphology and phonology. Argentinians evidently learned *jumper* and *lunch* from their written forms and thus give them spelling pronunciation as [xúmper] and [lúnč]. *Stretch* becomes [estríč] with epenthetic [e] and perhaps hypercorrective [i]. *Night club*, [nájklu], loses syllable-final [t] and [b], conforming to majority rule. And in *wash and wear*, w becomes [gw], d drops out, and n is velarized before the following [g], producing [gwaʃaŋgwéar].

Among the peculiarities of the speech of Buenos Aires is the widespread use of Cocoliche. A compromise between Spanish and Italian, it is a transitional language, according to some linguists, destined to disappear when speakers of Italian stock become fully fused with the general population. Other linguists, however, regard it as a sort of creole, odd because based on two European sister-languages. Beginning as a pidgin in the 1890s, it has for many generations been the first dialect learned by children in the Barrio de la Boca, near the port.

To what does Cocoliche owe its existence? In the 1880s, Argentina entered a period of rapid growth and immigration. In 1880 proper, there were over 1,500 miles of railroad built by the British, and this mileage was doubled by 1886. Ship tonnage increased threefold, and because of prosperity and peaceful conditions, a flood of European immigrants poured into the country. These were Spanish, Portuguese, German, Dutch, Yugoslav, Syrian, Austrian, French, British, American, and especially Italian. The newcomers from Italy, for the most part impoverished, settled in the *Barrio de la Boca*, where housing was within their reach. Thus was created an Italian community within the city of Buenos Aires. By 1930 there were six million immigrants from Europe, and by 1961 this number had swelled by 600,000 more, enhanced after 1924 by the imposition of immigration quotas in the United States. Further, after World War II, both Argentina and Brazil signed agreements with Italy to relieve that country of some of its excess population and to admit a large number of Italians every year.

Members of the first generation doubtless spoke Italian among themselves and with their neighbors, but as the process of acculturation began, their speech became increasingly Hispanized and from this interpenetration arose Cocoliche, a language which was neither Italian nor Spanish. The first stage in this development is exemplified in the following passage from *Los políticos*, a farce by Nemesio Trejo, written in 1907 (Robategli is an Italian immigrant, Prudencio an Argentinian of Spanish descent):

Text	Standard Spanish
Robategli. Perdonate, mio caro: ¿Voi siete de la parroquia?	Robategli. Perdone, amigo mío: ¿usted es de la parroquia?
Prudencio. No, señor, soy Prudencio García.	Prudencio. No, señor, soy Prudencio García.
Robategli. Ma estare de los nostros, corre. . . corre. . .	Robategli. Pero será de los nuestros, corre. . . corre. . .
Prudencio. Yo no corro.	Prudencio. Yo no corro.
Robategli. Correligionario.	Robategli. Correligionario.
Prudencio. ¡Ah!, sí (*Aparte.*) Este también es político. (*A él.*) Correligionario, sí señor, y amante decidido de la buena causa.	Prudencio. ¡Ah!, sí (*Aparte.*) Este también es político. (*A él.*) Correligionario, sí señor, amante decidido de la buena causa.
Robategli. Ecco, ¡la nostra causa! El pane por el pobrero.	Robategli. He aquí, ¡nuestra causa! El pan para el pobre.
Prudencio. Eco, el pan para nosotros; es decir, para el pobre. (*Aparte.*) Este no va a creer que yo tengo fortuna. (*A él.*) Mi brazo, y mi mano, y mis dedos, todo está a su disposición.	Prudencio. Eco, el pan para nosotros; es decir, para el pobre. (*Aparte.*) Este no va a creer que yo tengo fortuna. (*A él.*) Mi brazo, y mi mano, y mis dedos, todo está a su disposición.
Robategli. Grazie tanto.	Robategli. Muchas gracias.
Prudencio. ¿Sabe usted lo malo que tenemos? Que los vecinos son contrarios.	Prudencio. ¿Sabe usted lo malo tenemos? Que los vecinos son contrarios.
Robategli. Lo só.	Robategli. Lo sé.

Prudencio. Este almacenero y este barbero hablan mal de usted. (*Aparte.*) Yo no conozco al barbero, pero como todos hablan mucho. . .

Robategli. Lo só.

Prudencio. Bueno, usted lo sabe todo, ¿para qué se lo voy a contar?, yo lo que necesito es dinero para luchar. Si usted se interesa por la elección, sacrifíquese y el triunfo es seguro.

Robategli. ¡Io sono il candidato!

Prudencio. ¡Ah! ¿Usted es el candidato?

Robategli. Sí, signore.

Prudencio (*Aparte.*) Este es el de los tallarines. (*A él.*) Venga esa mano, vamos al atrio y allí verá usted cómo se ganan elecciones.

Robategli. El doctor González me fa la guerra. . .

Prudencio. El doctor González es un poroto para mí. Si yo tomo una mesa y un padrón, y quinientas boletas, y no hay partido contrario que vote, le gano la elección.

Prudencio. Este almacenero y este barbero hablan mal de usted. (*Aparte.*) Yo no conozco al barbero, pero como todos hablan mucho. . .

Robategli. Lo sé.

Prudencio. Bueno, usted lo sabe todo, ¿para qué se lo voy a contar?, yo lo que necesito es dinero para luchar. Si usted se interesa por la elección, sacrifíquese y el triumfo es seguro.

Robategli. ¡Yo soy el candidato!

Prudencio. ¡Ah! ¿Usted es el candidato?

Robategli. Sí, señor.

Prudencio. (*Aparte.*) Este es el de los tallarines. (*A él.*) Venga esa mano, vamos al atrio y allí verá usted cómo se ganan elecciones.

Robategli. El doctor González me hace la guerra. . .

Prudencio. El doctor González es un frijol para mí. Si yo tomo una mesa y un padfon, y quinientas boletas, y no hay partido contrario que vote, la gano la elección (Trejo 1907:n.p.).

The speech of Prudencio is Standard Argentine Spanish, while that of Robategli contains the seeds for the growth of Cocoliche. He either speaks in Italian, mixes Italian with Spanish, or invents what he supposes to be acceptable as Spanish words. When he inquires whether Prudencio is from the same ward (*parroquia*) as he, the predominant Italian leads Prudencio to think he has been asked if he is Mr. De la Parroquia. The second misunderstanding arises when Robategli, stumbling, produces only the first two syllables of *correligionario*, which Prudencio takes for the verb ¡*Corre*! 'Run!', which he refuses to do. Communication breaks down again when Robategli uses the word *ecco*, meaning 'behold' in Italian, and Prudencio understands it as *eco*, 'echo' in Spanish. In *pobrero* there is a blend of Italian *povero* and Spanish *pobre*. Most of the time Prudencio understands Robategli, because of the similarity of the two languages being combined.

A text from a recent Buenos Aires newspaper some 70 years later shows contemporary Cocoliche:

Desde el córner

Cocoliche	Standard Spanish
En la fonda El Pescadito, mientras tragan la buseca, el hincha del Boca Juniors y el del Ríver Plate se tiran el chico al fondo.	En la fonda El Pescadito, mientras tragan el menudo, el jaleador del (equipo) de los Boca Juniors y del Ríver Plate se jactan de sus equipos.
—Credo que a la prósima doménica cuesti miyonari . . . van a saber coánta son coatro, credo. . .	—Creo que el domingo próximo estos millonarios . . . van a saber cuántos son cuatro, creo. . .
—E ostede, los hinchaforro que se la dan de vivos e palman todo los domingo, ostede van a saber coántos son once tigres inocaos de adeveras. . .	—Y ustedes, los entusiastas que se la dan de vivos y aplauden todos los domingos, ustedes van a saber cuántos son once tigres enojados deveras. . .
—¡Ma sargan de ayí, sargan, propietarios de un bulín de tre pisos, e que se deben de acostar inti yuyi de la miseria que tiéneno a la caca de la tesorería!	—¡Pero salgan de allí, salgan, propietarios de un tugurio de tres pisos, y que se deben de acostar entre malezas de la miseria que tienen en la m. . . . de la tesorería!
—¿Quién te dico, Vichensín, qu'stamo propio en la vía?	—¿Quién te dijo, amigo Vincenzo, que estamos de veras en la calle?
—¡Ma se sabe, sacramento! ¿Acaso no tovieron que dir a tirarle de la manga hasta'l goberno?	—¡Pero se sabe por Dios! ¿Acaso no tuvieron que ir a pedir dinero prestado hasta el gobierno?
—¡Moñeca, que se tenemo! Ma, de todos modo, lo que se trata de descutir ahora é la insalada que se van' comer coando vayan ayá in casa. . . cunto al río. . .	—¡Muñeca, que sí tenemos (plata)! Pero, de todos modos, lo que se trata de discutir ahora es la ensalada que se van a comer cuando vayan allá en casa. . . junto al río. . .
—¡Descoidensé, e no toquen fierro, que a lo mecor la vaca se voelve toro. . .	—¡Descuídense, y no toquen fierro, que a lo mejor la vaca se vuelve toro. . .
—¿E sabés vos lo que deberían de hacer ostede, boquenses cachagrilas, si tovieran cinco guita de vergoña e de amistá per noialtri, y fratelli que siamo como ostede de la Buca?	—¿Y sabes tú lo que deberían hacer ustedes, boquenses cazabichos, si tuvieran cinco centavos de vergüenza y de amistad para con nosotros, hermanos que somos como ustedes de la Boca? (*La Prensa* n.d.:n.p.)

This conversation differs from the previous one in several ways. The two speakers are peers, Argentinians both, who are eating *menudo* and having a jocular argument about which of their respective teams will win next Sunday's soccer game, the Boca Juniors or the River Plate. The team names show again the association of English with sports, and *córner* in the title probably means 'neighborhood hangout'. With these exceptions, their language shows the complete fusion of Argentine Spanish and Italian—there is no sense of code switching nor difficulty in communication.

While a small part of one newspaper article hardly suffices to describe the phonology of a dialect, it can show through the spellings some of its phonological characteristics. Southern Italian influence can be observed in the treatment of vowels. Unaccented /u/ is often realized as [o] as in Ecuador: *coantos, ostede, tovieron, voelve*, and *moñeca*. Conversely, /o/ may become [u], as in *Buca*. Unaccented /e/ may become [i], as in *inocaos* ('*enojados*'), *insalada*, and *inti* ('*entre*'), perhaps because of analogy with the Italian prefix *in-*. *Mecor, dico*, and *cunto* indicate that since Italian lacks /x/, Cocoliche speakers have replaced it with their closest phoneme [k].

The phonological influence exerted by popular Argentine Spanish may also be seen in several spellings. Intervocalic or final /d/ is often omitted, as in *inocaos* and *amistá*. An intrusive [d] occurs in *dir* ('*ir*'), as in gaucho Spanish. Suggestive of Andalusian are the deletion of syllable- or word-final /s/ (*tenemo, diente, ostede*), and free variation of implosive /l/ and /r/, as in *sargan*. Cocoliche speakers, like most other Argentinians, are *yeísta*: *ayí, ayá*, and *miyonari*.

The suprasegmentals of Cocoliche also reflect the influence of both Italian and Spanish. As in Italian, the vowel of a stressed syllable is lengthened, and sentence intonation also is Italianate. Argentine Spanish, like South Italian, favors the accenting of an object pronoun when it is suffixed to an imperative, as in *descoidensé*.

In morphosyntax, masculine plurals in *-i* (*miyonari, yuyi*) and the affixing of *-o* to the third plural of some verbs (*quédano, tiéneno*) reflect Italian usage. General Argentine is responsible for *vos sabés*. The lexicon of Cocoliche has many Italian words: *buseca* from *bussecchia* 'menudo' ('tripe stew'), *ma* for '*pero*', *noialtri* '*nosotros*', *fratelli* '*hermanos*', and *siamo*, '*somos*'. Cocoliche as a term is used in Buenos Aires in contrast to the word *Lunfardo*, which is applied to that Cocoliche used by the *maffiosi*. In Montevideo, however, *Lunfardo* is used for both varieties of Cocoliche, and no effort is made to separate them (Veletti 1985).

Although a separate nation politically, most of Uruguay speaks a Spanish indistinguishable from that of Argentinian Buenos Aires. (Listen to Tape 2, selection k for cultivated Uruguayan or Argentinian, and see Appendix 5.) Historically a part of Argentina, then of Brazil, and then of Argentina again, Uruguay gained its independence after the intercession of the British in 1828 and has served as a buffer state between the two warring countries since that time (*The South American Handbook* 1979:477).

That part of Uruguay where Argentine Spanish is not spoken is the one third of the country which borders on Brazil. Right at the frontier is a narrow swath where Portuguese is spoken by the masses and both Portuguese and Spanish by the educated. In a wider swath to the southwest, '*fronterizo*' Portuguese is spoken, that is, Portuguese with a sprinkling of Spanish. Continuing southwest, there is a broad strip in which most people use '*fronterizo*' Spanish, that is, Spanish with an admixture of Portuguese.

The short story *Un peón*, by the famous Uruguayan Horacio Quiroga, provides examples of the mixed speech of this area. The central character, the *peón* Olivera, crosses the border into Argentina to work on Quiroga's farm. While no linguist, Quiroga had years of experience with such employees so that his knowledge of their speech can be assumed to be fairly accurate. He describes it as 'una lengua de frontera, mezcla de portugués-español-guaraní, fuertemente sabrosa' (Quiroga 1950:407). The following are some of Olivera's remarks in conversing with his *patrón*:

Para todo trabajo. Me sé tirar de hacha y de azada. . . Tengo trabalhado antes de ahora no Foz-do-Iguassú e fize una plantación de papas.

¡Oh! O sol no hace nada. . . Tené cuidado usted de mover grande la tierra con a azada. . . ¡Y dale duro ao yuyo! El yuyo es el peor enemigo por la papa.

No importa. . . . Me gusta esta casa. Es un lugar muito lindo. . . ¡Oh Paraná do diavo! . . . Si al patrón te gusta pescar te voy a acompañar a usted. . . Me tengo divertido grande no Fox con os mangrullús.

Ahora sí, cumplo. . . ¿Qué es para facer?

¡Está bueno! ¡Fica bon! . . .

¡Condenado! . . . No trabajo más allá. O pozo que vocé fizo. . . ¡No sabes hacer para tu pozo, usted! . . . Muito angosto.

¡Isto sí que está bon! ¡Lindo, Colin! ¡Ahora voy tener para mí machete macanudo!

¡Bicho ruin! No quería caminar direito. . .

Entao. . . ¿Vocé no quiere que yo le haga por tus pozos?

Ahí tenés para tus bocayás. . . ¡Así se faz un trabajo! . . .

¡Ah, no! ¡Usted sabés muito bien que yo no robo para vocé! ¡Ah, no! ¡Nao puede vocé decir eso!

¿Y cómo que vocé me prova que yo vine para a minina? ¡Vamos a ver!

¡Diavo con o patrón! ¡Pim! ¡Pam! ¡Pum! . . . ¡Barbaridade de revólver! . . .

O, patrón. . . , ¡Hay para ver! ¡Iste sí que es un home! ¡Dale caña y pirganato! (permanganato) Aprendé para usted.

¡Ah, ah! . . . ¡Yararacusú! Ya me tenía pensado. . . ¡No Foz-do-Iguassú tengo matadas barbaridade! . . . ¡Bonitinha, a condenada! (Quiroga 1950:406-423)

Although this sample does not reveal much about the phonology of the speaker, Quiroga's use of Portuguese or of Spanish spelling would provide some clues as to how Olivera must have sounded. He probably used Brazilian Portuguese to pronounce the words which have Portuguese spelling: *trabalhado* '*trabajado*', *fox* '*hoz*', *muito* '*muy*'/'*mucho*', *diavo* '*diablo*', *fica* '*queda*', *bon* '*bueno*', *socé* '*usted*'/'*tu*', *faz* '*hace*', *minina* '*muchacha*'. The Spanish spellings may or may not have had a distinctly Spanish phonology, probably not. The suprasegmentals, since Olivera comes from the southernmost part of Brazil, are doubtless the same as those in Uruguay and Argentina, not those of the northern part of the country nor those of Lisbon. One recalls the case of a professor of Portuguese from the south of Brazil who was thought by his students to be an Argentinian, only masquerading as a Brazilian, because of his intonation.

The morphosyntax of this border dialect is reminiscent of Cocoliche in its mixture of forms and constructions from two languages which are closely related. Some parts of Olivera's utterances are entirely in Portuguese:

> *¡Oh Paraná do diavo!*
> *¡Barbaridade de revólver!*
> *¡Bonitinha, a condenada!*

Some are entirely in Spanish:

> *Para todo trabajo*
> *Me sé tirar de hacha y de azada*
> *Me gusta esa casa*
> *Ahora sí, cumplo*
> *No trabajo más allá*

There is much code-switching:

> *¡Está bueno! ¡Fica bon!*

Others of his utterances may be analyzed as either Portuguese or Spanish; since the languages are so similar, it is difficult to tell.

> *¡Hay para ver!*
> *Ya me tenía pensado*

Occasionally, he violates both Spanish and Portuguese rules for *por* and *para*: *El yuyo es el peor enemigo por la papa.*

The great majority of his remarks, however, are mixtures—in syntax and/or morphology. Occasionally, a Portuguese definite article is used with a Spanish noun, as in *O sol*, or with a Hispanized Indian word such as *os mangrullús* or *ao yuyo*. Sometimes the article occurs in Spanish, as in *el peor enemigo* or *la tierra*, or alternately in Spanish and Portuguese, as in *la tierra con a azada*. Verb blends are numerous: *fazer* '*hacer*' appears as a Portuguese base with Spanish inflections in the preterite, such as *fize* '*hice*' (for *fiz*) and *fizo* '*hizo*' (for *fêz*). To form the present perfect tense, Olivera uses the Spanish present tense of *tener* (by analogy with Portuguese *ter*) followed by a Portuguese past participle: *tengo trabalhado* and *me tengo divertido*.

Second person singular verb forms and their corresponding pronouns are especially confusing to Olivera. This is doubtless because in popular Brazilian speech a distinction is no longer made between formal address (*o senhor*, etc. + 3rd person of the verb) and informal address (*tú* + 2nd singular of the verb). Their place has been taken by neutral *você*, neither formal nor informal. His problem is compounded by the Río Plata *vos*, which sounds misleadingly like Portuguese *você*. Because of this leveling and semihomophony, Olivera does not distinguish between *vos*, *você*, *usted* and their accompanying verbs: *Usted sabés muito bien que yo no robo para você*. Here the *peón* equates *usted* and *você* but says *sabés*, since he has heard Hispanics use this verb form with *vos*. Similarly, he makes no distinction between second person pronouns in the objective and the possessive. *Você no quiere que yo le haga por tus pozos* should be informal *Tu no quieres que yo te haga pozos para ti* or formal *Usted no quiere que yo le haga pozos para usted*. Here Olivera uses *tus* instead of *ti* as a prepositional object and he pluralizes it since he has heard native speakers of Spanish do so before a following plural noun. It is very likely that these amusing errors come from a sincere desire to be correct!

One characteristic of the literature of the Americas during the nineteenth and twentieth centuries has been the increasing use of the vernacular as a vehicle for serious literature. In the United States, writers of the stature of Mark Twain and Herman Melville have based masterpieces on the language of the common man. Their counterparts in Argentina are the nineteenth-century authors of *poesía gauchesca*. In these Argentinian adaptations of Peninsular folk poetry, the central figure of the knight errant is a new hero, the gaucho. The plains of Castile become the pampa; the enemies to be overcome are no longer the Moors but savage Indians and shrewd city slickers. The earliest gauchesque poems were oral improvisations composed by gauchos around their campfires or in the local *pulpería* 'general store and saloon'. In the early nineteenth century, during the Wars of Independence, this kind of poetry first appeared in print, designed to inspire the populace to resist the Spanish authorities. Later, it gained literary stature with the publication of *Martín Fierro* by José Hernández in 1872 and 1875. While this work is political in its purpose, it has been acclaimed as a masterpiece of Hispanic literature. Other authors who cultivated this genre were Bartolomé José Hidalgo, Hilario Ascasubi, and Estanislao Del Campo.

Once Argentinians recognized this rude speech as suitable for expressing the heroic virtues of the nation, authors of the calibre of Leopoldo Lugones, Benito Lynch, and Ricardo Güiraldes perpetuated it in the twentieth century novel, although the gaucho himself had shrunk from his symbolic stature to that of a hired hand. In the period between 1915 and 1930 there appeared several Argentinian classics, the greatest of these being *Don Segundo Sombra*, reminiscent at once of both *Don Quixote* and *Huckleberry Finn*. Don Segundo is the incarnation of ideal manhood, the apotheosis of the noble values that the old gauchos are supposed to have possessed. His grave and archaic speech recalls that of *Mío Cid*, and, while it is an artificial language, it serves as a recreation of the very real language spoken by the protagonist Martín Fierro, who like Huck Finn, tells us his story in his own words. Canto II of the first part describes the happy life of the gaucho before his domination by politicians and military men from the city.

Y apenas la madrugada
empezaba a coloriar,
los pájaros a cantar
y las gallinas a apiarse,
155 era cosa de largarse
cada cual a trabajar.

Éste se ata las espuelas,
se sale el otro cantando,
uno busca un pellón blando,
160 éste un lazo, otro un rebenque,
y los pingos relinchando
los llaman dende el palenque.

El que era pión domador
enderezaba al corral,
165 ande estaba el animal
bufidos que se las pela. . .
y más malo que su agüela
se hacía astillas el bagual.

Y allí el gaucho inteligente
170 en cuanto el potro enriendó,
los cueros le acomodó
y se le sentó en seguida,
que el hombre muestra en la
    vida,
la astucia que Dios le dio.

Y verlos al cáir la tarde
en la cocina riunidos,
195 con el juego bien prendido
y mil cosas que contar,
platicar muy divertidos
hasta después de cenar.

Cuando llegaban las yerras,
¡cosa que daba calor
tanto gaucho pialador
220 y tironiador sin yel!
¡Ah tiempos. . . pero si en él
se ha visto tanto primor!

Aquello no era trabajo,
más bien era una junción,
225 y despúes de un güen tirón
en que uno se daba maña,
pa darle un trago de caña
solía llamarlo el patrón.

Pues siempre la mamajuana
230 vivía bajo la carreta,
y aquel que no era chancleta
en cuanto el goyete vía,
sin miedo se le prendía
como güérfano a la teta.

Estaba el gaucho en su pago
con toda seguridá,
255 pero áura. . . ¡barbaridá!
la cosa anda tan fruncida,
que gasta el pobre la vida
en juir de la autoridá.

Pues si usté pisa en su
    rancho
260 y si el alcalde lo sabe
lo caza lo mesmo que ave
aunque su mujer aborte. . .
¡No hay tiempo que no se
    acabe
ni tiento que no se corte!

Y con el buche bien lleno
200 era cosa superior
irse en brazos del amor
a dormir como la gente,
pa empezar al día siguiente
las fáinas del día anterior.

205 Ricuerdo ¡qué maravilla!
cómo andaba la gauchada,
siempre alegre y bien montada
y dispuesta pa el trabajo;
pero hoy en el día. . . ¡barajo!
210 no se le ve de aporriada.

El gaucho más infeliz
tenía tropilla de un pelo;
no le faltaba un consuelo
y andaba la gente lista. . .
215 Tendiendo al campo la vista
no vía sino hacienda y cielo.

265 Y al punto dése por muerto
si el alcalde lo bolea,
pues áhi no más se la apea
con una felpa de palos.
Y después dicen que es malo
270 el gaucho si los pelea.

Y el lomo le hinchan a
golpes,
y le rompan la cabeza,
y luego con ligereza,
ansí lastimao y todo,
275 lo amarran codo con codo
y pa el cepo lo enderiezan
(Hernández 1941:32-36).

(Listen to Tape 2, selection 1.)

As can be seen, gaucho Spanish shares the phonological traits of rustic Spanish elsewhere, and Hernández, like other authors who write in dialect, misspells Standard Spanish in order to represent pronunciation, if inconsistently. For example, *goyete* instead of *gollete* illustrates *yeísmo* in accordance with gauchesque phonology, while the spelling *gallinas* does not (vv. 232. 154). Doubtless they were both pronounced with a [ʒ]. Again we see that intervocalic and final /d/ tends to weaken or disappear.

lastimao (v. 274)
ande ← *aonde* ← *adonde* (v. 165)
seguridá (v. 254)
barbaridá (v. 255)
autoridá (v. 258)
usté (v. 259)

When initial, Latin /f/ became aspirated [h] in Old Spanish, and this sound was preserved as [x] in Argentina, as in *juir* (v. 258). Spanish initial /f/ was also pronounced [x] before a back vowel, as indicated in *juego 'fuego'* and *junción 'función'* (vv. 195, 224). There was a confusion of fricatives before /w/: *agüela* ('*abuela*'), *güen* ('*buen*'), and *güérfano* ('*huérfano*') (vv. 167, 225, 234). Tiscornia adds that the front and back stops before another consonant were often lost:

p → Ø: *ecetuar* ('*exceptuar*')

b → ∅:   *osequiar* (*'obsequiar'*)
           oservar (*'observar'*)
           otener (*'obtener'*)
k → ∅:   *direción* (*'dirección'*)
           vitoria (*'victoria'*)
           dotor ('doctor')
g → ∅:   *inorancia* (*'ignorancia'*)
           indino (*'indigno'*)
           sinificar (*'significar'*)

The combination [ns] before another consonant lost [n] as in *circustancia*, *is-trumento*, and *istinto* (*instinto*) (Tiscornia 1941:19-20). Another important characteristic of gaucho Spanish was that [s] preceding the fricatives [β] and [γ] first caused these to devoice, and then [s] disappeared:

resbalar 'to slip' → *refalar*
amusgar 'to rust' → *amujar*
disgusto 'dislike' → *dijusto*
rasguido 'scratched'/'strummed' → *rajido* (Tiscornia 1930:48-49)

Two other phenomena may have occurred although neither is attested in *Martín Fierro* or other nineteenth-century works and, indeed, the second is impossible to represent in standard orthography. The first of these phenomena concerns syllable-final /s/. It may have been reduced to an aspirated unvoiced velar, i.e., the dorsum of the tongue rising toward the velum but not touching it, producing a sound similar to [h]. Before a following /f/, /s/, or /x/, a final /s/ might have been deleted entirely:

las fantasmas → [la fantáhma[h]]
los santos → [lo sánto[h]]
quinientos juntos → [kinjénto xúnto[h]] (Tiscornia 1930:46)

Gauchesque novelists of the twentieth century assume this phenomenon to have occurred and their fictitious dialogues reflect this belief in altered spellings:

. . . *vamoh' a buscar la tropa*
Cuando querráh 'ermano
Son medioh' idiosos no más, son (Güiraldes 1940:44, 50, 31)

Prominent linguists of the present time uphold these novelists in their suppositions.

The second phenomenon concerns both /r̄/ and /r/. In gauchesque Spanish, both might have been voiced fricatives, pronounced with less tension than in most dialects of the Peninsula. After /t/, /r/ may have devoiced, as in Chile and the Andean countries, becoming an affricate mistaken as [č] by foreigners. Between vowels /r/ may have been lax, but was not lost when final, unlike Andalusian. Initial or intervocalic /r/ tended to devoice and assibilate, as in the neighboring dialects. The gauchesque poets, with no phonetic alphabet, could not, of course, have indicated this pronunciation (Tiscornia 1930:45).

Abundant evidence exists, on the other hand, for the articulation of the vowels. In *Martín Fierro*, /i/ is often interchanged with /e/, and /o/ with /u/, as in Andean:

[i] for /e/
lición (I, v. 131)
siguro (I, v. 504)
ricuerdo (II, v. 205)
[u] for /o/
umbligo (I, v. 663)
lumbriz (I, v. 1475)
cubijas (II, v. 437)

[e] for /i/
recebir (I, v. 720)
menistro (I, v. 953)
polecía (I, v. 1393)
[o] for /u/
coyontura (I, v. 2062)
sepoltura (II, v. 960)
rigoroso (II, v. 2977) (Tiscornia 1930:14-23)

Other vowels interchanged but to a lesser extent. Further, when /i/ preceded a more open vowel, it became a semivowel [j], as can be seen in the above text in *coloriar*, *pión*, and *riunidos* (vv. 152, 163, 194). The text also shows that two contiguous vowels tended to become a diphthong with the stress on the more open of the two, as in *cáir*, *áura*, and *áhi* (vv. 193, 255, 267). Another trait, shared by nineteenth-century gauchesque speech and contemporary popular usage in the city, is the stressing of object pronouns suffixed to the infinitive, present participle, or imperative:

darmeló (II, v. 2254)
poniendomé (I, v. 4)
vamonós (II, v. 2647)
respondamé (II, v. 4346)

Tiscornia thinks that this accentuation may be Aragonese and also notes that it is attested in sixteenth- and seventeenth-century Peninsular literature (Tiscornia 1930:9-10).

The Spanish of the gaucho uses standard Río Plata *voseo*. At times, it contains aberrant prefixes such as the intrusive *a-* in *apiarse* and the substituted *en-* for *a-* in *enderezaba* (v. 164). Moreover, the form *enderiezan* for *aderezan* shows the common Latin American failure to distinguish between verbs that change their radicals and those which do not. Further, *enderezaba* (v. 164) is made nonreflexive, and *los pelea* (v. 270) is made transitive, again, typical of Latin American usage.

To be expected in rustic speech are the numerous archaisms in gaucho language. From our sample come:

pa ('*para*') (vv. 203, 208, 227, 276)
dende ('*desde*') (v. 162)
ande ('*adonde*') (v. 165)
mesmo ('*mismo*') (v. 261)
ansí ('*así*') (v. 274)
vía ('*veía*') (v. 216)

Standard Spanish terms have been adapted to the gaucho's activities, roles, equipment, and environment:

sentarse 'mount horse'
bolear 'down an animal with the *boleadora*'
tironear 'bulldog'
darse maña 'show skill'
gaucho pialador 'roper'
tironiador 'bulldogger'
pión domador 'bronc buster'
hacienda 'cattle'
tiento 'leather thong as for rein'
cueros 'equipment for horse'
carreta 'chuckwagon'
caña 'cheap rum'
mamajuana 'demijohn' (from French *dame Jeanne*)
cepo 'stakeout' ('gaucho stocks')
rancho 'hut'
pago 'district'
alcalde 'sheriff'/'mayor'

Many lexical items refer to horses:

animal 'unbroken horse'
potro 'pony'
tropilla 'herd of trained remounts'
de un pelo 'matched'

Pingo 'horse' probably comes from Aztec *penco* 'leaf of century plant' and *bagual* 'bronc' comes through *cagual* from the Pamperos' attempt to pronounce Spanish *caballo*. Also oriented to a life in which animals were important are *buche* 'belly' and *lomo* 'back', here used to refer to the bodies of humans. And the horse is personified in that he calls the gauchos ('*los llaman*') from his corral. *Gaucho* itself comes from Quechua *guacho*, meaning 'an orphan', and among its derivatives is *gauchada* 'a troop of gauchos'.

The similes and metaphors of gauchesque writers also refer to life on the pampa.

y si el alcalde lo sabe
lo caza lo mesmo que ave
'and if the sheriff finds out
he hunts you down like a wild fowl' (vv. 260-261)

y más malo que su agüela
se hacía astillas el bagual
'and worse than his grandmother
the bronc was turning himself into splinters' (vv. 167-168)

Pues siempre la mamajuana
vivía bajo la carreta
y aquel que no era chancleta
en cuanto el goyete vía,
sin miedo se le prendía
como güérfano a la teta.
'The little brown jug
always lived under the chuckwagon
and he who was not a little pig
as soon as he saw the neck of the jug
without hesitation pinned himself to it
like an orphan to the tit.' (vv. 229-234)

Although the Spanish of Paraguay, in general, shares most of the characteristics of the Río Plata dialect, in its phonology and lexicon it differs substantially enough from Argentine and Uruguayan usage to be considered a distinct subdialect (Malmberg 1947:3). The reasons for these differences are to be found in Paraguay's unique ethnic and cultural composition, which has led to a linguistic situation unparalleled elsewhere in South America. Paraguay is a truly bilingual nation, in which each of its two languages (Spanish and Guaraní) is used by speakers in well-defined and appropriate social contexts. Malmberg writes:

En el Paraguay de hoy, el español es la lengua oficial, la lengua de la administración, de la enseñanza, de los diarios y de los libros. Es también la lengua que se usa en los negocios y quehaceres corrientes de las ciudades. Pero no es la lengua de la intimidad. En el ambiente más íntimo, en las situaciones en las que los sentimientos predominan, los paraguayos prefieren el guaraní. El paraguayo, ya sea abogado, médico, profesor o ministro, una vez acabados los negocios oficiales del día, en su familia o con sus amigos, habla la lengua autóctona. El guaraní es la lengua que hablan los chicos que juegan en la calle, los trabajadores que descansan en la vereda y las mujeres que venden sus naranjas o sus ñandutys en la galería de la estación del Ferrocarril de Asunción (1947:7-8).

He adds that Spanish is 'una lengua reservada a la vida oficial y al contacto con gente poco conocida y con extranjeros', and is therefore 'más conservadora que una lengua completamente popular' (1947:8). Quite naturally, thus, the formal status accorded to Spanish has led to the desire to speak 'pure Castilian' and to avoid 'errors' made by Argentinians, whose speech they view as inferior (Malmberg 1947:16).

When Spanish words began to penetrate Guaraní in the sixteenth century, native speakers pronounced *morcilla* ('sausage') as [mbusiá], *cebolla* as [sebói], and *caballo* as [kabaǰú], showing that in Guaraní there was no phoneme equivalent to /ʎ/ (and that initial /m/ was always followed by /b/). As a result, /ʎ/ was either omitted or was realized as the nearest voiced palatal affricate, [ǰ]. When the Guaraní mastered the difficult foreign sound, they made a point of distinguishing it from /y/, creating an island of *lleísmo* in contrast to the *yeísmo* of the surrounding areas (Malmberg 1947:5).

Parallel treatment was given to /l/, which was pronounced [r]. After the Guaraní learned to pronounce /l/ in the Spanish way, the substitution of [r] for /l/ disappeared. Native /t/ and /d/ are alveolars, not dentals as in Spain, and Guaraní does not permit consonant clusters. Hence, the group /tr/ was articulated as an alveolar [t] followed closely by an assibilated retroflex [ř], producing a unitary sound very similar to [č]. The phoneme /r/ tends to be pronounced as a devoiced fricative, almost [ʒ], as in northern Argentina (Malmberg 1947:12-13).

Another example of the conservatism of Paraguayan Spanish is the treatment of syllable-final /s/. It is like the /s/ of Argentina and Uruguay in being aspirated, but unlike in that it is never lost. Also conservative is Paraguayan /v/, often a labiodental for people who 'affect a learned pronunciation, a habit acquired in school on the basis of orthography' (Malmberg 1947:15-16).

Both hypercorrection and the substratum are responsible for the articulation of words such as *baúl*, *país*, and *ahora*. Paraguayan speakers do not allow diphthongization of the vowels in hiatus on the basis of mere contiguity as in Argentina (Malmberg 1947:16-17).

Also conservative in Paraguay is morphosyntax. *Voseo* is avoided by many of the elite. Argentinian *che*, declared 'shocking to the ear', is reserved for the lower classes (Malmberg 1947:16).

Quite normal in a bilingual situation has been the exchange of words between Guaraní and Spanish, native words for native elements and imported words for cultural borrowings. It is to be regretted that many educated Paraguayans lament this intermixture that enriches the linguistic heritage of their nation, the only one in South America where both languages enjoy equal prestige.

References

Alonso, Amado. 1948. Lecture. University of Chicago.

Bioy Casares, Adolfo. 1978. Breve diccionario del argentino exquisito. Buenos Aires: Emecé.

Borges, Jorge Luis, and José Edmundo Clemente. 1968. El lenguaje de Buenos Aires. Buenos Aires: Emecé.

Canfield, D. Lincoln. 1981. Spanish pronunciation in the Americas. Chicago: The University of Chicago Press.

Desde el córner. n.d. [Probably in La Prensa. Buenos Aires.] n.p.

Güiraldes, Ricardo. 1940. Don Segundo Sombra. 2nd ed. Buenos Aires: Losada.

Hernández, José. 1941. Martín Fierro. 2nd ed. Ed. Eleuterio F. Tiscornia. Buenos Aires: Losada.

Kany, Charles E. 1945. American Spanish syntax. Chicago: The University of Chicago Press.

Malmberg, Bertil. 1947. Notas sobre la fonética del español en el Paraguay. Lund: Gleerup.

Muro, Gertrude. 1980. Some peculiarities of the Spanish language in Buenos Aires. Unpublished paper, The University of Texas at El Paso.

Quiroga, Horacio. 1950. Un peón. In: Cuentos escogidos. Madrid: Aguilar. 406-432.

Rosario, Rubén del. 1970. El español de América. Sharon, Connecticut: Troutman Press.

The South American Handbook. 1979. 55th ed. Eds. John Brooks and Joyce Candy. Bath, England: Trade and Travel Publications.

Tiscornia, Eleuterio F. 1930. La lengua de Martín Fierro. Buenos Aires: La Universidad de Buenos Aires.

Tiscornia, Eleuterio F. 1941. Advertencia lingüística. In: José Hernández, 'Martín Fierro'. Ed. Eleuterio F. Tiscornia. 2nd ed. Buenos Aires: Losada. 17-20.

Trejo, Nemesio. 1907. Los políticos. Buenos Aires: n.p.

Ullmann, Stephen. 1966. Semantic universals. In: Universals of language. Ed. Joseph H. Greenberg. Cambridge, Massachusetts: MIT Press. 217-262.

Veletti, Virgilio. 1985. Personal conversation.

Chapter 18
Southwestern United States

Spanish as one of the two dominant languages of the Western Hemisphere is not confined within the borders of Latin America proper, but has spread to the United States, where it plays an increasingly important role. It is estimated that in 1981 Spanish as a native language was spoken by more than fifteen million people north of the border. Some of the more recently arrived are the Puerto Ricans in the large cities of the Northeast and the Cubans in Florida. Both of these groups speak their own varieties of the Caribbean dialect. Their language differs considerably from the Spanish spoken in other areas of this country. Perhaps the most prominent of these other regions are, first, the southwestern United States from California to eastern Texas and, second, the more northern part of New Mexico and southern Colorado. The first of these is a wide swath which extends for 200 to 300 miles north of the border and includes a number of major metropolitan centers such as Los Angeles, Tucson, El Paso, and San Antonio. The Spanish of this region becomes increasingly similar to that of adjacent zones of Mexico as one approaches the *frontera*. The second of these dialect areas, historically and geographically isolated, differs markedly, although these differences are decreasing in number at the present time as a result of better transportation and communication.

Spanish has been spoken in the region which is now the southwestern United States since the sixteenth century. The first Spaniards here were Cabeza de Vaca and his men in 1536, who, after their shipwreck on Galveston Island, crossed Texas and turned south at a modest Indian pueblo where the river bent north, the present-day El Paso. Here they heard of impressive Indian 'cities' to the north, which the natives believed to be rich and powerful (among them, Acoma and Taos). These rumors excited the Spaniards, and two expeditions led by Francisco de Coronado brought other Spanish speakers into the Southwest, from 1540 to 1542. There were no permanent settlers, however, until 1598, when Juan de Oñate conquered the territory and claimed it for Spain (Espinosa 1975:99). Santa Fe was founded twelve years later and in 1630 had a population of 250 Spaniards, 700 Indians, and 50 mestizos. Exploited by the Spanish, the Indians revolted in 1680, and the would-be colonists were forced to withdraw until 1692, when Diego de Vargas retook the territory. The '*Camino Real*', actually a trail, was established for trade with Mexico City and was protected by Spanish garrisons in El Paso del Norte (now Ciudad Juárez), San Elizario, Senecú, Socorro, and Ysleta.

Since service in these remote military posts was far from attractive, they were manned, for the most part, by convicts from central Mexico who had chosen this tour of duty over jail in the capital. Some of these army personnel remained, and for the next two hundred years engaged in raising grapes for wine and herding sheep, products which they sold in the interior of Mexico. It can be assumed that they spoke a rustic Spanish flavored by occasional *germanía*.

In 1845, Texas was admitted to the United States, provoking Mexico and leading to the Mexican American War. This conflict ended with the annexation of the entire Southwest in 1848. American settlers, welcome for the most part, flocked into the newly won lands, Americanizing the culture and the language as they came (Espinosa 1975:99-100). Improved economic opportunities in the Southwest also drew immigrants from Mexico, and with the advent of the Mexican Revolution, 1910-1920, even more immigrants arrived, refugees from the ranks of armies defeated in recent battles. Most of these were uneducated men from ranches, farms, and small towns in the northern tier of states. A smaller group, however, consisted of highly educated professionals such as physicians, lawyers, and journalists. One of these was Mariano Azuela, who published the chapters of his famous novel *Los de abajo* in the columns of a South El Paso newspaper. Members of these two groups who chose to stay, as Azuela did not, had, of course, widely disparate linguistic histories. Many of the larger and less privileged group, hoping for better economic opportunities, assimilated to Anglo-American culture and language, losing Spanish altogether by the second or third generation. Other members of this group have continued to maintain Spanish in the family, orally, to this day, but speak serviceable English as well. Still other members of this group, farm workers for the most part, have felt no need to acquire English at all.

In contrast, the professionals in many cases saw at once the disadvantage of continuing to use Spanish in an English-dominant society and adopted their second language for home use by the second generation—like their less privileged fellows. Others of this second group, because of pride in their Mexican heritage, trained their children in the prestige dialect of their mother tongue, saw to it that they read the Hispanic classics, and sent them to private schools where instruction was conducted in Spanish.

In characterizing Mexican American Spanish, one is obviously not concerned with the speech of those who have been formally educated in Standard Spanish nor with that of those who depend primarily on English. Of more interest is the Spanish of the families who have kept it alive through oral transmission without the benefit of being literate in it. This language is impoverished in two ways in comparison with that of speakers of like socioeconomic status in Mexico. Its morphosyntax is devoid of constructions and forms which are learned through reading, both in and out of school. Its lexical items, when they refer to domestic matters such as the family and the household, are relatively standard, but they deviate in other semantic areas such as literature, the sciences, and technology.

It is easy to see the reasons for this impoverishment if we compare the acquisition of language by two children, one in Chihuahua and one in El Paso. At first, both children are limited to oral language, to topics which are immediately and physically present, and to people and animals in their home and neighborhood. Their linguistic development begins to diverge when they are seven and enter school. The child in Mexico is introduced to the wider world, the academic and social organizations and functions, with the Spanish structures and terminology which are appropriate. The little Spanish speaker in El Paso learns about the same subjects, but all in English. Later on, when both children leave school, they look for jobs. In Chihuahua, work-related syntax and vocabulary are Spanish, but, in El Paso, may be Spanish or English, depending on the type of management and clientele. The young person, as a result, may be forced into using a readapted Spanish word or an adopted English term, a situation reminiscent of the linguistic plight of his Hispanic forebears when confronted with the New World and its new language.

The quality of the Spanish used by Mexican Americans has varied considerably during the past several decades. The flood of immigrants who came to the Southwest in the early twentieth century were naturally Spanish-dominant, but the speech of following generations has become increasingly anglicized. This trend was reinforced by laws in several states forbidding the use of anything but English in the public schools. Also, an individual's success in the 'Anglo' world of business was presumably a measure of his assimilation to the wealthier culture and its ways.

The subordinate status of Spanish in the Southwest did not begin to change until World War II. Mexican Americans in California were confronted by servicemen from all over the United States, and ethnic friction was inevitable. As a reaction to discrimination, Hispanic teenagers began to be aware of their separate identity: they were spurned by their fellow-Americans and ridiculed by Mexicans as *pochos*, 'dummies' or 'copycats'. Thus was born the Pachuco, a rebel against both societies. He was identifiable by his attire, the zootsuit: a very long jacket with enormous lapels and padded shoulders, blousy pants drawn in at the ankle, elevated shoes, and a gold watch chain looping down around his knees. His outfit was completed by his *tando* 'a wide brimmed felt hat' like those worn in the movies by gangsters. His costume, according to Octavio Paz, was 'an exaggeration of the models', the middle-class American businessmen against whom he sought to rebel and not 'a return to the costumes of his ancestors' (Paz 1963:14). His speech was no less a parody, a double-edged sword striking against the dominant English and the Spanish spoken by his detractors in Mexico. (Listen to Tape 2, selection m for Pachuco speech of the 1950s, and see Appendix 5.) Further, it confirmed his independent identity.

The inarticulate protest represented by the Pachuco was succeeded in the 1950s by the Chicano Movement, a generation of Mexican American youngsters consciously aware of their social and political situation and of their potential for power. With this perception of their new identity came a rebirth of pride in the Spanish language, more interest in Standard Spanish and its use as a medium for writing, both literary and political, in support of the Chicano cause. As a result, the quality of Mexican American Spanish is today considerably higher than it was at its low ebb in the 1940s and early 1950s. Another group of Mexican Americans who are keenly aware of their heritage and the need to maintain it is composed of *cholos*, the spiritual descendants of the Pachucos, whose language is made up on the one hand of *pachuquismos* and on the other of in-group neologisms.

Spanish is frequently used in border regions such as Laredo, El Paso, Nogales, and Calexico which are in active daily contact with Mexico. It is the language of the majority in more remote areas such as Española in New Mexico and San Antoñito in Colorado. Also important is the ethnic composition of the district. Spanish predominates in places where Hispanics outnumber Anglo-Americans, at times from 20 or 50 to one. In other places, such as the newer cities of Albuquerque, Roswell, and Durango, where there are 20 Anglo-Americans to one Hispanic, English predominates, especially for speakers below the age of fifty. Where the population is ethnically more evenly divided, as in San Antonio, most of the Hispanic youngsters are bilingual and so are many of their Anglo counterparts (Espinosa 1975:100-101).

The kind of Spanish spoken in the Southwest is, in general, homogeneous and like rustic Spanish elsewhere. As in most of Latin America, it is characterized by *seseo* and *yeísmo*. Further, initial /f/ is realized as [ɸ] or [x]: *fui* becomes [ɸwí] or [xwí], and *fogata* becomes [ɸoɣáta] or [xoɣáta]. Where initial *h* comes from Latin initial /f/, it is pronounced [h]: *hervir* → [herβír] and *humo* → [húmo]. Intervocalic or final /d/ is often lost: *tapado* → [tapáo], and *verdad* → [berðá] (Cobos 1983:ix). As in Andalusia, /č/ is often materialized as [ʃ]: *chamaco* → [ʃamáko], and *muchacho* → [muʃáʃo]. Another general rustic trait is that vowels in hiatus tend to become diphthongs: *cae* → [káj], and *país* → [pájs]. Also general is metathesis:

SW Spanish:	Standard:
catágolo	*catálogo*
estógamo	*estómago*
murciégalo	*murciélago*
polvadera	*polvareda*
probe	*pobre*
suidad	*ciudad* (Baker 1966:39)

Particular to New Mexico is the metathesis *pader* for *pared*.

And there are other differences, from one place to another. In Texas, Hispanics are heavily influenced by the speech of the adjacent parts of Mexico. In Los Angeles, some levelling has taken place since speakers there have come from different parts of the Southwest. It is, however, very like the Spanish of Texas because of the constant movement from one state to the other and back. In contrast, the Hispanics of northern New Mexico and southern Colorado are far from the border and have shown little inclination to leave home, as is reflected in some distinctive traits of their dialect. In Texas, for example, syllable-final /s/ is not aspirated, vibrant /r̄/ does not assibilate, and /x/ does not become [h] but is pronounced as a postpalatal fricative, as in nearby Mexico. Some features of the speech of New Mexico and southern Colorado, however, are more like those of Guatemala and Costa Rica than of Mexico: syllable-final /s/ and, less frequently, intervocalic /s/ are aspirated (*esta* → [éhta] and *casa* →[káha]). There, vibrant /r̄/ is assibilated (*tierra* → [tjér̆a]), /r/ in a few words becomes [l] (*cerebro* → [selébro] and *coriandro* → [kulántro]), and /x/ becomes [h] (*gente* → [hénte]).

Intervocalic /j/, spelled *ll* or *y*, is either deleted or becomes a vowel: *capilla* is [kapía], and *ella* is realized as [éa] or [éja]. As to vowels, /o/ and /u/ are sometimes confused, as are /i/ and /e/.

codicia → [kudísja]
arrullar → [ařoiár]
despertar → [dispertár]

Another vocalic peculiarity is the addition of /i/ to words stressed on the final syllable ending in /r/, /l/, /s/, and /n/: *beberi, papeli, despuesi, quieni* (Cobos 1983:ix).

Southwestern Spanish in its morphology differs but little from popular usage throughout Latin America. A recent study, 'Spanish Verb Form Usage in El Paso and Mexico City: A Comparison', was based on a corpus of 7,063 items produced by Spanish-dominant Texas teens and a Mexican corpus of 15,880 analyzed by Moreno de Alba. It was discovered that the frequency of appearance of most tenses was very similar. For instance, in the El Paso sample, the imperfect indicative accounted for 9% of the total, and in Mexico 11%. The Texas preterite comprised 11% and that of Mexico 12%. Surprisingly, the conditional was used more often by the Texas informants, possibly because of its frequent occurrence in the protasis, or 'if' clause, of the conditional sentence. The present perfect and pluperfect are used more in Mexico City. The future and conditional perfect are almost nonexistent in both areas. Synthetic subjunctives are similar in frequency, except for the present perfect and pluperfect which are rare in El Paso. Neither group uses the *-se* subjunctive. The one difference, 25% to 8%, lay in the frequent appearance of the infinitive in Texas speech (Moreno de Alba 1978:passim; Cotton and Sharp 1983). (This overuse of the infinitive arose from the circumstances of the data gathering.)

In Southwestern Spanish, as elsewhere, there is no second person plural familiar form of the verb. Also, in the imperfect, three *-er* verbs preserve the extremely archaic *-ba-* tense marker.

Latin:	SW Spanish:	Standard:
cadebam	*caiba*	*caía*
credebam	*creiba*	*creía*
trahebam	*traiba*	*traía*

In the preterite, the second singular familiar may contain an epenthetic /s/ through analogy (*hablastes, comistes, vivistes*) and may lose the first /s/ through dissimilation (*hablates, comites, vivites*) (Cobos 1983:ix). As a result of the general tendency to form diphthongs from two vowels in hiatus, the future tense forms of *-er* verbs whose stem ends in a vowel usually change *-er-* to *-ir-*, giving forms such as *cairé, creirá, leiremos,* and *trairán* (for *caeré, creerá, leeremos,* and *traerán*) (Baker 1966:65-66). As in the Andes and Chile, an infinitive tends to lose *r* if it is followed by a third person pronoun beginning with *l*: *darles* → *dales* and *escribirle* → *escribile* (Baker 1966:70). Infixing an object pronoun before *-n* of the third plural in the subjunctive imperative creates:

delen 'give (it) to him' (*denle*)
hágamen 'do (it) for me' (*háganme*)
siéntesen 'be seated' (*siéntense*)
vállasen 'go' (*vállanse*) [sic] (Baker 1966:60)

Spanish verbs of New Mexico differ from those of Texas and resemble those of the Andes in three ways. The personal ending *-mos* for many speakers becomes *-nos*, by analogy with the pronoun *nos*, in the imperfect indicative and the present subjunctive. Also, there is a shift of accent in the subjunctive.

hablábanos (for *hablábamos*)
háblenos (for *hablemos*)

This accent shift occurs in all three conjugations. Finally, in third conjugation verbs, the first person plural of the present tense is signalled by *-emos* and thus serves to distinguish the present from the preterite.

vivemos 'we live'
vivimos 'we lived'
salemos 'we go out'
salimos 'we went out' (Cobos 1983:x)

Widespread in the Spanish of the Southwest, as in all of Latin America, is gender confusion among nouns, especially for common words borrowed from Greek. When these end in *-a*, Southwestern speakers treat them as feminine although they are masculine in Standard speech.

cinema	*panorama*	*sistema*
clima	*poema*	*telegrama*
drama	*problema*	*tema*
idioma	*programa*	*mapa* (Baker 1966:71)

Another trait which Southwest Spanish shares with other dialects is the pluralization with *-ses* of nouns ending in a stressed vowel:

cafeses (for *cafés*)   *sofases* (for *sofás*)

Because of the lengthy coexistence of Spanish and English speakers in the same geographic area, it is inevitable that southwestern Hispanics exhibit varying degrees of competence in both languages. A study by George Ayer classifies Mexican American speakers as follows:

(1) virtually monolingual in English
(2) English-dominant bilinguals
(3) balanced or coordinate bilinguals
(4) Spanish-dominant bilinguals
(5) virtually monolingual in Spanish (Ayer 1974:3-4)

Peñalosa describes bilinguals as compound or coordinate. The compound bilinguals come from bilingual homes 'where two languages [are] spoken more or less interchangeably by the same people in the same types of situations. Hence, they have fused two meaning systems'. In contrast, coordinate bilinguals 'learn their two languages in different contexts . . . , so that they have somewhat different meanings for corresponding words in the two languages; they are said to have separate meaning systems'. A well-known example is the term for Christmas. When a coordinate bilingual refers to gifts and decorated trees on the 25th, he says /krísmes/; but if he is thinking of *posadas*, *piñatas*, and presents on Epiphany, he says *Navedad*. This distinction is less frequent in the speech of compound bilinguals (Peñalosa 1980:45-46).

Typically, a Chicano, whether compound or coordinate, may use English at work or in school, but Spanish at home or out on a date. Or he may combine the two languages, especially in informal situations. This combination is not a mere matter of inserting a lexical item from one language into a matrix from another, although that practice is very popular. In general, the categories of words borrowed are restricted to nouns in abundance, some verbs, and a very few adjectives and adverbs. They are likely to refer to concrete objects and have simple grammatical functions (Sobin 1976:15-47). A Mexican American, in ordering a hamburger, will use the English word just as an Anglo will ask for *tortillas* with his Mexican plate. More complex than the borrowing of a single word is the mixture of two grammatical systems, code switching, which is subject to complex syntactic strictures and must be learned. This is to say, a Colombian with control of both English and Spanish grammar, if he finds himself in Tucson, will be unaware of combinatorial possibilities and, thus, unable to code switch acceptably.

One of the most basic strictures is that a speaker may not violate the syntax of the matrix language, which is the language he thinks of as basic to a given utterance (Lawrence 1982:21). In a Spanish matrix with English insertions, for example, the word order must be Spanish, as in:

Tenían patas flacas y pechos flat.
Las palabras heavy duty *bien grandes se me han olvidado.*
Daban unos steaks *tan sabrosos.*
Me huele a toast *quemado* (Lawrence 1982:17).

The matrix language is that of the finite verb. Therefore, in the noun phrases of these sentences, adjectives will tend to come after the nouns they modify: *patas flacas*, *pechos* flat, steaks *tan sabrosos*. Seeming violations of this rule are:

Me hace un cheese sauce.
y un scoop *pa' la* potato salad
en una paper cup
No creo que son fifty-dollar suede ones.
¿Cómo se llama la otra con la short hair?

Lawrence comments: 'In these examples, there is no question of the inserted English phrase matching Spanish word order. The phrase, rather, is incorporated into the Spanish speech segment unanalyzed—i.e., as if it were a single item' (1982:26). In an isolated noun phrase, with no attendant verb, it is the function words such as determiners that indicate the matrix language of the segment. Thus, acceptable are *un libro* yellow (Spanish matrix) and two *borracho* butterflies (English matrix). Less acceptable is two *borrachas* butterflies (Lawrence 1982:63), doubtless because the adjective shows concordance, not admissible in English syntax.

Another stricture is the prohibition of a mixture of English and Spanish forms in one verbal element. One cannot say *He is *trabajando* or *If you are going to *tomar* (Peñalosa 1980:58). In Texas Chicano Spanish, English interrogative forms may not be used in questions with a Spanish matrix: *How *lo hizo*? or *When *vino*? But *Lo hizo* slowly and *Vino* early are acceptable.

In a Spanish segment, an English predicate adjective is sometimes used for emphasis: *Está muy* heavy, *Este es el más* simple, *Es muy* wild. It may be that English *heavy*, *simple*, and *wild* are pronounced with English stress, and that suprasegmentals are free from restrictions, but one would have to investigate this matter further. Also open to investigation are conversations in which speakers alternate Spanish and English in complete sentences, one segment in one language and the next segment in the other.

In contrasting Mexican American Spanish with other dialects, we find that its most prominent feature is the abundance of English loan words. In this respect, it is by no means alien to the genius of the Spanish language, since Spanish, like English, has readily incorporated words from other languages throughout its history, from Visigothic, Arabic, Italian, French, and the American Indian languages.

One reason for the massive number of English terms in Southwestern Spanish is that speakers, initially of rural origin, moved north into the United States and found themselves faced with the need to name new things and concepts for which they had no linguistic resources. If it be objected that there are in Mexico perfectly good Spanish words for many of these referents, it is equally clear that they did not exist on the *rancho* and the Spanish terms, therefore, were never learned (Sharp 1970:210-211). Or, it may be that the speaker did know the Spanish word but felt that his listener might not. Finally, he may have used the English term in order to enhance the prestige of what he was saying (Peñalosa 1980:36). As Labov points out: 'Whenever a subordinate dialect is in contact with a superordinate one, linguistic forms produced by a speaker of the subordinate dialect in a formal context will shift in an unsystematic manner to the superordinate. . .' (Labov 1971:450).

English words incorporated into the Mexican American lexicon fall into several categories. First, there are words which are modified to conform to basic Spanish patterns in phonology:

gasolín	*daime*	*taipear*
balún	*nicle*	*chequear*
magazín	*lonche*	*driblear*
bil	*yonque*	*flonquear*

Next, there are words which are made to follow less common phonological patterns, such as *grábel* 'gravel'. Third are those which form new phonological patterns, such as *deit* 'date'. A fourth type consists of words which contain English phonemes, such as

[ǰéle] 'jelly'   [ʃampú] 'shampoo'
[ǰábe] 'job'   [ʃerífe] 'sheriff'
[ǰímes] 'Jimmy'   [ʃaráp] 'shut up'
[ǰín] 'Jean'   [guáʃa] 'washer'
[los ánheles] 'Los Angeles'   [sæn æntówn] 'San Antonio'

Another group contains English words Hispanized beyond recognition:

quiande 'candy'   *gorejel* 'go to hell'
jare 'howdy'   *jarirusa* 'how do you do, sir'
guirepe 'get up'   *reganche* 'rail gang'
buri/buti 'very'   *sanamagón* 'son of a gun'

A different type, the loan-blend, adapts morphologically as well as phonologically, with borrowed bases and native affixes: *cuitar* 'quit' and *boxeador* 'boxer'. In loanshifts, the phonology and morphology remain Spanish but the semantic value is altered to that of an English cognate. *Aplicación*, in Standard Spanish 'to apply oneself to whatever he is doing', has shifted to 'a form to fill out'. *Educación* 'upbringing' has narrowed to 'schooling'. *Atender* 'to pay attention', 'attend to something' has switched to the English meaning of 'be present'; *realizar* 'complete a task' is to Chicanos 'to be aware of'; and *correr* is 'run for office'. Very similar are calques or loan translations at the phrasal level.

buen tiempo 'good time'
va para tras 'he goes back'
telefonear para tras 'to call back'
escuela alta 'high school'
esperar niño 'to be expecting a child'
cambiar la mente 'change one's mind'
hacer la mente para arriba 'make one's mind up' (Baker 1966:24-25; Cobos
    1983:xiv; Espinosa 1975:109-113; Peñalosa 1980:60-62; Cotton and
    Sharp 1980b:440-444).

Although the lexicon of New Mexico and Southern Colorado resembles that of the Southwest in general, the relative isolation of this area accounts for a number of clearly discernible differences. One is the archaic character of many lexical items, some of which are no longer in use in Mexico or in other varieties of Mexican American Spanish. Some of these are:

alverjón 'peas'   *desafuciado* 'discouraged'
cuerpo 'blouse'   *empeloto* 'naked'
estafeta 'post office'   *ñudo* 'knot'
camalta 'bed'   *turco* 'gypsy'
¡a redo vaya! 'good heavens!'
en silla de manos 'regally'

¿La gracia de su merced? 'Your name, please?'
¡Bal ni que juera el rey! 'Gee, as if you were a king!'

Also archaic are many *Nahuatlismos* brought in during the early seventeenth century by colonial settlers. These are still pronounced much as they were then, whereas if they have survived in Mexico, their pronunciation has been so Hispanized as to camouflage them almost completely. Some examples of these archaic Nahuatlismos are:

shocoque 'sour'	*tinamaishte* 'trivet'
nesha 'yellowish'	*chichincle* 'fawner'
chincual 'diaper rash'	*guajolote* 'salamander'
jumate 'dipper'	*tapeshte* 'hayloft'
tazol 'straw'	*metlacahuitl* 'pole for hanging hides out to dry'

In addition to words from Nahuatl, Spanish settlers in New Mexico added to their vocabulary a few terms from local tribes living along the Rio Grande. Many of these words refer to local plants, clothing, housing, foods, rites, and topography:

cachina 'ceremonial doll'	*kiva* 'ceremonial chamber'
comanche 'Comanche'	*pujacante* 'witch doctor'
chiguata 'squaw'	*conchelle* 'buffalo skin'
aguapá 'cattail'	*chigüil* 'dale' (Cobos 1983:ix-xi)

The building of the railroads in the 1880s attracted many Spanish-speaking laborers from the south. As new communities sprang up, *braceros* were lured by opportunities for employment on farms and ranches. These newcomers brought with them nineteenth century Spanish, at times modified by Mexican Indian loan words.

arrancado 'penniless'	*cuate* 'twin'/'pal'
la arranquera 'the Depression'	*papalote* 'kite'
bolillo 'gringo'	*petaquilla* 'trunk'
cócono 'turkey'	*sacate* 'grass'
chapulín 'grasshopper'	*trastes* 'dishes'
chiple 'spoiled child'	*zoquete* 'mud' (Cobos 1983:xi-xii)

Because of their isolation and widespread illiteracy, the Hispanics in this area often were forced to coin new expressions based upon existing Spanish words. Many of these were highly imaginative. *Ratón volador*, for example, is 'bat', literally a 'flying mouse', like German *fledermaus*. From 'armpit' *sobaco* came *sobaqueras* 'crutches'. *Callado* from *callar* 'to be quiet' was given the meaning of 'illegitimate child', as was *de los pajaritos del monte* '[gift] of the birds of the woods'. *Pinta* 'penitentiary' was perhaps suggested by the striped uniforms of the inmates, as *varillero* 'peddlar' may have been by the pole on which a hawker carried his wares. Humorous exaggeration is seen in the use of *poros* ('pores') for 'nostrils'. *Quedadas*, literally 'those who were left behind' became 'old maids', perhaps from the Spanish phrase *quedarse para vestir santos* since it was customary for spinsters as well as young girls to sew clothes for the images in the church (Cobos 1983:xiii).

After the creation of the New Mexico Territory and the pacification of the non-Pueblo Indians, many *americanos* moved in, providing a new source of vocabulary from which were chosen and Hispanized many terms such as

bequenpaura 'baking powder'
bísquete 'biscuit'
cacombre 'cucumber'
cute 'coat'
espauda 'yeast powder'
fecha 'date' in the sense of 'rendezvous'
güiso/-a 'boy/girl friend' from 'sweetheart'
granpo 'grandpa'
mula 'corn liquor'
pope 'puppy'
sobrechuses 'overshoes'

In our own times, the increasing dominance of English has resulted in the frequent and spontaneous use of a multitude of 'non-incorporated' (i.e., non-Hispanized and unpredictable) words and phrases. Among these are:

average rainfall	reversible sweater
ballpoint pen	skiing
corduroy pants	special delivery
frostless refrigerator	station wagon
insurance premium	unleaded gasoline
pencil sharpener	windshield sticker (Cobos 1983:xiv-xv)

Despite the partial assimilation of the Mexican American to English-dominated society, his speech shows an imaginative creativity closely akin to that found in other dialects of Spanish. This creativity is especially manifested in slang, *caló*. Each generation introduces neologisms into this lexical category and at the same time continues to use many of those invented by forebears, in Mexico and earlier in Spain. The majority of these neologisms share a number of traits. They come from different sources. They are often humorous. Subjective, they frequently refer to kinds of people or behavior. They tend to be figurative and at the same time judgmental, either derisive or laudatory, depending on the relationships of the people involved. In many cases, the coinages are in-group terms (Cotton and Sharp 1980a:passim).

A brief sample of Mexican American nouns and adjectives can be seen in Table 24.

Table 24 Neologistic nouns and adjectives in Mexican American slang.

Nouns (20)

Lexical item	Derived meaning	Original meaning	Figure	Judgmental derisive	Judgmental laudatory
bote	'jail'	'can'	met.	X	
calco	'shoe'	*V.L. *calcus*?	meton.		
cantón	'house'	'barracks'	meton.	X	
carnal/-a	'brother'/'sister'	'cousin'	meton.		
frajo	'cigarette'	'rolled'	meton.		
gabacho/-a	'gringo'	'French soldier of Napoleon'	meton.	X	
grifa	'reefer'	'rolled sail'	met.		
jaina	'sweetheart'	'honey'	met.		
jefe/-a	'father'/'mother'	'boss'	met.	X	
lisa	'shirt'	'smooth'	meton.		
maderista	'bull-slinger'	'wood'	met.	X	
manopla	'hand'	'maniple'	met.		
mono	'movie'	'monkey'	an.met.		
presidio	'tenement house'	'penitentiary'	met.	X	
ranfla	'car'		onom.		
refín	'meal'	'refine'	met.		X
simón/sirol	'yes'	'*sí* + suffix			
tacuchi	'suit'	?			X
tramos	'pants'	'RR track'	met.		
vato/-a	'guy'/'gal'	'young goat'	an.met.		

Adjectives (5)

Lexical item	Derived meaning	Original meaning	Figure	Judgmental derisive	Judgmental laudatory
cuero/-a	'good-looking'	'leather'	met		X
changa	'pretty'	'monkey'	an.met.		X
dioquis	'unemployed'	'at leisure' (Latin *de otiis*)	meton.	X	
huevón	'lazy'	'setting hen'	an.met.	X	
ruco/-a	'old person'	'old person' (Sp. *vejarruco*)		X	

All of these entries have referents that are important to people in their personal lives. *Refín* has to do with eating well, and four items (*calco, lisa, tacuchi,* and *tramos*) with clothing. Three more personal items are *frajo*, *dioquis*, and *manopla*. Interpersonal relations are suggested in the kinship terms *jefe/-a* and *ruco/-a*, 'father', 'mother', 'my old man', 'my old woman'. *Carnal* and *carnala* are 'brother' and 'sister'. *Vato* and *vata* are slightly despective, 'guy' and 'gal'. *Jaina* is an affectionate term for 'girl' or 'sweetheart', *changa* is 'a pretty girl' and *cuero*, 'a handsome man'. Terms reflective of social disapproval are *gabacho*, *maderista*, and *huevón*. *Bote* and *grifa* belong to the domain of the lawless. Popular amusements are going to the *mono* or riding around in a *ranfla*. If one is poor, he or she is likely to live in a *cantón* or, worse, a *presidio*.

These slang terms are without exception humorous, and one may be sure that speakers use them with comic intent. Such is certainly true of *manopla* and of *simón* and *sirol*, in the mouth of a teenager. *Simón* may be a play on the name *Simón*, while *sirol* may come from the Hispanic pig-Latin which inserts either *-ol* or *-ul* between syllables. Of the 25 items, seven come from varied sources: *dioquis* and *calco* probably from Latin, *grifa* and *jaina* from English, *gabacho* from Basque, *changa* from West Africa, and *tacuchi* likely an Amerindian derivative. The majority (22, or 88%) are figurative, and, of these, 14 are metaphoric (63.6%), seven are metonymic (31.8%), and one is onomatopoeic (4.5%). Among the 14 metaphors, four are animalian: *changa* and *mono* from monkeys, *huevón* from a hen, and *vato* from 'young goat'. Of the 13 terms which are judgmental (52%), nine are derisive (69%) and four are laudatory (30.8%). Several are in-group Pachuco or Cholo: *frajo*, *grifa*, *jaina*, *simón/sirol*, and possibly *cuero* and *ruco*.

In addition to nouns and adjectives such as the ones in this brief sample, the lexicon of Mexican American Spanish has many neologistic verbs, whose characteristics are even more clearly defined. Further, they are extremely numerous. As in other Hispanic dialects in the New World, Southwestern Spanish has adapted many verbs by simply altering their semantic value to fill local needs. *Guisar*, in Standard Spanish a generic for 'to cook', is specifically 'to fry' in the Southwest and northern Mexico. *Chingar*, which in the Cono Sur has a number of meanings, some of which are 'to gyp', 'to tease', and 'to annoy', in Mexico and the Southwest has come to signify 'have sexual intercourse'. *Refinar*, 'refine' elsewhere, in Chicano Spanish means 'to eat'. Also numerous and quite distinctive are the new verbs in the Southwest which have not only novel meanings but novel forms. One prominent subgroup of these is composed of verbs with a base plus a palatal plus *-ar* conjugational endings. The palatal is usually /j/, which becomes /e/ when stressed: *brujear* → [bruxjár] but [bruxéa]. These verbs fall into two main groups, those with English bases and those whose bases are native Spanish. The English-based verbs are less numerous than one would expect. An analysis of every verb of this type in *The Dictionary of the Spanish of Texas* (Galván and Teschner 1975) shows that of the total of 355, only 147 (41.4%) contain English bases, while 208 (58.6%) are Spanish-based. Among those with Spanish bases, 166 (79.8%) are based on nouns, whereas those based on verbs number only 31 (14.9%). For Spanish, adjective bases are found in only six verbs, 2.9%, while the remaining five verbs are based on interjections or pronouns. Among those with English bases, however, 127 or 86.4% are verb-based, while only 20 or 13.6% are based on nouns; 17.7% are ambiguous: two counted as noun-based and 24 counted as verb-based might actually be considered as either noun or verb-based, i.e., from words like *comb*, *step*, and *work* (see Appendices 6 and 7) (Cotton and Sharp 1980b: passim).

It is evident from these figures that the percentages of noun-based verbs and verb-based verbs are almost exactly the opposite in the case of coinages of Hispanic versus English origin. One may surmise that a Spanish-dominant speaker might be inclined to create new verbs based on nouns already known to him and merely to copy verbs to which he is exposed in the 'Anglo' culture. As in Quechua, it seems to be true that it is easier to be creative in one's own language and also easier simply to imitate forms of a second language. The verbs with Spanish bases also differ from those of English derivation in that they come from sources that are linguistically more varied: Medieval Spanish, Standard Spanish (modified semantically and/or phonologically), Standard Spanish slang, rogue slang, Nahuatl, and Pachuco.

Perhaps the most interesting difference among these verbs is the contrast between their respective areas of semantic application, as shown in Appendix 8. The figures in this Appendix indicate that of the verbs in Category I, Behavior, the number with Spanish bases is three times greater than that of those with English bases (156 vs. 47). In Category II, Sports and play, and Category III, Work, it is the English-based verbs which predominate, two to one (32 vs. 17 and 66 vs. 29). Terms in Category IV, Weather, and V, Medical, are all Spanish-based, and in Category VI, General and/or unclassifiable, there are two verbs with English bases and only one with a Spanish base.

Category I, Behavior, is divided into five subcategories. The first, Personal behavior, general, contains 30 Spanish-based terms, most of which deal with physical activities such as *cararaquear* 'chatter', *chanquilear* 'walk', *sofacear* 'lie on sofa', *papalotear* 'excel', and *nortear(se)* 'go crazy'. The English-based verbs in this category number only seven, but they refer to some of the same activities: *toriquear* 'talk', *shoflear* 'shuffle', and *bonquear* 'hit the bunk'. The second subcategory, Personal behavior, domestic setting, has 18 from Spanish: ten for eating and drinking, such as *martillar* 'eat voraciously' and *pistear* 'have a drink', and eight for grooming and dressing, such as *pintorreguear* 'do a poor paint job' and *entacucharse* 'dress up'. The ten verbs from English in this category include *birronguear* 'drink beer', *lonchar*, and *shainear* 'shine shoes'.

The third subcategory, Interpersonal behavior, general, contains 38 Hispanic bases, several of which refer to sexually oriented activities ranging from *cachumbear* 'neck' to *chopetear* 'have intercourse'. Concomitantly, six more terms refer to child raising, such as *apapachar* 'spoil' and *sonajear* 'spank'. Interpersonal behavior general also includes positive, neutral, and negative terms, such as *ahuichotear* 'encourage'/'stimulate', *baratear* 'mix with a crowd', and *barajear* 'make a fool of'. The English-based verbs in Interpersonal, general, only 12, are similar: *flirtear* 'flirt', *jainear* 'make love', *tisear* 'tease', positive *tritear* 'treat someone', neutral *espatear* 'recognize', and negative *chatapear* 'shut somebody up'. The fourth subcategory of Interpersonal, general contains social formulas such as *matrimonear* 'to marry' and *pronuncear* 'declare that something is so'.

The last subcategory of Behavior has 45 Spanish-based verbs and 17 with English bases which refer to widely varied activities that are socially disapproved. Some Spanish-general examples are *sanchar* 'commit adultery', *huevonear* 'be lazy', *chisquear* 'drive crazy', *torear* 'spree', *cachuquear* 'double cross', and *jacalear* 'gossip'. Some of the Spanish-criminal are *colear* 'tail somebody', *mañanear* 'steal', *pildorear* 'take dope', *filetear* 'knife', and *cuetear* 'shoot'. The disapproved-general verbs with English bases include *pompear* 'fornicate', *ponchar* 'punch', and *muchar* 'mooch'. The disapproved-criminal verbs include *freimear* 'frame', *rolear* 'roll somebody', *capear* 'prepare heroin in capsules', and *chutear* 'shoot'. Not only are the Spanish-based verbs in the criminal category more numerous but they also include seven terms for 'to knife', continuing the Spanish tradition of attaching great prestige to the use of a blade to settle differences.

In the second major Category II, Sports and play, there are approximately twice as many verbs of English derivation (32) as of Spanish (17), and this category is clearly English-dominated. There are 14 verbs with English roots naming activities typical of team sports. Of these, the greatest number (six) refer to baseball, three to football-soccer, three to basketball, and one to any team sport. Some are:

batear 'bat'	*driblear* 'dribble'
quiquear 'kick'	*quechar* 'catch'

Team sports, excepting soccer, have only recently become popular among Latin Americans and their terminology hence has been borrowed from the English-speaking countries in which they originated. The verbs with Spanish bases in this semantic area, *capotear* 'snatch ball'/'leave team scoreless', *cañonear* and *garrotear* 'defeat' are less specific than their English counterparts. The six terms for boxing and wrestling, all of which have English bases, are, again, specific, such as *naquear/noquear* 'to knock out'. In the next subcategory of Sports and play, Card playing and gambling, English-based verbs outnumber Spanish four to one with items such as *blofear* 'bluff' and *poquear* 'play poker'. The one verb derived from Spanish, *barajear*, is very general, 'play cards'. Immigrants from rural Mexico apparently acquired their taste for card games in the United States.

Five lexical items concerning other social amusements are also from English, with terms such as *cabaretear* 'go nightclubbing' and *campear* 'go camping'. Like the terms for sports, the Spanish verbs here are less specific, e.g., *banquetear* 'to party'. A subcategory of verbs referring to dancing is especially interesting because it contains six Spanish-based verbs and none from English, probably because the love of dancing is a Hispanic cultural trait of long standing and also one which continues to be of primary importance in the life of the Mexican American teenager. Some of these are specific, such as *taconear* 'dance, stamping one's heels', and some are more general such as *bolevear* 'dance'.

Highly reflective of both traditional values and activities taken from Anglo America are new verbs in Category III, Work. Here, there are only 29 from Spanish, but 66 from English. This disproportion grows larger as the technicality of the work increases. There are no terms for secretarial work derived from Spanish, but six come from English: *check*, *dial*, *sign*, *staple*, *tape*, and *type*. There is one electrical term, *ploguear*, and one military, *machinganear*. A contrast may also be noted between the referents of Spanish-based and English-based automotive verbs. Those from Spanish are adaptations of Standard forms for horsemanship, boating, or flying:

arrear 'giddap' → 'start a car'
manear 'hobble a horse' → 'put on the brakes'
talonear 'spur a horse' → 'hurry up'
orillar 'reach the shore' → 'park'
pilotear 'pilot' → 'drive'

Most of those from English come from specifically automotive activities such as *bompear* 'bump into' and *yequear* 'jack up', because of the Mexican Americans' acculturation to mechanization in the United States.

As to Work, domestic, the eight verbs with Spanish bases involve the preparation of food, while the 13 from English have to do primarily with cleaning chores, e.g., *lamprear* 'to roast', versus *waxear*. The Spanish-based verbs may have been coined by bilinguals while the English bases probably came from the pidgin spoken by Anglo-American housewives to their maids.

Work in the educational field has yielded only one verb from Spanish (hypocoristic *colear* 'color') but 19 from English, which reflect life in a typical Anglo-American school. Some of these are *espeletear* 'spell', *impruvear* 'improve', *flonquear* 'flunk', and *juquear* 'play hooky'. In the financial realm, verbs which derive from Spanish are noninstitutional but those from English concern the Mexican-American's dealings with businesses which are often dominated by Anglos, e.g., Spanish *feriar* 'make change', in contrast to English *charchear* 'charge'.

In the semantic area of labor relations there are no terms from Spanish but four from English. These fall into two groups, those which refer to unemployment (*cuitear*, *discharchar*) and those to do with conflicts with employers (*estraiquear* and *piquetear*). Words for manual labor and work in general are more frequently Spanish, such as *azadonear* 'to hoe', and several verbs which mean 'to blow a job', such as *cachuquear*.

Neologistic verbs for weather or medicine are from Spanish (*grajear* 'sleet' and *moretear* 'bruise'). Only six verbs are unclassifiable, such as Spanish *afrañar* 'understand' and *craquear* 'crack', from English.

These neologistic *-ear* and *-iar* verbs with Spanish bases are especially likely to be figurative. One of these verb forms, indeed, may have several meanings, each of which may derive from a different figurative process. Among the 208 verbs of Hispanic origin, 192 are figurative, and among these are found 226 separate figures of speech (Cotton and Sharp 1980a: passim; 1980b: passim).

According to Ullmann, figures are motivated according to three different categories: phonetic, morphological, and semantic (1966:221). Phonetic motivation is often seen in primary onomatopoeia, 'the imitation of sound by sound', as in *jirimiquear*, connotatively as well as denotatively 'to whine'. *Cacaraquear* is like English 'cackle' or 'chatter'. *Chipear* 'drizzle' probably comes from Nahuatl *chipi-chipi* 'sound of falling rain'.

Secondary or metalinguistic onomatopoeia occurs in the Southwest in neologistic verbs that 'talk about talking' (Bolinger 1975:292). *Chiquear* 'spoil a child' reflects a doting mother's constant use of the endearment *chico/-a*. *Totachar*, 'speak unintelligibly', like a Pachuco in the presence of the uninitiated, comes from *to tatli* ('Our Father'), a term used by the Indians to deride the Latin used in the Mass by the priests. Secondary onomatopoeia and morphological motivation are also to be found in stem augments, that is, additional syllables such as *-iz-*, *-ac-*, *-ul-* between the stem and the conjugational ending. Front vowels, mid to high, suggest smallness in size or in value in many languages (Ullmann 1966:226; Bolinger 1975:24; Langacker 1973:26). This notion can be seen in *pintorreguear* 'put on heavy makeup', *titiritear* 'shiver', and *lambizquear* 'nibble between meals'. The low or back vowels *-o-* and *-u-* suggest large size, heaviness, or that which is foolish or repugnant, as in:

Augment:	Verb:	Meaning:
-ot-	*borlotear*	'dance wildly'
-uq-	*cachuquear*	'mess up'
-ol-	*chismolear*	'do a job poorly'
-oj-	*mirojear*	'ogle'
-ul-	*pagulear*	'pay poorly'
-on-	*temponear*	'waste time'

If phonology and morphology play an important role in the heightening of meaning, figurative language resulting from semantic motivation provides even greater emotional intensity. It also adds multidimensional suggested meanings and gives sensuous pleasure. Such effects are often produced in language by synecdoche, metonymy, metaphor, and irony, the figures which we found to predominate in these popular coinages. Indeed, of the 226 figurative devices found in the sample, 161 are of semantic motivation, 71.2%. Synecdoche, the use of an important part for the whole, occurs in 11 verbs, 6.8%. One example, *chanclear* 'dance wildly', is based upon *chancla* 'slipper' and suggests that one is dancing so furiously that his shoes are flying off.

Metaphor results from a sudden leap of seeing 'likenesses between unlike things' (Perrine 1973:66) while metonymy, in which one term is replaced by another closely associated with its referent, is based on analogies and similarities as well. Metaphoric verbs in the sample number 93, 57.8%, and metonymic verbs 52, or 32.3%. The two groups together represent 90.1% of the total number of figurative examples.

As Ullmann notes, 'subjects prominent in the interests and activities of a community tend to attract a large number of synonyms'. He adds that, if we are interested in a subject, 'it will provide us with analogies for the description of other experiences' (1966:231, 240). In the data, these analogies have come from sources which have the features (1) [− animate], (2) [+ animate] [− human], and (3) [+ human]. The largest of these groups falls within (1). Many of these terms (14) are based on foods and plants. Most of them are despective, and some are jocular. Some are euphemisms, and some are dysphemisms:

Verb:	Meaning:	Source:
abolillar	'act like a gringo'	*bolillo* 'white roll'
filetear	'slash'	*filete* 'filet'
sacatear	'dodge'	*sacate* 'grass'
tomatear	'ogle'	*tomate* 'tomato'
tortillar	'slap'/'applaud'	*tortilla*

Tools or instruments are the source of 11 verbs:

Verb:	Meaning:	Source:
alfilear	'stab'	*alfiler* 'pin'
garranchar	'bludgeon'	*garrancha* 'heavy hook'
machetear	'eat voraciously'	*machete*
martillar	'eat voraciously'	*martillo* 'hammer'
cuetear	'shoot'	*cohete* 'firecracker'

Four verbs are drawn from clothing:

Verb:	Meaning:	Source:
capotear	'steal the ball'	*capote* 'bullfighter's cape'
casquetear	'masturbate'	*casqueta* 'skull cap'
chaquetear	'be a turncoat'	*chaqueta* 'jacket'
taconear	'dance, stomping'	*tacón* 'heel'

Verbs which derive from the house and its furnishings number seven, most of which are jocular. Some are:

Verb:	Meaning:	Source:
encantonear	'marry'	*cantón* 'house'
jacalear	'carry gossip'	*jacal* 'hut'
lamparear	'ogle'	*lámpara* 'lamp'
petatear	'die'	*petate* 'straw mat'
sofacear	'lounge'	*sofá*

Also within this domain lie three verbs based on children's toys:

Verb:	Meaning:	Source:
chopetear	'fornicate'	*chopete* 'baby's pacifier'
papalotear	'excel'	*papalote* 'kite'
sonajear	'spank'	*sonaja* 'baby's rattle'

Some of the remaining terms in the category [− animate] have their sources in words originally designating line or shape:

Verb:	Meaning:	Source:
alinear	'go straight'	*línea* 'line'
camellar	'do manual labor'	*camellón* 'mound of dirt or gravel'
canalear	'slash, head to toe'	*canal*
chambear	'slash, head to toe'	*chamba* 'ditch'
esquinear	'assent'	*esquina* 'corner'

The second category, [+ animate] [− human], contains figurative references to human behavior based on names or activities of birds or beasts. According to Philbrick, 'zoological metaphors, as applied to people, are deservedly popular as being obvious and usually insulting' (Philbrick 1967:178). Insulting—in a jocular way—are those verbs which have birds as their source: gossiping and chattering women are likened to chickens and parrots in *cacaraquear, periquear*, and *cotorrear*; people who overeat are said to *gusjear* 'be like a vulture'. *Pajarear*, literally 'to bird', means 'keep an eye on', and *copetear* 'fill to the brim' comes from *copete*, literally the 'topknot of a fowl', analogous to the English 'head' on a glass of beer. *Huevonear* 'to be lazy' comes from *huevo* 'egg' and its derived meanings in Mexico. Of this group, only *pichonear* 'pigeon' in its meaning of 'engage in sexual foreplay' is a euphemistic term, somewhat analogous to the English 'bill and coo'.

Animal names have contributed an equal number of terms, all of which are despective, and most of which are jocular. Three concern the activities of criminals: *coyotear* 'steal', *torear* in its meaning of 'defy the law', and *colear* in the sense of 'to tail somebody'. *Changuear* 'to mimic' is the obvious outgrowth of *chango* 'ape'. Two verbs are associated with intimidation, and both have their origin in animals that are weak and inoffensive: *azorrillar* (from Castilian 'small fox') and *chivear* (from 'she-goat'). The two remaining verbs in this category are *lambizquear* and its variant spelling *lambuzquear* 'eat between meals' from 'lick', and *jetear* 'to pout' from an 'animal's muzzle'.

Moving to the category [+ human], one class of verbs is created from bases representing different sorts of people. Here we find the existence of several cultural stereotypes. Moreover, the stereotypes frequently have connotations which are either positive or negative. There are only a very few human-based terms which are neutral. Among those with positive connotations are *pilotear* 'drive a car' from 'pilot', and *mecanear* 'do mechanical work', probably from *mecánico*. Two which are ambivalent, according to the point of view of the speaker, are *chicanear* and *chotear*. If one defines *chicano* favorably, it is euphemistic, 'to do one's thing' or 'act like a Chicano'. On the other hand, *chicanismo* is often used derogatorily. Similarly, *chota*, an old slang word in many Latin American countries, means 'cop' and exists as a jocular term for law-and-order people but as a derisive epithet for the lawless. Other verbs here with unfavorable connotations derive from *chipil* ('whiny child'), 'to pamper a youngster', *bruja* ('witch'), 'to go sleepless', *cuzca* and *puta*, 'to act as if on the make', and *chulo*, 'to pimp'.

Verbs which attribute a sense of the ridiculous to the referent are *totachar* and *sanchar*, *totachar* from the Nahuatl *to tatli* ('Our Father') and *sanchar* 'commit adultery' from *sancho*, an innocent, guileless man and hence one easily deceived by his wife—a verb which is limited to feminine subjects. Also in this group is the term *chiquear*, which has unfavorable connotations in meaning 'to spoil a child' although it is formed on a neutral base.

A second class of the category [+ human] contains verbs whose etymons refer not to individuals but to the activities of different groups. The first of these are drawn from horsemen's language. Two of these are the jocular *chicotear* and *pafuelear*, both of which stem from 'whip' and mean 'excel'. Also meaning 'excel' is the macho term *rayar*, from 'stopping one's horse on the line'. The three terms used for automobiles, *arrear* ('to say giddap') 'to start a car', *manear* ('hobble') 'to put on the brakes', and *talonear* ('spur') 'to step on the gas', are all jocular and macho. Two terms with negative connotations are *manzanear* 'to bribe' and *retobear* 'to sass an adult', both originating from bases which refer to parts of the saddle, the pommel and strips of leather used to secure a load.

Two terms come from sailors' language: *anclear* 'to settle down', from 'anchor', and *orillar* 'to curb a car', from 'shore'. Two more terms that have their origin in other means of transportation are *acarrear* from a 'cart', figuratively 'to spread tales', and *carruchar* from *carrucha*, a despective form of *carro*, figuratively 'to joy ride'. All of these are jocular.

Language concerning people who deceive contains five terms, the first two of which are jocular: *chotear* in its meaning of 'play a dirty trick' from *chota* 'stool pigeon' and *chancear* 'commit adultery' from *chanza* 'joke', influenced possibly by English 'chance'. *Chapucear* from *chapuza* 'work of little importance and poorly done' and *pacotear* from *pacota* 'goods of little value' both have the figurative meaning of 'betray'. *Trampear*, originally 'to trick', now has the meaning of 'enter without paying'.

Social gatherings provide a number of jocular terms, some previously mentioned. *Baratear* 'mix with a crowd' originates in *barata* 'bargain sale'; *banquetear* 'have a good time' comes from *banquete* 'banquet'. *Borlotear* 'dance rock style' evolved from *borlote* 'a wild and disorderly party', and *mitotear* 'raise hell, spree, make trouble, or attend a noisy gathering' has its origin in *mitote*, an Indian 'powwow'.

A term which has its antecedent in music is *tamboretear* 'to drub or beat someone up' from *tamborete*, the diminutive of *tambor* 'drum', and it is jocular as well as euphemistic.

The last subdivision of the category [+ human] is composed of terms which are anthropomorphic, that is, borrowed from parts of the human body or from physiological functions, figures of speech extremely common worldwide.

One group of these verbs derives from names of reproductive organs or erotic stimuli, but these terms are not all sexually oriented in their figurative meanings: two examples are *chisquear* 'drive crazy' from *chisgo* 'sex appeal', and *huevonear* 'be lazy'. Anthropomorphic terms that are sexually oriented are *caldear* 'to heat in anger or love', *cachumbear*, from *cacho* 'surf', meaning 'to neck', and *casquetear* and *puñetear* 'to masturbate'. All are noun-based, and all except *caldear* are jocular in varying degrees; one, *cachumbear*, is euphemistic as well.

Another group of these verbs derives from other parts and functions of the human body and none of these are sexually oriented in their figurative meanings. Two refer to the face: *barbear* 'flatter', from the phrase *hacer la barba*, literally 'to stroke someone's beard', and *cachetear* 'slap', from *cachete*, 'cheek'. *Nalguear* 'spank' is based on *nalga* 'buttock'. These three are jocular, and somewhat macho is the teenage *talonear* 'step on the gas' from *talón* 'heel'. All are noun-based.

Descended from bodily functions are three verbs: the euphemistic *babiarse por* 'covet' or 'steal' from the Standard Spanish verb *babiar* 'drool'; jocular *jaspear* 'eat' from *jaspia* 'hunger'; and the jocular dysphemism *pedorrear* 'to raise a stink' from *pedo*.

Perhaps the strongest of the figures to be observed among these verbs is irony, the use of a word in the exact opposite of its literal meaning. Irony is characteristic of only five verbs in the sample, or 3.1% of the total of semantically motivated figures. These verbs, all of which are jocular, include *ahuichotear* 'encourage' or 'stimulate', which is of uncertain derivation but may come from *ahuizote*, an Aztec noun meaning 'pest' or 'nuisance', from the name of a Mexican king who irked his subjects with countless rules and regulations. *Calcear* 'go barefoot' appears to have originated in *calzar* 'put on shoes'. *Chulear* in its meaning 'to pimp' is based on *chulo* 'whoremonger', a nominalized form of the adjective *chulo/-a* 'dear'. *Nortear* and its reflexive form, *nortearse*, which in Standard Spanish mean 'to orient' (or 'give directions') and 'locate oneself', have the ironic meanings of 'drive crazy' and 'go crazy'.

Spanish in the Southwest thus provides a wealth of linguistic structures which allow for the creation of hypersemantic neologisms—phonologic, morphologic, and semantic in their motivation. The native speaker is aware of these resources and makes active use of them. Whether he is literate or not is beside the point. Indeed, these terms are not usually coined by the learned, but in general by those who are underprivileged and undereducated but, nonetheless, lively artists in the creation of vivid language.

References

Ayer, George W. 1974. A tentative classification of language performance categories of Spanish surnamed students. Teaching Spanish to the Spanish Speaking: Newsletter 1.1.3-4.

Baker, Paulline. 1966. Español para los hispanos. Skokie, Ill.: National Textbook Company.

Bolinger, Dwight. 1975. Aspects of language. 2nd ed. New York: Harcourt, Brace, and Jovanovich.

Cobos, Rubén. 1983. A dictionary of New Mexico and southern Colorado Spanish. Santa Fe: Museum of New Mexico Press.

Cotton, Eleanor Greet, and John M. Sharp. 1980a. Hypersemanticization in neologistic Mexican Spanish verbs. Papers in Romance 2.4.229-246.

Cotton, Eleanor Greet, and John M. Sharp. 1980b. Neologistic palatal + -ar verbs in Mexican-American Spanish. In: Speaking, singing, and teaching: A multidisciplinary approach to language variation. Eds. Florence Barkin and Elizabeth Brandt. Tempe: Arizona State University. 422-444.

Cotton, Eleanor Greet, and John M. Sharp. 1983. Spanish verb form usage in El Paso and Mexico City: A comparison. Conference on Research Needs in Chicano Spanish: A Major Ethnic Dialect.

Espinosa, Aurelio M. 1975. Speech mixture in New Mexico: The influence of the English language on Mexican American Spanish. In: El lenguaje de los chicanos; Regional and social characteristics used by Mexican Americans. Eds. Eduardo Hernandez-Chavez, Andrew Cohen and Anthony F. Beltrano. Arlington, Virginia: Center for Applied Linguistics. 99-113.

Galván, Roberto A., and Richard V. Teschner. 1975. The dictionary of the Spanish of Texas. Silver Spring, Maryland: Institute of Modern Languages.

Labov, William. 1971. The notion of system in creole languages. In: Pidginization and creolization of languages. Ed. Dell Hymes. London: Cambridge University Press. 447-472.

Langacker, Ronald W. 1973. Language and its structure. New York: Harcourt, Brace, and Jovanovich.

Lawrence, Timothy James. 1982. Language mixing in modified noun phrases. M.A. thesis, The University of Texas at El Paso.

Moreno de Alba, José G. 1978. Valores de las formas verbales en el español de México. México: Universidad Nacional Autónoma de México.

Paz, Octavio. 1963. El laberinto de la soledad. 3rd ed. México: Fondo de Cultura Económica.

Peñalosa, Fernando. 1980. Chicano sociolinguistics: A brief introduction. Rowley, Massachusetts: Newbury.

Perrine, Laurence. 1973. Sound and sense: An introduction to poetry. 4th ed. New York: Harcourt, Brace, and Jovanovich.

Philbrick, F. A. 1967. Bias words. In: Introductory readings on language. Eds. Wallace L. Anderson and Norman C. Stageberg. New York: Holt, Rinehart and Winston. 176-184.

Sharp, John M. 1970. The origin of some non-standard lexical items in the Spanish of El Paso. In: Studies in language and linguistics, 1969-1970. Eds. Ralph W. Ewton, Jr., and Jacob Ornstein. El Paso: Texas Western Press of The University of Texas at El Paso. 207-232.

Sobin, Nicholas. 1976. Texas Spanish and lexical borrowing. Papers in Linguistics 9. 1 and 2. 15-47.

Ullmann, Stephen. 1966. Semantic universals. In: Universals of language. Ed. Joseph H. Greenberg. Cambridge, Massachusetts: MIT Press. 217-262.

Chapter 19
A look toward the future of Spanish

In 1977, Spanish was the native language of no less than 213,000,000 speakers, a sizeable proportion of the world's population. By 1983 this figure had risen to 297,000,000. The total is projected to reach 422,000,000 by the year 2000, an increase of 42% in 15 years. At present, Spanish is the fourth language in the world in numbers of speakers, and it will become the third if it outdistances Russian. Only Chinese and English are spoken natively by a greater number. These statistics lead one to hypothesize what the prospects are for Spanish to become a truly international language (Wallechinsky, Wallace, and Wallace 1977:169).

Several characteristics of Spanish speakers and their language seem to favor its growth and spread. For one, the population explosion in Latin America that began around World War II has continued and may be expected to expand. For instance, it is projected that by 2025 there will be 93 metropolitan areas with a population of over five million, and 15 of these are either in Mexico or South America; it is thought that the number of residents in Mexico City, Buenos Aires, and Santiago will almost have doubled (McDowell 1984:181). The rate of growth in Mexico in 1982 was 2.4%. Therefore, it can be estimated that its present population, some 75 million, will grow to more than 125 million by the year 2000 (McDowell 1984:148).

There are a number of reasons for this increase. One of these is that the median age of Spanish speakers is relatively young—in Mexico, 18 (McDowell 1984:139). McDowell comments:

> Third world countries . . . now hold very youthful populations, and the populations will continue to soar because there are more women of childbearing age. Hence the paradox of modern population growth: even as the birthrate continues to fall, the population will rise (1984:182).

Two other reasons for the burgeoning number of Spanish speakers in Latin America are the tendency to have large families and the substantial drop in the mortality rate.

Another characteristic which favors the spread of the Spanish language is that the prestige of Hispanic culture, once low, has climbed high with the acclaim accorded to many twentieth-century philosophers and authors such as Federico García Lorca of Spain, Pablo Neruda of Chile, Jorge Luis Borges of Argentina, Carlos Fuentes of Mexico, and Nobel laureates Miguel Ángel Asturias of Guatemala and, most recently, Colombian Gabriel García-Márquez, who has drawn a great deal of attention worldwide, with his novel *Cien años de soledad*.

The Spanish language, moreover, is well suited for use as a lingua franca or second tongue. Its phonology shares features common to many other languages which are not contiguous or historically akin. Its five vowels, for example, are the same as or similar to their counterparts in the majority of languages the world over. When spoken by nonnatives, Spanish can be distorted by mistakes and still be understood. This maintenance of communication is due to its phonological structure. It has fewer phonemic vowels and consonants than many other languages. Phonemes are spread widely enough apart so that the foreigner need not worry about fine distinctions which are often to him inaudible. The five-vowel system of Spanish, for instance, may be compared with the 17 of English (Stockwell and Bowen 1965:117-118). Its consonants, generally agreed to number about 19, may be contrasted with the 24 of English (Stockwell and Bowen 1965:116) and the 23 of Mandarin Chinese (Chao 1968:22).

Phonemic contrasts are not only fewer but also simpler in type. The foreign speaker of Spanish is not faced with the problem of differentiation between open and close *e*, as in French *été* 'been' /eté/ versus *était* 'was' /etέ/. These two sounds exist in Spanish, but are not in phonemic contrast. The same is true of *s* and *z*, as in English *sip* and *zip*. A foreign speaker of Spanish who says [zapáto] instead of [sapáto] will sound odd, but he will not be misunderstood. Spanish does not present subtle phonemic contrasts such as the difference between prepalatal and postpalatal [s] in Polish that causes foreigners to say 'pigs' (*prosze*) when they mean 'please' (*prosie*). Nor does one have to distinguish between sibilants that are retroflex and those that are not, as in Chinese. Unlike Italian, geminate consonants in Spanish are rare, and the vowel harmony of the typical Finno-Ugric languages is nonexistent. Another vocalic-suprasegmental difficulty that does not have to be mastered is vowel length, phonemic in Czech, Finnish, and Japanese. Indeed, vowel duration varies from dialect to dialect in Spanish. Tones do not distinguish the meanings of individual words as they do in Serbo-Croatian and Chinese. Chinese *ma*, for example, if pronounced with a falling tone, means 'to scold'; if with a rising tone, 'hemp'; if with a level tone, 'mother'; and if with a dipping tone, 'horse' (Wang 1980:58).

Spanish morphology admittedly is far more complex than that of many other major languages such as English and Chinese. The maximum number of verb forms in English, for example, is eight for *be*. Other irregular verbs have five, and regular forms have only four. Chinese has only one! However, the example of Papiamento, the Spanish-based creole of the Caribbean, shows that this morphological complexity can be reduced without significant loss to the transmission of meaning.

Obviously, in the case of any lingua franca, whether artificial like Esperanto or natural like English or nineteenth-century French, there will always be a problem with lexicon. Vocabulary must be based on the language of some group or groups of people. Speakers who do not belong to these groups must necessarily find the language exotic. The dimensions of this problem, however, will be reduced if the lexical items are at least in part familiar to other speakers. The fact that Spanish is Latin-based means that it shares much of its lexicon with a fairly large number of other tongues. The largest group of these is, of course, the Romance languages. A recent study on linguistic demography notes that the correspondences among these are extensive, from 97% between Spanish and

Portuguese to 67% between French and Rumanian. The same study predicts that by the year 2000, a billion people, or one-sixth of humanity, will be speaking a neo-Latin tongue, according to Carlos Barral (1984:19).

Of the European languages that do not belong to the Romance group, the largest in terms of speakers is English, and, even though English is a descendant of Germanic, it has a lexicon so Latinate in nature that of the 20,000 words of highest frequency today, the Anglo-Saxon element accounts for less than one-fifth, while the Graeco-Roman represents over three-fifths (Robinson and Cassidy 1954:173). And if one ignores frequency of use and simply compares the number of Graeco-Latinate elements to the total of the English lexicon, the percentages for Anglo-Saxon would decrease even further. The English language is a Germanic skeleton with Latin flesh. Accordingly, if one speaks English as a first or a second language, he will find learning Spanish vocabulary fairly easy.

In the case of other European languages, especially the Germanic and Slavic, elements from Latin and Greek have been introduced into the lexicon through science, technology, and education. In speaking of the resultant impact on human language, Bodmer says that

> the growing stock of internationally current terms for machinery, instruments, chemicals, electrical appliances, and manufactured products, [as well as] the vocabulary of modern technics is equally the word material of the United States and the U.S.S.R., of modern Iran and of Italy. It is already invading the Far East [cf. Japan] and must do so more and more, if China and India emerge from their present miseries as free and modernized societies (1944:502).

The Latin and Greek roots used as constituents of these scientific terms worldwide are identical to those of Spanish.

For Spanish to become a second world language, rivalling English in this respect, thus seems possible. However, there are powerful factors that militate against it. One of these is that Spanish, unlike some other languages, was not spread throughout the world but was limited to the Western Hemisphere. English and French, in contrast, became implanted not only in the West but also in Africa, India, Asia, and Polynesia, where they continue to serve as second languages today. According to editor Carlos Barral, 'the weakness of Spanish is in its lack of a more or less balanced distribution on several continents' (1984:19). Even Portuguese outdoes Spanish in more regions outside of the Americas—as in Angola, Mozambique, Goa, and Macao. Outside of the Americas, in places where Spanish was introduced in the heyday of its empire, it has all but disappeared. For example, it has been replaced by English and Tagalog in the Philippines and by French in most of North Africa.

Spanish also suffers in that 'it is not the language of an industrial power of world rank', but, except for Spain, belongs to the economically underdeveloped Third World. The countries of Latin America are, on the whole, producers of raw material and only now are beginning to develop their technology and heavy industries. The economic plight of Hispanic America is worsened by perennial political instability. Outsiders, rightly or wrongly, view it as a region plagued by dictatorship, terrorism, and corruption. Further, the rate of illiteracy is still very high: for southern Europe 8.5% and for Latin America 20.3% (Barral 1984:19).

Traditionally, few Europeans have been interested in the study of Spanish as a part of their general education. Instead, they choose English, French, or German, languages which have served as vehicles for literary works of great merit and universality. A French novel can be read in Japan or Africa, and a reader can identify with its characters. Shakespeare is thought to be more universal than Cervantes and Molière more so than García Lorca. Goethe and Thomas Mann have no counterparts in Hispanic letters.

Some Spanish writers find their homelands picturesque and romantic and emphasize these traits—just the opposite of the universal. Moreover, this practice perpetuates the stereotype of a Latin country as populated almost entirely by bullfighters, guitar players, sombreroed bandits, and beruffled *señoritas* with flashing eyes, who click their heels to the rhythm of castanets. Surely, the language of these speakers is not to be taken seriously!

Another stereotype, older and less pleasant, was invented by Spaniards themselves—always their own worst critics, as was succinctly recognized by Joaquín María Bartrina in his 'Arabesco':

> Oyendo hablar a un hombre, fácil es
> acertar donde vió la luz del sol;
> si os alaba a Inglaterra, será inglés,
> si os habla mal de Prusia, es un francés,
> y si habla mal de España, es español (1932:385).

This second stereotype was begun by Bartolomé de las Casas and other Spanish humanitarians in Latin America. These writers, in their attempts to defend the Indians against exploitation, exaggerated the accounts of their fellow countrymen's mistreatment of the natives. These highly colored descriptions, intended for Spain, were seized upon by two of her principal enemies, France and England. The French had sporadically been at war with Spain for over two centuries, from the time of the Reyes Católicos until the Treaty of the Ladies and the accession of a French Bourbon king to the Spanish throne. The English, from the time of Henry VIII, had viewed Catholic Spain as the mortal foe of their faith and had narrowly escaped invasion by the Invincible Armada in 1588. Hostile authors in both countries magnified the supposed misdeeds of the Conquistadores to such an extent that these tales developed into the Black Legend, which portrayed all Spaniards as monsters of cruelty and intolerance. Neither of these stereotypic views is calculated to further the spread of Spanish as a second language.

Even though Spanish may not become a lingua franca, as English is and as French was, it is already showing signs of becoming a second language in the non-Romance areas of the Western Hemisphere. The United States receives hundreds of thousands of Hispanic immigrants annually. (Approximately 60% of the Spanish speakers in this country are of Mexican origin, 14% are from Puerto Rico, 5% are from Cuba, and 21% from other parts of Latin America)

(Solé 1985:283). Between the years 1970 and 1980, there were 1.3 million newcomers from Latin America. In 1980, the number of Spanish speakers in this country was 14,608,673, 6.4% of the total population. In 1985, they may be estimated at 17,000,000, the second largest minority group in the United States (U.S. Bureau of the Census 1983:119).

Prior to 1950, the majority of these Hispanics were to be found in the Southwest, especially in rural areas. By 1980, however, they had established themselves in substantial numbers in all other regions of the nation as well.

Table 25 Population of Spanish origin by area, 1980.

Region	Population of Spanish origin	Percentage of the total of area
Northeast	2,604,170	5.3%
North Central	1,295,045	2.2%
South	4,446,969	5.9%
West	6,260,011	14.5% (U.S. Bureau of the Census 1983:124).

The states with the largest numbers of Spanish speakers are California, with 31% of the Hispanics in this country, Texas, with 20%, and New York, with 11%; Arizona, Colorado, and New Mexico have 6% each. The remaining 24% are spread throughout the nation (Solé 1985:296). There are enormous concentrations of Latin Americans in the three urban centers of Los Angeles (over three million), New York (nearly two million), and Miami (almost a million). Percentages represented by Hispanics in 1980 in several major cities are shown in Table 26.

Of the seventeen million Hispanics here, approximately 90% use Spanish with their families, making it the most widespread foreign language in the United States. Bilingualism is also widespread. In 1980, one-half of those of Spanish origin claimed to be very proficient in English, and one-fourth claimed to have adequate mastery. In the least proficient one-fourth, one of six had problems, and one of ten spoke no English at all (Solé 1985:284). English ability varies with age: the youngest, from five through 24 years, the best; and the oldest, 65 years and up, the weakest. The speakers with the highest degree of mastery (the youngest) also comprise the largest group of the Hispanic population. In 1980, almost one-half of the Mexican Americans and Puerto Ricans, plus one-third of those from Cuba, one-third from Central America, and another third from South America, were under twenty years of age (Solé 1985:294). Those over 65 numbered 708,880, while those under 18 totaled 5,627,956 (U.S. Bureau of the Census 1983:51).

These young Latin Americans tend to marry within the Hispanic group and, like Hispanics in general, to have larger families (3.48 persons per household) than the United States average (2.75) (U.S. Bureau of the Census 1983:51).

Table 26 Population of Spanish origin by city, 1980.

City	Percentage of population	City	Percentage of population
El Paso	61.9%	New York	20.0%
San Antonio	53.7%	Austin	17.6%
Corpus Christi	48.5%	Phoenix	15.0%
Albuquerque	36.8%	Houston	14.7%
Fresno	29.3%	Chicago	14.0%
Los Angeles	27.5%	Denver	11.4%
Jersey City	26.1%	Dallas	8.5%
Tucson	25.0%	Colorado Springs	8.1%
Miami	23.5%	(U.S. Bureau of the Census 1984: 19-21)	

Most of their children grow up in areas with a high density of Spanish speakers, and are thus quite likely to retain their native culture and speech (Solé 1985:296). Further, except for those from Cuba and other Central and South American areas, Spanish speakers are likely to receive less education than their 'Anglo peers'. In the Southwest, 14.6% have under five years in school, only 45.6% graduate from high school, and a mere sprinkling (6.5%) complete college (Solé 1985:295). As a result, they are often handicapped economically. Most of them occupy the lower strata of the labor force, and many live below the poverty line. Solé comments: 'The low educational attainment and low occupational profile of Hispanics retard their social mobility within the mainstream society, which in turn fosters ingroup cohesiveness and the maintenance of the minority language' (Solé 1985:295).

An even more important motivation for this linguistic continuity is the 'inevitable involvement of these speakers with their mother-tongue as they learned it in childhood' (Solé 1985:296). So Spanish continues, in contrast to the fate of other languages such as Italian and German. In the past and at present, this loyalty has posed a problem in public education, particularly in places in which large numbers of Spanish-speaking pupils are a novelty. With the advent of the Castro regime in Cuba, southern Florida received thousands of refugees, many of whom belonged to the highly literate professional class. In the course of two decades, Miami was transformed into a city of two languages with an immediate and urgent need for bilingual education. Dade County, indeed, was the pioneer in this pedagogical endeavor, and it is the forerunner of many such programs which now, by law, exist wherever there are children who need to learn English. And their monolingual English-speaking peers, who have largely been ignored in these programs, are now showing increased interest in the benefits of bilingualism as well. This attitude is reflected in a letter to *The El Paso Times* of May 13, 1985:

Favors bilingualism

I heard the El Paso public schools intend to drop Spanish instruction, at least in the lower grades, next year. I was hoping they would hire qualified Spanish teachers, develop a good course of study and intensify their instruction.

The value of speaking Spanish in El Paso and the Southwest cannot be overemphasized. We should all be bilingual.

I have had many chances to learn the language, but I was always so "smart," I made my friends speak English. Now they're bilingual, and I'm paying for private Spanish lessons (Healy 1985).

Spanish instruction, thus, is sought after, for more effective communication in both languages. This can be seen in the enrollment figures in language classrooms at all levels. Spanish used to trail French and German, but now heads the three, and speakers no longer feel their language symbolic of subordinate rank.

There have been concomitant changes in attitudes toward Hispanic culture and history, which can be seen in a new Mexican American literature, an example of which is 'We've Played Cowboys':

We've Played Cowboys

We've played cowboys
   not knowing
nuestros charros
   and their countenance
con trajes de gala
   silver embroidery
on black wool
   Zapata rode in white
campesino white
   and Villa in brown
y nuestros charros
   parade of sculptured gods
on horses
   of flowing manes
proud
   erect
they galloped
and we've played cowboys
   as opposed to indians
when ancestors of mis charros abuelos
indios fueron
   de la meseta central
and of the humid jungles of Yucatán
   nuestros Mayas
if we must
   cowboys play

        con bigotes
            y ojos negros
                negro pelo
        let them be
    let them have cheekbones
    de firmeza y decisión
    of our caballeros tigres (Alurista 1972:31-32).

Like the foregoing poem, most Mexican American literature until recently has been written in a mixture of Spanish and English or in English alone. Publishers in the United States could see no profit in the publication of works in a 'foreign language'. Thus, serious writers in Spanish, such as Alejandro Morales, were obliged to publish in Mexico or to search out a marginal press in the United States with limited funds for promotion and distribution. Now, however, literature in Spanish is coming out in this country and is being encouraged as a medium for the establishment of a new 'standard' dialect. This will reflect both traditional values and the adaptation of Chicanos to life in this nation. Further, it is designed to serve as the language for literature of real artistic value. In support of this trend is *Palabra Nueva*, a collection of contemporary Mexican American short stories in Spanish. Its themes vary widely, from migratory workers to memories of the past from the point of view of two generations, to problems of adjustment of new immigrants. Its authors, both well known and novice, come from regions as widely separated as California and New Jersey, Texas and Minnesota. In addition, this anthology is not an in-house Chicano publication but the work of a state university press (*Palabra Nueva: Cuentos Chicanos* 1984:x-xi).

The Mexican American and the Hispanic world in general are increasing their influence on other aspects of life in the United States. Professional men—especially physicians and lawyers—and businessmen in general have come to realize the economic importance of being bilingual, in areas where there is a large Hispanic population to be served. Along the border, quite important is the twin plant program, in which goods partially finished in the United States are sent across the border for assembly in Mexico, to the benefit of both countries. This venture proves to be a powerful stimulus to the development of bilingualism among the personnel, both Mexican and American. Another institution which spans the border is the church. Many denominations based in one country have joint programs in the other. In many cases, services are conducted in both languages. Over 900 churches use Spanish for all or part of their service (Fishman and Milán 1983:176).

In daily living in the United States, clothing and food from Latin America are no longer felt to be unusual. Men in *guayabera* shirts and women in embroidered cottons are as likely to be seen in Chicago as in Tijuana. A well-known fast food chain has made *tacos* and *enchiladas* familiar to diners who a few years ago would have been hard pressed to distinguish a *frijol* from a *jalapeño*. *Gazpacho* frequently appears on menus in Midwestern restaurants, which is unfortunate for the reputation of Spanish cuisine, and the reader is forewarned that it bears no resemblance to the original. The same is true of the *Margaritas* innocent of *tequila* served far north of the border. Be this as it may, one must at least recognize that imitation is the sincerest form of flattery! This no doubt explains the growing popularity of Hispanic cookbooks. In the past, these were in Spanish for use by maids. Nowadays they are in English, sponsored by leading publishers, for use by the lady of the house (or the gent, if he does the cooking!).

Also influential are the 850 Spanish radio stations, and television is now broadcast from one coast to the other of the United States by more than 100 TV and cable stations affiliated with S.I.N., the Spanish International Network (Fishman and Milán 1983:176). The programs, all in Spanish, are produced for the most part in Mexico, Argentina, and Spain. *Telenovelas* ('soap operas') are extremely popular, as are the newscasts, especially '24 Horas' from Mexico City.

Tourism is another source of Hispanization. Spain, once almost ignored by vacationers, is now attracting more than 35,000,000 tourists a year. And the Mexican borders are so congested with traffic from the United States that the shoppers must often wait more than an hour to cross an international border.

The growing closeness between Mexico and the United States has led to increasing intermarriage, with consequent bicultural-bilingual families, where parents insist that their offspring be exposed to both languages. Spanish, once frowned upon in polite society in the United States, is now taking its place with French as a hallmark of the well-traveled, well-educated person.

Whatever the eventual fate of Spanish as a lingua franca, there can be no doubt that it is a major force ensuring the unity of the entire Hispanic world, once breached by the bitter Wars of Independence. Spanish speakers in the Americas recognize in their noble language a rich inheritance that binds them together not only with their brethren in the New World but also with those in Spain. The following verses from 'La Lengua Castellana', by José Mercado, a Puerto Rican and United States citizen, epitomize the Hispanics' feeling for their mother tongue:

Lengua inmortal, idioma de Cervantes,
el colono de ayer tu gloria canta.
  Eres raudo torrente. Te despeñas
y caes en deslumbrante catarata,
llenando de sonidos el espacio
y de notas de fuego, que se apagan
con ese ritmo vago y misterioso
de un suspiro de amor. Sonora y clara,
expresas la pasión; y el pensamiento
por ti se viste con brillantes galas.

   .   .   .

  Ese lazo que ayer rompió la fuerza,
¡átalo tú, mi lengua castellana!

Immortal language, tongue of Cervantes,
yesterday's colonist sings thy glory.
Thou art a rushing torrent. Thou castest thyself down
and fallest in a blinding cascade
filling space with sound
and with notes of fire quenched
in the melody impenetrable and mysterious
of a lover's sigh. Resounding and clear,
thou voicest thy passion; and thought
by thee is clad in dazzling garb.

¡Mensajera perenne de concordia,
cruza el inmenso mar que nos separa
y lleva de la América española

  .   .   .

The bond yesterday severed by force,

make fast anew, my lengua castellana.

el beso fraternal de nuestras almas!

Perennial envoy of harmony,
cross the vast sea between us
and receive from Spanish America

  .   .   .

the fraternal kiss that unites our souls!
(Mercado 1969:539-540)

References

Alurista. 1972. We've played cowboys. In: Literatura Chicana: Texto y contexto. Eds. Antonio Castañeda Shular, Tomás Ybarra-Frausto and Joseph Sommers. Englewood Cliffs, New Jersey: Prentice-Hall. 31-32.

Barral, Carlos. 1984. El País. Madrid. April 9, p. 19, col. 2.

Bartrina, Joaquín María. 1932. Arabesco. In: The Oxford book of Spanish verse. Ed. James Fitzmaurice-Kelly. Oxford: Clarendon. 385.

Bodmer, Frederick. 1944. The loom of language. New York: Norton.

Chao, Yuen Ren. 1968. A grammar of spoken Chinese. Berkeley: University of California Press.

Fishman, Joshua A., and William Milán. 1983. Spanish language resources of the United States: Some preliminary findings. In: Spanish in the U.S. setting: Beyond the Southwest. Ed. Lucía Elías-Olivares. Rosslyn, Virginia: National Clearinghouse for Bilingual Education. 167-179.

Healy, Nellie. 1985. Letter. The El Paso Times. August 15, A, p. 2, col. 3.

McDowell, Bart. 1984. Mexico City: An alarming giant. National Geographic. August. 138-185.

Mercado, José. 1969. La lengua castellana. In: Las mil mejores poesías de la lengua castellana. 22nd ed. Ed. José Bergua. Madrid: Ediciones Ibéricas. 537-540.

Palabra nueva: Cuentos Chicanos. 1984. Eds. Ricardo Aguilar, Armando Armengol, and Oscar V. Somoza. El Paso: Texas Western Press of the University of Texas at El Paso.

Robertson, Stuart, and Frederic G. Cassidy. 1954. The development of modern English. 2nd ed. Englewood Cliffs, New Jersey: Prentice-Hall.

Solé, Yolanda Russinovich. 1985. Spanish/English mother-tongue claiming: The 1980 Census data, a subsample, and their sociodemographic correlates. Hispania. 68.2.283-297.

Stockwell, Robert P., and J. Donald Bowen. 1965. The sounds of English and Spanish. Chicago: The University of Chicago Press.

U.S. Bureau of the Census. 1983. 1980 Census of population. vol. 1. General population characteristics, part I U.S. summary. Washington, DC: U.S. Department of Commerce.

U.S.Bureau of the Census. 1984. Statistical abstract of the U.S. 1985. Washington, DC: U.S. Department of Commerce.

Wallechinsky, David, Irving Wallace, and Amy Wallace. 1977. The book of lists. New York: Morrow.

Wang, William S-Y. 1980. The Chinese language. In: Human communication: Language and its psychobiological bases. San Francisco: Freeman. 50-62.

Appendix 1: Dialect questionnaires

Questionnaires are frequently used by field workers to gather information about a dialect under study. Following are four examples.

The first is part of an unpublished mimeo designed to elicit samples of Texas English for the Linguistic Atlas of the United States. It contains useful instructions on procedures as well.

Questionnaire 1. For investigation of Texas English

INSTRUCTIONS:

Record the informant's terms for the words and phrases that are printed in capital letters on the work sheets. Write each word beside or under the item on the work sheet, using the conventional spelling. If the word has no written form that you know of, or if it is given with an unusual pronunciation, use the phonetic alphabet in transcribing it. Try in every case to determine the informant's usage without yourself using the word in question. If you find it necessary to 'suggest' the term to the informant, always write 's.' or 'sug.' before the word, thus: 's. Dutch cheese'.

Items are arranged topically to help give coherence to the interview. Please add any further words that you think to be of interest; use the back of the sheet or a separate sheet if necessary. If the informant uses a number of interesting cookery terms, ranching or farming terms, etc., record as many as you can whether they are on the work sheets or not.

If the informant uses more than one term for a single item, record all terms used. If one of the terms is regarded by the informant as 'older', or 'old-fashioned', or 'familiar', please indicate this fact. *Please give definitions in all cases where variation in meaning is encountered.*

Note: Words enclosed in parentheses (#) are suggestions as to the kind of variants to watch for. They are by no means a complete listing of the possibilities.

THE WEATHER

0101. TIME WHEN THE SUN COMES UP (sun-up)
  02. AT SIX IN THE MORNING YESTERDAY, THE SUN (riz, raised, rised, come up)
  03. CLEARING UP (fairing up, fairing off, etc.)
  04. STORM WITH RAIN & THUNDER & LIGHTNING (electrical storm, etc.)
  05. VERY HEAVY RAIN THAT DOESN'T LAST LONG (gulley-washer, goose-drownder, etc.)
  06. THE WIND IS NOT BLOWING SO HARD (easing up, laying)
  07. STRONG COLD WIND FROM NORTH (blizzard, norther, wet norther, blue norther, etc.)

08. LONG PERIOD OF DRY WEATHER (drouth, dry spell)

Other terms:

THE HOUSE

0301. ROOM AT FRONT WHERE GUESTS ARE ENTERTAINED (parlor, sitting room, etc.)
02. FLOOR OF FIREPLACE
03. SHELF OVER FIREPLACE (mantel, mantelpiece, fireboard, etc.)
04. TROUGHS TO TAKE WATER OFF ROOF (eaves troughs, spouts, gutters, etc.)
05. CLOSET FOR CLOTHING
06. UNFINISHED SPACE AT TOP OF HOUSE (attic, garret, etc.)
07. PORCH (*at front door*; *at back door*; *describe*) (piazza, veranda, gallery, stoop, etc.)
08. OVERLAPPING BOARDS ON OUTSIDE OF HOUSE (*horizontal*) (clapboards, siding, weatherboards)
09. ROOM FOR STORING DISUSED ARTICLES
10. MAIN RANCH HOUSE (big house, hacienda, etc.)
11. SHINGLES OR BOARDS SPLIT FROM A LOG (shakes, clapboards)

Other terms:

HOUSEHOLD GOODS

0401. CHEST OF DRAWERS (*describe*) (dresser, bureau, chiffonier, armoire, etc.)
02. WINDOW COVERING ON ROLLERS (blinds, curtains)
03. SMALL ROOM OFF THE KITCHEN TO STORE FOODS AND EQUIPMENT
04. LONG PIECE OF FURNITURE TO SIT OR LIE ON (lounge, couch, davenport, etc.)
05. HOUSEHOLD GOODS (*particularly worthless stuff*) (plunder, etc.)
06. IRONS TO HOLD LOGS FOR BURNING (dog irons, fire dogs, etc.)
07. WOODEN VESSEL FOR WATER (bucket, pail)
08. METAL VESSEL FOR WATER, MILK, etc. (bucket, pail)
09. METAL CONTAINER FOR CARRYING DINNER OR LUNCH
10. GARBAGE CONTAINER (for scraps, slop, etc.)
11. CONTAINER TO CARRY COAL INTO HOUSE
12. CLOTH FOR DRYING DISHES (tea towel, cup towel, dish towel)
13. CLOTH USED FOR WASHING FACE OR BATHING (washrag)
14. HEAVY IRON PAN USED FOR FRYING (skillet, etc.)
15. DEVICE TO TURN ON WATER (*in kitchen or bathroom*; *outdoors*) (tap, spigot, spicket, faucet, hydrant)
16. LARGE JAR FOR DRINKING WATER (olla, etc.)
17. CLOTH COVER USED TO COVER A BED PILLOW

THE FAMILY

1201. He RESEMBLES his father in appearance; in other traits (takes after, etc.)
02. Her RELATIVES (relations, folks, kinfolks, etc.)
03. Her PARENTS (folks, etc.)
04. She has BROUGHT UP three children (raised, reared, etc.)
05. GRANDMOTHER (usual term and terms of affection)
06. GRANDFATHER (usual term and terms of affection)
07. MOTHER (usual term and terms of affection)
08. FATHER (usual term and terms of affection)
09. MY WIFE (also familiar and facetious terms) (the Missus, etc.)
10. MY HUSBAND (familiar)
11. ILLEGITIMATE CHILD
12. WOMAN WHO HELPS AT CHILDBIRTH (granny woman, partera)

Other terms:

SOCIAL LIFE

1301. STRING OF BEADS (strand, pair)
02. He is COURTING her (wooing, etc.)
03. KISSING (bussing)
04. NOISY BURLESQUE SERENADE AFTER A WEDDING (describe) (shivaree, belling, skimmelton, callathump, etc.)
05. HARMONICA (mouth organ, harp, mouth harp, French harp)
06. BOYS' WEAPON MADE OF RUBBER STRIPS ON A FORKED STICK (sling, slingshot, beanie, nigger-shooter, etc.)
07. GREETING EARLY ON CHRISTMAS MORNING (Christmas gift)
08. BONUS OR GIFT GIVEN WITH A PURCHASE OR WHEN BILL IS PAID (pilon, lagniappe)
09. May I TAKE you home (*on foot*; *in a vehicle*) (carry)
10. STORE WHERE ALL KINDS OF CHEAP THINGS ARE SOLD (racket store, etc.)
11. THE LOCAL PREACHER; AN UNPROFESSIONAL, PART-TIME, LAY PREACHER (parson, dominie, the reverend, Brother so-and-so, jackleg preacher, yardax, chair-backer, Bible banger, etc.)
12. YOU (*plural*) (you-all, you-uns, you folks, etc.)
13. HELLO! (*familiar term*) (hi, hey, etc.)

Other terms:

VARIOUS ACTIVITIES; VERB FORMS AND SYNTACTICAL PECULIARITIES

1501. I WANT TO GET OFF (I want off)
02. I'LL WAIT FOR YOU (on you)

03. LEAVE VERY FAST (light a shuck, etc.)
04. She CLEANS UP the house (tidies up, reds up, etc.)
05. WASH OFF (DISHES) IN CLEAR WATER (rinse, rench)
06. He DRAGGED a log (drug)
07. BALANCED BOARD FOR CHILDREN TO PLAY ON
08. IT WASN'T ME
09. GAME IN WHICH HORSESHOES ARE PITCHED; RINGS, ETC.
10. A GOOD DEAL (right much, right smart, etc.)
11. JAIL (*jocular terms*) (calaboose, hoosegow, etc.)
12. He THREW a STONE at a dog (throwed, flung, chunked; a rock, etc.)
13. SWITCH (for punishing children)
14. TO WHIP SOUNDLY
15. HE OUGHTN'T TO GO (hadn't ought, ortn't, etc.)
16. He walked DIAGONALLY across a field (catty-cornered, antigodlin, etc.)
17. HE DIVED IN (dove, div, etc.)
18. The baby MOVES ON ALL FOURS across the floor (creeps, crawls)
19. He CLIMBED up a tree (clum, clim, etc.)

NAME OF INFORMANT
AGE   EDUCATION
OCCUPATION
BIRTHPLACE
LENGTH OF RESIDENCE IN PRESENT COMMUNITY
LENGTH OF RESIDENCE IN OTHER PLACES (Specify)
BIRTHPLACE AND HOME OF PARENTS
NAME AND LOCATION OF COMMUNITY IN WHICH INFORMANT NOW
    LIVES (including name of county)
TYPE OF COMMUNITY
FURTHER CHARACTERIZATION OF INFORMANT (Anglo, Latin, or Negro? Foreign language background? Types of social and religious contacts. Principal interests, activities, reading.)

Other topics:
—*Topography*: what terms are used for various types of land, streams, hills, etc.
—*Time and distance*.
—*The premises*: farm and ranch: buildings, equipment, types of workers.
—*Animals*: what are they called; what word or sound is used to call a dog, a cat, chickens, hogs, etc.
—*Crops and foods*.
—*Persons*: personal characteristics; how people are described; terms used for various foreigners.

The second example was prepared by students at The University of Texas at El Paso in a course on Latin American dialectology. (These students used Questionnaire 1 as a model.) Included is general information about the informant which will be of use in the analysis of the data.

Questionnaire 2. For investigation of El Paso Spanish

Dialectología Hispánica: Informantes

Nombre del (la) informante:
País:
Edad aproximada:
  niño: ( )
  adolescente: ( )
  maduro joven: ( )
  maduro mediano: ( )
  anciano/a: ( )
Educación formal:
  primaria ( )
  secundaria (y/o preparatoria) ( )
  universidad ( )
Oriundo de: la ciudad ( )
  del campo: ( )
Conocimiento de idiomas:
  monolingüe ( )
  bilingüe ( )
  sabe varios idiomas: ( ) (indíquese cuáles son:)
Tiempo que lleva aquí en El Paso:
  muy poco tiempo:
  varios meses (¿cuántos?):
  muchos años (¿cuántos?):

OTROS COMENTARIOS:

LA CASA

0101. ¿Cómo se llama una casa muy humilde, donde vive una familia muy pobre?

02. ¿Cómo se llama el cuarto donde se reúne la familia para platicar, leer, o ver televisión?

03. ¿Dónde pone usted cosas, trastos, o aparatos que no están en uso?

04. ¿Cómo se llama la cosa que se usa para apagar o encender la luz eléctrica?

05. ¿Cómo se llama el cuarto donde se duerme?

06. ¿Cómo se llama la cosa que se usa para calentar la casa (o, si no toda la casa, un cuarto) durante el tiempo frío?

07. ¿Cómo se llama la pieza subterránea, entre los cimientos de la casa (cuando ésta la tiene)?

08. ¿Cómo se llama el sitio donde se puede encender una lumbre (de leño o carbón) en la sala de la casa?
09. ¿Cómo se llama una silla grande de brazos, con cojines?
10. Tratándose de una cosa de dos o más pisos, ¿cómo se llama la parte más alta de la casa, inmediata al techo?
11. ¿Dónde guarda usted la ropa?

LA COCINA

0201. ¿Cómo se le llama a la comida que no se consume durante la comida?
02. ¿En qué se lavan los utensilios de cocina?
03. ¿Qué se utiliza para lavar estos utensilios?
04. ¿Cómo se llama el aparato de donde sale el agua?
05. ¿Cómo se llama el aparato donde se guarda la leche, la carne, etc.?
06. ¿En qué se prepara el te?
07. ¿Cómo se llama el aparato en el cual se coce (cuece) o se calienta la comida?
08. Cuando le ha gustado una comida, ¿qué expresión usa?
09. ¿Cómo se llama lo que se come por la mañana, al levantarse?
10. ¿Cómo se llama la comida que se toma por la noche?
11. ¿Cómo se llama la comida ligera que se hace por la tarde antes de la cena?

PERSONAS Y RASGOS PERSONALES

0301. ¿Cómo se refiere a la persona con quien está casado?
02. ¿Cómo se refiere a la persona con quien se va a casar?
03. ¿Cómo se refiere a la madre de su madre?
04. ¿Cómo se refiere a:
(a) los padres de su esposo?
(b) los padres de su esposa?
05. ¿Cómo se le llama a una persona que no es de su país?
06. ¿Cómo se le dice a la persona por quien se trabaja?
07. ¿Cómo se le llama a una persona que vende cosas de casa en casa?
08. ¿Cómo se le llama a una persona que habitualmente pide limosna?
09. ¿Cómo se le llama al representante de la ley que anda en motocicleta?
10. ¿Cómo se le llama a una mujer que es todo lo contrario de fea?
11. ¿Cómo se le llama a un hombre que es todo lo contrario de feo?
12. ¿Cómo se le llama a una persona que es de ascendencia nórdica (angloamericano, inglés, germánico, etc.)?
13. ¿Cómo se le llama a un estudiante muy inteligente y aplicado, que hace a los demás quedar mal?
14. ¿Cómo se le llama a un estudiante poco inteligente y aplicado, que generalmente saca malas notas, o fracasa?
15. ¿Cómo se refiere a una persona que es todo lo contrario de amable, que no se lleva bien con la gente?
16. ¿Qué palabra se le aplica al que es todo lo contrario de *flaco*?

17. ¿Qué palabra se le aplica al que es todo lo contrario de *gordo*?
18. ¿Qué término(s) de cariño se usan entre novio(s) (o esposos)?
19. ¿Qué palabra se le aplica a un hombre que tiene 70 años o más?
20. ¿Qué palabra se le aplica a una mujer que tiene 70 años o más?
21. ¿Cómo se le llama a un niño que tiene menos de dos años?
22. ¿Cómo se le llama a una persona que tiene unos 10 a 12 años?
23. ¿Cómo se le llama al empleado que le sirve la mesa en los restaurantes?
24. ¿Cómo se le llama al empleado que sirve en los hoteles para cargarles el equipaje a los clientes?
25. ¿Cómo se le llama al técnico que compone las tuberías, las llaves de agua, los lavabos, etc.?

LOS TRATAMIENTOS

¿A cuál de los siguientes se le dirige de *tú* (o de *vos*), y a cuál de *usted*?

	tú/vos	Usted
0401. El padre a los hijos		
02. Los hijos al padre		
03. La madre a los hijos		
04. Los hijos a la madre		
05. Entre hermanos		
06. Entre amigos		
07. Entre condiscípulos de la misma escuela		
08. El profesor a sus estudiantes		
09. Los empleados a su jefe		
10. El jefe a un empleado		
11. Los niños a sus abuelos		
12. Entre novios		
13. A la doméstica (sirvienta, criada)		
14. Al mozo en el restaurante		
15. A un chófer de taxi		

COMENTARIOS:

LA ROPA Y LAS PRENDAS PERSONALES

0501. ¿Cómo se llama el calzado de verano?
02. ¿Cómo se llama la especie de sombrero que usan los jugadores del béisbol?
03. ¿Cómo se llama la cosa que prensa el cabello de una mujer?
04. *Ilustraciones.*—Se le interrogará al (a la) informante en cuanto a la palabra que se les aplica a los siguientes mediante ilustraciones (grabados, fotos, etc.):
(a) las piyamas (pijamas)
(b) camisa de dormir
(c) swéter (suera)
(d) chamarra (chaqueta)

(e) abrigo ligero (para otoño)

(f) abrigo pesado (para el tiempo muy frío)

(g) bata

(h) calzado pesado y fuerte, como el que usan los obreros industriales

(i) chaqueta de hombre

MISCELÁNEA

0601. ¿Cómo se le saluda a un amigo (cuando no se refiere a la hora del día)?

02. ¿Algo que no es frecuente pasa . . . .?

03. Cuando un profesor le encarga a su clase un tema sobre el cual hay que escribir, ¿cómo se llama el resultado escrito?

04. Cuando comienza a llover, y el agua es poca, ¿cómo se le dice?

05. ¿En qué carga un estudiante sus libros y papeles, o un negociante sus papeles?

06. ¿Cómo se le refiere al empleo u oficio de una persona?

07. ¿Si se le avienta una pelota, usted la _____?

08. ¿Cómo se describe *mucho ruido*?

09. ¿Qué nombre se le da al acto de discutir precios?

10. ¿Qué nombre se le aplica al dinero menudo que se le devuelve a uno que ha pagado su compra con un billete que vale más de lo que debe por lo que ha comprado?

11. ¿Con qué verbo se describe el acto o estado de emborracharse?

12. ¿Con qué palabra o frase se describe el estado en el cual se encuentra uno que se ha emborrachado la noche anterior?

13. ¿Qué palabra o frase se aplica a la condición de una persona que se halla sin dinero?

14. ¿Qué palabra o frase se le aplica a una persona a quien habitualmente le va muy mal en la vida, o que siempre tiene muy mala suerte?

15. ¿Qué palabra o frase se le aplica a una persona a quien habitualmente le va muy bien en la vida, o que siempre tiene muy buena suerte?

The third example was designed by Adela Berry Dávila, who was interested in lexical differences among people of four different age groups in northern Mexico.

Questionnaire 3. For investigation of generational differences in the speech of Ciudad Juárez

CONTENIDO DEL CUESTIONARIO

El cuestionario contiene lo siguiente:

1. Sobrenombres que se dan a personas de aspecto un poco fuera de lo normal, como personas altas, bajas, delgadas, gordas, niños recién nacidos y ancianos.

2. Los sobrenombres que les dan a los agentes del gobierno como a los policías o agentes secretos.
3. Sobrenombres a prendas de vestir como camisa, pantalón o zapatos.
4. Sobrenombres a partes del cuerpo, como cabello, cabeza.
5. Expresiones idiomáticas como cuando alguien se muere, o está enamorado, lo que le hacen cuando lo llevan a la cárcel, lo que le diría a una persona que miente.
6. Nombres de objetos o lugares como un carro policíaco, un cerillo, un cigarro, una cerveza, el cine, la mariguana, las drogas.

En la siguiente página se encontrará el cuestionario que se usó. La letra R. significa la respuesta que se esperaba que los informantes dieran, en varias ocasiones todos dieron la respuesta esperada y en otras usaron diferentes palabras.

1. ¿Cómo te llamas?
2. ¿En dónde naciste?
3. ¿Cuántos años tienes?
4. ¿Estás casado?
5. ¿Hasta qué año llegaste?
6. ¿Eres mexicano?
7. ¿Sexo?
8. ¿Trabajas?
9. ¿Qué tanto tiempo has estado aquí en Juárez?
10. ¿Qué tanto tiempo has estado fuera de Juárez?
11. ¿Qué haces cuando no tienes nada que hacer?
12. ¿Qué haces el fin de semana?
13. ¿Qué te gusta leer?
14. ¿Qué periódico te gusta leer?

CUESTIONARIO

1. ¿Cómo le dices a este?   R. un mordelón
   (foto de un policía)
2. ¿Y esto?   R. la julia
   (foto de una patrulla)
3. ¿Cuando estos te levantan a dónde te llevan?   R. al bote
4. ¿Y luego qué te hacen?   R. te tuercen
5. ¿Qué está haciendo este?   R. tocando el piano
   (foto de una persona tomando las huellas digi-
   tales)
6. Si tú quieres algo que yo ando comiendo, ¿qué   R. mochilas
   me dices?   pásala
7. Al levantarte, vas a la cocina y ¿qué pides?   R. el refín
                                                      el pipirín
                                                      la alfalfa

8. ¿Cómo está este?   R. abollado
   (foto de una persona golpeada)   cateado

9. ¿Cómo está esta persona?   R. ahuitada
  (foto de una persona triste)   aplatanada
10. Si una persona te hace enojar, ¿qué le dices? R. que se la calme
               que se la corte
11. Si te gusta mucho una cosa, ¿qué dices? R. que está muy
               padre
12. ¿Qué ves aquí?   R. una morra
  (foto de una muchacha)   una chava
               una changa
13. ¿Qué ves aquí?   R. un chavo
  (foto de un muchacho)
14. ¿Te gusta?   R. simón
  (si es hombre se le apunta a la muchacha)
  (si es mujer se le apunta al muchacho)
15. Si la (lo) vieras en la calle, ¿qué le dirías a tus R. que vi una cosota
  amigos?   un papasote
               un mango
16. ¿Qué están anunciando aquí?   R. el mono
  (se le señala el anuncio de un cine)
17. ¿Qué están haciendo aquí?   R. tirando chancla
  (foto de una pareja bailando)
18. Si vas a bailar, ¿con quién vas?   R. con mi morra
               con mi chava
19. ¿Cómo está este?   R. hasta la manitas
  (foto de una persona borracha)
20. ¿Cómo le dices a una persona como esta? R. la liga
  (foto de una persona delgada)   la víbora
21. ¿Cómo le dirías a una persona como esta? R. aguayón
  (foto de una persona gorda)   pulpa bola
               mantecosa
22. Si en la escuela hay alguien que sabe más que R. lumbrera
  los otros, ¿cómo le dirías?   chicho
23. Si hay otro que no sabe nada, ¿cómo le dirías? R. burro
24. ¿Qué se esto?   R. un frajo
  (foto de cigarros)
25. ¿Y esto?   R. la tetera
  (una cerveza)   el chupón
26. ¿Y esto?   R. un toque
  (foto de unas drogas)
27. ¿Cómo te pones con esto?   R. buti suave
  (con las drogas)   todo aplatanado
28. ¿Cómo les dices a estos?   R. los calcos
  (apuntando a los zapatos)   las herraduras
29. ¿Cómo le dices a una persona que huele mal? R. apestoso
30. ¿A qué van las muchachas a las maquilas? R. a camellar

31. ¿Cómo le dices a tu mamá?   R. jefa
32. ¿Cómo le dices a tu papá?   R. jefe
33. ¿Cómo le dices al que te manda en el trabajo?   R. jefe
34. ¿Cómo les dices a tus hermanos?   R. carnales
35. ¿Cómo le dices a tu mejor amigo (-a)?   R. carnal
36. Si una persona no tiene ni qué comer, ni dinero,   R. bien jalado
    ¿cómo dirías que está?   amolado
37. ¿Qué es esto?   R. un chavalo
    (foto de un niño de 12 años)
38. ¿Cómo le dirías a alguien como este?   R. un chicharrón
    (foto de un anciano)
39. ¿Y a este?   R. una araña
    (foto de un niño recién nacido)   un ratón
40. ¿Cómo dices cuando una persona pasa a mejor   R. se petateó
    vida?   colgó los tenis
41. ¿Qué haces cuando te quieres conseguir a una   R. le caigo
    muchacha?   me la amarro
42. ¿Cómo le dirías a una persona como esta?   R. nopal
    (foto de una persona alta)
43. ¿Por qué?
44. ¿Y a una persona así?   R. zotaco
    (foto de una persona de estatura baja)   chori
45. ¿Cómo les dices a los que son de la policía pero   R. los molones
    no traen uniforme, casi siempre traen gabardina?
46. ¿Cómo le dices a esta?   R. el coco
    (apuntando a la cabeza)   la maceta
47. ¿Cuando terminas de trabajar adónde te vas?   R. a mi cantón
                                                                   a mi chante
48. Si ahorita vinieran y te dijeran que vas a ir a la   R. me ciscaba
    cárcel, ¿cómo te sentirías?
49. Cuando a una persona le dicen que es "cócono"   R. que tiene miedo
    ¿qué quiere decir?
50. ¿Cómo le dices a una persona que no es muy   R. federal
    guapa, más bien lo contrario?
51. ¿Cómo le dices a estos?   R. tramos
    (apuntando a los pantalones)
52. Si alguien te dice algo que tú sabes que no es   R. que diga la neta
    cierto, ¿qué le dices?
53. ¿A qué van los niños al parque los domingos?   R. a los huevitos
54. ¿Comó le dices a esta?   R. la lisa
    (apuntando a la camisa)
55. Si te vas a fumar un cigarro, ¿qué necesitas?   R. mecha
                                                                   lumbre
56. Si una persona te quiere decir algo, pero le dé   R. que no se maderée
    muchas vueltas al asunto, ¿qué le dices?

57. Si quieres mucho a una persona, ¿cómo le dices? R. mi gorda
58. Si ves a alguien que está muy enamorado, ¿cómo le dices? R. que lo traen rebotando el pavimento

59. Si ves a la novia de tu amigo con otro, ¿qué le dirías a tu amigo? R. que le andaban haciendo de chivo los tamales

60. ¿Cómo le dices a esto? (apuntando al cabello) R. la greña

61. ¿Cómo le dices a ese? (apuntando a un carro) R. una ranfla

The final sample was prepared by Marcia Lagos-Sandoval for the study of lexical differences in Temuco, Chile, with respondents who come not only from different age groups but also from different socioeconomic backgrounds. It contains 100 questions which fall into five semantic areas.

Questionnaire 4. For investigation of generational and socioeconomic differences in Temuco, Chile

Semantic area no. 1: School
1. ¿Cómo llama Ud. a una persona que en el colegio siempre tiene buenas notas (calificaciones), siempre sabe y siempre está estudiando?
2. ¿Y a la persona que es todo lo contrario?
3. ¿Qué se dice que hace una persona que falta a clases sin avisar ni pedir permiso?
4. ¿Qué diría si tuviera un examen o una prueba y no se hubiera preparado?
5. ¿Cómo llama a ese papel con datos para un examen que los estudiantes tratan de ver a escondidas y que, por supuesto, no está permitido mirar?
6. ¿Cómo llama Ud. a la acción de usar ese papel en un examen o tratar de ver lo que escribe el compañero?
7. ¿Cómo dice que le fue en un examen si recibe éste con nota dos (2: F)?
8. ¿Y si la nota es un siete (7: A)?
9. ¿Qué dice cuando no le entiende a otra persona lo que explica o lo que dice?
10. ¿Qué le puede pasar a una persona si es desobediente o si no hace lo que se le ordena?
11. ¿Qué le dice a alguien que lo molesta para que deje de hacerlo?

Semantic area no. 2: Work
1. ¿Cómo llama a su superior en el trabajo?
2. ¿Qué nombre le da al dinero mensual que recibe por su trabajo?
3. ¿Cómo llama a las personas que trabajan con Ud. en la misma actividad?
4. ¿Cómo dice que se siente después de trabajar mucho y quedar sin energías?
5. ¿Cómo dice que está cuando no tiene dinero para nada?
6. ¿Qué dice que le pasa cuando no puede recordar algo?

Semantic area no. 3: Home

1. ¿Cómo le dice a su madre?
2. ¿Y a su padre?
3. ¿Cómo los trata, los tutea?
4. ¿Qué nombre le da a la persona a la cual se le paga por hacer los quehaceres domésticos?
5. ¿Con qué nombre designa Ud. el mueble donde se lavan los platos?
6. ¿Qué nombre le da a esta habitación? (picture of a living room)
7. ¿Cómo llama Ud. a la habitación donde duerme? (picture of a bedroom)
8. ¿Y a la habitación donde comen? (picture of a dining room)
9. ¿Cuál es la primera comida del día y en qué consiste?
10. Y, ¿cómo llama Ud. a la comida del mediodía?
11. ¿Qué otras comidas hay?
12. ¿Qué nombre le da Ud. a esa habitación donde se guardan cosas viejas, sin uso, papeles, etc.?
13. ¿Qué nombre le da a esto? (picture of a dress)
14. ¿Y a esto? (picture of a skirt)
15. ¿Y cómo se refiere a las dos prendas juntas?
16. ¿Qué es esto para Ud.? (show a T-shirt)
17. ¿Qué nombre le da a esta prenda de ropa? (show a sweater)
18. ¿Cómo llama a los zapatos que se usan en verano, ésos que son muy abiertos?
19. ¿Y a los zapatos que usan los uniformados en el regimiento, muy cerrados y subidos?
20. Si una persona no lleva ropas puestas, ¿cómo dice que está?
21. ¿Y si por el contrario llevara demasiadas prendas de ropa?
22. ¿Cómo dice que se ve una persona mal vestida, con las ropas en desorden, sin planchar, cómo anda?
23. ¿Cómo dice que se siente si no tiene nada que hacer y eso le desespera?
24. ¿Cómo dice que estaba algo que comió y le gustó mucho?
25. ¿Qué hace cuando quiere escuchar música?
26. ¿Cuánto dice Ud. que tiene de algo, si la cantidad es más que abundante?

Semantic area no. 4: Social life

1. Si quiere pasarlo bien, ¿qué hace, adónde va?
2. Si va al cine, ¿come Ud. algo?, ¿qué?
3. ¿Qué nombre le da a una reunión pequeña de amistades en la cual se conversa, o se baila, o se bebe un poco?
4. ¿Y a ese tipo de reunión a la cual cada invitado debe llevar algo?
5. ¿Y si la reunión es más grande, con cena y baile, mucha gente, algunas personas incluso desconocidas para Ud.?
6. ¿Qué hacen estas personas? (picture of people eating ice cream)
7. ¿Cómo saluda a sus amigos?
8. ¿Y a las personas que sólo son conocidos?
9. ¿Con qué nombre(s) se refiere Ud. a este personaje? (picture of a policeman)
10. ¿Cómo le dice al vehículo que utilizan para llevar los detenidos?

11. ¿Con qué nombre se refiere Ud. a esos policías que no usan uniforme, los que van de civil?
12. Cuando detienen a una persona, ¿adónde la llevan?
13. ¿Para qué la llevan a ese lugar?
14. Cuando alguien va de compras y no quiere pagar todo el valor de la compra sino poco menos, ¿qué puede hacer?
15. ¿Cómo llama Ud. a los vehículos de locomoción colectiva urbana, de dos puertas?
16. ¿Y a los más pequeños que sólo tienen una puerta?
17. ¿Cómo se llama el sitio donde venden verduras, también frutas y pescado al aire libre?
18. ¿Cómo llama Ud. la parte por donde deben transitar los peatones?
19. ¿Y la parte por donde deben transitar los vehículos?
20. Cuando Ud. necesita algo y no tiene, ¿qué hace? (¡Tampoco lo puede comprar!)
21. ¿Cómo se refiere a algo, por ejemplo, una noticia que es muy vieja o ya sabida desde hace mucho tiempo?
22. Cuando algo le divierte mucho, ¿cómo dice que es?
23. ¿Y si fuera lo contrario?
24. ¿Qué está haciendo esta persona? (picture of a woman in bathing suit under the sun)
25. ¿Qué son éstos? (show a box of cigarettes)
26. Y estas personas, ¿qué hacen con ellos? (picture of people smoking)
27. ¿Qué necesita para fumar?
28. ¿Cómo dice que llueve si la lluvia es fuerte y con viento?
29. ¿Cómo dice que se siente una persona que está en un ambiente diferente al suyo propio y en el cual no se siente cómoda?
30. ¿Cómo llama Ud. a una persona que no es de Temuco?

Semantic area no. 5: Physical characteristics of human beings
1. ¿Cómo le dice a una persona a la que estima mucho y a la que considera amiga?
2. ¿Cómo dice que es una persona que cuando Ud. está en apuros siempre le ayuda?
3. ¿Cómo llama a una niña de 17 años?
4. ¿Y a una niña de 8 años?
5. ¿Con qué nombre llama Ud. a éste? (picture of an old man)
6. ¿Y a éste? (picture of a baby)
7. ¿Cómo llama Ud. al hecho de sentirse atraído por una persona del otro sexo y darse cuenta que la atracción es recíproca?
8. Y si Uds. empiezan a salir juntos formalmente, ¿qué nombre le da a esa relación?
9. ¿Cómo dice que está esta persona? (picture of a drunk person)
10. ¿Y este otro? (picture of a man beaten and wounded)
11. ¿Cómo llama Ud. a una persona que es todo lo contrario de flaca?

12. ¿Cómo dice que está esta joven? (picture of a young woman laughing)
13. ¿Y cuando una persona está todo lo contrario?
14. ¿Qué dice cuando una persona deja de existir?
15. ¿Cómo se refiere a una persona del sexo femenino que es muy atractiva?
16. ¿Y si la persona es del sexo masculino?
17. ¿Y si la persona es todo lo contrario de atractiva?
18. ¿Qué nombre(s) le da a una persona que cree mentalmente anormal, retrasada?
19. Cuando Ud. se siente físicamente mal, ¿cómo dice que se encuentra?
20. ¿Cómo le dice a una persona que usa lentes? ¿Le pone un sobrenombre?
21. ¿De qué manera expresa su desagrado por una persona, qué dice sobre ella?
22. ¿De qué otras maneras llama Ud. a esto? (show the head)
23. Para referirse a los pies, ¿usa Ud. alguna otra palabra?
24. ¿Cómo dice que está esta señora? (picture of a woman expecting a baby)
25. El último día del embarazo, ¿qué pasa?
26. ¿Cómo dice que siente si tiene mucho frío?

Appendix 2: Glossary of linguistic terms

Adlative: A suffix added to a noun or noun phrase that indicates movement toward.

Affix: A bound morpheme added to a base, occurring before it (prefix), after it (suffix), or within it (infix).

Affricate: A consonant made up of a stop plus a fricative.

Allative: See adlative.

Allomorph: One of several realizations of a morpheme, e.g., /-s/ and /-es/ as allomorphs of the Spanish morpheme 'plural'.

Allophone: One of several realizations of a phoneme, conditioned by adjacent sounds, e.g., the Spanish phoneme /n/ becoming [m] before /p/ or /b/.

Alveolar: Pronounced with the tip or apex of the tongue on the ridge behind the upper front teeth, e.g., English /t/ and /d/, Spanish /n/.

Analytic: A language which is analytic depends on free morphemes and/or word order to express relationships, rather than on inflections, e.g., English *John gave a rose to Mary* and *John gave Mary a rose*. Similarly, a structure which is analytic is composed of free morphemes rather than bound ones, e.g., English *they will eat* as opposed to Spanish *comerán*.

Apex (adj. apical): The tip of the tongue.

Apico-alveolar: Pronounced with the apex of the tongue in contact with the alveolar ridge, e.g., English /t/ and /d/, Spanish /n/.

Archaism: An antiquated speech element.

Articulator: Speech organ, usually movable, such as the tongue or lower lip.

Aspiration: Pronounced with a puff of air accompanying the release of a stop consonant before the voicing of a following vowel, e.g., English /p/, /t/, and /k/ when word-initial, and Quechua /pʰ/, /tʰ/, and /kʰ/.

Assibilation: Pronounced with a hiss or shush, e.g., Spanish [ř] or [ř̬;] after a stop, especially /t/, in Chile and in the Andes.

Assimilation: A feature of one sound is anticipated by a preceding one, e.g., the voicing of the /s/ in Spanish [mízmo].

Base (stem): The form, free or bound, to which affixes are added, e.g., Spanish *sal* 'salt' and *dij-* in *dijo*.

Bilabial: Pronounced with the lips either closed or nearly so.

Bound morpheme: One which cannot occur alone, e.g., Spanish plural *-s* in *puertas* 'doors'.

Caló: Slang spoken by Gypsies or Mexican Americans.

Chicano/-a: Mexican American.

Cholo/-a: Teenage Mexican American fringe group.

Creole: A former pidgin which has become the first language of a speech community.

Dental: Pronounced with the tip or apex of the tongue on the upper front teeth, e.g., Spanish /t/.

Diachronic: A view of language at a succession of stages in time.

Dialect: A variation of a language, usually social or regional.

Dorsovelar: Pronounced with the dorsum of the tongue on the velum, e.g., /k/ or /g/.

Dorsum (adj. dorsal): The blade of the tongue.

Free morpheme: One which can occur alone.

Fricative: Speech sound produced by the friction of the air stream restricted by an articulator held close to a point of articulation, e.g., English or Spanish /s/.

Germanía: Peninsular rogue slang spoken during the colonial period.

Glottal stop: Pronounced by a quick closing and opening of the vocal cords, e.g., English [bɑʔl] 'bottle' in Scots or Brooklynese.

Glottis: The opening between the vocal cords.

Hypocoristic: Pertaining to a form which has been shortened or modified as in the speech of children.

Idiolect: Speech which is characteristic of one person.

Imperfect (adj. imperfective): Verb form descriptive of action or state without reference to its conclusion.

Infix: A morpheme inserted within a word, e.g., *-me-* in *dígamen* for *díganme* 'tell me' and *-it-* in *chiquito* 'little one'.

Intonation: The rise and fall in pitch of successive syllables. Intonation contour is the customary pitch pattern of a language.

Jargon: Special language of an in-group.

Juncture: The pause or lack of pause between contiguous segmentals.

Labial: Pronounced with the lips.

Labiodental: Pronounced with the upper teeth on the lower lip, e.g., English /f/ and /v/.

Larynx (adj. laryngeal): The cylindrical cavity at the upper end of the trachea containing the vocal cords.

Lateral: Speech sound pronounced with passage of air between the edges of the tongue and the lower molars.

Lexicon (adj. lexical): The wordstock of a language.

Morpheme: The smallest meaningful or functional element of a language, e.g., Spanish *habl-*, *-a-*, *-ba-*, and *-mos* in *hablábamos* 'we were talking'.

Morphology: The forms or study of the forms of a language at the level of the affixes and bases.

Morphosyntax: The study of the forms of a language and how they are combined at the phrase, clause, and sentence levels into meaningful utterances.

Pachuco/-a: Teenage Mexican American of a fringe group, World War II to the end of the 1950s, a term later displaced by *cholo*.

Palatal: Pronounced with the blade of the tongue against the palate.

Perfect (adj. perfective): Verb form that refers to an action or state viewed as completed.

Phone: Any speech sound.

Phoneme (adj. phonemic): A speech sound considered significant in a language, e.g., Spanish /r/ and /r̄/ in *pero* and *perro*.

Phonology: The sounds or study of the sounds of a language.

Pidgin: A combination of two or more languages for communication between different linguistic groups.

Point of articulation: Location in the vocal tract where the air may be constricted by the articulator, e.g., for /s/, the alveolar ridge.

Polysynthetic language: One which combines in a single word several semantic elements which are grammatically related, e.g., Nahuatl *chika-wka-tahto-htinemi* 'talk forcefully while walking' (Bolinger 1975:28).

Postalveolar: Pronounced with the apex of the tongue at the back of the alveolar ridge, e.g., Castilian intervocalic [ş].

Postposition (adj. postpositional): A function marker which is analogous to a preposition but which follows a word or phrase rather than preceding it, e.g., Japanese *o* which marks the preceding word or phrase as direct object.

Postvelar: Pronounced with the dorsum of the tongue against the uvula.

Prefix: A bound morpheme occurring before a base.

Prepalatal: Pronounced with the blade of the tongue against the front of the palate, e.g., German *ch* in *ich*.

Prestige dialect: That spoken by people considered to be successful and influential.

Regional dialect: Speech characteristic of a geographic area.

Retroflex: Pronounced with the apex of the tongue curling back on itself, e.g., Midwestern U.S. English /r/.

Rustic dialect: Speech characteristic of a rural area.

Segmental: Term used to refer to consonants and vowels in the stream of speech.

Sephardic: Spanish dialect spoken by the descendants of the Jews expelled from Spain in 1492.

Sibilant: Pronounced with a hiss, e.g., /s/ and /z/.

Social dialect (sociolect): Speech characteristic of a social level.

Stem: See Base.

Stop: Speech sound produced by stopping the air stream with an articulator held against a point of articulation, e.g., [p], [b], [t], [d], [k], [g].

Stress: Degree of intensity or loudness of a syllable.

Subdialect: Manner of speaking within a dialect according to factors such as age, sex, or profession.

Suffix: A bound morpheme occurring after a base.

Suprasegmental: Term used to refer to stress, pitch, and juncture in the stream of speech.

Synchronic: A view of language at one particular point in time.

Syntax (adj. syntactic): How words are related to each other in phrases, clauses, and sentences.

Synthetic: A synthetic language does not depend on free morphemes but on inflections, e.g., Spanish *comería* as opposed to English *he would eat*.

Uvula (adj. uvular): Small fleshy projection hanging at the back of the velum.

Velar: Pronounced with the dorsum of the tongue on the velum, e.g., /k/ and /g/.

Velum: Soft muscle tissue behind the hard palate.

Voiced: Speech sound pronounced with vibration of the vocal cords, e.g., /z/ as opposed to /s/.

Voiceless: Speech sound pronounced without vibration of the vocal cords, e.g., /s/ as opposed to /z/.

Appendix 3: Phonetic symbols for segmentals in Latin America

Consonants

Point of articulation:

	Bilabial		Labio-Dental		Inter-Dental		Dental		Alveolar		Post-Alveolar		Prepalatal & Palatal		Velar		Postvelar		Laryngeal	
	Voiceless	Voiced	Voiceless	Voiced	Voiceless	Voiced	Voiceless	Voiced	Voiceless	Voiced	Voiceless	Voiced	Voiceless	Voiced	Voiceless	Voiced	Voiceless	Voiced	Voiceless	Voiced
S:	p	b					t Sp.	d	t Eng.	d					k	g	q		ʔ	
F:	ɸ	β	f	v	θ	ð	ş ṛ̌ r̃	z̧ r̃	s	z	s R	z̧	ç ʃ	j ʒ	x	ɣ			h	ḥ
A:									c				č	ǰ						
L:							ḻ		ḷ	l			ʎ̥	ʎ			ɫ			
V:									r r̄											
N:	m̥	m			m̰		ṉ		n				ɲ		ŋ					

Manner of Articulation:

S: Stops   A: Affricates   V: Vibrants
F: Fricatives   L: Laterals   N: Nasals

These symbols are for the most part those used by the International Phonetic Association except for a few which have been modified either for typographic simplicity or for easy recognition by the reader.

A cedilla below a symbol indicates dental articulation except for [ç], which is used generally to represent a palatoalveolar unvoiced fricative, as in the standard German pronunciation of *ich*.

A superscript ^{h} following a stop, such as [t^h], shows aspiration.

As in Lenz, a scarcely audible consonant is symbolized by raising it: [tra^{β}axá] 'trabajar'.

Among the stops, *t* and *d* are dental in Spanish but alveolar in Guaraní, as in English.

The symbol /q/ is used for the sound similar to /k/ but with an occlusion farther back, between the postdorsum of the tongue and the uvular region of the velum.

There are several possible realizations of /r/ and /rr/:

1. We transcribe the flap /r/ as [r] and the vibrant /rr/ as [r̄].
2. Assibilation of either of these is marked with a haček: [ř] or [ř̄].

3. [R] represents retroflex articulation like that of the midwestern United States.

A dot below /s/ or /z/ signifies that the point of articulation is apicoalveolar.

The laryngeal, whether it be /h/ or [h], may occur voiceless or voiced.

Among the affricates, /c/ is pronounced *ts*. We have used the symbols /č/ and /ǰ/ instead of the I.P.A. [tʃ] and [dʒ] as more accurate representations of these two Spanish sounds.

Velar *l*, often called 'dark *l*', is written [ł].

Vowels

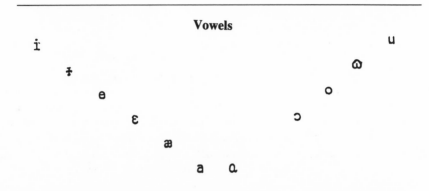

All of these symbols except one are standard in I.P.A. usage. The [ɨ] has been added because it is more easily discerned than [I], and also it is standard in the orthography of Mapuche.

A tilde (˜) over a vowel indicates nasalization.

Appendix 4: Word list for practice with Tape 1

The words recorded on Tape 1 are illustrative of the sounds of Castilian Spanish described in Chapter 2. The speaker is a cultured Spanish professor from Madrid. The listener should bear in mind that despite the high prestige of Castilian it is but one of many varieties of Spanish, and that educated speakers from other areas of the Hispanic world pronounce many of these sounds differently.

The Vowels

While Standard Spanish, unlike French, Italian, and Portuguese, makes no phonemic distinction between open and close vowels, phonologists have noted a relative 'openness' and 'closeness' in the vowels of Spanish in a number of predictable environments. For this reason, in the following presentation both the 'open' and the 'close' pronunciation of each of the five vowels is illustrated, using the terminology of Navarro Tomás. In the special notation used in the following list a comma below a vowel symbol indicates an open quality.

Close [i]	Open [i̦]
mira	rico
dice	hijo
silla	silba
pisada	sentir
millón	asignar

Close [e]	Open [e̦]
noche	guerra
compré	regla
peña	oreja
atento	seis
vengo	belga
	técnica

Medial [a]	Velar [a̦]
caro	causa
escaso	cacao
compás	caldo
cortar	igual
contacto	caja

Close [o]	Open [o̦]
boda	gorra
poco	ropa
adobe	hoja
bodega	soy

posada

golpe
ahora

Close [u]

cura
tuvo
puño
pureza
mudanza

Open [y]

discurre
rumor
bruja
insulto
instructor

The Consonants

Voiceless

Voiced

Stops

[p]
pío
Pepe
papá
popa
pupilo

[b]
(after a pause)
basta
vasta
(after a nasal)
ambos
hombre
un vecino

[t]
Tito
tente
tata
total
tuteo

[d]
(initial)
doy
diente
(after a nasal)
andando
(after [l])
falda
molde

[k]
kilo
qué
coca
cucú
Quica

[g]
(after a pause)
gato
goma
(after a nasal)
tengo
ganga

Voiceless

Voiced

Fricatives

[β]
(initial, no pause)
está bien
ya vino

(medial)
suba
alba
polvo

[f]
(initial)
favor
fiebre
(medial)
enfermo
gafas

[θ]
(initial)
zapato
cielo
(medial)
dice
hizo
(final)
capaz
luz

[ð]
(initial, no pause)
su dedo
la dama
(medial)
todo
cada
(final)
verdad
Madrid

[ʂ]
(before a dental)
está
estudio

[z̧]
(before a dental)
desde
los dedos

[s]
(initial)
solo
son
(medial)
ese
visita
(final)
nos
comes

[z]
(before a voiced consonant)
mismo
disgusto
los burros
las mujeres

[j]
(initial)
yo
hielo
(medial)
vaya
oye
(final)
estoy

ley

[x]
(initial)
jamón
gemir
(medial)
dije
trajo
(final, rare)
boj

[γ]
(initial, no pause)
la guerra
el golpe
(medial)
lago
higo
(final, rare)
Magog

Affricates

[č]
chino
cheque
chata
muchacho
Blanch

[ǰ]
(after [n] or [l])
inyección
cónyuge
con hierro
el yunque
el yerno

Laterals

[ļ]
caldo
alto

[l]
(initial)
lado
leche
(medial)
cola
isla
doble
(final)
sol
Brasil

[λ]
(initial and medial only)
lleno
llama
villa
calle
colchón

Vibrants

[r]
(intervocalic)
mira
coro
(preconsonantal)
cuerda
cerca
(postconsonantal)
Pedro
potro
(final)
sentir
flor

[r̄]
(initial and medial only)
risa
raso
rosa
tierra
corre

Nasals

[m] (initial and medial only)
mina
mono
cima
cama
hombre
admirar

[m̭]
informar
inflación

[ŋ]
(before a dental consonant)
indio
entero
un tío

[n]
(initial)
nido
nada
(medial)
cena

zona
(final)
comen
orden
examen

[ɲ]
(initial, rare)
ñoño
(medial)
señor
año
sueño
(final when followed by palatal)
poncho

[ŋ]
(medial)
inca
tengo
inglés
(final when followed by a velar)
en casa
ven corriendo

Appendix 5: Tape transcriptions not included in text

Tape 2, selection b (Contemporary Peruvian Quechua)

The Lord's Prayer (*Yayaiku*)

Yayaiku hanac Pachakunapij kaj
Hapaj-Rainiki, noq'aikunan hamuch'un
nunainiki rurasja kachun, amainan
hapaj pachapi hinapaj kai Pachapipas
saga P'unchau tantaikuta kunan Raiku
hunchaikutari p'ampachawaiku imainan
noj'aikupas huchaikuta p'ampachawaiku
hina amataj pachari raikuchu, wataj kainan
hurmainukaikupaj yuyanraj nanan allin
manta hespichiwaiku. Imainaj kachun.

Tape 2, selection c (Guaraní)

'Cerro Kora' by Félix Fernández,
from Antonio Guash. 1956. *El idioma guaraní.* Asunción: América-Moreno.
(Prose translation by Víctor Sánchez)

Campaménto, Campaménto
Amoite "Cerro Korápe"
Pyhareve ko'etī jave
Pe ñorairōpa hague.

Campamento, Campamento, allá en Cerro
Kora, al amanecer en el día en que la
contienda terminaba, encima de su caballo,
con la espada en la mano,

Henda ári Mburuvixa
Ha ikyse puku okápe:
"Amanóta, añeme'ē rangue
He'i hape, ohuvaitī umi
kamba."

nuestro Líder, alzándola arriba, gritaba,
"¡Morir antes de entregarse!" y con este
grito encontraba a los kambas.

Mariscal rire, Mariscal jevy,
Mamópa oime nde rasaharā.
Nemboxyryry, nereñeme'ēi
Nde ko Paraguái mombe'u-
pyrā.

Mariscal, después de ti solamente, Mariscal,
otra vez, ¿dónde habrá quien será mejor
que tú? Alguna vez tú serás el que hará
conocer al Paraguay y harás escribir
historias de él.

Osyry upe Akidavan
Culantrilloeta apytépe;
Iñe'ēme omombe'u
ñande Ru omano hague.

Corre el río Akidavan entre Culantrillos,
y con sus corrientes va contando la
historia de que el Padre Máximo ha muerto.

Ha yvyra piru-tiníre
Yvyty hū pa'ū mbytépe,

Y entre palos y espinillas, entre vientos
y en el medio del campo, con la corriente

Ysyrype omoirūvo
Ojahe'opa umi guaimingue.

del agua, todas las mujeres llorando la
pérdida del Padre Máximo,

Guyra jepeve ombopurahéi
Omomba'ete Paraguái ruguy.
Nokirirīvéi maymáro guyra
Oñembo'epa oike pytumby.

los pájaros al volar, la gloria del
Paraguay, y contando con ello la gloria
del Mariscal. ¿Adónde habrá otro igual?
Pasarán muchas horas de oscuridad y nunca
morirás.

Campaménto, Campaménto
Amoite "Cerro Korápe"
Yvyty pa'ū mbytépe
Yvyty hérava Amambái.

Campamento, Campamento, allá en Cerro
Kora, entre vientos y en el medio del
campo, allí estarán las flores para
mirarte; allí estará el Amambay, nuestra
flor, para estar cerca de ti.

Omano Tendota López
Tetā ao ovevehápe:
Ao karai no me'eiva
Oñuvāvo Paraguái.

Ha muerto nuestro padre, el Supremo López
murió queriendo a su patria, murió como
un señor que nunca se entregó, para
abrazar a su querido Paraguay.

Toñembo'e joa pyhare ha ára
To jerure hese ita'yra eta:
Ha! Cerro Kora, Loma
   Valentina
Ha! xe rendumína, Sauce,
   Bokerō.

Por ahora que se acerca la mañana, al
venir a pedir la gente su cuerpo, todo
mundo implorando y diciendo, "¡Oh, Cerro
Kora, oh Loma Valentina, oh gran padre,
oh Sauce y Boquerón!"

Tape 2, selection d

From lecture by Joaquín Piñeros Corpas on the history of the national anthem
of Colombia, n.d. Bogotá, Colombia: Emisora H.J.C.K. (Cultivated
Colombian Andean)

El primer ensayo del himno colombiano está representado por la canción
nacional de José de María Salazar, escrita en 1814, y por algunas canciones
patrióticas de Juan Antonio Velasco, que conservan referencia histórica, sin
partitura conocida. Debido a su dirección pseudoclásica en días de alba romántica,
y a la falta de música adecuada, escasa resonancia tuvo en el medio emancipador
la oda de Salazar, que así comienza:

> A la voz de la América unida,
> de sus hijos se inflama el valor,
> sus derechos el mundo venera,
> y sus armas se cubren de honor.

A falta de himno, o de canción de seductor sentido heroico, el soldado de la
Independencia buscó su música capitana en los géneros populares como la contradanza y el bambuco. En la tarde del 7 de agosto de 1819, en el propio campo
de Boyacá, cuando el caos de los escombros heráldicos y los caballos sin gobierno

aún no habían permitido hacer el inventario de la victoria, el alférez payanés, José María Cansino, organizó una pequeña fanfarria para festejar con música la jornada gloriosa. La obra elegida fue la contradanza "La Vencedora", de autor incógnito, que después de muchos lustros de olvido vuelve a oídos colombianos. . . .

Tape 2, selection e

'Heroísmo americano' by Emilio Castelar,
from Isabel K. MacDermott and M. Fernández Juncos. 1944. *Libro cuarto de lectura.* New York: Silver Burdett. (Cultivated Peruvian Andean)

Los Estados Unidos han invocado el Dios de la libertad; han aceptado la guerra como un gran castigo por el pecado nacional de la esclavitud; han hablado a los dueños de esclavos en el sublime lenguaje de los antiguos profetas; se han desposeído de sus bienes para romper sus ergástulas; han dado su pura sangre sajona, su blanca piel por la dignidad y por la libertad de aquellos negros, menos estimados que los perros; han ensangrentado el Misisipí; han cubierto de ruinas las llanuras y las montañas de Virginia; han inmolado en la cruzada de la dignidad y de la igualdad humanas un millón de hombres que, las madres americanas, inclinadas las frentes sobre el Evangelio, han visto morir en la tierra, pero renacer en el cielo; y sobre las ruinas de Richmond, entre el choque de dos mundos, se han derretido las cadenas de tres millones de esclavos y se ha levantado, como el epílogo de un gran poema, que está aguardando el genio de Homero aumentado por el genio del Dante, rejuvenecidos ambos por la savia del Nuevo Mundo; se ha levantado como epílogo de este poema el sacrificio de Lincoln, de ese segundo Cristo de los negros.

Tape 2, selection f

From lecture by José Antonio Portuondo, 'Filosofía y Cultura Latinoamericana', from *De la cultura latinoamericana.* n.d. México, D.F.: Universidad Nacional Autónoma de México. (Cultivated formal Cuban Spanish)

Martí significa en el proceso del pensamiento latinoamericano, la más constante y profunda afirmación de la unidad esencial de nuestra América, frente a la expansión imperialista de la América del Norte. Acaso el más preciso y agudo, el más bello también de los planteamientos martianos del problema latinoamericano, sea el que con el título definitorio de *Nuestra América* publicara él en el partido liberal de esta misma ciudad de México en enero de 1891. Este ensayo, escrito en la más bella prosa modernista por Martí, plantea desde el comienzo la necesidad de la unidad latinoamericana a través del conocimiento mutuo de nuestros pueblos. Escribió él: "Los pueblos que no se conocen han de darse prisa para conocerse, como quienes van a pelear juntos." He aquí el más bello y rotundo lema de la unidad latinoamericana que pudiera haber sido utilizado por los numerosos congresos que se han celebrado entre nosotros ya moderna-mente, para conocernos, para pelear juntos contra el imperialismo. Para Martí: "Conocer el país, y gobernarlo conforme al conocimiento, es el único modo de librarlo de tiranías"—y añade inmediatamente—: "La Universidad Europea ha de ceder a la Universidad Americana. La historia de América, de los incas a acá, ha de enseñarse al dedillo, aunque no se enseñe la de los arcontes de Grecia. Nuestra Grecia es preferible a la Grecia que no es nuestra. Nos es más necesaria"—y aclara inmediatamente—: "Los políticos nacionales han de reemplazar a los políticos exóticos." Y luego esta fórmula que es la que hemos adoptado todos los que luchamos por una América mejor, por la América antiimperialista, la América que ocupa ya ahora un lugar importantísimo en el proceso histórico de nuestro tiempo. Este lema martiano fue esgrimido en el reciente congreso de Educación y Cultura celebrado en La Habana en abril del año pasado. "Injértese en nuestras Repúblicas el mundo; pero el tronco ha de ser el de nuestras Repúblicas." Obsérvese que Martí no rechaza, no podría hacerlo, la gran herencia cultural que nos vino desde la hora misma de la conquista; no rechaza tampoco todo lo que hay de aprovechable en el gran desarrollo cultural de los pueblos del mundo. América no vive aislada. América no vive metida en una campana neumática; coexiste con otros pueblos y al mismo tiempo participa de sus angustias, de sus esperanzas, de sus anhelos. América vive en el mundo y por lo tanto debe aprovechar todo lo que hay de aprovechable en el mundo, todo lo conquistado por el hombre a través de las edades; pero eso sí, debe mantenerse fiel a sus propias raíces, debe de ser esencialmente americana y todo esto se resume bellísimamente en el aforismo martiano: "Injértese en nuestras República el mundo; pero el tronco ha de ser el de nuestras Repúblicas." Esa posición de Martí que consuena admirablemente bien con su pronunciamiento anterior de la necesidad de que la Universidad Americana sea eso, esencialmente americana, que en ella se estudien nuestros problemas, se reitera constantemente a lo largo del ensayo que estamos comentando. Pero él, además, en este ensayo reconoce la condición de la clase hegemónica a las masas populares: esto es una de las novedades notables en el pensamiento martiano. En el tiempo en que Martí vive, todavía perduran los rasgos democrático-burgueses de los grandes caudillos o los grandes fundadores del siglo XIX. Sin embargo, Martí ve ya cómo va surgiendo una nueva clase que va a encargarse de dirigir la historia, y no vacila en señalarlo así, aunque para la guerra que está preparando en Cuba tenga que apoyarse en un frente unido de clase social. Aunque en su artículo admirable a la muerte de Marx se oponga un tanto a la idea de la lucha de clases, porque no tenía sentido de aplicación inmediata a la lucha cubana de entonces. Pero él sabe demasiado bien que son los de abajo, que son los hombres del pueblo, las masas populares las que comienzan a manejar la historia, las que tienen el sentido progresivo de la historia y por eso en este ensayo que comentamos dice esto: "¡Bajarse hasta los infelices y alzarlos en los brazos! ¡Con el fuego del corazón deshelar la América coagulada! ¡Echar, bullendo y rebotando por las venas, la sangre natural del país! En pie con los ojos alegres de los trabajadores, se saludan, de un pueblo a otro, los hombres nuevos americanos." Es decir, es el énfasis puesto en los trabajadores, en la masa proletaria y así fue. Ya sabemos bien que

Martí, edificó el Partido Revolucionario Cubano fundado en 1892 con los trabajadores cubanos fundamentalmente, es decir, con los tabaqueros de Tampa, Cayo Hueso, Nueva York, Filadelfia y otras grandes ciudades americanas.

Tape 2, selection g

From lecture by Félix Bultrón on the history of Puerto Rico
(cultivated informal Puerto Rican Spanish)

Les voy a hablar de, más o menos, de la historia de Puerto Rico antes de llegar los españoles. La isla, como ustedes saben, fue llamada por los indios que habitaban en aquel entonces, arahuacos o taínos, y también en una . . . en la parte del sur habitaban también los caribes; ellos le llamaban a la isla "Borinquén" [sic].

Los españoles en el 1497 (the speaker here inadvertently made an error, as he meant '1897') le dieron la autonomía a Cuba y a Puerto Rico, pero fue muy tarde, porque ustedes sabrán que en el 1898 ocurrió la guerra de los Estados Unidos con España, y entonces los Estados Unidos tomaron posesión de Puerto Rico, Cuba, y las Filipinas. En ese entonces vinieron los americanos a ser dueños de la posesión de Puerto Rico, que es la que más nos interesa ahora.

En el 1917, los Estados Unidos le dió la ciudadanía a los puertorriqueños, viniendo a ser que todo aquel que nace en Puerto Rico o que tuviera padres que (allí) habían nacido son ciudadanos americanos. Los Estados Unidos para entonces, el Presidente, apuntaba cada cuatro años un Gobernador a la isla. Era así que más tarde, cuando ocurrieron unas votaciones, que llamó [sic] el Partido Popular Democrático, vino a ser un Gobernador, pero ya no era americano el que apuntaba él . . . el Presidente, sinó que el primero fue puertorriqueño, fue don Jesús Tepiñero (que en paz descanse), pero fue—no fue nominado por el pueblo, sino que fue mandado por el Presidente de los Estados Unidos. . . .

Tape 2, selection i

Seis Villarán, Jíbaro folksong (rustic Puerto Rican Spanish)

Tengo una novia trigueña	
que es como *l'alba* tropical:	el alba
es la rosa de un rosal	
desde mi tierra *borinqueña*	puertorriqueña
Mi novia solo en la *güeya*	huella: camino
dejó todo mi corazón.	
Cuando de mi *lira* al son	guitarra
coplas de amor yo le canto	
me devuelve con encanto	
besos llenos de pasión.	
Tengo *una alazana*	yegua color de canela

de andadura y paso fino
que galopa en el camino
como majestad soberana
(domingo por la mañana,
como me marca la ley).
La llevo bajo un *mamey* árbol frutal tropical
que da sombra a una quebrada,
y la traigo bien *bañá* bañada
a *trenzarla* en el *batey*. atarla patio

Tengo un pollito en la valla
que *tá en calle'e* Isabela: está en la calle de
es muy ligero a la escuela
y siempre pica en la raya.
Mi pollo es de mucha talla
y nunca extraña gallera.
Al verlo en la *talanguera* reñidero de gallos
medirse con su rival,
yo apuesto mi capital
a otro capital cualquiera.

Ve ya cómo de un *capá* madera de un árbol tropical del
            Caribe
mi *tiple* yo fabriqué, guitarra pequeñita y rústica
y las clavijas yo formé
desde las ramas de un *guamaga*. *guamaca*, árbol de madera fine

¡En *Colagüilito* ya me voy nombre de un caballo
pa' 'onde mi trigueña!
Y al verla tan *halangüeña* halagüeña
y tan llena de primores,
entónole en mis canciones
¡eh!, es decir, más borinqueña(s).

Tape 2, selection k:1

From 'Rea Silvia' by Horacio Quiroga
(cultivated Uruguayan or Argentinian Spanish)

Hay en este mundo naturalezas tan francamente abiertas a la vida que la desgracia puede ser para ellas el pañal en que se desenvuelven al nacer. Permítaseme esta ligera filosofía en honor a la crítica infancia de una criatura que nació para los más tormentosos debates de la pasión humana, y cuya vida pudo ser desgraciada como puede serlo el ramo de los más costosos jarrones.

Sus padres le dieron por nombre Rea Silvia y la conocí en su propia casa.

Era una criatura voluntariosa, de ojos negros y profundos. Su alma expuesta al desquicio la hizo adorar (era muy pequeña) los cuadros, los brocatos oscuros de los sillones, las cortinas de terciopelo en que se envolvía tiritando como en un grande abrazo.

Era alegre, no obstante. Su turbulencia pasaba la medida común de las hijas últimas a que todo se consiente. Las amigas queridas de su mamá (señorita de Almendros, señorita de Joyense, señora de Noblecorazón) soñaban—unas para el futuro, otra para esos días—un ángel igual al de la blanca madre. El canario— que era una diminuta locura, los mirlos más pendencieros de la casa vecina, vivían en gravedad, si preciso fuera compararlos con las carcajadas de Rea—. ¿Cómo pues, tan alegre perdía las horas en la sala oscura, sombra y desgracia de las hijas que van a soñar en ellas? Problemas son éstos que sólo una noble y grande alma puede descifrar.

Tape 2, selection k:2

From *Ariel* by José Enrique Rodó
(cultivated Uruguayan or Argentinian Spanish)

Aquella tarde, el viejo y venerado maestro, a quien solían llamar Próspero, por alusión al sabio mago de "La Tempestad" shakespiriana, se despedía de sus jóvenes discípulos, pasado un año de tareas, congregándolos una vez más a su alrededor.

Ya habían llegado ellos a la amplia sala de estudio, en la que un gusto delicado y severo esmerábase por todas partes en honrar la noble presencia de los libros, fieles compañeros de Próspero. Dominaba en la sala—como numen de su ambiente sereno—un bronce primoroso, que figuraba al Ariel de "La Tempestad." Junto a este bronce se sentaba habitualmente el maestro, y por ello le llamaban con el nombre del mago a quien sirve y favorece en el drama el fantástico personaje que había interpretado el escultor. Quizá en su enseñanza y en su carácter había, para el nombre, una razón y un sentido más profundos.

Ariel, genio del aire, representa, en el simbolismo de la obra de Shakespeare, la parte noble y alada del espíritu. Ariel es el imperio de la razón y el sentimiento sobre los bajos estímulos de la irracionalidad; es el entusiasmo generoso, el móvil alto y desinteresado en la acción, la espiritualidad de la cultura, la vivacidad y la gracia de la inteligencia, el término ideal a que asciende la selección humana, rectificando en el hombre superior los tenaces vestigios de Calibán, símbolo de sensualidad y de torpeza, con el cincel perseverante de la vida.

La estatua, de real arte, reproducía al genio aéreo en el instante en que, libertado por la magia de Próspero, va a lanzarse a los aires para desvanecerse en un lampo. Desplegadas las alas; suelta y flotante la leve vestidura, que la caricia de la luz en el bronce damasquinaba de oro; erguida la amplia frente; entreabiertos los labios por serena sonrisa, todo en la actitud de Ariel acusaba admirablemente el gracioso arranque del vuelo; y con la inspiración dichosa, el arte que había dado firmeza escultural a su imagen, había acertado a conservar en ella, al mismo tiempo, la apariencia seráfica y la levedad ideal.

Próspero acarició, meditando, la frente de la estatua; dispuso luego al grupo juvenil en torno suyo, y con su firme voz—voz "magistral," que tenía para fijar la idea e insinuarse en las profundidades del espíritu, bien la esclarecedora penetración del rayo de luz, bien el golpe incisivo del cincel en el mármol, bien el toque impregnante del pincel en el lienzo o de la onda en la arena—, comenzó a decir, frente a una atención afectuosa: . . .

Tape 2, selection m

Conversación entre dos Pachucos y una Jaina, en un borlo paseño
(teenage Mexican American Spanish of 1950)

Pachuco 1:   Ese, ¿ónde está su carnal?

Pachuco 2:   Nel, pos no pudo venir, siempre está con la jaina.

P. 1:   ¿Con la jaina? ¿Que no dijo que iba a venir con usted?

P. 2:   Pos ya había quedado en venir, pero la jaina no le dejó venir, porque lo tiene bajo el teni.

P. 1:   Bueno, ¿quién es esa jaina que anda contigo?

P. 2:   Es mi carnala—¿la quieres conocer? Nomás que se cree muy buena.

P. 1:   Y ¿quién te preguntó cómo se crea? A mí, cuando me gusta una chavala, a mí no me importa cómo se crea.

Jaina: Oh, pues ustedes están conmigo: ¡a poco se creen muy buenotes! ¿Vamos a tirar chancla pues, o no? Ya me estoy ahuitando aquí. Se me hace que me los tirotea pa' l'otra vez.

P. 2:   Nel, cálmela. Esta jaina no quiere borlotear contigo.

Jaina: Chale, chale, ya me ahuité. Ahi los huacho. Parece que están tirados a todos los vicios ustedes.

P. 1:   ¡Cállese o le agarro el chongo! No madera, que esta jaina ahuita; ahuita demás, ese, jijo, y es tu carnala.

P. 2:   Se lo dije.

P. 1:   Bueno, ese, ahi te huacho.

P. 2:   Nel, pos, ¿aónde va, ese?

Jaina: Ya era tiempo.

P. 1:   Era tiempo, ¿pa' qué?

Jaina: Pa' que se fueran.

P. 2:   ¡Uh, cómo nos quieres!

P. 1:   ¡Uh, tú de a tiro que ahuita tu carnala!

P. 2:   Pues, comienza, ese . . . el comienzo.

P. 1:   ¿El comienzo?

P. 2:   Pos, yo creía que vamos a borlotear. . .

P. 1:   Pues, sabe poquito, ¡no vote! Esa jaina, ¡venga pa'cá, dígame algo!

Jaina: Pues que ¡no!, ¿eh?

P. 1:   Pues, véngase nomás y verá, enséñeme cómo se tirotea.

P. 2:   (con sarcasmo, imitando la pronunciación de Nuevo México): Oh, tú sabes, yo no sé, ese, ¿vusté sabe?

P. 1:   ¡Oh, tú pareces manito de Nuevo México¡

P. 2:	¡Oh, tá bueno, no me necesitas insultar!
P. 1:	Bueno, dile a la jaina que se venga, y tú, vete a tu chante, ese.
P. 2:	Oh, sí, y tú que dijites y tú lo que quieres es pleito, ¿verdad?
P. 1:	¡A ver! ¡Pues, vente!
Jaina:	¡Ya, ya, ya!
P. 2:	¿Cómo? ¡Aquí tengo un machete!
P. 1:	¡¿Eh?! ¡Traigo mi fila también! A ver, ¡vente y verás!
P. 2:	¡Nel, pues tú no duras ni un *round*!
P. 1:	¿Cómo que un *round*?
P. 2:	Nel, pos, ¡lo verá con mi carnal!
P. 1:	¡¿Con tu carnal?! Pues, quién se creerá tu carnal, cuando vengas conmigo?
P. 2:	¿Cómo? ¿Por qué? ¡A poco te crees muy buenote!
P. 1:	Me creo muy buenote, ese, pero comoquiera tú estás bastante grande pa' mí.
P. 2:	¡Verá! ¡Barbas de lión!
P. 1:	¡Barbas de lión, ¿eh?! ¡Voy a sacar mi fila, y tú verás qué te voy a dar!
P. 2:	Bueno, ¿qué me haces?
P. 1:	¡Te voy a hacer bastante, ese! Fuera, ¡quítate del camino, esa!
Jaina:	Pues se callen, o ¡les hago!
P. 1:	¡Tú nos haces!—¿Qué nos haces?
Jaina:	¿Ven estas uñas? ¡Pues, ya verán lo que saben hacer!
P. 1:	¡Nel!

Appendix 6: Mexican American lexical items with Spanish bases

Semantic area	Meaning	Figure of speech
I. Behavior		
A. Personal behavior, general		
1) *anclear*	'settle down'	met
2) *bostecear*	'yawn'	freq
3) *brujear*	'go without sleep'	met
4) *cacaraquear*	'cackle'/'chatter'	stem aug, freq, prim onom
5) *calcear*	'go barefoot'	irony
6) *coyotear*	'goof off'	met
7) *chanquilear*	'walk'	meton
8) *chapear*	'blush'	met
9) *chicanear*	'do one's thing'/'act like Chicano'	hypocor, meton
10) *chicotear*	'excel'	met
11) *chisquearse*	'go crazy'	met
12) *chistear*	'complain'	metal onom, meton
13) *chivear*	'be bashful'	met
14) *chotear*	'use to excess'	meton
15) *frajear*	'smoke cigarette'	little hyp
16) *jirimiquear*	'complain'	stem aug, freq, prim onom
17) *lamparear*	'eye'	met
18) *nortearse*	'go crazy'	irony
19) *papalotear*	'excel'	met
20) *periquear*	'talk incessantly'	met
21) *petatear*	'die'	met

Key to abbreviations:
back form: back formation
blend
deplet: depletion
freq: frequentative
hypocor: hypocoristic
irony
lit: literal
little hyp: little hypersemanticization
met: metaphor

metal onom: metalinguistic onomatopoeia
meton: metonymy
poss freq: possible frequentative
prim onom: primary onomatopoeia
sec onom: secondary onomatopoeia
stem aug: stem augment
syn: synecdoche
?: unknown

22) *planchar*	'sleep'	met
23) *sofacear*	'lounge'	met
24) *talonear*	'hurry'	met
25) *temponear*	'be used to'	meton
26) *titiritear*	'shiver'	freq, prim onom
27) *tomatear*	'stare at'	met
28) *torear*	'make an attempt'	met
29) *totachar*	'speak in Chicano slang'/'talk in mixed English and Spanish'	poss freq, metal onom
30) *trafiquear*	'walk'/'ride'	freq

B. Personal behavior, domestic setting

  1. Eating and drinking

1) *cusquear/cuzquear*	'snack constantly'	met
2) *gusjear*	'eat like vulture'	met
3) *jaspear*	'eat'	meton?
4) *lambizquear/ lambuzquear*	'eat between meals'	stem aug, meton
5) *machetear*	'eat voraciously'	met
6) *martiar/martillar*	'eat'	met
7) *mastiquear*	'chew'	freq
8) *pajuelear*	'take a shot of liquor'	met
9) *pistear*	'drink alcohol'	poss freq
10) *tortear/tortillar*	'eat tortillas'	little hyp

  2. Grooming and dressing

1) *chapear*	'put on rouge'	met
2) *chapetear*	'put on rouge'	met
3) *entacucharse*	'dress up'	syn
4) *florear*	'dress up'	met
5) *laquear*	'spray hair'	met
6) *pintorreguear*	'use cosmetics to excess'	stem aug, poss freq
7) *polvear*	'powder self or nose'	little hyp
8) *trajear*	'dress up'	syn

C. Interpersonal behavior, general

1) *ahuichotear*	'encourage'/'stimulate'	met, irony
2) *apapachar/papachar*	'spoil a child'	met
3) *azorrillar*	'frighten'	met
4) *babiarse (por)*	'covet'	meton
5) *barajear*	'make a fool of'	met

6) *baratear*	'mix with a crowd'	meton
7) *barbear*	'flatter'	meton
8) *borruquear*	'confuse'	stem aug
9) *cachetear*	'slap'	stem aug, meton
10) *cachumbear*	'neck'	syn
11) *caldear*	'anger'/'make love'	meton
12) *capear*	'dodge'	met
13) *carrerear*	'hurry someone'	meton
14) *colear*	'grab'/'borrow'	met
15) *corretear*	'run someone ragged'	stem aug, freq
16) *cotorrear*	'converse'	met
17) *changuear*	'imitate'	met
18) *chiplear*	'spoil a child'	meton
19) *chiquear*	'pamper a child or a pet'	metal onom, meton
20) *chistear*	'hush someone up'	metal onom, meton
21) *chivear*	'back down'	met
22) *chopetear*	'have intercourse'	stem aug, met
23) *chotear*	'pet heavily'	met
24) *chulear*	'caress'/'speak sweetly'	metal onom
25) *encantonear*	'marry'	meton
26) *enseñar*	'show one's bad side'	deplet
27) *esquinear*	'assent'/'agree'	met
28) *nalguear*	'spank a child'	meton
29) *ningunear*	'debase', 'kill'	metal, metal onom
30) *pafuelear/pajuelear*	'whip'/'excel'/ 'take shot of liquor'	met
31) *pajarear*	'keep an eye on'	met
32) *pandear*	'retract'	meton
33) *pedorrear*	'warn'	met
34) *pichonear*	'engage in sexual foreplay'	met
35) *rayarse*	'repeat'/'excel'	met
36) *sacatear/zacatear*	'dodge'	meton
37) *serenatear*	'serenade'	little hyp
38) *sonajear*	'spank a child'	met
39) *tortear/tortillar*	'slap'	met

D. Interpersonal behavior, social formulas

1) *sentenciar*	'warn of revenge'	met

E. Socially disapproved behavior
  1. Socially disapproved behavior, general

1) *abolillar*	'act like a gringo'	met
2) *acarrear*	'gossip'	met
3) *cachuquear*	'double cross'	met
4) *capear*	'tattle'/'catch'	met
5) *casquetear*	'masturbate'	stem aug, meton
6) *corbear*	'sponge'/'free-load'	met?
7) *cusquear/cuzquear*	'be nosy'	met
8) *chacotear*	'behave lewdly'	prim onom
9) *chancear*	'commit adultery'	meton
10) *chapetear*	'fornicate'	met
11) *chapucear*	'cheat'	little hyp
12) *chaquetear*	'betray'	met
13) *chismolear/chismorrear*	'gossip'	stem aug, freq
14) *chisquear*	'drive someone crazy'	met
15) *chotear*	'defame'/'make fool of'	meton
16) *chulear*	'pimp'	irony
17) *disgracear*	'impregnate'/'ruin'	meton
18) *enchinchar*	'waste someone's time'	met
19) *engarruñar*	'brawl'/'shrink in anger'	meton
20) *feriar*	'defecate in fear'	met
21) *garrotear*	'beat up'	met
22) *huevonear*	'be lazy'	stem aug, met
23) *idear*	'daydream'	meton
24) *jacalear*	'gossip'	syn
25) *jetear*	'pout'	met
26) *lambizquear/lambuzquear*	'bootlick'	stem aug, met
27) *lamparear*	'ogle'	met
28) *maderear*	'flatter'/'brag'	met
29) *manzanear*	'bribe'	met
30) *maromear*	'betray'	met
31) *mirojear*	'peek lustily'	stem aug
32) *mitotear*	'raise hell'	met
33) *nortear*	'drive someone crazy'	irony
34) *pacotear*	'betray'	stem aug, meton
35) *patalear*	'kick in rear'	stem aug, deplet
36) *pedorrear*	'scold'/'raise stink'	stem aug, met

37) *pirfantear*	'be sassy'	met
38) *politiquear*	'play politics'	poss freq? lit
39) *puñetear*	'masturbate'	stem aug, met
40) *rajolear*	'back down'	stem aug, poss freq, meton
41) *retobear*	'(child) sass adult'	poss freq met
42) *sanchar*	'commit adultery'	met
43) *tamboretear*	'beat up'	stem aug, met
44) *temponear*	'waste time'	stem aug, meton
45) *torear*	'go on spree'	met

2. Socially disapproved behavior, criminal
  a. Crime, general

1) *alinear/linear*	'go straight'	met
2) *colear*	'tail someone'	met
3) *coyotear*	'be a shrewd law-breaker'	met
4) *cusquear/cuzquear*	'solicit as prostitute'	met
5) *muraguear*	'murder'	blend?
6) *torear*	'defy the law'	met
7) *trampear*	'enter without paying'	poss freq, meton

  b. Crime, stealing

1) *babiarse (por)*	'steal'	met
2) *coyotear*	'steal'	met
3) *mañanear*	'steal'	meton
4) *talonear*	'steal'/'hustle'	met

  c. Crime, with dope

1) *pildorear*	'ingest narcotics'	little hyp

  d. Crime, with knife

1) *alfilear*	'cut with knife'	met
2) *canalear*	'cut with knife'	met
3) *charrasquear*	'cut with knife'/'leave scar'	little hyp
4) *filerear*	'cut with knife'	syn
5) *filetear*	'cut with knife'	met
6) *garranchar*	'cut with knife'	met
7) *navajear*	'cut with razor or knife'	little hyp
8) *pacotear*	'stab'	stem aug, meton

  e. Crime, with weapon other than knife

1) *cuetear*	'shoot someone'	met
2) *macanear*	'bludgeon'	meton

3) *plomear*	'shoot someone'	met

II. Sports and play
    A. Sports, general

1) *carruchar*	'ride around'	stem aug, meton
2) *fonchar*	'cheat at marbles'	?
3) *maromear*	'somersault'	meton
4) *pichonear*	'easily defeat a novice'	met
5) *trampear*	'hunt animals'	little hyp

    B. Team sports

1) *cañonear*	'defeat'/'throw a pass'	met
2) *capotear*	'snatch ball'/ 'leave team scoreless'	met
3) *garrotear*	'defeat'	met

    C. Boxing and wrestling

    D. Card playing and gambling

1) *barajear*	'play cards'	little hyp

    E. Social amusements

1) *banquetear*	'have a good time'	meton
2) *tortear/tortillar*	'applaud'	met

    F. Dancing

1) *bolevear*	'dance'	stem aug, met
2) *borlotear*	'dance'	stem aug, meton
3) *chanclear*	'dance wildly'	meton
4) *polquear*	'dance polka'	poss freq, little hyp
5) *taconear*	'dance'/'dance Western'	meton
6) *valsear*	'dance waltz'	poss freq, little hyp

III. Work
    A. Work, general

1) *cabulear*	'complete a chore'	stem aug
2) *cachuquear*	'blow a job'	stem aug, meton
3) *camear/camillar*	'work'	meton

4) *cascarear*	'work for low pay'	meton
5) *chambear*	'work'	syn
6) *chambonear*	'work awkwardly'	stem aug, syn
7) *machetear*	'work clumsily'	met
8) *reganchar*	'contract for work'	met

B. Work, technological
   1. Automotive

1) *arrear*	'start a car'	met
2) *manear*	'brake'	met
3) *mecanear*	'do mechanical work'	little hyp
4) *orillar*	'curb a car'	met
5) *pilotear*	'drive a car'	met
6) *talonear*	'step on the gas'	met

   2. Secretarial

   3. Electrical

   4. Military

C. Work, domestic

1) *cachumbear*	'nick a dish'	met
2) *cocinear*	'cook'	poss freq, little hyp
3) *copetear*	'fill to brim'	met?
4) *chicharronear*	'burn to a crisp'	meton
5) *lamprear*	'roast'	met
6) *tasajear*	'slice'	lit
7) *trastear*	'wash dishes'	lit
8) *tortear/tortillar*	'make tortillas'	little hyp

D. Work, educational

1) *colear*	'color'	hypocor

E. Financial transactions

1) *feriar*	'make change'	lit
2) *feriar*	'barter'	meton
3) *pagulear*	'pay poorly'	stem aug
4) *rayar*	'pay wages'/ 'write checks'	meton

F. Labor relations

G. Manual labor

1) *bolear*	'shine shoes'	poss freq, met

2) *pegostear* 'spread with little hyp
sticky
substance'

IV. Weather and natural phenomena
1) *candelear* 'sleet' met
2) *chipear* 'drizzle' prim onom
3) *grajear* 'sleet' met

V. Medical
1) *moretear* 'bruise' back form, little
hyp
2) *sangrear* 'bleed' little hyp

VI. General and/or unclassifiable
1) *afrañar* 'understand' met?

Appendix 7: Mexican American lexical items with English bases

I. Behavior
  A. Personal behavior, general

1) *bloquear*	'block'
2) *bonquear*	'sleep'
3) *chusear*	'choose'
4) *guachar*	'watch'
5) *shoflear*	'shuffle'
6) *stepear*	'step'
7) *toriquear*	'talk'

  B. Personal behavior, domestic setting
    1. Eating and drinking

1) *bironguear*	'drink beer or other alcohol'
2) *liquear*	'lick'
3) *lonchar*	'eat lunch'

    2. Grooming and dressing

1) *combiar*	'comb'
2) *mechar*	'match'
3) *permanentear*	'give a permanent'
4) *setear*	'set'
5) *shainear*	'shine'
6) *tatu(y)ar*	'tattoo'
7) *trimear*	'trim'

  C. Interpersonal behavior, general

1) *chatapear*	'shut up'
2) *espatear*	'spot'/'recognize'
3) *flipear*	'flip'/'go crazy'
4) *flirtear*	'flirt'
5) *fulear*	'fool'
6) *jainear*	'make love'
7) *pinchar*	'pinch'
8) *tisear*	'tease'
9) *tochar*	'touch'
10) *tritear*	'treat'
11) *trostear*	'trust'
12) *yonkiar*	'junk'/'throw away'

  D. Interpersonal behavior, social formulas

1) *pronuncear*	'declare that something is so'

E. Socially disapproved behavior
   1. Socially disapproved behavior, general

1) *canquear*	'beat somebody up'
2) *mochar/muchar*	'mooch'
3) *monquear*	'monkey around'
4) *parquear*	'overstay one's welcome'
5) *pinchar*	'pinch'
6) *pompear*	'fornicate'
7) *ponchar*	'punch'
8) *swinguear*	'swing'

   2. Socially disapproved behavior, criminal
     a. Crime, general

1) *estulear*	'stool on someone'
2) *freimear*	'frame'
3) *joslear*	'hustle'
4) *licorear*	'look over'/'case the joint'

     b. Crime, stealing

1) *requetear*	'steal'
2) *rolear*	'roll'/'steal'

     c. Crime, with dope

1) *capear*	'put heroin in capsules'
2) *estufear*	'sniff residue of narcotics'

     d. Crime, with knife
     e. Crime, with weapon other than knife

1) *chutear*	'shoot'

II. Sports and play
  A. Sports, general

1) *escrachar*	'scratch'/'eliminate'
2) *jonchar*	'move marble shooter closer to target'
3) *trapear*	'go hunting'

  B. Team sports

1) *batear*	'bat'
2) *cachar/quechar*	'catch'
3) *cañonear*	'throw a cannonball pass'
4) *chutear*	'shoot'
5) *driblear*	'dribble'
6) *estraiquear*	'strike at and miss'/'strike someone out'
7) *fanear*	'fan'/'strike out'
8) *fildear*	'play position of fielder'
9) *golear*	'make a goal'
10) *golfear*	'play golf'

11) *pichar*　　　　　　'pitch'
12) *rachar*　　　　　　'rush'
13) *swinguear*　　　　'swing'
14) *quiquear*　　　　　'kick'

C. Boxing and wrestling
　　1) *catear*　　　　　'give someone an uppercut'
　　2) *fletear*　　　　　'flatten someone'
　　3) *naquear/noquear*　'knock out'
　　4) *ponchar*　　　　'punch'
　　5) *ringuear*　　　　'ring a bell'
　　6) *soquear*　　　　'sock'

D. Card playing and gambling
　　1) *betear*　　　　　'bet'
　　2) *blofear*　　　　　'bluff'
　　3) *dilear*　　　　　'deal'
　　4) *poquear*　　　　'play poker'

E. Social amusements
　　1) *cabaretear*　　　'go night clubbing'
　　2) *campear*　　　　'go camping'
　　3) *clapear*　　　　'applaud'/'cut in, while dancing'
　　4) *plujear*　　　　'plunge'
　　5) *swimear*　　　　'swim'

F. Dancing

III. Work
　A. Work, general
　　1) *güerquear*　　　'work'
　　2) *puchar*　　　　'push'
　　3) *pulear*　　　　'pull'
　B. Work, technological
　　1. Automotive
　　　1) *baquear*　　　'back'
　　　2) *bompear*　　　'bump'
　　　3) *brequear*　　　'brake'
　　　4) *choquear*　　　'choke'
　　　5) *crenquear*　　'crank'
　　　6) *draivear*　　　'drive'
　　　7) *estartear*　　'start'
　　　8) *fletear*　　　'flatten a tire'
　　　9) *güeldear*　　　'weld'
　　　10) *parquear*　　'park'
　　　11) *ponchar*　　'puncture a tire'
　　　12) *puchar/apuchar*　'push'

13) *raitear*   'give or get a ride'
14) *requear*   'wreck'
15) *yequear*   'jack up'

2. Secretarial
   1) *chequear*   'check'
   2) *dailear*   'dial'
   3) *esteiplear*   'staple'
   4) *sainear*   'sign'
   5) *taipear*   'type'
   6) *teipear*   'tape'

3. Electrical
   1) *ploguear*   'plug in'

4. Military
   1) *machinganear*   'shoot, with machine gun'

C. Work, domestic
   1) *clinear*   'clean'
   2) *cuquear*   'cook'
   3) *dompear*   'dump'
   4) *dostear*   'dust'
   5) *flochar*   'flush'
   6) *guarear/warear*   'water (plants)'
   7) *laquear*   'lock'
   8) *mapear/mopear*   'mop'
   9) *mixear*   'mix'
   10) *polichar*   'polish'
   11) *pompear*   'pump'
   12) *teipear*   'tape'
   13) *waxear*   'wax'

D. Work, educational
   1) *copear*   'copy'
   2) *cuitear/quitear*   'quit'
   3) *charpear*   'sharpen (pencil)'
   4) *chitear*   'cheat'
   5) *dropear*   'drop (course)'
   6) *espelear/espeletear* 'spell'
   7) *esquechar*   'sketch'
   8) *esquipear*   'skip'
   9) *feilear*   'fail'
   10) *flipear*   'flip out in a course'
   11) *flonquear/flankiar* 'flunk'
   12) *impruvear*   'improve'
   13) *instructear*   'instruct'
   14) *juquear*   'play hookey'

15) *mistear*   'miss'
16) *practicear*   'practice'
17) *ringuear*   'ring (bell)'
18) *testear*   'test'
19) *tichar*   'teach'

E. Financial transactions
  1) *buquear*   'enter a purchase as debit against
             future wages'
  2) *cleimear*   'claim'
  3) *charchear*   'charge'

F. Labor relations
  1) *cuitear/quitear* 'quit'
  2) *discharchar*   'discharge'
  3) *estraiquear/straiquear* 'go on strike'
  4) *piquetear*   'picket'

G. Manual labor
  1) *shainear*   'shine'

IV. Weather and natural phenomena

V. Medical

VI. General and/or unclassifiable
  1) *craquear*   'crack'
  2) *cheiquear*   'shake'

Appendix 8: Mexican American lexical items with Spanish and with English bases: A comparison

Categories	Spanish bases	English bases
I. Behavior		
A. Personal behavior, general	30	7
B. Personal behavior, domestic setting		
1. Eating and drinking	10	3
2. Grooming and dressing	8	7
C. Interpersonal behavior, general	39	12
D. Interpersonal behavior, social formulas	1	1
E. Socially disapproved behavior		
1. Socially disapproved behavior, general	45	8
2. Socially disapproved behavior, criminal		
a. Crime, general	7	4
b. Crime, stealing	4	2
c. Crime, with dope	1	2
d. Crime, with knife	8	0
e. Crime, with weapon other than knife	3	1
Totals	156 (76.8%)	47 (23.1%)
II. Sports and play		
A. Sports, general	5	3
B. Team sports	3	14
C. Boxing and wrestling	0	6
D. Card playing and gambling	1	4
E. Social amusements	2	5
F. Dancing	6	0
Totals	17 (34.6%)	32 (65.3%)
III. Work		
A. Work, general	8	3

B. Work, technological		
1. Automotive	6	15
2. Secretarial	0	6
3. Electrical	0	1
4. Military	0	1
C. Work, domestic	8	13
D. Work, educational	1	19
E. Financial transactions	4	3
F. Labor relations	0	4
G. Manual labor	2	1
Totals	29	66
	(30.5%)	(69.4%)
IV. Weather and natural phenomena	3	0
V. Medical	2	1
VI. General and/or unclassifiable	1	2
	6	2
	(75%)	(25%)
Grand Totals	208	147
	(58.6%)	(41.4%)

References

Academia Chilena. 1978. Diccionario del habla chilena. Santiago de Chile: Editorial Universitaria.

Alonso, Amado. 1940a. La interpretación araucana de Lenz para la pronunciación chilena. In: El español en Chile. Eds. Amado Alonso and Raimundo Lida. Buenos Aires: Universidad de Buenos Aires. 279-289.

Alonso, Amado. 1940b. Rodolfo Lenz y la dialectología hispanoamericana. In: El español en Chile. Eds. Amado Alonso and Raimundo Lida. Buenos Aires: Universidad de Buenos Aires. 269-278.

Alonso, Amado. 1948. Lecture. University of Chicago.

Alonso, Amado. 1967a. De la pronunciación medieval a la moderna en español. 2 vols. Madrid: Gredos.

Alonso, Amado. 1967b. Estudios lingüísticos: Temas hispanoamericanos. 3rd ed. Madrid: Gredos.

Alurista. 1972. We've played cowboys. In: Literatura Chicana: Texto y contexto. Eds. Antonio Castañeda Shular, Tomás Ybarra-Frausto and Joseph Sommers. Englewood Cliffs, New Jersey: Prentice-Hall. 31-32.

Álvar, Manuel. 1960. Textos hispánicos dialectales: antología histórica. Madrid: Revista de Filología Española, anejo LXXIII. 2 vols.

Álvares de Villasandrino, Alfonso. 1967. Desexoso con desexo. In: Francisco da Silveira Bueno, A formação histórica da língua portuguesa. São Paulo: Paraiva. 296.

Álvarez Quintero, Serafín y Joaquín. 1923. Teatro completo. vol. 1. Primeros ensayos. Madrid: Imprenta Clásica Española.

Amastae, Jon. 1983. An investigation of the phonemic distinction between /b/ and /v/ in Bogotá. Colloquium Series lecture, University of Texas at El Paso.

Ayer, George W. 1974. A tentative classification of language performance categories of Spanish surnamed students. Teaching Spanish to the Spanish Speaking: Newsletter 1.1.3-4.

Bachiller y Morales, Antonio. 1883. Desfiguración a que está expuesto el idioma castellano al contacto y mezcla de las razas. Revista de Cuba 14. 97-104.

Baker, Paulline. 1966. Español para los hispanos. Skokie, Ill.: National Textbook Company.

Baroja, Pío. 1928. Zalacaín el aventurero. Eds. S. L. Millard Rosenberg and Laurence D. Bailiff. New York: Knopf.

Barral, Carlos. 1984. El País. Madrid. April 9, p. 19, col. 2.

Bartrina, Joaquín María. 1932. Arabesco. In: The Oxford book of Spanish verse. Ed. James Fitzmaurice-Kelly. Oxford: Clarendon. 385.

Benavente, Jacinto. 1942. La fuerza bruta y lo cursi. Buenos Aires: Espasa-Calpe Argentina.

Benavente, Jacinto. 1947. Señora Ama. Buenos Aires: Espasa-Calpe Argentina.

Bernal, Ignacio. 1964. Lecture. Texas Western College, El Paso, Texas.

Bioy Casares, Adolfo. 1978. Breve diccionario del argentino exquisito. Buenos Aires: Emecé.

Blansitt, Edward. 1984. Private conversation.

Bodmer, Frederick. 1944. The loom of language. New York: Norton.

Bolinger, Dwight. 1975. Aspects of language. 2nd ed. New York: Harcourt, Brace, and Jovanovich.

Borges, Jorge Luis, and José Edmundo Clemente. 1968. El lenguaje de Buenos Aires. Buenos Aires: Emecé.

Bowen, J. Donald, and Robert P. Stockwell. 1960. Patterns of Spanish pronunciation. Chicago: University of Chicago Press.

Boyd-Bowman, Peter. 1953. Sobre la pronunciación del español en el Ecuador. Nueva Revista de Filología Hispánica 7. 221-233.

Boyd-Bowman, Peter. 1960. El habla de Guanajuato. México: Universidad Nacional Autónoma de México.

Brend, Ruth. 1968. A tagmemic analysis of Mexican Spanish clauses. The Hague: Mouton.

Breyne, Marcel R. 1956. Lehrbuch des Afrikaans. Munich: Pohl.

Brun, Gerard. 1966. La lingüística aplicada a la enseñanza del español como lengua extranjera. Madrid: Instituto de Cultura Hispánica.

Brundage, Burr Cartwright. 1967. Lords of Cuzco. Norman: University of Oklahoma Press.

Buesa Oliver, Tomás, and Luis Flórez. 1954. El atlas lingüístico-etnográfico de Colombia. Bogotá: Caro y Cuervo.

Bull, William E. 1965. Spanish for teachers: Applied linguistics. New York: Ronald Press.

Caballero, Ramón C. F. 1961. La juega de gallos o el negro bozal. In: El elemento afronegroide en el español de Puerto Rico. Ed. Manual Álvarez Nazario. San Juan: Instituto de Cultura Puertorriqueña. 387-393.

Canfield, D. Lincoln. 1981. Spanish pronunciation in the Americas. Chicago: The University of Chicago Press.

Carter, Henry Hare. 1942. Contos e anedotas brasileiros. Boston: Heath.

Catalá, Víctor. 1930. Conversió. In: Contrallums. Barcelona: Gost. 9-68.

Catrileo, María Rayen. 1972a. Influencia del mapuche en el español de Chile. Unpublished paper, The University of Texas at El Paso.

Catrileo, María Rayen. 1972b. A tagmemic sketch of Mapuche grammar. M.A. thesis, The University of Texas at El Paso.

Chao, Yuen Ren. 1968. A grammar of spoken Chinese. Berkeley: University of California Press.

Chavero, Alfredo. n.d. Explicación del Lienzo de Tlaxcala, 1892. México, D.F.: Artes de México.

Cobos, Rubén. 1983. A dictionary of New Mexico and southern Colorado Spanish. Santa Fe: Museum of New Mexico Press.

Colón, Cristóbal. n.d. Diario de navegación. Buenos Aires: TOR.

Consejo Superior de Investigaciones Científicas. 1960-1967. Enciclopedia lingüística hispánica (E.L.H). 2 vols. Madrid: Consejo Superior de Investigaciones Científicas.

Corominas, Joan. 1961. Breve diccionario etimológico de la lengua castellana. Madrid: Gredos.

Cotton, Eleanor Greet, and John M. Sharp. 1980a. Hypersemanticization in neologistic Mexican Spanish verbs. Papers in Romance 2.4.229-246.

Cotton, Eleanor Greet, and John M. Sharp. 1980b. Neologistic palatal + -ar verbs in Mexican-American Spanish. In: Speaking, singing, and teaching: A multidisciplinary approach to language variation. Eds. Florence Barkin and Elizabeth Brandt. Tempe: Arizona State University. 422-444.

Cotton, Eleanor Greet, and John M. Sharp. 1983. Spanish verb form usage in El Paso and Mexico City: A comparison. Conference on Research Needs in Chicano Spanish: A Major Ethnic Dialect.

Cotton, Eleanor Greet, and John M. Sharp. 1985. The social function of humorous figures in Mexican speech. Paper read at The Western Humor and Irony Membership and excerpted in Whimsy III: Contemporary Humor. Eds. Don L. F. Nilson and Alleen Pace Nilson. Tempe: Arizona State University. 211-212.

Dante Alighieri. 1940. The 'De Vulgari Eloquentia'. In: A translation of the Latin works of Dante Alighieri. Trans. A.G.F.H. London: J.M. Dent and Sons, Ltd. 3-115.

Dávila, Adela B. 1975. El habla popular de Ciudad Juárez. M.A. thesis, The University of Texas at El Paso.

Desde el córner. n.d. [Probably in La Prensa. Buenos Aires.] n.p.

Díaz del Castillo, Bernal. 1943. Historia verdadera de la conquista de la Nueva España. Ed. Ramón Iglesias. vol. 1. México: Nuevo Mundo.

Du Bellay, Joachim. 1966. La deffence et illustration de la langue francoyse. Ed. Henri Chamard. Paris: Didier.

Edmonson, Munro S. Classical Quiche. In: Handbook of Middle American Indians. Ed. Robert Wauchope. Austin: The University of Texas Press. vol. 5. 249-310.

Entwistle, William J. 1951. The Spanish language together with Portuguese, Catalan and Basque. London: Faber and Faber.

Ercilla y Zúñiga, Alonso de. 1945. The Araucaniad. Trans. Charles Maxwell Lancaster and Paul Thomas Manchester. Nashville, Tenn.: Vanderbilt University Press.

Ercilla y Zúñiga, Alonso de. 1947. La Araucana. Buenos Aires: Espasa-Calpe Argentina.

Escobar, Alberto. 1976. Bilingualism and dialectology in Peru. The International Journal of the Sociology of Language 9. 85-96.

Espinosa, Aurelio M. 1975. Speech mixture in New Mexico: The influence of the English language on Mexican American Spanish. In: El lenguaje de los chicanos; Regional and social characteristics used by Mexican Americans. Eds. Eduardo Hernandez-Chavez, Andrew Cohen and Anthony F. Beltrano. Arlington, Virginia: Center for Applied Linguistics. 99-113.

Ferns, H. S. 1969. Argentina. New York: Praeger.

Fishman, Joshua A., and William Milán. 1983. Spanish language resources of the United States: Some preliminary findings. In: Spanish in the U.S. setting: Beyond the Southwest. Ed. Lucía Elías-Olivares. Rosslyn, Virginia: National Clearinghouse for Bilingual Education. 167-179.

Flórez, Luis. 1963. El español hablado en Colombia y su atlas lingüístico. Bogotá: Caro y Cuervo.

Flornoy, Bertrand. 1958. The world of the Incas. Garden City, N.Y.: Doubleday.

Galván, Roberto A., and Richard V. Teschner. 1975. The dictionary of the Spanish of Texas. Silver Spring, Maryland: Institute of Modern Languages.

Garcilaso de la Vega, El Inca. 1950. Comentarios reales. 3rd ed. Buenos Aires: Espasa-Calpe Argentina.

Gili Gaya, Samuel. 1961. Curso superior de sintaxis española. 13th ed. Barcelona: Biblograf.

Gili, Joan. 1967. Catalan grammar. Oxford: Dolphin.

Goilo, E. R. 1962. Papiamentu textbook. Aruba, Netherlands Antilles: D. J. de Wit.

González Zeledón (Magón), Manuel. 1920a. El clis de sol. In: La propia. San José de Costa Rica: García Monge y Cía. 157-162.

González Zeledón (Magón), Manuel. 1920b. Un día de mercado en la Plaza Principal. In: La propia. San José de Costa Rica: García Monge y Cía. 36-49.

Guasch, Antonio. 1956. El idioma guaraní: gramática y antología de prosa y verso. 3rd ed. Asunción: América-Moreno.

Güiraldes, Ricardo. 1940. Don Segundo Sombra. 2nd ed. Buenos Aires: Losada.

Hammond, Norman. 1982. Ancient Maya civilization. New Brunswick, New Jersey: Rutgers University Press.

Hasler, Juan. 1964. Étimos latinos, griegos, y nahuas. Xalapa, México: Universidad Veracruzana.

Healy, Nellie. 1985. Letter. The El Paso Times. August 15, A, p. 2, col. 3.

Henríquez Ureña, Pedro. 1938. El español en Méjico, los Estados Unidos y la América Central. Buenos Aires: La Universidad de Buenos Aires.

Henríquez Ureña, Pedro. 1940. El español en Santo Domingo. Buenos Aires: La Universidad de Buenos Aires.

Hernández, José. 1941. Martín Fierro. 2nd ed. Ed. Eleuterio F. Tiscornia. Buenos Aires: Losada.

Hyams, Edward, and George Ordish. 1963. The last of the Incas. New York: Simon and Schuster.

Juilland, Alfonse, and E. Chang-Rodríguez. 1964. Frequency dictionary of Spanish words. The Hague: Mouton.

Kany, Charles E. 1945. American-Spanish syntax. Chicago: The University of Chicago Press.

Kany, Charles E. 1947. Some aspects of Bolivian popular speech. Hispanic Review 15. 193-205.

Karsten, Rafael. 1949. A totalitarian state of the past: The civilization of the Inca empire of ancient Peru. Helsingfors: Societas Scientarum Fennica.

Labov, William. 1971. The notion of system in Creole languages. In: Pidginization and creolization of languages. Ed. Dell Hymes. London: Cambridge University Press. 447-472.

Lagos-Sandoval, Marcia. 1980. Non-standard lexical usage in the Spanish of Temuco, Chile: A case study. M.A. thesis, The University of Texas at El Paso.

Langacker, Ronald W. 1973. Language and its structure. New York: Harcourt, Brace, and Jovanovich.

Lapesa, Rafael. 1968. Historia de la lengua española. 7th ed. Madrid: Escelicer.

Lastra, Yolanda. 1958. Cochabamba Quechua syntax. The Hague: Mouton.

Lawrence, Timothy James. 1982. Language mixing in modified noun phrases. M.A. thesis, The University of Texas at El Paso.

Lenz, Rodolfo. 1940a. Estudios chilenos (Fonética del castellano de Chile). In: El español en Chile. Eds. Amado Alonso and Raimundo Lida. Buenos Aires: Universidad de Buenos Aires. 197-208.

Lenz, Rodolfo. 1940b. Para el conocimiento del español de América. In: El español en Chile. Eds. Amado Alonso and Raimundo Lida. Buenos Aires: Universidad de Buenos Aires. 209-268.

Lenz, Rodolfo, Andrés Bello, and Rodolfo Oroz. 1940. El español en Chile. Eds. Amado Alonso and Raimundo Lida. Buenos Aires: Universidad de Buenos Aires.

León, Luis de. [1585] 1944. Los nombres de Cristo. In: Obras completas castellanas. Ed. Félix García, O.S.A. Madrid: Biblioteca de Autores Cristianos. 339-759.

Lope Blanch, Juan M. 1968. El español de América. Madrid: Ediciones Alcalá.

Lope Blanch, Juan M. 1972. Estudios sobre el español de México. México: Universidad Nacional Autónoma de México.

Lope Blanch, Juan M. 1976. El habla popular de la Ciudad de México. México: Universidad Autónoma de México.

Lope Blanch, Juan M. 1979. Investigaciones sobre dialectología mexicana. México: Universidad Nacional Autónoma de México.

López de Escalera, Juan. 1964. Diccionario biográfico y de historia de México. México: Editorial del Magisterio.

López Morales, Humberto. 1971. Estudios sobre el español de Cuba. Long Island City, N.Y.: Las Américas Publishing Company.

Mallent, Visént. 1914. Una vida romántica.In: El Cuento del Dumenche. 1.15.283-298.

Malmberg, Bertil. 1947. Notas sobre la fonética del español en el Paraguay. Lund: Gleerup.

Marqués, René. 1971. La carreta. 8th ed. Río Piedras, Puerto Rico: Editorial Cultural.

McDowell, Bart. 1984. Mexico City: An alarming giant. National Geographic. August. 138-185.

McQuown, Norman A. 1967. Classical Yucatec (Maya). In: Handbook of Middle American Indians. Ed. Robert Wauchope. Austin: University of Texas Press. vol. 5. 201-247.

Mejías, Hugo A. 1980. Préstamos de lenguas indígenas en el español americano del siglo XVII. México: Universidad Nacional Autónoma de México.

Meliá Lliteras, Bartolomé, Alfonso Pérez Peñasco, and Luis Farré Maluquer. 1960. El guaraní a su alcance. Asunción: Ediciones Loyola.

Menéndez Pidal, Ramón. 1941. Manual de gramática histórica española. 6th ed. Madrid: Espasa-Calpe.

Mercado, José. 1969. La lengua castellana. In: Las mil mejores poesías de la Lengua Castellana. 22nd ed. Ed. José Bergua. Madrid: Ediciones Ibéricas. 537-540.

Montes Giraldo, José Joaquín. 1970. Dialectología y geografía lingüística. Bogotá: Caro y Cuervo.

Moreno de Alba, José G. 1978. Valores de las formas verbales en el español de México. México: Universidad Nacional Autónoma de México.

Morley, Silvanus Griswold. 1975. An introduction to the study of the Maya hieroglyphs. New York: Dover.

Mosterín, Jesús. 1981. La ortografía fonémica del español. Madrid: Alianza.

Munro, Dana Gardner. 1942. The Latin American republics: A history. New York: Appleton-Century.

Muro, Gertrude. 1980. Some peculiarities of the Spanish language in Buenos Aires. Unpublished paper, The University of Texas at El Paso.

Muysken, Pieter. 1977. Syntactic development in the verb phrase of Ecuadorian Quechua. Lisse: Pieter de Ridder Press.

Nathan, Deborah Ruth. 1978. The influence of African slave speech on the phonology of Caribbean and coastal Latin American Spanish. M.A. thesis, The University of Texas at El Paso.

Navarro Tomás, Tomás. 1932. Manual de pronunciación española. 4th ed. Madrid: Centro de Estudios Históricos.

Navarro Tomás, Tomás. 1948. El español en Puerto Rico. Río Piedras, Puerto Rico: Universidad de Puerto Rico.

Navarro Tomás, Tomás. 1968. Studies in Spanish phonology. Trans. Richard D. Abraham. Coral Gables, Florida: University of Miami Press.

Oroz, Rodolfo. 1966. La lengua castellana en Chile. Santiago: Universidad de Chile.

Palabra nueva: Cuentos Chicanos. 1984. Eds. Ricardo Aguilar, Armando Armengol, and Oscar V. Somoza. El Paso: Texas Western Press of The University of Texas at El Paso.

Palmer, L. R. 1968. The Latin language. 6th ed. London: Faber and Faber.

Past, Ray. 1970. Language as a lively art. Dubuque, Iowa: Brown.

Patterson, William, and Hector Urrutibéheity. 1975. The lexical structure of Spanish. The Hague: Mouton.

Paz, Octavio. 1963. El laberinto de la soledad. 3rd ed. México: Fondo de Cultura Económica.

Peffer, Randall. 1984. Catalonia: Spain's country within a country. National Geographic. January. 95-127.

Peñalosa, Fernando. 1980. Chicano sociolinguistics: A brief introduction. Rowley, Massachusetts: Newbury.

Perissinotto, Giorgio Sabino Antonio. 1975. Fonología del español hablado en la Ciudad de México. México: El Colegio de México.

Perrine, Laurence. 1973. Sound and sense: An introduction to poetry. 4th ed. New York: Harcourt, Brace, and Jovanovich.

Philbrick, F. A. 1967. Bias words. In: Introductory readings on language. Eds. Wallace L. Anderson and Norman C. Stageberg. New York: Holt, Rinehart and Winston. 176-184.

Picón-Salas, Mariano. 1958. De la Conquista a la Independencia. México: Fondo de Cultura Económica.

Prescott, William H. 1966. The conquest of Mexico, the conquest of Peru, and other selections. Ed. Roger Howell. New York: Twayne.

Quiroga, Horacio. 1943. Sus mejores cuentos. Ed. John A. Crow. México: Editorial Cvltvra.

Quiroga, Horacio. 1950. Un peón. In: Cuentos escogidos. Madrid: Aguilar. 406-432.

Ramage, Edwin S. 1973. Urbanitas: Ancient sophistication and refinement. Norman: University of Oklahoma Press.

Ramsey, Marathon Montrose, and Robert K. Spaulding. 1960. A textbook of modern Spanish. New York: Holt.

Recó, D'en Jordí des. 1953. Aplec de rondaies mallorquines. Palma de Mallorca: Gráfiques Miramar.

Reed, Carroll E. 1977. Dialects of American English. Amherst: University of Massachusetts Press.

Rincón, Antonio del. 1885. Gramática y vocabulario mexicanos, 1595. México: Oficina Tipográfica de la Secretaría de Fomento.

Robelo, Cecilio de. n.d. Diccionario de aztequismos. México: Ediciones Fuente Cultural.

Robertson, Stuart, and Frederic G. Cassidy. 1954. The development of modern English. 2nd ed. Englewood Cliffs, New Jersey: Prentice-Hall.

Robinson, Kimball L. 1979. On the voicing of intervocalic s in the Ecuadorean highlands. Romance Philology 33. 1.137-143.

Rojas, Ricardo. 1937. Himnos quichuas. Buenos Aires: Imprenta de la Universidad.

Rosario, Rubén del. 1970. El español de América. Sharon, Connecticut: Troutman Press.

Ruvalcaba, J. Melquíades. 1968. Manual de gramática náhuatl. Guadalajara, Jalisco: n.p.

Saciuk, Bohdan. 1980. Estudio comparativo de las realizaciones fonéticas de /y/ en dos dialectos del Caribe Hispánico. In: Dialectología hispanoamericana. Ed. Gary E. Scavnicky. Washington, D.C.: Georgetown University Press. 16-31.

Salas, Alberto M. 1959. Tres cronistas de Indias. México: Fondo de Cultura Económica.

Santamaría, Francisco J. 1942. Diccionario general de americanismos. 3 vols. Méjico: Pedro Robredo.

Santamaría, Francisco J. 1978. Diccionario de mejicanismos. Méjico: Porrúa.

Santana, Ruperto. 1960. Glossaries of Nahuatl and Mayan loanwords.

Sharp, John M. 1970. The origin of some non-standard lexical items in the Spanish of El Paso. In: Studies in language and linguistics, 1969-1970. Eds. Ralph W. Ewton, Jr., and Jacob Ornstein. El Paso: Texas Western Press of The University of Texas at El Paso. 207-232.

Shuy, Roger, Walter A. Wolfram, and William K. Riley. 1968. Field techniques in an urban language study. Washington, D.C.: Center for Applied Linguistics.

Silveira Bueno, Francisco da. 1967. A formação histórica da língua portuguêsa. São Paulo: Paraiva.

Sobin, Nicholas. 1976. Texas Spanish and lexical borrowing. Papers in Linguistics 9. 1 and 2. 15-47.

Solá, Donald F. 1967. Gramática del quechua de Huánuco. Lima: Universidad Nacional Mayor de San Marcos.

Solé, Yolanda Russinovich. 1985. Spanish/English mother-tongue claiming: The 1980 Census data, a subsample, and their sociodemographic correlates. Hispania. 68.2.283-297.

The South American handbook. 1979. 55th ed. Eds. John Brooks and Joyce Candy. Bath, England: Trade and Travel Publications.

Stockwell, Robert P., and J. Donald Bowen. 1965. The sounds of English and Spanish. Chicago: The University of Chicago Press.

Tiscornia, Eleuterio F. 1930. La lengua de Martín Fierro. Buenos Aires: La Universidad de Buenos Aires.

Tiscornia, Eleuterio F. 1940. Poetas gauchescos: Hidalgo, Ascasubi, Del Campo. Buenos Aires: Losada.

Tiscornia, Eleuterio F. 1941. Advertencia lingüística. In: José Hernández, 'Martín Fierro'. Ed. Eleuterio F. Tiscornia. 2nd ed. Buenos Aires: Losada. 17-20.

Torres-Rioseco, Arturo. 1946. The epic of Latin American literature. New York: Oxford University Press.

Toscano Mateus, Humberto. 1953. El español en el Ecuador. Madrid: Revista de Filología Española, Anejo LXI.

Trejo, Nemesio. 1907. Los políticos. Buenos Aires: n.p.

Ullmann, Stephen. 1966. Semantic universals. In: Universals of language. Ed. Joseph H. Greenberg. Cambridge, Massachusetts: MIT Press. 217-262.

Undurraga, Antonio de. 1947. Prólogo a Alonso de Ercilla y Zúñiga, La Araucana, 9-24. Buenos Aires: Espasa-Calpe Argentina.

U.S.Bureau of the Census. 1983. 1980 Census of population. vol. 1. General population characteristics, part I U.S. summary. Washington, D.C.: U.S. Department of Commerce.

U.S.Bureau of the Census. 1984. Statistical abstract of the U.S. 1985. Washington, D.C.: U.S. Department of Commerce.

Vela, A. Orlando. 1965. Gramática y diccionario Quechua. Lima: Studium.

Veletti, Virgilio. 1985. Personal conversation.

Wallechinsky, David, Irving Wallace, and Amy Wallace. 1977. The book of lists. New York: Morrow.

Wang, William S-Y. 1980. The Chinese language. In: Human communication: Language and its psychobiological bases. San Francisco: Freeman. 50-62.

Zamora Vicente, Alonso. 1979. Dialectología española. 2nd ed. Madrid: Gredos.

Index

African, 47, 203, 211-212, 217-219
African slave immigrants, 132
Alba, Moreno de, 280
Almagro, Diego, 124
Alonso, Amado, 81, 82, 147-148, 154, 223, 224, 238
Alurista, 304-305
Álvar, Manuel, 156
Álvares de Villasandrino, Alfonso, 67-68
Álvarez, Nazario, 207
Álvarez Quintero, Serafín and Joaquín, 59-61
Amerindian, 47, 52, 89-90
Andalusian, 59-61
Andalusian lexicon, 59; influence of Gypsy caló and Arabic, 59
Andalusian phonology, 59-60; apocope, 59-60; *ceceo* of all sibilants, 59; /d/ and /l/ deletion, 60; /h/ as velar, 59; /r/ deletion, free variation with /l/, 59-60; /r/ as fricative, 59; /s/ reduction, effect on preceding vowel, 59; /x/, 59; *yeísmo*, 59, 81
Andalusian, text, 60-61
Andean Spanish, 176-202; geographical zones of, 176; highland and lowland, subdialects, 176-177; highlands, influence on coast, 177; rustic vs urban usage, 177, 184-185;

similarities to and differences from Castilian and Andalusian, 177-178; similarities to Mexican Spanish, 177; *voseo*, except for Central Peru, 177
Andean Spanish lexicon, 196-201
Andean Spanish lexicon, Colombia, 196-198; English influence on, 198; figures of speech, 198; forms of address, 197; marine terms, 198; regionalisms, 198; semantic shift, 196-197; similarities to speech of Mexico and Argentina, 196-198
Andean Spanish lexicon, Ecuador, Peru, and Bolivia, 198-201; neologisms, 199; personal names, 200; Quechua influence on, 198-199; terms of address, 200
Andean Spanish morphosyntax, 184-196; adjective, 193; adjective, adverbialized, 193; adjective, affixation, 193; analytical tendencies, 185-186; imperative, 190-191; noun, 192-193; noun, elision in, 193; noun, gender, 192; noun, number, 192-193; noun, suffixation, 193; noun determiner, 194; noun determiner, Quechua influence on, 194; preposition, 195-196; pronoun, 194-195; pronoun, Quechua influence on, 195; Quechua influence on morphosyn-

 GEORGETOWN UNIVERSITY PRESS
Romance Languages and Linguistics Series

ROMANCE COLLOQUIA

1975 COLLOQUIUM ON HISPANIC LINGUISTICS
Frances M. Aid, Melvyn C. Resnick, Bohdan Saciuk, editors

SPANISH AND PORTUGUESE IN SOCIAL CONTEXT
John J. Bergen and Garland D. Bills, editors

LINGUISTIC SYMPOSIUM ON ROMANCE LANGUAGES: 9
William W. Cressey and Donna Jo Napoli, editors

STUDIES IN CARIBBEAN SPANISH DIALECTOLOGY
Robert M. Hammond and Melvyn C. Resnick, editors

COLLOQUIUM ON SPANISH AND LUSO-BRAZILIAN LINGUISTICS
James P. Lantolf, Francine Wattman Frank, Jorge M. Guitart, editors

CURRENT STUDIES IN ROMANCE LINGUISTICS
Marta Luján and Fritz G. Hensey, editors

1974 COLLOQUIUM ON SPANISH AND PORTUGUESE LINGUISTICS
William G. Milan, John J. Staczek, Juan C. Zamora, editors

LINGUISTIC APPROACHES TO THE ROMANCE LEXICON
Frank H. Nuessel, Jr., editor

DIALECTOLOGIA HISPANOAMERICANA: ESTUDIOS ACTUALES
Gary E. A. Scavnicky, editor

ON SPANISH, PORTUGUESE, AND CATALAN LINGUISTICS
John J. Staczek, editor

CONTEMPORARY STUDIES IN ROMANCE LINGUISTICS
Margarita Suñer, editor

DATE DUE FOR RETURN

30 APR 1992
19 JAN 2001
14 JAN 2005

11. MAR

29 MAR 2005

94

26 FEB 2001

03. OCT 94
4 MAY 2001
19 MAY 2006

21 FEB 2002
14 MAY 2008

29 NOV 1995
25 MAR 2002

09 JAN 2009

3 MAY 1996

19 DEC 1997
-3 MAY 2002

-2 APR 2003

16 JAN 1998
19 NOV 2007